Contents

Healing Your Thyroid Naturally

Manage Symptoms, Lose Weight and Improve Your Thyroid Health

Dr Emily Lipinski,
Doctor of Naturopathic Medicine

To my children and all the other future leaders of the world.
May you have the courage to seek the truth, take the time to find peace, and
always connect with the innate wisdom of your body, mind, and spirit.

First published in the United States in 2020 by Hachette Go,
An imprint of Hachette Books
A division of Hachette Book Group, Inc

First published in Great Britain in 2020 by Yellow Kite
An Imprint of Hodder & Stoughton
An Hachette UK company

1

Interior design by Trish Wilkinson

A CIP catalogue record for this title is available from the British Library

Trade Paperback ISBN 978 1 529 34706 7
eBook ISBN 978 1 529 34855 2

Printed and bound in Great Britain by Clays Ltd, Elcograf S.p.A.

Hodder & Stoughton policy is to use papers that are natural, renewable and recyclable products and made from wood grown in sustainable forests. The logging and manufacturing processes are expected to conform to the environmental regulations of the country of origin.

Yellow Kite
Hodder & Stoughton Ltd
Carmelite House
50 Victoria Embankment
London EC4Y 0DZ

www.yellowkitebooks.co.uk

A Journey to Thyroid Health and Healing

I can still remember how I felt when I was finally diagnosed with Hashimoto's thyroid disease at the age of twenty-seven. It was a mix of emotions: sadness and fear that I could be sick for the rest of my life living with an autoimmune condition. Not to mention lifelong medication and monitoring. On the other hand, I also felt relief to finally have an answer after years of fatigue and the inability to lose weight despite a healthy lifestyle.

My journey with hypothyroidism began long before my diagnosis. I was the kid who reacted to everything: pollen, grass, and dust—just to name a few. If I came into contact with cats or dogs, I was sneezing within a few minutes, and half an hour later, my body was littered with hives. I had chronic eczema on my face, hands, and legs. By the time I was ten, I was diagnosed with asthma and I also began to have chronic issues with strep throat. Clearly, my immune system was struggling, but my medical doctor did not have any answers except to give me antihistamines for the allergies, puffers for my asthma, and multiple rounds of antibiotics for my strep throat. Little did I know that my allergies and asthma represented an overreacting immune system that could predispose me to autoimmune disease (such as Hashimoto's hypothyroidism) later in life. Not to mention the plethora of antibiotics I was exposed to that were harming my microbiome and could have also set me up for autoimmune issues.

During my high school years, my health was fairly good. However, once I moved away from home for my undergraduate studies, began to have less home-cooked food, stayed up late, and took on a large course load, my sore throats returned. I also began to constantly feel cold and I started to gain weight. My doctors chalked it up to the "freshman fifteen" and fewer home-cooked meals. Fair enough—but when my blood work was taken, not only were my ferritin levels (the marker of a person's iron stores) low, but my TSH (thyroid-stimulating hormone) was often slightly elevated. If I only knew then what I know now, I would have challenged my doctor and pushed for more tests to be run. Like countless patients I have met over the years, I trusted the expertise of my physician and assumed that everything was "normal."

Fast-forward to my last year at naturopathic medical school. My weight was at an all-time high, my face was puffy, I was cold, and my fatigue was unbearable. After learning about how to treat and diagnose patients with thyroid issues, I knew I had to retest my thyroid. This time around, armed with new information, I requested that not only my TSH be tested but also other blood markers of thyroid health: T3 hormone, T4 hormone, and thyroid antibodies. When the results came back, my new doctor was shocked. My TSH levels were now significantly elevated, my thyroid hormones were low, and my thyroid antibody levels were sky-high! I was told that I would now need to be on the thyroid medication known as Synthroid (levothyroxine) for the rest of my life and there was nothing else I could do. There was no mention about my high levels of antibodies. But by that point, I had my own medical knowledge and I knew better. Elevated thyroid antibodies meant I had an autoimmune issue—Hashimoto's thyroiditis. High levels of certain antibodies (we'll explain more later in Chapter 1) have also been associated with anxiety and obsessive-compulsive syndrome. Additionally, if the autoimmune disease is not addressed, there is an elevated risk of developing other autoimmune diseases, such as pernicious anemia, rheumatoid arthritis, and lupus. I also knew that women living with elevated thyroid antibodies can have difficulty with fertility and with becoming pregnant. Essentially, if I did not address my immune system, my health could get a lot worse.

Although I started on the levothyroxine thyroid medication, many of my symptoms persisted. I was still having difficulty losing weight, I was always freezing, and my fatigue was only marginally improved. Deep down, I knew that medication was only part of the puzzle. I began to search out any and every possible way to lower my antibodies and improve the state of my immune system. My journey included dietary changes, such as the removal of gluten and other grains from my diet, changing my beauty care routine, addressing my stress head-on, and using herbs and other supplements to help support my immune system and my thyroid gland. I also stopped using the levothyroxine medication and switched to desiccated thyroid medication. Slowly but surely, my symptoms of hypothyroidism began to subside and my levels of antibodies gradually reduced. I am now a healthy body weight, my face no longer looks puffy, and my energy is much better. Thankfully, I did not have any trouble conceiving and I welcomed a beautiful baby boy in 2018 without complications. By addressing my immune system and using natural therapies, I am now essentially in remission from Hashimoto's. I have also been able to help many other patients reduce their antibody levels, improve their thyroid function, and reduce the frustrating symptoms of hypothyroidism.

Making dietary and lifestyle changes may not be the simple route; it certainly isn't as easy as just taking a pill every morning. But the recommendations made in this book have helped not only myself but countless patients overcome debilitating fatigue, dark mood swings, and unbearable cold intolerances. I wrote this book for anyone who is suffering as my patients and I did—looking for answers aside from medication alone and just not sure where to turn. If you have—or think you have—thyroid disease, I want to help you improve your health and wellness and help you thrive. Or, as my patients have said, help you get your life back.

I am a naturopathic doctor (ND). Naturopathic doctors are trained as primary care providers who blend modern scientific knowledge with traditional and natural forms of medicine. The naturopathic philosophy is to stimulate the healing power of the body and treat the underlying cause of disease. Naturopathic doctors use dietary and lifestyle changes, herbs, supplements, and in some cases prescription medicines to treat the patient. In Canada and the US, the naturopathic medical profession's structure includes accredited naturopathic medical programs, standardized North American Board Exams, national standards of practice, and regulation in many provinces and states. Prescription rights vary depending on which province or state the naturopathic doctor is practicing.

In addition to the care of a traditional medical doctor, many of my patients over the years have found tremendous benefit in seeking care from a naturopathic doctor or a functional medical doctor. Functional medical doctors are medical doctors who have had extra training in natural medicines and, like naturopathic doctors, aim to address the root cause of the medical issue by using natural therapies in combination with prescription medicines when needed.

HOW TO GET THE MOST OUT OF THIS BOOK

Some of the information provided in this book will be brand new, and some of it may sound intuitive. With that said, when you embark on healing your thyroid, it is vital that you listen to your intuition, that little voice that helps guide you through life. Many patients who come to me start off a conversion with "I know I'm not supposed to be doing this, or eating that, but . . ." It is time to stop doing the things you know you shouldn't be doing, for the sake of your health. This could be anything from fast food to cigarettes, too much coffee, not enough sleep, or even using cleaning products that you know give you a headache (and aren't good for your health) but they "just make everything so clean!" It is time to make some big changes. Your thyroid (and the rest of your body) will thank you.

This book is divided into three parts. Part 1 discusses all the potential contributing factors to the onset of autoimmune thyroid disease, including toxins, stress, electromagnetic fields (EMFs), genetics, infections, and food. Each of these chapters outlines how you can reduce the impact of these factors to promote healing. In Part 2, we discuss the multiple ways thyroid disease can be improved: the Thyroid-Healing Diet, microbiome, medications, natural herbs and supplements, and ancient and emerging therapies. Part 3 helps you put it all together with strategies and simple recipes to get you started on your thyroid-healing journey.

You can read this book from start to finish or begin by focusing on a chapter that you are currently in need of as you attend to your thyroid.

Many people like a "plan," and although I truly do not believe that "one size fits all," these are the general thyroid-healing steps that I used with my patients and myself to overcome thyroid disease; these steps will be explained in depth throughout the book.

THYROID-HEALING STEPS:
1. First, have blood work tests performed:
   - A complete thyroid panel blood test will help you understand whether you are positive for thyroid antibodies and/or have low T3 or high RT3.* If you already know you have Hashimoto's, retesting your hormones and your antibodies before starting the program can give you a baseline for you to track your improvement in addition to tracking your symptoms.
   - Ask your health-care provider to test for the following potential nutrient deficiencies: vitamins B_{12} and D, and iron. If you have deficiencies, use supplements to correct them; we'll cover supplements in Chapters 11 and 13.
2. Adopt the Thyroid-Healing Diet (pages 131–173). If you are not ready to take on the Thyroid-Healing Diet in its entirety, focus on increasing thyroid-healing foods and reducing thyroid-harming foods (see chart, page 147).
3. Address stress and environmental triggers, including toxins and electromagnetic fields. Take some time to explore ancient and emerging therapies.
4. Use supplements tailored to your needs. If you are having issues converting T4 to T3, or you have positive antibodies, use supplements to help increase this conversion or reduce antibodies (page 249).
5. Heal your gut and keep your microbiome happy; we'll talk more about the microbiome in Chapter 9.
6. Address potential chronic infections that could be contributing to an autoimmune response (see Chapter 6).

---

*If you are unable to test all your markers of thyroid health, that is okay! Just start with adopting the Thyroid-Healing Diet.

Before we begin, I want to share some words that I think are so very important: *When you embark on your healing journey, you must first believe that your body has the ability to heal. This is such a simple concept, but sometimes difficult to believe, especially when we are feeling so sick. I often have my patients recall a time they have cut their finger. The wound bleeds, scabs, and then heals, without our having to even think much about it! Our body is made for recovery and there is tremendous power in believing that we can be well again.*

An Important Note Before You Get Started

IF you are currently taking medication and begin to take supplements to support thyroid hormone conversion, support the adrenal glands, and/or stimulate the thyroid gland, it is important that you monitor the thyroid hormone levels in your blood, ideally every 6 to 8 weeks, until stable, especially if you have a change in symptoms. Additionally, please be sure to consult with your health-care professional in advance of making any dietary changes and/or taking any supplements. Some supplements could cause an allergic response, cause side effects, or may be contraindicated to take with other medications you may currently be using, so you should always talk with your health-care provider first.

PART 1

The Thyroid Disease Epidemic: What You Need to Know

CHAPTER 1

Thyroid 101

I t has been estimated that thyroid issues have doubled or tripled since the 1950s. In fact, a medical textbook from the '60s reported that "diseases of the thyroid are not common in medical practice." It is now estimated that over 12 percent of the US population will develop a thyroid disorder at some point in their life. The most common reason for hypothyroidism is an autoimmune disease called Hashimoto's thyroiditis. It is estimated that over 90 percent of people in the United States living with hypothyroidism have Hashimoto's and many of them do not even know it because they have never been tested for the antibodies! These antibodies essentially attack the thyroid, and over time can cause thyroid damage.

> **IT** is now estimated that 200 million people in the world suffer from thyroid disease. Hypothyroidism is more common in women and it is believed that 1 in 8 women worldwide will develop a thyroid condition in their lifetime! Unfortunately, over 50 percent of people with hypothyroidism are undiagnosed and may be suffering with symptoms without proper treatment. Understanding the thyroid's important function in the body, along with knowing the signs and symptoms to look out for, can help raise awareness about hypothyroidism.

The thyroid is a small but powerful butterfly-shaped gland located in the neck just below the larynx. In healthy individuals, the thyroid gland cannot be typically felt or seen by just looking at or touching the neck.

The thyroid is only .79 inches (2 cm) thick and has two lobes connected by a narrow piece of tissue known as the isthmus. Each little lobe measures only about 1.8 inches (4.6 cm) in length and the total weight of the thyroid can be up to around 2 ounces. Despite its tiny size, the thyroid is known as the "body's thermostat" and regulator of metabolism. In fact, it produces hormones that provide energy for every one of the cells in your body! These thyroid hormones control breathing, alertness, heart function, body temperature, cholesterol level, nervous system function, how easily you gain or lose weight, skin moisture, brain development, and menstruation. Needless to say, the thyroid hormones play an incredibly significant role in the body.

The two primary hormones produced by the thyroid are T3 and T4. The thyroid hormones are synthesized from the amino acid tyrosine and the mineral iodine. Approximately 90 percent of the hormone released by the thyroid gland is T4, also known as the inactive thyroid hormone, and 10 percent is the active hormone T3. When T4 is released into the body's circulation, it is converted into the active form of T3 by way of a process called deiodination. This process of converting inactive T4 to active T3 happens in the liver, kidneys, and brain. (In some cases, instead of converting T4 into T3, the body changes T4 into the mirror image of T3, called reverse T3 [RT3]. Unfortunately, RT3 is not an active hormone and the body cannot use this form of T3. This is often more likely to happen when a person is fasting, is exposed to lots of toxins, has diabetes, is under a high amount of stress, or has a chronic illness.)

The body regulates the production of these important hormones by sending signals from the pituitary gland (located in your brain), by way of another hormone known as TSH (thyroid-stimulating hormone). This means that the thyroid hormones can exert a negative feedback on your TSH. When the T3 and T4 levels are too high in the body, TSH goes down; when the T3 and T4 hormones are too low, TSH increases to help produce more thyroid hormones. Typically, when the thyroid begins to function abnormally, the brain should respond by communicating to the thyroid and increasing or decreasing the amount of TSH released, and therefore either decreasing or increasing the amount of T3 and T4 hormones in the body.

One of the most common reasons for abnormal thyroid gland function in North America is the development of autoimmune thyroid disorders (AITD). When this immune disease develops in the body, antibodies develop and attack the thyroid gland. The most common antibodies that develop in Hashimoto's hypothyroidism are thyroid peroxidase antibodies (TPOAb) and thyroglobulin antibody (TgAb). These antibodies can cause swelling and damage to the thyroid and can result in thyroid dysfunction.

TYPES OF THYROID DYSFUNCTION, SYMPTOMS, AND DIAGNOSIS

First up, here are the six most important blood tests that properly assess low thyroid function. Most conventional doctors only run one of these tests and this is part of the reason many cases of autoimmune hypothyroidism are not properly assessed. If you are suffering from symptoms of thyroid disease (see page 13) but your TSH is normal, you should have these other blood tests run. I will discuss markers specific to various thyroid conditions.

BLOOD TEST NAME	WHAT IT LOOKS AT
Thyroid-stimulating hormone (TSH)	Measures blood levels of TSH. This hormone, sent from the pituitary gland, should increase when thyroid hormone levels (T3 and T4) are too low in the body.
Free T4 hormone (thyroxine)	Measures blood levels of T4 hormone, produced by the thyroid gland; the "free T4" is the biologically active form of T4. Too little T4 can indicate that the thyroid gland is not functioning properly, or it is hypoactive.
T3 hormone (triiodothyronine)	Measures blood levels of T3 hormone, produced in small amounts from the thyroid, but primarily produced by converting T4 into T3 hormone in other tissues, such as the liver and kidneys. Too little T3 can indicate that the thyroid gland is not functioning properly, or it is hypoactive. However, low T3 levels can also indicate that the T4 hormone is not converting properly to T3 in the body.

continues

continued

Thyroid peroxidase antibodies (TPOAb)	Measures antibodies against TPO in the blood. TPO is an enzyme found in the thyroid gland and helps produce thyroid hormones. High levels of TPO antibodies could indicate Hashimoto's hypothyroidism.
Thyroglobulin antibodies (TgAb)	Measures antibodies to thyroglobulin in the blood. Thyroglobulin is a protein made by the thyroid gland. This test detects antibodies against this thyroid protein. High levels of thyroglobulin antibodies could indicate Hashimoto's hypothyroidism or Graves' disease.
Reverse T3 (RT3)	Measures reverse T3 hormone in the blood, another form of T3 hormone that has no biological activity. High levels of reverse T3 can indicate that the body is undergoing high amounts of stress but can also help guide a treatment protocol.

Hypothyroidism

Hypothyroidism develops when the thyroid gland becomes underactive and does not produce enough thyroid hormones. In turn, the TSH from the brain begins to increase in the body due to the reduction of T4 and T3 hormones in circulation. In essence, the brain starts to yell at the thyroid to "hurry up and make more hormones!" In developed countries, the development of AITD and Hashimoto's thyroiditis is the most common cause of hypothyroidism. (In underdeveloped countries, lack of iodine intake is at the root cause of the development of an underactive thyroid. Due to the addition of iodized salt in Canada, the US, and Europe, lack of iodine is typically not thought to be an issue in these nations [however, this isn't always so clear cut; read more about the iodine issue on page 204]. When someone develops hypothyroidism due to a lack of iodine, the thyroid often becomes swollen and can become visible by looking at the neck. Any swelling of the thyroid is referred to as a goiter and can also be present in individuals with Hashimoto's, Graves', or other thyroid diseases, even if the patient is not iodine deficient.)

Symptoms of hypothyroidism include:

- Inability to lose weight
- Fatigue
- Increased sensitivity to cold
- Low body temperature (see Appendix B, pages 306–307, for more information on monitoring your body temperature as an indicator of thyroid function)
- Puffy face
- Dry skin
- Thinning hair
- Constipation
- Hoarseness
- Mood changes
- Brain fog/memory problems
- Muscle weakness
- Goiter
- Stiff joints

It is important to note that many individuals with hypothyroidism may only have one or two of the listed symptoms.

Common Blood Tests to Diagnose Hypothyroidism

TSH: Less than 4.0 to 4.5 mIU/L* is indicative of an underactive thyroid gland.

T4 hormone: Less than 9 pmol/L indicates that the thyroid gland is not making enough T4 hormone.

---

*The normal TSH value is debated in medicine and the upper limit of TSH has consistently lowered over the last few years. The American Association for Clinical Chemistry (AACC) reports that 95 percent of people living without hypothyroidism have a TSH value of under 2.5 mIU/L. In Canada, conventional practitioners still generally adhere to the upper limit being 4.0 to 4.5 mIU/L; however, whenever I see a TSH value of over 2.5 mIU/L and the patient reports any symptoms of hypothyroidism, I definitely begin to dig a little deeper and run more blood tests.

T3 hormone (not as commonly tested): Less than 2.6 pmol/L indicates that the thyroid gland is not making enough T3 hormones.

Reverse T3 (RT3): As mentioned earlier, RT3 can be produced by the body when it is trying to convert T4 into the active T3 hormone and instead produces RT3, a form of T3 that the body cannot utilize. Ideally, we want to make sure that RT3 levels are low in the body, otherwise many patients still experience symptoms, especially related to energy and weight gain. I often test RT3 with a full hormone panel for people who are suffering from hypothyroid symptoms (whether they have previously been diagnosed with hypothyroidism or not), as it can be very helpful to guide treatment. Normal RT3 levels are 9.2 to 24.1 ng/dl.

Subclinical Hypothyroidism and Overt Hypothyroidism

Subclinical hypothyroidism is often considered a "mild" form of hypothyroidism, whereby the TSH becomes elevated but the T3 and T4 thyroid hormones are still within normal levels. Oftentimes, especially if the TSH is only mildly elevated, patients are told they will be monitored but no medical intervention is necessary. Usually medical doctors wait to treat the patient with medication until the patient is "overtly hypothyroid" (increased TSH and decreased thyroid hormones). Once a patient is on thyroid medication, it can be very difficult to discontinue the medication as the thyroid gland becomes "lazy" and stops producing its own hormones. As a naturopathic doctor focused on preventative medicine, I find this extremely frustrating! Many patients still have annoying and debilitating symptoms of hypothyroidism when they are only "subclinically hypothyroid" and may likely be mounting an autoimmune response that has yet to be uncovered with blood tests. I honestly believe that if I had had my thyroid antibodies tested in my early twenties when I first was experiencing thyroid symptoms, I may have been able to reduce the progression to full-blown Hashimoto's by addressing my immune response. I have seen countless patients who have complained to their doctors for years about thyroid symptoms despite their TSH levels being normal. When they arrive in my office and we test antibodies, I am never surprised to see them elevated.

MANY natural therapies and interventions can be extremely beneficial for those with subclinical hypothyroid disease and may prevent the need for medication if the overt hypothyroid disease can be prevented from progressing. If you have an elevated TSH level (even if it is only mildly elevated), I strongly encourage you to have your thyroid antibodies checked and seek out a naturopathic doctor or functional medical doctor who can address the disease before it progresses.

Hashimoto's Thyroiditis

As previously mentioned, Hashimoto's is an autoimmune disease and the most common reason in the Western world for the development of hypothyroidism. Individuals with Hashimoto's may have very mild symptoms of hypothyroidism at the beginning stages of the disease. In these early stages TSH, and T3 and T4 hormones, will likely be normal, but thyroid antibodies will be elevated in blood test results. As the disease progresses, TSH often becomes slightly elevated and the T3 and T4 hormones may still read in the normal level. This is often referred to as subclinical hypothyroidism. As discussed, because thyroid antibodies are not as commonly tested, many individuals in the early stages of Hashimoto's will be told there is nothing wrong despite their mounting symptoms of hypothyroidism. As the disease progresses, TSH, T3, and T4 will eventually become abnormal. People who are already diagnosed with an autoimmune disorder, such as lupus, rheumatoid arthritis, Addison's disease, vitiligo, pernicious anemia, type 1 diabetes, or if they have a family history of autoimmune disorders are at greater risk of developing Hashimoto's.

Common Blood Tests to Diagnose Hashimoto's Thyroiditis

TSH: Normal in early stages of disease; greater than 4 to 4.5 mIU/L in later stages of Hashimoto's disease.

T4 hormone: Less than 9 pmol/L indicates that the thyroid gland is not making enough T4 hormone.

T3 hormone (not as commonly tested): Less than 2.6 pmol/L indicates that the thyroid gland is not making enough T3 hormone.

TPO antibody: Over 30 kIU/L indicates that the body is making an abnormal number of antibodies against TPO.

Tg antibody: Over 40 kIU/L indicates that the body is making an abnormal number of antibodies against Tg.

Note: Although Tg antibodies can be elevated in Hashimoto's, TPO antibodies are the most commonly elevated antibody.

Complications of Untreated Hypothyroidism

As the thyroid gland is responsible for so many vital processes in the body, leaving thyroid disease untreated can result in some serious side effects. First and foremost, the heart can become negatively affected when there are not enough thyroid hormones in the body. Thyroid hormones control every component of the cardiovascular system necessary for normal healthy heart function. Typically, when cardiovascular disease is first identified in a patient, thyroid function tests are usually examined to see overt thyroid disorders or even whether subclinical thyroid dysfunction exists. The kidneys are also controlled by the thyroid hormones and therefore lack of sufficient hormones can lead to renal complications and kidney disease. Neurological changes, such as severe anxiety, headaches, memory losses, and tremors, can also be a result of low levels of thyroid hormones.

Untreated hypothyroidism also reduces fertility in both women and men. This is because the T3 and T4 thyroid hormones regulate the metabolism of sex hormones, estrogen and progesterone, which affect the production of eggs and sperm. When thyroid levels are too low in men, sperm can become abnormally shaped, libido can decrease, and even erectile dysfunction can result. Women with hypothyroidism may have abnormal periods or reduced levels of progesterone (important for conception) and may experience menstrual cycles with no ovulation. Interestingly enough, research has shown that even subclinical hypothyroidism may affect a woman's ability to conceive.

Hyperthyroidism and Graves' Disease

Hyperthyroidism develops when the thyroid produces too much thyroid hormone and becomes hyperactive. Typically, as the body's metabolism begins to go into overdrive, individuals can experience rapid heartbeat, increased sweating, and anxiety. As a result, the TSH released from the brain slows as the body attempts to reduce how much thyroid hormone is made from the thyroid gland. Graves' disease, another AITD, is the most common reason someone develops hyperthyroidism. Because Graves' is also an autoimmune thyroid condition, some individuals may develop Hashimoto's as a result of Graves' syndrome or may develop Graves' as a result of Hashimoto's.

Common symptoms of hyperthyroidism include:

- Anxiety and irritability
- Weight loss
- Menstrual cycle changes
- Increased perspiration/constantly feeling warm or hot
- Racing heart/palpitations
- Fatigue
- Bulging eyes
- Tremors
- Increased blood pressure
- Goiter

Common Blood Tests to Diagnose Hyperthyroidism and Graves' Disease

TSH: Less than 0.4 mIU/L is indicative that the thyroid gland is overactive.

T4 hormone: Over 19 pmol/L indicates the thyroid gland is making too much T4 hormone.

T3 hormone (not as commonly tested): Over 5.8 pmol/L indicates the thyroid gland is making too much T3 hormone.

Thyroid-stimulating immunoglobulin (TSI): This antibody is diagnostic for Graves' disease and therefore a positive result suggests Graves' disease.

Thyroid-stimulating hormone receptor antibody (TrAb) Less specific for Graves' disease; however, a positive result also often indicates Graves' disease.

TPO antibodies: May be elevated in Graves' disease, as well as Hashimoto's disease. (Over 30 kIU/L indicates that the body is making an abnormal amount of antibodies against TPO.)

Other Tests to Diagnose Hyperthyroidism and Graves' Disease

Radioactive iodine uptake (RAIU): This test requires individuals to swallow either a pill or a liquid containing radioactive iodine. Because the thyroid gland requires iodine to make thyroid hormones, the iodine will naturally accumulate in the thyroid gland. In individuals with "hyperactive glands," more iodine will accumulate and can be indicative of hyperthyroidism or Graves' disease. After a stated period of time, a special scanner is placed over the thyroid and the amount of radioactivity is compared to the amount that the patient ingested.

As this test exposes the body to radiation (albeit small amounts), some patients decline this test. Additionally, if people have shellfish allergies, they may react to the iodine substance. It is thought that allergies to shellfish could be a result of the iodine found within the shellfish. Due to the radiation, this test is also not recommended for women who are pregnant or breastfeeding.

Ultrasound: Ultrasounds are often run to check whether the thyroid gland is enlarged, or for patients who are not taking the radioactive iodine test.

THE IMMUNE SYSTEM AND THE DEVELOPMENT OF AITD

As I am sure you realize by now, autoimmune disease has become the most common reason for abnormal thyroid function. *Autoimmune* essentially means that molecules created by the immune system begin to attack your own body, instead of a foreign invader, such as germs and other microbes. To truly understand why autoimmune disease develops, we need to address first how the immune system operates.

The immune system works in your body to protect you from bacteria, viruses, fungi, parasites, and other foreign invaders. The immune system

Thyroid Nodules

THYROID nodules are common growths of thyroid cells that cause a lump to form in the thyroid gland. It is suspected that much of the normal, healthy population have thyroid nodules. Approximately 50 percent of patients with Hashimoto's disease have thyroid nodules and about 25 percent of patients with Graves' disease have them. Sometimes these nodules can be seen or felt when looking at or touching the area of the neck where the thyroid gland is located. The majority of thyroid nodules are not cancerous (benign), but about 5 percent may contain thyroid cancer cells. For this reason, thyroid nodules should always be properly addressed and evaluated by a doctor.

A fine-needle biopsy is sometimes ordered for thyroid nodules to make sure they are not cancerous. This is a test that removes a small sample of tissue from your thyroid gland. Cells are removed through a needle. The sample is then sent to the lab for analysis.

response is divided into two features: the innate response and the adaptive response. The innate immune system is the first responder if bacteria or toxins enter the body. It responds by creating inflammation to destroy the invader. This response should be quick, attacking the unwanted guest and then retreating from the scene. The acute inflammation that develops from the innate response often results as redness, swelling, and pain, which generally appear soon after the injury. The innate immune system has no memory but will react and attack every invasion that is deemed unwanted by the body. The adaptive immune response, on the other hand, has a memory of what has invaded the body in the past. This response also results in inflammation and creates a special system once it has been exposed to certain foreign pathogens, so it can attack them the next time they are identified in the body. However, sometimes this adaptive response gets confused and begins to attack "self-antigens." When this happens, it is usually impossible for the immune system to then eliminate the antigen completely, and so a sustained inflammatory response occurs. The consequence is chronic inflammatory injury to tissues, and the development of autoimmune disease. Over eighty autoimmune diseases have now been identified and their occurrence is on the rise.

The reason one person develops autoimmune disease and another person does not often depends on genes, exposure to certain triggers, and the health of their gut.

Genetics play a large role in the development of an autoimmune disease. But even if you have inherited the genes, you may not necessarily develop the disease. In fact, research has been done in twins where one twin has Hashimoto's and the other twin does not. It was discovered that in these patients with Hashimoto's, only about 50 percent of the identical twins also had Hashimoto's. This means genetics are only part of the puzzle. Exposure to certain triggers can increase the chance of developing autoimmune diseases.

However, research shows that intestinal permeability (otherwise known as leaky gut) helps control the way the immune system regulates itself and is a very important factor to the development of autoimmune disease. The intestines are protected by a single layer of special skin cells that are linked together by tight junction proteins. These tight junctions act as the gateway between your intestines and your bloodstream. Leaky gut is a consequence of intestinal tight-junction malfunction. When leaky gut begins, little cracks or openings through these tight junctions allow partially digested food, toxins, and bacteria to penetrate the tissues beneath it. When you have leaky gut, particles that should never be able to enter your bloodstream start to make their way through. Once these particles enter the bloodstream, inflammation and changes in the immune system begin to take place. Interestingly enough, the majority of our immune system is actually found in the gut! So, damage to the gut essentially damages an epicenter of immune functioning and therefore can present a large problem that may cascade into the development of autoimmune disease.

Leaky gut is so crucial to the development of an autoimmune disease that essentially, without it, even if you have the genes and have been exposed to the triggers, you may not develop autoimmune disease.

As Izabella Wentz, PharmD, and Dr. Alessio Fasano, director of the Center for Celiac Research and Treatment at Massachusetts General

Hospital, explain, you must have all three factors to develop autoimmune disease: the genetic disposition, exposure to triggers, and leaky gut.

Symptoms of leaky gut are often very similar to the symptoms of hypothyroidism (not surprisingly!) and include fatigue, headaches, bloating, constipation or diarrhea, memory changes, acne and other skin disorders, and food sensitivities.

Triggers for the development and progression of autoimmune diseases include the following:

- Eating a Western diet, including high fat and cholesterol, high protein, high sugar, and excess salt intake, as well as frequent consumption of processed and fast foods
- Exposure to toxins and heavy metals
- Certain infections and parasites, such as recurrent strep throat, Epstein-Barr virus (EBV), cytomegalovirus (CMV), and *Yersinia enterocolitica*
- Stress; in fact, some studies show that over 80% of patients report an incidence of high stress before the onset of the disease
- Exposure to radiation
- Certain medication use, such as antibiotics and nonsteroidal anti-inflammatory drugs (NSAIDs)
- Elevated iodine intake in foods and other supplements

If autoimmune disease has been triggered, addressing intestinal permeability may be a key factor in the recovery of AITD, as research has shown intestinal barrier function reestablishment can be used in prevention or treatment of autoimmune disorders.

DID you know? Women are more likely to develop an autoimmune disorder. Approximately 6.4 percent of women as opposed to 2.7 percent of men are at risk of developing an autoimmune response; however, Hashimoto's disease is seven times more likely to develop in women compared to men.

INFLAMMATION AND AITD

To address the root cause of the most common cause of thyroid disease, we must address inflammation. When someone develops an autoimmune disease, the inflammation in the body becomes chronically elevated due to the immune system changes. In the case of Hashimoto's disease, markers of inflammation in the blood, known as c-reactive protein (CRP) and erythrocyte sedimentation rate (ESR), can be elevated compared to the normal population. Additionally, the reaction from the immune system causes what is called lymphocytic infiltration, inducing thyroid tissue damage and causing inflammation of the thyroid gland. In conventional medicine, the symptoms of other autoimmune diseases, such as lupus or rheumatoid arthritis, are controlled with anti-inflammation or immune-suppressant medications. These medicines help reduce the inflammation in the body, but often come with many undesirable side effects. Although these medications are not commonly used in the treatment of AITD, addressing the inflammatory response through natural means can significantly reduce the symptoms of the disease and the need for increased medication, and in some cases may help reverse the thyroid disease altogether.

Dietary changes are vital when addressing inflammation. Not only is the conventional Western diet a trigger for inflammation and autoimmune disease, but changes in diet and nutrients have shown to reduce overall inflammation in the body *and* help decrease leaky gut! Another important factor that I have found when addressing the immune response in AITD is addressing the potential triggers for autoimmune disease with the use of certain herbs, supplements, and lifestyle changes.

CAN YOU REVERSE AUTOIMMUNE THYROID DISEASE?

Many conventional doctors believe that due to the inflammation and antibody attack on the thyroid, hypothyroidism is irreversible and results in lifelong thyroid cell damage. However, there have been reports of healthy thyroid function spontaneously returning in some 20 percent of patients. Another study showed that once the autoimmune attack reduces in the body, the damaged thyroid actually has the ability to regenerate and return

CIARA, age 25, arrived in my office with the classic symptoms of hypothyroidism. She had gained 10 pounds over the last six months without many changes to her diet or exercise routine. She reported her energy level to be a 2 out of 10 (10 would represent the energy of a fully charged battery) and her face was puffy. She also believed that her neck appeared bigger when she looked in the mirror. She had previously been diagnosed with irritable bowel syndrome (IBS) and she suffered from anxiety. She also reported her stress level to be about a 9 out of 10. She was out of a job and was in the process of moving to a new home after returning from living abroad for many years. To top it all off, she had very painful and heavy periods. She mentioned that her medical doctor had noted that her TSH level was elevated in the past, but that her thyroid hormone levels were normal and she was not to worry at this point; he would check the TSH level again in another eight months.

I immediately knew I had to run blood tests to check for hypothyroidism. Not surprisingly, her TSH and TPOAb were elevated (indicative of Hashimoto's), and although her T4 had been normal in the past, it was now just below normal. I explained to Ciara that at this point, a need for thyroid medication was indicated, given her low T4 level. I spoke about the risks of not treating the hypothyroidism and how all the cells in the body required the thyroid hormones. Although she understood the risks, she refused medication. She did not want to be on lifelong medication, especially given her young age of twenty-five. She was open to trying any other natural therapy and would comply with regular follow-ups and close monitoring.

Ciara began on a high dose of an herbal formula and a probiotic, adhered to some strict dietary changes, and practiced daily stress-reduction exercises. After a mere four weeks, her T4 was already back in the normal range and her TSH value had now dropped by 5 points. Six weeks later, her TSH was 4 (still not ideal but normal) and her T4 was 14. Although she still had elevated antibodies, she was no longer in a hypothyroid state. She stuck to the routine, and three months later, she had lost 10 pounds, she no longer felt puffy, and her energy was a 7 out of 10.

to normal function! Ultrasounds have confirmed that once the thyroid gland returns to a normal state, the previously elevated TPO antibodies are normal. I have worked with many patients who are able to significantly reduce their thyroid medication after using natural herbs and making diet and lifestyle changes. Many patients have reported that they never knew they could feel so energetic again or participate in life like the way they used to prior to being diagnosed with hypothyroidism. And, although dietary and lifestyle changes can be a learning curve to adopt, I find most people eventually find them easy to maintain, especially given their health improvements! Personally, I have used natural therapies to take my TPO antibodies from over 400 kIU/L to under 35 kIU/L (normal levels are <35 kIU/L). Although I still use desiccated thyroid hormone daily, I no longer struggle with daily symptoms of hypothyroidism. I take certain herbs known to boost thyroid function and help reduce inflammation in the diet. Previously, I removed all grains from my diet for three months, was strictly gluten-free for four years, and now eat a diet that is 90 percent gluten- and dairy-free. I rarely eat packaged foods and, I have to say, I don't miss them. The few times I do eat them, they are never as good as I remember them being in my childhood and teenage years. The point here is that even if you need to be on medication, it is not the only answer.

CHAPTER 2

Toxins

The thyroid gland is extremely sensitive to toxins. Unfortunately, we now live in a day and age where toxins are literally everywhere. Without even thinking about it, we breathe them, eat them, drink them, and sleep on them every day and night. You may find that hard to believe, but it's true.

Let's start with the beginning of the day. Most of us wake up after a night's rest having slept on a mattress sprayed and treated with chemicals. The sheets we slept in may also contain certain perfumes and chemicals, depending on the detergent they were washed in. Then, we shower and maybe have a glass of water, which has most likely been treated with fluoride and chorine and may contain a few other chemicals that could not be filtered out in the water treatment plant. Did you wash your hair this morning? Conventional shampoos and conditioners contain a slew of chemicals that may not be so great for your health. Are you putting on a dry-cleaned outfit for work? If so, you will be exposing yourself to perchloroethylene (known as perc), a chemical that has been associated with some not-so-nice side effects. The International Agency for Research on Cancer classifies perc as a probable human carcinogen that can increase the risk of cervical and esophageal cancers, as well as non-Hodgkin's lymphoma. And what about conventional makeup and hair spray? These products can contain perfumes and phthalates, known to be harmful to the thyroid and able to wreak havoc on the hormonal system. Conventional deodorants contain aluminum, which has been linked to health concerns. Next up, we may commute to work. Whether we walk or drive, we are exposed to fumes from vehicles and other airborne pollutants, including potential pesticides from neighboring lawns as we walk out the door. As we arrive at work, we sit down in our office and begin our day. But what kind of chemicals was the office cleaned with last night? Moreover, if your office is carpeted, you could be exposing yourself to even more chemicals, such as formaldehyde, often found in furniture and carpets. And we haven't even mentioned the potential pesticide and chemical exposure that we can be subjected to by eating conventional produce, fish laden with heavy metals, or packaged foods.

I don't mean to instill fear or scare you; however, it is important to understand just how many chemicals we are now exposed to on a daily basis. It is hard to truly quantify how many chemicals are manufactured today. As a best estimate, we can refer to the Environmental Protection Act (EPA), similar to the National Environmental Policy Act (NEPA), which was tasked by the Toxic Substances Control Act (TSCA) of 1976 with creating an inventory of chemicals being produced in the United States. That said, TSCA did not cover food and food additives, drugs, cosmetics, firearms and ammunition, pesticides, tobacco, and "mixtures." Nonetheless, it provides us with an idea of the amount of chemicals in manufacture. To create the initial chemicals inventory, TSCA required all manufacturers and processors of chemicals to report those chemicals to the EPA between 1978 and 1982. During that period, the EPA received reports on approximately 62,000 chemicals. The law also required that, when manufacturing a new substance, the manufacturer had to bring it to the EPA for review and to add it to the inventory. Chemicals added are referred to as "new chemicals." From 1982 to 2012, the agency added 22,000 new chemicals to the inventory. As of 2018, the TSCA Inventory showed over 86,000 chemicals available for commercial production and use in the US. And the most unfortunate part about all of this is that many of these chemicals in commercial use, and in our food supply, have never been tested for safety. Although we are beginning to understand that quite a number of them may be unsafe, they still remain in manufacture. And simply put, most of us have never given much consideration to the chemicals that we are exposed to, let alone think about the health effects they may carry. We assume they are safe.

Of the chemicals that have been tested for safety, typical toxicity studies are looking for something known as the lowest observed adverse effect level (LOAEL) or no observed adverse effect level (NOAEL). Many

WHEN Isla first appeared in my office, her eczema was so severe that she had patches on her face and around her eyes, and was experiencing multiple itchy, fluid-filled blisters on her hands, arms, legs, and torso. Two blisters on her arms were as big as golf balls. Isla had been suffering with eczema for over forty years but it had "never gotten this bad." She took pills orally to help control the itch, applied different types of corticosteroids and other over-the-counter anti-itch creams, but she was still scratching her body as she spoke to me. Originally from Scotland, Isla had traveled a lot with her husband and had seen doctors all over the world. When I asked her about the chemicals she used in her home she reported, "Just the usual: Mr. Clean, Vim, bleach for the bathrooms and toilets, Tide for washing clothes, and dryer sheets." Isla also loved using a perfume that her son would send her from Italy. I explained that there could be a link to her symptoms and the chemicals that she uses. Although she seemed skeptical as she had never heard something like this from any of the many doctors she had seen over the years, she was willing to try anything. I suggested she stop using any perfume (except for essential oils), and change her laundry detergent, body creams, body wash and hand soap, and cleaning products. I also recommended lukewarm oatmeal baths and that she start taking a few key dietary oils to help reduce the symptoms of eczema, but warned that these oils might take four to six weeks to have true effect. Two weeks later, Isla was back in my office and reported that she was already 60 percent better! She could not believe that no one had ever mentioned that the chemicals in conventional products could contribute to allergic symptoms and that these products don't come with warning labels.

chemicals on the market aren't necessarily "safe"; they are just lowered to levels that scientists deem to be acceptable. The trouble is that chemicals can accumulate over time with multiple exposures and become much more elevated in our body compared to the initial lower level that was deemed to be "safe." What is also troubling is that researchers have found that low doses of chemicals, over time, can sometimes act differently than high doses. What happens to the body at high doses may not accurately predict what happens to the body at chronic low exposure.

Bruce Lanphear, a medical doctor and researcher, explains the impact in his recently published article in *PLOS Biology* entitled "Low-Level Toxicity of Chemicals: No Acceptable Levels?":

> During medical school, I was taught to categorize patients with or without a disease. I learned that diseases were usually the result of exposure to a single agent and that toxic chemicals, like lead, exhibited a threshold; low concentrations of chemicals that we are regularly exposed to—which are now typically measured in parts per billions—were considered safe or innocuous. In my postdoctoral training, it became clear that most chronic diseases, like autism and heart disease, exist on a spectrum, and they usually result from the cumulative impact of many subtle risk factors. Over the past 15 years, I've also learned that exposure to exceedingly low concentrations of toxic chemicals, like lead, pesticides, and flame retardants, can be hazardous, especially if exposure occurs during early brain development; in many cases, there is no apparent threshold or safe level.

Chronic exposure to low levels of chemicals in our environment has been linked with hormonal and fertility problems, chronic inflammation, developmental delays in children, Alzheimer's, and cancer.

Conventional cosmetic and body care products, such as makeup, shampoos, and fragrances, may be more dangerous to the health than ever before. A study published in the *Journal of the American Medical Association* found that from 2004 to 2016, a total of 5,144 adverse health-related events were submitted to the US Food and Drug Administration (FDA) over the use of beauty products (an average of 396 events per year). Currently, cosmetics companies have no legal obligation to report health problems from their products. The authors of the study concluded that better cosmetic surveillance is needed as the data suggests that a significant portion of adverse health outcomes can be attributed to the use of cosmetics.

This is not to say that all these chemicals cause harm or that, if you are exposed to one of them, you will develop a disease. However, increased exposure to chemicals over time can provide a higher likelihood that adverse reactions could develop. As many environmental chemicals can either interfere with the thyroid's ability to uptake iodine, alter thyroid function, or change thyroid hormone production, the thyroid gland can be especially sensitive to pollutants. It is not surprising that those of us with thyroid disease need to reduce our toxic exposure.

TOXIC BODY BURDEN

Such experts as environmental toxicologists refer to the amount of chemicals and toxic substances in our body at any time as our "body burden." Our body is designed to deal with chemical insults, as long as our detoxification system is not overloaded with too many substances to process. And it appears that many of us have a lot of chemicals pumping through our blood. A study conducted by the Environmental Working Group (EWG) found 287 chemicals in the umbilical cord blood of babies. Of these chemicals, 180 are known to cause cancer in humans and animals, 217 are toxic to the brain and nervous system, and 208 can cause birth defects or abnormal development in animal tests.

The reason some people may become sick from chemicals and others may not depends on a few key factors:

- The type of chemical
- The amount of the chemical
- The duration of exposure
- The frequency of exposure

Adverse effects and reduced detoxification can also be dependent on other variables, such as age, gender, pregnancy, other current health conditions, gastrointestinal health, and genetics. Single neucleotide polymorphisms (SNPs, pronounced "snips") are genetic mutations that can affect many different processes in the body, including detoxification. Specifically, SNPs in the MTHFR gene or the GSTM1 and CYP1A2 genes can slow how fast someone processes toxins in the body. Although MTHFR mutations do not seem to be more common in people with Hashimoto's, the gene variation seems to be more common in people with hypothyroidism. Furthermore, hypothyroidism can also reduce the rate at which the liver metabolizes toxins.

Our primary organ of detoxification is the liver, which uses enzymes to transform potential toxins to less harmful substances that are then released from the body through sweat, urine, or stool. This process is referred to as biotransformation. If the liver cannot keep up with the exposure to toxins and chemicals, symptoms can arise and cause unwanted effects in the body. The greater the toxic burden, the larger the potential harm.

Do You Have a High Toxic Body Burden?

1. I drink water out of plastic bottles. yes/no
2. I often use plastic products, such as plastic containers and plastic wrap, to store or cover my food. yes/no
3. I often wear clothes that have been dry cleaned. yes/no
4. I often wear perfumes and/or use conventional perfumed body lotions. yes/no
5. I eat conventional produce and conventionally raised animal products much more than organic produce and animal products. yes/no
6. I regularly eat junk food, such as chips, candy, chocolate bars, and/or fast food. yes/no
7. I often eat farmed fish, especially farmed Atlantic salmon or tuna. yes/no
8. I have mercury fillings in my mouth. yes/no
9. I use fluoridated toothpaste daily. yes/no
10. I live in a house that was built before 1978. yes/no
11. My house is often damp and/or humid or I have discovered mold in my house. yes/no
12. I have carpeted floors in my house. yes/no
13. I grew up in an area where pesticides were commonly sprayed and/or I now live in an area where pesticides are allowed and often used. yes/no
14. I use insecticides in my house and/or have a contract with a pest control company. yes/no
15. I am currently taking the oral birth control pill or I previously took it for more than 6 months OR I often take painkillers, such as acetaminophen or NSAIDS (ibuprofen). yes/no
16. I wear drugstore or designer-brand makeup. yes/no

continues

continued

17. I use conventional cleaning products in my house (e.g., bleach). yes/no
18. I am a smoker or I am regularly exposed to secondhand smoke. yes/no
19. I drink more than 14 alcoholic drinks a week. yes/no
20. I use conventional brands of clothes detergents. yes/no
21. I drink tap water without filtering it. yes/no
22. I have a known mutation in my genes responsible for detoxification, such as MTHFR. yes/no
23. I have chronically low or low-normal WBC and/ or platelets of "unknown origin" on blood testing. yes/no
24. I have mildly elevated CRP on blood testing. yes/no
25. I am overweight. yes/no
26. I am very sensitive to the smells of perfumes, hair sprays, and/ or cleaning chemicals. yes/no
27. I struggle with constipation and often have a day or two where I do not have a bowel movement. yes/no

If you answered yes to at least eight of these questions, you most likely have an elevated toxic body burden. Some people will have an increased body burden but only have answered yes to one or two of the questions.

MOLD Sensitivity (also known as Toxic Mold Syndrome) is different than a true mold allergy. Symptoms include headaches, sneezing, itchy eyes, fatigue, and reduced immunity upon mold exposure. Although not a readily accepted diagnosis in conventional medicine, a study has found that people may experience different unwanted responses from mold aside from a true allergic response.

Many Naturopathic practitioners believe that mold sensitivity can result from a high toxic body burden. People with mold sensitivity may also experience more pronounced effects from EMF exposure and may want to explore Electromagnetic hypersensitivity syndrome (see pages 69–71). If you have had adverse reactions upon mold exposure, it may be another clue that it is time to detox your body. Working on improving your microbiome (see Chapter 9) may also be of benefit.

HOW TO LOWER YOUR BURDEN

We now live in a world where it is truly impossible to avoid all toxins, but we have the ability to reduce our body burden by encouraging healthy detoxification and by avoiding more harmful toxins in our daily lives.

10 Ways to Detox Your Day

1. Filter your water or choose reverse osmosis water and add back minerals.
2. Choose organic as much as possible, especially avoiding the EWG Dirty Dozen (go to ewg.org).
3. Incorporate "liver-loving" foods into your diet. These include dandelion greens, dandelion root tea, kale, broccoli, green tea, leafy green veggies, and beets and beet greens.
4. Consider dry brushing. It not only encourages gentle detoxification but is also invigorating and is great for the skin (see page 34).
5. Avoid the use of conventional deodorants and antiperspirants. Choose a natural alternative with no perfumes, propylene glycol, and aluminum, or make your own with coconut oil, essential oil, and baking soda.
6. Rethink your beauty routine. Look at the labels of the shampoos, conditioners, hair sprays, soaps, body lotions, face creams, perfumes, and nail polishes you use. Are they packed with chemicals and fragrances? You may want to change some (or all) to more natural products. When your current products run out, replace with natural options.
7. Avoid dry-cleaning your clothes. Better options include dry cleaners that offer CO_2 cleaning or "wet cleaning" (if you opt for wet cleaning, ask about what type of cleaning products are used). Organic dry cleaners are not regulated and may not actually be a better option, despite marketing.
8. Ditch the common household cleaners. Make your own cleaning products with vinegar, baking soda, hydrogen peroxide, lemon, rubbing alcohol, water, and essential oils. You can find a number of my favorite DIY household cleaning recipes by visiting

www.emilylipinski.com/resources, or purchase cleaning products at your local health food store.

9. Consider filtering the air of your house (and possibly your office) with a HEPA filter. Make sure your vacuum cleaner is outfitted with a HEPA filter too.

10. Do not use pesticides, herbicides, or fungicides in your home or on your garden. Try natural alternatives, such as diatomaceous earth, or make your own sprays by experimenting with mixes of vinegar, water, insect- and pest-repelling herbs and spices (e.g., garlic, essential oils, and/or cayenne pepper). Find my favorite DIY natural pest control recipes (including a thyroid-friendly bug spray) at www.emilylipinski.com/resources.

ELIMINATION AND DETOXIFICATION

Normal, healthy, and daily bowel movements are an important part of detoxification. Just like we need to take out the garbage in our house, our body regularly should be eliminating the things it doesn't need. Many thyroid condition sufferers struggle with constipation for many reasons. If you are not having daily, complete bowel movements that are well formed and easy to pass, you may want to work on healthy bowel habits as well as work on your microbiome (see Chapter 9).

Here are some of my top tips to ease constipation:

1. Our bodies are very much attuned to the cycle and rhythms of the day so aim to have a bowel movement at the same time every day. If you struggle with constipation, just sitting on the toilet, relaxed for 10–15 minutes is a good habit to begin to encourage a bowel movement.

2. Increase water consumption, even by 1 glass daily.

3. Try using a "squatty potty" or stool when using the toilet. Lifting the legs relaxes some of the muscles around the rectum and can improve healthy evacuation.

4. Add 1–2 tablespoons of chia or ground flax seeds to ⅓ cups of water. Let soak for 10 minutes and then eat (or slurp down) the

mixture, followed by a cup of water, before going to bed to improve the chance of a movement in the morning.

5. Incorporate relaxation into every day. Having a bowel movement requires the parasympathetic nervous system to be activated (the part of the nervous system that is responsible for resting and digesting). Try one of the stress-relieving activities discussed in the next chapter, outlined on pages 57–64.

6. Consider using a castor oil pack; see page 35.

7. Probiotics and other supplements can be game changers when dealing with constipation. See pages 181–184 for more on these supplements.

Sauna Detoxification

HUMANS all over the world have used saunas for many reasons, including hygiene, health, and spiritual reasons. Saunas (especially infrared saunas) can help reduce chemical body burden. Saunas not only increase sweating, helping to release toxins, but they also increase internal body temperature, and may encourage fat cells to release stored chemicals. People suffering from chemical sensitivities or other health issues may have to be cautious with sauna treatment. Check with your health-care provider about whether this treatment could be an option for you.

Dry Brushing

Dry brushing is a naturopathic and Ayurvedic technique to encourage the body to detoxify by improving lymphatic flow; dry skin brushing removes dead skin cells from the pores, so it also allows for easier detoxification via the skin and sweat glands (additionally, it improves skin tone and texture). Dry brushing is exactly as it sounds—it is the process of brushing the skin in a particular pattern before showering. Dry brushes can be found at the drugstore, online, or at a health food store. As the bristles of a dry brush are firm, it is important not to brush too hard, resulting in red or stinging skin.

1. Starting at the feet, brush the bottom and tops of your feet in long, smooth upward strokes. It is recommended to brush toward your heart chest area when dry brushing.
2. Repeat the same process with your arms, starting with the palms of your hands and brushing up your arm toward your heart.
3. On your stomach and armpits, brush in a circular clockwise motion.
4. Then, repeat the process on your abdomen and back.
5. It is not generally recommended to dry brush over delicate areas of your body, such as the face or nipples.

Castor Oil Pack

THE use of castor oil packs, a simple holistic detoxification treatment, dates back to ancient times. Castor oil is a thick fatty oil that is derived from the castor bean. Historically, castor oil has been taken internally (however this route of administration is not generally recommended), rubbed on the skin externally, or made into a poultice or pack and placed on the body. Traditionally castor oil applications have been used for everything from improving skin and digestion, relieving constipation and pain, inducing labor, shrinking fibroids, and benefiting the immune system. In terms of detoxification, a small study has found that lymphocytes increased when patients placed a castor oil pack on their abdomen, compared to placebo packs. Lymphocytes are an integral part of both the immune system and the body's detoxification system. Many people also find that castor oil packs are an excellent way to get the bowels moving—another important aspect of detoxification!

I find people generally benefit from incorporating a weekly or even monthly castor oil pack to encourage healthy detoxification.

continues

continued

How to make and use a castor oil pack:

Materials:

- Organic Castor Oil
- Glass pan or storage container, with lid
- An old piece of flannel or cotton cloth large enough to cover your upper abdomen and cut into a square (typically 8in x 8in)
- An old dry cloth large enough to cover the upper abdomen
- Hot water bottle or heating pad with a low setting

Method:

- Pour a ¼ cup of castor oil into the glass pan.
- Soak the square piece of flannel or cotton in the castor oil; squeeze out extra oil.
- Place the soaked square over your liver (on the top right side of your abdomen, just below your rib cage) and cover the square completely with the dry cloth.
- Place the hot water bottle or heating pad over the cloth and set on low heat for 50–60 minutes.
- Rest, read, or watch a good show while the pack is in place. But be careful not to fall asleep with the heating pad on as it could lead to a burn.
- After removal, clean the area with warm water.
- Store the pack and the extra oil in a covered container in the refrigerator to reuse 1–2 times.

NOTE: Castor oil may leave a stain on your clothing, bedding, or upholstery. Make sure that you are either sitting on an old sheet or that excess oil does not drip out while using the pack. Additionally, do not use a castor oil pack on your liver or abdomen while pregnant or while menstruating.

If these detoxifying adjustments sound like a lot, you are not alone. Many of my patients feel overwhelmed when they first start making a switch to a greener lifestyle. But once you make the switch and form new habits, it becomes so much easier!

> **HEALING TIP:** The mind is a powerful tool in healing. Use the power of thought to help increase your body's resistance to toxins. During a meditation, or at some point throughout the day, begin to envision your body's being able to easily remove and detoxify chemicals that may be harmful to your body and to your thyroid and eliminate them through sweat, urine, stool, and even breath.

CHEMICALS AND YOUR THYROID

Certain chemicals on the market are known to be problematic to thyroid function. Aside from the chemicals and heavy metals found in our conventional food supply, problem chemicals for the thyroid are primarily found in:

- Antibacterial soaps, gels, and other products
- Conventional perfumes and body care products
- Conventional toothpastes and mouthwashes
- Sunscreens
- Plastics (such as shower curtains, plastic wrap and storage containers, and water bottles)
- Tap water
- Receipts

Seven chemicals in particular are harmful: The following sections explain what they are and where you find them. It is important to make yourself familiar with where these substances are found, so you can reduce your exposure and find healthier alternatives.

1. Triclosan

Studies have shown that triclosan decreases the thyroid hormone T4, therefore lowering thyroid function.

Triclosan, commonly known as a "disinfectant," has been banned by the US Food and Drug Administration in certain products, after many years of controversy surrounding its safety. Although this chemical will no longer be present in a variety of soaps and body washes, it is still allowed in many products. Triclosan can be disguised in many other consumer products, so it is time to start reading your labels carefully!

Key terms to look for that should make you suspect triclosan:

- Antibacterial
- Odor-fighting
- "Keeps food fresher, longer"
- Triclocarban
- Biofresh
- Microban

Products that often contain triclosan:

- Hand sanitizers
- Deodorants
- Antibacterial face washes and hand soaps
- Antibacterial wipes
- Toothpastes and mouthwashes
- Some cutting boards and mops

Healthy alternatives: vinegar, hydrogen peroxide, and rubbing alcohol. Two of the most powerful nontoxic disinfectants are readily available: vinegar and food-grade 3 percent hydrogen peroxide. One study found that 6 percent acetic acid (acetic acid is the active component in vinegar) effectively kills *M. tuberculosis* and 10 percent acetic acid kills more resistant mycobacteria, both after a dwell time of thirty minutes. The study also mentions that not only is vinegar an effective mycobactericidal disinfectant, but it may also be active against most other bacteria. Hydrogen peroxide works by releasing oxygen when applied to the affected area and thereby cleaning the area. Food-grade hydrogen peroxide is a 3 percent concentration and is commonly found at grocery stores or drugstores. The 3 percent concentration means that it is extremely diluted: only 3 percent of the solution is hydrogen peroxide and the remaining 97 percent is water. Because this formula is already diluted, there is no need to further dilute it for cleaning (although you can, and many DIY recipes suggest diluting). However, keep in mind that it can still act as a bleaching agent.

Although vinegar and hydrogen peroxide act as great cleaning agents on their own, it is best to not mix the two together, as it creates paracetic acid. This acid can cause irritation of the skin, eyes, and throat. Rubbing alcohol (isopropyl alcohol 70 percent), although not as commonly thought of to clean the house with, can be a great addition to DIY cleaning mixtures or homemade natural hand sanitizers. Alcohol is often used to disinfect small surfaces and is known to be effective against the influenza virus.

Other healthy alternatives to antibacterial products:

- Good old-fashioned soap and water
- Natural hand sanitizers found at health food stores, containing water, essential oils, and a little isopropyl rubbing alcohol
- Mouth rinses and toothpastes made with safer ingredients, such as non-GMO xylitol, clove oil, and cinnamon
- Salt water. Gargling with warm water and salt can also be helpful to control bacteria in the mouth.

2. Phthalates

Phthalates disrupt thyroid function by inhibiting the binding of the thyroid hormones to its receptors.

Phthalates are chemicals that are typically added to plastics to make them flexible, but are commonly found in conventional makeup and perfumes. They have also been found in children's toys, sex toys, vinyl, lotions, insecticides, dairy, packaged foods, and pharmaceutical medications.

A 2017 Korean study looking at 6,003 Korean adults found that exposure to phthalates and BPA (another toxic chemical) caused altered thyroid hormone levels. Specifically, increased concentrations of phthalates in the urine was associated with lower T3 and T4 hormone levels and increases in TSH levels. Phthalates have also been linked to obesity, infertility, birth defects, allergies, asthma, developmental delays, type 2 diabetes, and cancer.

According to estimates by the EPA, today over 470 million pounds of phthalates are produced each year. There are many different types of phthalates, such as DMP (dimethyl phthalate), DEP (diethyl phthalate), and DBP (dibutyl phthalate). Although you can check labels to see whether there are phthalates in the product, it is not foolproof. Conventional fragrances and perfumes are often full of phthalates, but manufacturers aren't required to list the actual ingredients in fragrances because they're considered proprietary formulas.

Although we cannot possibly avoid phthalates, here are some top tips to help reduce your exposure:

- Fragrances, or "parfums," are a major source of phthalates and are often found in beauty care products, such as makeups, perfumes, body lotions, shampoos, and conditioners. Make the switch to organic, chemical-free beauty care products that do not contain synthetic fragrances or perfumes.

- Do not store or heat your food in plastics (especially plastic #3). When plastics touch your food, phthalates leach out into it. They do so more readily when exposed to heat (when warming up food in a plastic storage container, for example) and also continue to leach out over time. It is best to store and warm food in glass, ceramic, or stainless-steel containers. Transfer packaged store-bought food into glass containers.

- Stop using plastic wrap and try a nontoxic alternative, such as a beeswax wrap.

- Flexible cutting boards also contain phthalates, so opt for wood, bamboo, or glass cutting boards.

- Use glass or stainless-steel water bottles and coffee mugs.

- Supplements and prescription medications with enteric coating and time-release pharmaceuticals contain phthalates. Phthalates can also leach out of soft plastic medical devices into stored liquids, such as IV fluids, blood, and plasma. Start asking for detailed information about any medication and supplements you are given and request phthalate-free options when possible.

- Vinyl shower curtains unfortunately contain a whole bunch of chemicals, including phthalates. Opt for a nylon, cotton, or bamboo shower curtain without a liner.

- Choosing a diet that is primarily fresh, organic food as opposed to packaged, nonorganic food will significantly help reduce your exposure to phthalates. Keep in mind that even organic dairy, because of the plastic devices used to pump and store the milk, can still be a source of phthalates.

3. Parabens

Parabens have been linked to abnormal thyroid function in pregnancy. Another study revealed that thyroid levels were lower in people who had higher levels of parabens in their body, especially in females.

Parabens are commonly added to cosmetics and creams to prevent bacterial growth and to extend shelf life. The most common parabens in manufacturing are methylparaben, butylparaben, and propylparaben. Parabens are known xenoestrogens, meaning they mimic the natural estrogens in our body and can cause unwanted side effects and hormonal imbalance. Parabens have also been found in tumors from cancerous breast tissue.

The easiest way to avoid parabens is to check labels and choose beauty care products without parabens listed, or ones that advertise that they are paraben-free.

4. Oxybenzone

New research is showing that a chemical commonly used in sunscreens, oxybenzone, can disrupt thyroid function.

Oxybenzone has been used since 1960 for its ability to protect against a broad spectrum of ultraviolet light, including UVB and short-wave UVA rays. However, this chemical does not just stay topically on the skin; it becomes absorbed into the bloodstream, like many other chemicals, and has some nasty side effects. In fact, sunscreens often include ingredients that act as "penetration enhancers" to help the sunscreen product to adhere to skin, especially when the person sweats or goes into the water. This chemical is also harmful to our environment. Oxybenzone is readily absorbed by wildlife, such as coral, and has been shown to disrupt the coral life cycle, leading to bleaching.

Oxybenzone is part of the benzophenone family of chemicals. Although these benzophenones help protect against UV light, they are known endocrine disruptors and have been shown to alter levels of estrogen, progesterone, testosterone, and thyroid hormones.

The story with chemicals in sunscreens is very similar to that of other industrial and commercial chemicals—many of them have never been properly tested for safety and efficacy.

According to the FDA, the only ingredients in sunscreens that are actually recognized as safe based on existing data are titanium dioxide and zinc oxide.

Higher sun-protection factor (SPF) values may not give you the protection you think. Studies show that many people who use sunscreen and have a false sense of security end up getting burned, and this increases the risk of melanoma (skin cancer). Although some studies have reported positive results for sunscreens, others reveal that sunscreens may not offer as much protection as one would hope. At this point, scientists are not certain whether sunscreen can help prevent melanoma. Exposing yourself to sun does help with vitamin D absorption and boosts mood, but the intensity of sun and the length of time that you are in the sun should be monitored.

Tips for sun safety:

- Wearing long-sleeved, lightweight, or breathable shirts and pants significantly helps shield your skin from UV rays and reduces your chance of burning.
- Make sure to put on a hat—the wider brimmed, the better!
- Choose your outdoor time wisely. Getting outside in the early morning and late afternoon is ideal, as the sun's rays are weaker compared to late morning and early afternoon.
- Find the shade or make your own. Use the shade from trees, umbrellas, or canopies to shield yourself from the sun.
- Check the UV index and be extra cautious on days with higher ratings.
- Choose sunscreens that contain titanium dioxide and/or zinc oxide for UV protection. You may need to reapply after swimming or any activity causing sweating.

5. Perchlorate

The thyroid gland is the primary organ of perchlorate toxicity in humans. High levels of perchlorate in the urine have also been associated with lower levels of the T4 hormone in the body.

Perchlorate, used in the manufacturing of many man-made materials, including batteries, gunpowder, paint, and rubber, can accumulate in the water and soil. This chemical is the explosive ingredient in solid rocket fuel, and has unfortunately leaked from multiple military bases and defense and aerospace contractors' plants in at least twenty-two states, contaminating drinking water for millions of Americans. Studies have shown that even low levels of perchlorate, which were previously deemed to be safe, have been found to be harmful to the thyroid gland in women who have low iodine levels—a recent study suggests emergent iodine deficiencies, particularly in women of childbearing age in the US.

My top tip for avoiding as much perchlorate as possible? Install a reverse osmosis water filter in your home. This will filter perchlorate out of the water. (Note that reverse osmosis filters also filter out many minerals. Many people choose to remineralize their reverse osmosis water.)

6. Bisphenol A (BPA) and Bisphenol S (BPS)

Bisphenol A (BPA) has been found to alter thyroid structure and act as an antagonist to T3 at thyroid hormone receptors. Bisphenol S appears to interfere with thyroid gland function.

BPA is found primarily in plastic bottles, the lining of many canned foods, and thermal paper, such as receipts, paper currency, transit passes, and movie ticket stubs. BPA use in baby bottles was banned in 2012 by the FDA after concerns were raised when studies revealed BPA mimics estrogen, causing hormonal havoc and potentially harming a baby's developing brain. Since then, many "BPA-free" plastic bottles have replaced BPA with another plastic called bisphenol S (BPS). Unfortunately, research is now revealing that this latter plastic may not only be just as harmful, but may cause damage at lower doses compared to BPA.

Most plastic water bottles contain BPA or BPS, which leaches into the water you drink. Levels of BPA and BPS have been shown to skyrocket in cashiers who regularly handle receipts. This is important—just touching the receipt increases the chemicals in our bloodstream! Likewise, we can assume the same process happens when we handle paper money.

Here are some tips to reduce exposure to BPA and BPS:

- Bring your own water, instead of buying bottled water. Use filtered water from your home and pour into a stainless-steel or glass reusable water bottle for on-the-go hydration.
- Use fresh or dried foods instead of canned foods, to avoid the chemicals found in canned products.
- If you don't need a receipt, don't take it, or ask for an e-receipt.
- After handling receipts and paper money, wash your hands well (I wash my hands as soon as I get home). BPA and BPS move from the fingers onto food, and then into the mouth, where it can be even more readily absorbed.
- Topical agents, such as creams and sanitizers, may increase the penetration of BPA or BPS. Avoid using creams and sanitizers (hopefully, you have switched to natural sanitizers!) right before handling receipts or paper money; wash your hands after, then apply the cream or sanitizer.

7. Fluoride

If you have ever done a little research online regarding fluoride and hypothyroidism, you know that the debate around fluoride is a serious issue! Wherever you stand on it, you—like me!—probably do not want to compromise your oral health, so here's what you need to know:

Fluoride does help prevent tooth decay, but it is only particularly effective among children and babies.

A Cochrane Review conducted in 2015 looked at twenty studies on the effects of fluoridated water on tooth decay and 135 studies on dental fluorosis. The report revealed that fluoridation is effective at reducing levels of tooth decay, specifically among children. The introduction of water fluoridation resulted in children having 35 percent fewer decayed, missing, and filled baby teeth and 26 percent fewer decayed, missing, and filled permanent teeth.

It is interesting to note that the evidence was stronger for baby teeth compared to permanent adult teeth.

Fluoride has been linked to multiple adverse health effects.

Another recent study published in 2014 concluded that "the available evidence suggests that fluoride has a potential to cause major adverse human health problems, while having only a modest dental caries prevention effect."

These adverse effects of fluoride include:

- Hypothyroidism when exposed to high levels
- Reduced cognitive development in children with high exposure to fluoride
- There have also been a number of studies that link fluoride and cancer. More than 50 population-based studies that have examined the potential link between water fluoride levels and cancer have been reported in the medical literature.
- Fluoride can interact with a wide range of enzymes, interfering with your body's ability to carry out important processes when you are exposed to toxic levels.

The harmful effects on the thyroid appear to be dependent on the amount of exposure.

Just like most adverse reactions, the more you are exposed to a potentially harmful substance, the higher the risk for harm. The same is true with fluoride and the thyroid. High amounts of fluoride have been linked to reduced thyroid function, including reduced production of T3 and T4 hormones. Harmful effects appear to be more prevalent in iodine-deficient individuals (iodine seems to help protect the thyroid from the adverse effects of fluoride). In fact, high amounts of fluoride used to be a treatment for hyperthyroidism as the substance was known to slow the thyroid down.

If you drink a lot of tap water, you are exposed to more fluoride.

The World Health Organization (WHO) guideline for fluoride in the water is 1.5 mg/L of water.

It is thought that chronic human exposures to levels above 1.5 mg/L of water could potentially cause health issues. Many people have never given it a second thought, but the more water you drink, including water that is used to boil your tea or make your coffee, the more fluoride you will be exposed to. It is hard to know for sure whether someone who drinks 4 to 5 liters of water a day (like myself) is exposed to too much fluoride, as each city and town has different levels of fluoride in their respective water system. However, it is safe to say that my exposure to fluoride would be much higher compared to someone who drank 1 to 2 liters of water a day, assuming the water is coming from fluoridated city tap water.

I now filter the fluoride out of my water at home. I still brush with fluoridated toothpaste on occasion, but I choose natural toothpaste more often. To keep up with oral hygiene, I rinse my mouth with warm water and sea salt, brush and floss at least twice a day, and visit the hygienist multiple times a year.

Tips to reduce your fluoride exposure include:

- Choose a water filtration system that filters fluoride out of your water. Common popular water filters (such as Brita) do not filter fluoride out.
- If you would like to completely reduce your fluoride exposure, ask your hygienist to use pumice instead of fluoride to clean your teeth during dental hygiene visits.
- If you are choosing a fluoride-free toothpaste, look for other ingredients that encourage oral health and reduce bacteria in the mouth, such as cloves, tea tree oil, and probiotics.

IF you have known long-term exposure to pesticides or other chemicals, a history of mercury or lead poisoning, or are suffering from serious environmental sensitivities, detoxing using intravenous (IV) vitamin C and possible chelating agents may be key in helping you heal. Many NDs and functional MDs have an IV license and may offer these services.

A SPIRITUAL CONNECTION TO TOXINS

A chapter on toxins would not be complete without addressing toxic relationships or any potentially toxic people who may be causing added stress in your life.

As we'll discuss more in the following chapter, countless studies have addressed how stress can make us ill. I have seen many patients in toxic relationships who, as a result, become sick. If you struggle with difficult relationships, I highly suggest seeking out a good therapist to help you create healthy boundaries, or to end relationships if they are no longer serving you. Just like the other toxins noted throughout this chapter, no toxic relationship is worth your health!

CHAPTER 3

Stress

If you can for a moment, imagine you are a bunny rabbit being chased by a fox. Your heart is pumping, you are sweating, and you are running for your life. There are two main outcomes to this scenario. Either the fox catches you for dinner, or he doesn't. If he doesn't catch you, then unless you were injured in the pursuit, you would most likely go back to a field and happily begin eating some clover again. Your heart rate would slow down, your muscles would relax, and you would begin to digest your food. Although during the height of the chase your stress hormones (such as cortisol) would have been elevated, allowing you to run as fast as you can, these hormones would drop and return to normal levels soon after your escape.

Now picture yourself dealing with a personal stressful situation. It could be your morning commute or a recent fight with a loved one. After this incident took place, did you go somewhere and relax? Just dive into a tasty meal and forget all about it? Chances are you may not have been able to rest, relax, and quickly forget about that highly stressful event. Although some of us thrive on persistent stress, most of my patients have a difficult time balancing the many stressors of today's lifestyle. Not surprisingly, financial stress is the number one worry of many North Americans. Other worries and stressors include family stress, relationship stress, and work-life balance (including commuting to and from the office). On top of our many constant and complex stressors, we tend to ponder and relive stressful situations. Over the years, I have realized that part of the stress issue with many of my patients is "perceived stress." The stress response in our body can activate whether something stressful is *actually* happening to us, or we are just worrying that it *could* happen to us. When we combine this constant worry with a busy lifestyle, the effect on the body—and the thyroid—can be dramatic.

Stress can be good or bad. It can propel us to complete tasks, meet deadlines, and think quickly on our feet. In essence, our stress response activates our fight-or-flight response when a stressful event arises. Studies have shown that although animals in the wild face many stressors (the bunny rabbit may face multiple potential predatory attacks a day), wild animals have adapted to handle chronic stress as they continue to breed and their stress response functions normally.

However, in humans, chronic stress has been shown to cause damage to the immune system, influencing changes to autoimmunity, increasing blood pressure, and causing hormonal havoc. It may lead to anxiety, depression, and even addiction. Many of my patients with autoimmune diseases, myself included, have had difficulty balancing stress at some point in their health journey.

THE STRESS RESPONSE

Humans function on a continuum between a sympathetic (fight-or-flight) and a parasympathetic (rest-and-digest) response.

Our stress response is primarily mediated by the hypothalamic-pituitary-adrenal (HPA) axis. The hypothalamus and the pituitary gland are both located in the brain. The adrenal glands are tiny endocrine organs that are found on top of our kidneys in our abdomen. The HPA axis is a dynamic combination of both the central nervous system and the endocrine system. When we encounter a stressful situation, the hypothalamus sends a signal to the pituitary gland, which sends another signal to the adrenal glands to produce cortisol, also known as the main "stress hormone." Essentially, the brain tells the adrenal glands to be on alert and they produce cortisol in response to the call. This is the fight-or-flight response. Other hormones that are produced in response to stress include adrenaline (epinephrine) and norepinephrine.

Cortisol, although it has a bad rap, is a pretty amazing hormone. Released in response to the sympathetic nervous system, cortisol is essential for proper water, carbohydrate, protein, and fat metabolism. Without this hormone, animals die within a week! The function of cortisol is to prepare the body for action in response to stress. Cortisol releases glucose (sugar) from your liver. Glucose gives your cells the energy they need to respond to a stressful situation as well as promoting arousal, alertness, motivation, and goal-directed behavior. When the bunny is being chased by the fox in the woods, or when we need to meet a tight deadline for work, cortisol levels surge in the body, promoting performance, concentration, and drive. Cortisol's other effects are to increase blood pressure, increase blood sugar, and suppress the immune system. Cortisol is actually a very potent anti-inflammatory hormone, helping to prevent nerve damage associated with inflammation.

The parasympathetic nervous system, on the other hand, promotes growth, repair, and healing in the body. This system helps restore energy reserves and is important for longevity. The parasympathetic response is necessary for digestion and is also crucial for optimal sexual function and orgasm. If the body is in a constant "alert" state, it will not be able to relax and have an enjoyable sexual experience. Studies have shown that stress is often the main reason men experience erectile dysfunction. This can also be true of women who are unable to reach an orgasm and/or have a low sex drive. It makes sense—sex is not ideal if you have a fox chasing after you in the woods!

SHORT-TERM VS. LONG-TERM STRESS

Cortisol's effects are ideal when a stressful situation is short term. For example, the bunny rabbit that ran away from the fox experienced a short period of stress. During this time, the blood pressure would have been raised in its body and sugar may have been released, allowing for quick energy, focus, and quick response time. The cortisol surged as a response from the brain's alarm system and would allow the body a good attempt at an escape. After a stressful situation or threat is over, cortisol should decrease and the parasympathetic system slows the stress response by increasing relaxing hormones, allowing the body and mind to rest, relax, and restore.

However, when stress becomes chronic, the brain constantly tells the adrenal glands to release cortisol. As previously mentioned, chronic stress can not only be a response to our busy modern lifestyle, but also in part because of our thoughts of worry, rumination, and magnification. I cannot begin to tell you how many patients have told me over the years that their thoughts are "their own worst enemy." Common themes seem to be constantly worrying about their children (even when they know they are going to be fine) or about their mortgage payments (despite having a good job with a reliable monthly paycheck). Our recurrent thoughts can continue to activate the stress response and prolong cortisol secretion.

Long-lasting activation of the stress response causes constant cortisol surges and results in cortisol dysfunction. After cortisol is consistently elevated, your body can become resistant to the cortisol and so may no longer have a proper response to stress. Over time, these continuous elevations in cortisol can cause the adrenal glands to "burn out" and significantly reduce the amount of cortisol that can be released. Both high and low cortisol levels in the body can cause unwanted symptoms and are a result of extended periods of stress (again, physical or mental).

Functional medical doctors and naturopaths often refer to this cortisol dysfunction (which encompasses either too-high or too-low elevations of cortisol) as adrenal fatigue or adrenal burnout. Dysfunction is not a disease, but an abnormal response in the body. Many conventional medical doctors do not accept this term, and tend to only address adrenal diseases, such as Addison's or Cushing's disease. Nonetheless, I have found that in both myself and my patients, addressing the dysfunction in the adrenal glands is paramount to healing the thyroid gland, especially when we are focusing on improving symptoms of fatigue.

SYMPTOMS OF CORTISOL DYSFUNCTION (ADRENAL FATIGUE)

I would argue that every single one of my patients with thyroid issues has also had some form of cortisol dysfunction or adrenal fatigue. This is especially true of those with Hashimoto's thyroiditis (the vast majority of patients with thyroid disease). Many patients with Hashimoto's recall that their symptoms of hypothyroidism started after a very stressful or traumatic event. If you are unsure where to start, first look at these symptoms, which are key indicators of adrenal fatigue, to truly assess cortisol levels in your body.

Symptoms are a key indicator that you are experiencing adrenal fatigue by way of either high or low cortisol levels. This assessment will help you determine whether you may have adrenal fatigue.

ELEVATED CORTISOL

1. Do you have constant sugar cravings? yes/no
2. Do you experience thinning skin or eczema? yes/no
3. Do you feel "wired but tired"? yes/no
4. Do you carry extra weight around your stomach? yes/no
5. Do you have high blood pressure? yes/no
6. Do you have elevated blood sugar (elevated fasting blood sugar or HbA1c greater than 5.8)? yes/no
7. Do you have difficulty getting to sleep at night and/or wake often throughout the night? yes/no
8. Do you constantly worry and/or feel a constant level of anxiety and worry? yes/no
9. Do you feel overwhelmed? That you have constant responsibilities or jobs so that you cannot take time for yourself or rest? yes/no
10. Have you had difficulty with fertility? yes/no
11. Have you experienced purplish stretch marks (also known as striae) on your tummy and/or back? yes/no

LOW CORTISOL

1. Are you constantly fatigued and do you especially have difficulty getting out of bed in the morning, even after a good night's rest (7 to 9 hours uninterrupted)? yes/no
2. Do you feel depressed and can you cry easily? yes/no
3. Do you constantly feel stressed? yes/no

4. Have you noticed you are using more caffeine or stimulants just to get through the day? yes/no
5. Do you crave chips, crackers, olives, or other really salty foods? yes/no
6. Do you have low blood pressure, or often feel dizzy when you stand up from a seated or lying position? yes/no

If you answered yes to three or more of the questions for either high or low cortisol, consider further testing.

Testing. I recommend a four-point cortisol saliva test. It can be ordered through an MD or ND. Labs offering this test include ZRT Laboratory, Genova Diagnostics, and Rocky Mountain Analytical. Cortisol can also be accurately measured via the urine in either a twenty-four-hour urine test, or a Dutch test. The Dutch test is also a comprehensive urine test that can offer great insights into hormone function, including cortisol.

Treatment. Simply put, lifestyle modifications (such as the ones discussed on page 57) are the most important when addressing adrenal fatigue and burnout. How can the body repair and recharge without rest?

Certain herbs, referred to as adaptogens, can also be extremely helpful. See page 217 to learn more.

THYROID, STRESS, AND ADRENAL FATIGUE

As with most hormones in the body, a delicate balance exists between the thyroid hormones and stress hormones, such as cortisol. High cortisol levels can suppress thyroid function. The opposite is also true; untreated hypothyroidism (both overt and subclinical) can cause cortisol levels to rise in the body. This begs the question: Does someone develop thyroid disease because of stress? Or does thyroid disease itself cause stress in the body? I believe both scenarios can be true (but keep in mind stress is only one piece of the puzzle for the development of the disease). It is also thought that normal thyroid function helps regulate and balance adrenal function. As stress has been shown to reduce the activity of the thyroid gland, T3 thyroid hormone levels have been shown to be reduced after

CLAUDIA showed up in my office looking for an alternative to conventional thyroid medication. Her MD had recently run her blood work for the second time and it was found that her TSH was high (18), and her T4 was just below the conventional normal range (8). She had been diagnosed with hypothyroid. At 28 years of age, she really did not want to be "put on medication for the rest of her life." Claudia described her current symptoms as being very tired, worrying more than usual, constantly craving sugar, having difficulty getting to sleep most nights, and having recently gained 8 pounds. Not only were Claudia's symptoms reflective of hypothyroidism, but she also had some classic symptoms of adrenal fatigue. When I asked her when she could remember these symptoms starting, she said it was about nine months earlier, when she quit her job and had to move back into her parents' house. Her relationship with her boyfriend had also become strained around this time and she was more stressed out than she ever had been before. She was now practicing deep breathing, which was helping, but she still felt that daily stress was harder to manage than it had been a year ago. I made a deal with Claudia than we would try a high dose of a specific adaptogenic herb known as withania, to help balance her adrenal glands and raise T4 levels in her thyroid gland. She would have to have her thyroid monitored every four to six weeks, and if after twelve weeks there was no improvement in her TSH and T4 levels, we would need to trial thyroid medication. Adaptogens are specific herbs that help the body adapt to stress and have been used to either lower cortisol or increase it back into balance. Withania also has a specific benefit to the thyroid gland. After four weeks, Claudia's blood work showed that her TSH had already been reduced to 6.2 and her T4 was back in range (10). After another five weeks, her TSH was normal (3) and her T4 was improved to 11. Claudia reported that she felt more like herself and her anxiety was gone. She also had a lot more energy and was sleeping better again. (You'll learn more about adaptogens and herbs and how to use them in Chapter 11.)

a stressful event. Stress also causes increased inflammation in the body, further reducing thyroid function.

Multiple studies have also shown that both physiological and psychological stress can cause immune changes in the body. These changes can lead to the development of autoimmunity and the onset of such conditions as Graves' or Hashimoto's. As noted in Chapter 1, stress is also a key factor in the development of intestinal permeability (leaky gut), which can lead to autoimmune disease.

Are Women More Stressed Out?

MEN and women handle stress differently. Women are more likely than men to report that their stress levels are on the rise and that they are dealing with chronic stress. They are also more likely to ruminate about their stressors. Although many men report that they feel "nothing" when stressed, most women report that they feel like they could cry when really stressed out. I don't think it is any coincidence that autoimmune disease and thyroid disease are also much more common in women compared to men.

TIPS FOR MANAGING STRESS

Step 1: Assess Your Daily Routine

There is no escaping stress. And, to be fair, stress truly is a powerful motivator and can be a key aspect to success. The goal is to manage stress and find a balance that works for you. My thyroid recovery would not have been possible without long-term lifestyle changes and key herbs and vitamins (covered in Chapter 11). I know this is true of many of my patients' returns to health; stress management is paramount.

When addressing stress management, it is important to look at your entire day, from start to finish, to incorporate changes that work for you. Stress-reduction techniques that are only practiced on weekends, once a month, or on vacations are not long-term solutions. Just as you would take a medication *daily* for a disease, stress reduction needs to be incorporated like a prescription for health and practiced every day. The following are some of most common daily stressors that I see in practice, with easy tweaks for stress management.

- **Upon waking:** Do you check your phone as soon as you wake up? This common habit can send our brain and body into high drive with answering emails, responding to messages, or comparing ourselves to others on numerous social media platforms. Instead of checking your phone immediately when you wake, do something for yourself that is enjoyable and relaxing. Try 5 to 10 minutes of deep breathing or stretching, making yourself a tea or coffee, and mindfully enjoying it before your day gets started, or getting outside for a quick morning walk.

- **Breakfast:** Unless you are intermittently fasting, eating breakfast is key for mood balance, especially if you are drinking caffeine. I cannot begin to tell you how many of my patients have reported that their anxiousness and irritability reduced after incorporating even a small breakfast (a piece of fruit or a handful of seeds) when they drank their morning coffee. Many people don't realize how caffeine can be overstimulating, especially when taken on an empty stomach in the morning.

- **Commute:** If you are driving, and in traffic, what are you doing? Ruminating? Worrying? Cursing at other drivers? Many North Americans now spend over two hours a day in their cars, and this can be a perfect time to work on stress reduction. Meditation is often not recommended while driving (no one wants to fall asleep at the wheel!); however, deep breathing can be practiced while driving, as well as listening to relaxing music or nature sounds. I also encourage patients to monitor the amount of time they listen to the news on the radio (or watch on the TV, for that matter). Rarely is the news positive, and often it can cause more worry and anxieties. If you take public transit, you can use that time to meditate, practice deep breathing, or listen to relaxing music.

- **Lunch break:** Are you eating at your desk? If you are, I encourage you to take a small break elsewhere to eat your lunch. As mentioned earlier in this chapter, relaxation by way of the parasympathetic nervous system is required for digestion. In other words, we need to rest to digest. Working while eating keeps us stimulated and can lead to indigestion, bloating, and gas.

- **After work:** Are you making time after work for yourself? Or do you have multiple commitments that take up your time? Many of my patients have told me that they feel uncomfortable saying no when asked to volunteer or get involved in a group of some kind. Don't get me wrong; extracurricular activities can be wonderful and fulfilling—if they are bringing you joy. But if you feel overwhelmed and as if you don't have enough downtime, it may be important to start saying no to activities that do not bring you joy.
- **Before bed:** Sleep helps repair our tissues and balance our hormones. Nighttime rituals (also known as sleep hygiene practices) are important factors for optimizing sleep. Please see page 74 for more on how to have a good night's rest. If you are on your phone or computer within one hour of going to sleep, it could be interfering with your ability to get that rest. Alcohol before bed can also disrupt your ability to get restorative sleep.

HEALING TIP: Put yourself first. Let go of the guilt you may feel if you prioritize taking a bath instead of going out on the town; decide to sleep in, or indulge in a good book. Allow yourself to have quiet time and revel in it—rest is required for healing.

Step 2: Stress-Reduction Activities

Over the last few decades, relaxation activities, such as yoga, meditation, and mindfulness, have become more commonly practiced and incorporated into our lives. I will say, the majority of patients who show up in my office with adrenal fatigue report that although they know they *should* be doing something more often to lower their stress levels, they aren't. The reasons can be multifactorial: they feel too tired, it is too expensive, or they simply don't want to join a class or run out of the house yet again for something like yoga as soon as they finish dinner.

Activities focused on relaxation, rejuvenation, and self-care should be enjoyable and easy to implement—that is the whole point! Many things can be done from the comfort of your own home (or office) that do not require money or travel time. First and foremost is mindfulness meditation.

Mindfulness meditation is the act of simply being present in the moment, and observing but not judging our thoughts and feelings. Although meditation sounds so straightforward, it can be difficult for many people, myself included. I still struggle with my to-do list when I start my practice, and some days I find that I am constantly working to bring myself back to listening to the sound of my heartbeat. However, meditation has some incredible benefits and is a powerful way to reduce the stress in our body. Meditation can help put us in a relaxed state and encourage the body to heal. *This benefit of meditation is key: meditation may cause physical changes in the body to promote healing.* Research has shown that meditation may actually slow, stall, or even reverse changes in the brain that happen with normal aging!

Even better, mind-body therapies, such as mindfulness, appear to support the immune system by encouraging immune balance, and may even be helpful in fighting off viruses. This aspect of mindfulness is one of the main reasons it can be so advantageous for thyroid recovery. It fosters an environment in the body for healing, while promoting positive immune system changes. I cannot even begin to imagine the changes in disease we would see if people could just quit their stressful jobs, stop commuting, and start meditating for hours every day. This, of course, is not reality for most of us, but meditation is a powerful tool to incorporate in the healing process.

Other benefits of meditation include lowering blood pressure, reducing anxiety, improving sleep, and increasing our ability to feel happiness.

A study conducted by Georgetown Medical Center in 2014 found that individuals who practiced eight weeks of mindfulness meditation had a reduction in stress hormones (and other inflammatory markers) and also had reductions in self-reported stress compared to a control group. Another study found that mindfulness meditation lowers the cortisol levels in the blood of medical students, suggesting that it can lessen stress and may decrease the risk of diseases that arise from stress.

As mindfulness meditation can be difficult for many, especially beginners, I find guided meditation a great place to start. You can still practice the meditation just about anywhere, but you will need either your smartphone, computer, or good old-fashioned boom box and CD player. Many meditation gurus suggest sitting cross-legged with a straight back when practicing meditation; however, don't let this hold you back. You can still meditate while lying down (however, you may fall asleep!) or while walking. Benefits of meditation are exponential; the more your practice, the more you will notice a change. I suggest starting with at least five minutes, three times a week, and increase the time and/or frequency as you see fit. Remember that meditation is a skill and it does take time to learn. Your meditation practice will most likely never be perfect, so don't expect it to be. Every effort toward attempting meditation and focusing on relaxation counts!

You can find an app (I like Calm, Headspace, and Jon Kabat-Zinn's apps) or use guided meditation from YouTube or other places online. UCLA also provides free guided meditations on its website at https://www.uclahealth.org/marc/mindful-meditations. Guided meditation CDs can be found at most bookstores or at many secondhand stores and libraries. I recommend finding a quiet room, turning off your cell phone, and letting yourself be led through the meditation for at least five minutes. You can set a timer if you like, as five minutes can feel like a long time, especially if you are just starting your meditation practice.

Deep Breathing

Another technique that is affordable and easy to practice anywhere is "breathwork," or deep breathing (also referred to as diaphragmatic breathing). Studies have shown that deep breathing can increase mood and reduce anxiety, depression, and stress. Research has also found that regular deep-breathing practices can lower cortisol levels. Whether we are aware of it or not, when we are stressed, our breathing changes and we begin to take more rapid, shallow breaths. This sends a signal to the brain that can trigger the sympathetic nervous system and activate the fight-or-flight response. By simply changing our breathing to take slower, deeper, and more rhythmic breaths, we can override this response and turn on the parasympathetic nervous system, which helps calm our body down.

There are many ways of deep breathing. In my practice, I generally focus on diaphragmatic breathing and alternate nostril breathing. Both of these forms of breathwork are easy, and their benefits are well researched. As with meditation, the more you practice deep breathing, the greater the results and the easier (and frankly more enjoyable) the practice will become. Just as with mindfulness meditation, if you are up to trying breathwork, I suggest giving it a try for at least five minutes a day, three times a day, and work your way up. Breathwork is also a great tool to use on the spot in a stressful situation. If you are uncomfortable deep breathing in public, and you would like to practice during your workday, you can always find somewhere more private, such as a quiet place in the park or on a park bench, or an available private conference room or boardroom, or practice in your car.

Diaphragmatic breathing can be practiced anywhere, but is best learned lying down.

1. To begin, lie comfortably on your back with your knees slightly bent. A pillow can be helpful under your knees for support.
2. Place one hand on your chest over your heart and the other hand on your stomach, above your belly button but below your rib cage. This is the area of your diaphragm.
3. Inhale slowly through your nose, feeling your stomach move outward into your hand as you inhale, and then pull in your stomach as you exhale through the mouth. Your chest should remain as still as possible. Go at your own pace but exaggerate the exhale through your mouth. Your body will relax more when you practice longer exhales.

After you have the hang of diaphragmatic breathing, try it sitting up.

1. Start by sitting comfortably (in a chair, on your knees, or cross-legged).
2. Again, place one hand on your belly and one hand on your chest. Feel your hand that is placed on your stomach expand out into your hand. Remember to try to keep your chest as still as possible.
3. Inhale slowly through your nose and exhale through your mouth, trying to ensure your exhales are longer than your inhales.

Alternate nostril breathing (also known as *anuloma viloma pranayama*) is a form of slow, rhythmic, breathing where you use your finger to block one nostril and then the other nostril.

1. Begin by either sitting or lying in a comfortable position. Block your right nostril with your thumb. Breathe through your left nostril for a count of 6 seconds.
2. Then, use your index finger to block your left nostril (both nostrils will be closed). Count to 6 seconds if you can, but do not hold your breath for this long if it feels uncomfortable.
3. Release your right thumb from your right nostril and breathe out for a count of 6 seconds.
4. Now, breathe in from your right nostril for a count of 6 seconds (your index finger will still be holding your left nostril closed).
5. Then, block your right nostril with your right thumb (again both nostrils will be closed) and hold your breath for as long as feels comfortable but only up to 6 seconds.
6. Now, open your left nostril by releasing your right index finger and breathe air out of your left nostril for 6 seconds. This completes 1 cycle.

Ideally, alternate nostril breathing is practiced for thirty minutes, but just like the other mind-body therapies discussed here, even a few minutes can have an impact.

Spend Time in Nature

This is another wonderful (and free!) activity to lower stress. A recent study showed that by spending just twenty minutes in nature reduced cortisol levels. And for people who spent longer than twenty minutes in nature, their cortisol levels dropped even further! The study, conducted at the University of Michigan, asked research participants to choose any time of day, during daylight hours, to spend in nature. The participants also chose their own place for their nature experience and was defined as anywhere outside where they could interact with nature. During this time, participants were asked to avoid the use of social media and internet, and to not take phone calls. They were also asked not to participate in conversation or reading. Aerobic exercise was also not suggested. The key here is to really take in nature and your natural surroundings—to observe the sky, the trees, or the birds, even if you are sitting on a park bench in the middle of a noisy city. If you live in a cooler climate, this activity is still absolutely possible, but just requires a bit of bundling up before venturing out, especially on cold days.

MARK, a 43-year-old executive, showed up in my office knowing he needed to work on his stress reduction. His blood pressure was at an all-time high, he had gained over 20 pounds in the last two or three years, he was experiencing daily headaches, and he constantly felt anxious. On top of this, his medical doctor had mentioned that his thyroid hormone levels had recently been a little "off" and he would need to run them again in four to six weeks. Due to his high-stress job, he needed some stress-reduction solutions that could somehow fit into his busy lifestyle. He also reported that he really did not want to be on conventional medication, nor did he like the idea of taking supplements. I asked Mark to commit to spending twenty-five minutes a day, on his lunch break, observing nature. He could sit on a park bench, lie on a grassy area in the small park close to his work, or simply go for a gentle stroll while observing the clouds and feeling the sunshine on his back. However, he had to either leave his cell phone at the office or turn it off for the duration of his "nature time." A month later, Mark could not believe the dramatic effect such a small intervention was having on his health. His blood pressure had already dropped, he was sleeping better at night, and his headaches had also reduced. He had even lost a few pounds and noticed he wasn't craving sweets in the same way as he was a few weeks earlier. Two weeks later, upon blood testing, his thyroid levels had also improved, closer to a normal range again. Even better, he was encouraging some of his colleagues and other employees in the office to practice their own nature time.

Exercise

Multiple studies have shown that exercise and physical activity helps lower stress and reduce anxiety. But note that while exercise is healthy, more isn't necessarily better. Too much aerobic exercise can increase cortisol levels and can also reduce thyroid hormones, thus affecting thyroid function over time. In fact, high-intensity endurance athletes such as long-distance runners, triathletes, and cyclists, are exposed to higher cortisol levels over longer periods. Overtraining, whether you are a professional athlete or someone who loves to hit the gym hard multiple days a week, can actually lead to symptoms of hypothyroidism, such as fatigue, anxiety, weight gain, and depression.

Low-intensity exercise, on the other hand, does not appear to raise cortisol levels in the body and may help reduce cortisol levels. Short bursts of high-intensity exercise, such as HIIT training or sprinting, are generally okay for cortisol levels as long as rest periods in between sets are long enough.

If you feel worse after exercising and/or feel extremely fatigued the following day postexercise, you may want to seriously consider switching to a lower intensity form of physical activity. I still remember feeling hung over one day after I really pushed myself in the gym. Even worse, I was pretty sure I was gaining weight despite exercising for one hour, four to five times a week! As soon as I began to exercise less often, do less cardio, and began to practice resting more in between weight-lifting sets, I not only had more energy, but my weight began to shift.

There are many different forms of low-intensity (or low-impact) exercise. Some of my favorites include:

- Yoga
- Pilates
- Walking
- Swimming
- Tai chi
- Strength training (weight lifting)
- Gentle biking/cycling

- If you love cardio, opt for shorter periods (no more than 30 minutes at a time) or take a few minutes to rest between periods of aerobic activity.

When choosing an exercise, choose something you enjoy, and something that still makes you sweat. Dr. Valter Longo, professor and director of the Longevity Institute at UCLA, says that exercise should not only be enjoyed, but that the best exercise for longevity is something that you can incorporate into your daily routine and that you can practice until your hundredth birthday—and beyond!

CHAPTER 4

Electromagnetic Fields (EMFs)

Technological advances now offer us incredible benefits and conveniences. Although the internet has only been around since 1989, I cannot imagine a world without it! The plethora of information that can be accessed in a split second is amazing, not to mention how I am able to connect with friends, family, colleagues, and patients all over the world. Then, there are the benefits from credit cards (who needs to carry cash?!), hair dryers, high-speed blenders (I love my green smoothies), medical screening tools, cell phones (remember when we had to go to a pay phone to make a call when we were out of the house?), and Netflix—these are just a few that immediately come to mind. However, these advances in technology have also brought an increased exposure to a form of radiation commonly known as EMFs (electromagnetic fields).

An electromagnetic field is exactly what it sounds like: a physical field produced by electrically charged objects. Electric and magnetic fields are invisible areas of energy (also called radiation) that are produced by electricity. EMFs are organized on a spectrum and classified by their wavelength and frequency. Higher-frequency EMFs have higher energy and shorter wavelengths. These types of higher-frequency EMFs produce ionizing radiation. Lower-frequency EMFs have lower energy and longer wavelengths. The lower-frequency EMFs produce non-ionizing radiation.

EMFs are essentially found everywhere is nature. Visible light from the sun is a type of EMF, as is UV light and infrared light. These are naturally made EMFs, but the majority of the EMFs we are now exposed to are from man-made electronic devices. If you just take a look around your environment right now, you are most likely sitting in a room that contains multiple forms of EMFs.

Common sources of EMF, from lowest to highest frequency, include:

LOWER FREQUENCY (NON-IONIZING RADIATION)

- AC power (50 to 60 Hz)
- TV and radio waves
- Cell phone signals
- Wi-Fi
- Microwaves
- Infrared rays
- Visible light

HIGHER FREQUENCY (IONIZING RADIATION)

- Ultraviolet (UV) light
- X-rays
- Gamma rays
- Cosmic rays

EMFs are used not only for technological applications, such as computers, power lines, cell phones, and household appliances, but are also widely applied for medical purposes, such as imaging for diagnostic reasons.

Unless you never use a smartphone, never have medical imaging of any kind, live off the grid, and do not use Wi-Fi, you are constantly being exposed to high levels of these lower-frequency man-made EMFs at levels millions of times greater than what we would naturally be exposed to in nature. Our bedrooms, where most of us spend a great many hours over our lifetime, are particularly reflective of this relatively new increase in EMF exposure. Not only do many of us have TVs, modems, and Bluetooth applications in our bedroom, lots of us are sleeping with our phone.

As these sources of man-made EMFs have increased in number over the last few years, many health-care professionals and scientists have raised concerns about the health implications of this amplified amount of radiation on our body. Granted, many of us may not realize it, but our body also contains electric currents due to the multiple chemical reactions that are constantly taking place for normal human function. Elements in our body, such as magnesium, calcium, sodium, and potassium, have a specific electrical charge. Nearly all our cells can use these charged elements, known as ions, to generate electrical currents. For example, the nervous system consistently sends and receives electric impulses, the heart pumps blood due to electric activity, and even digestion and many other biochemical processes require charged particles for functioning. When we come into contact with EMFs, changes are seen in the voltage gated calcium channels (VGCC) in our body. These VGCCs are found in multiple types of tissues, including some cells of the thyroid gland. This means the energy transmitted from these devices can affect the electrical charges of humans (including the thyroid gland) and in theory affect biological processes. Or more simply put, the electric currents outside are affecting the electric currents inside.

Concerns about EMFs are not a new phenomenon. Back in the 1950s, researchers found that microwaves could damage the lens of the eye in animals. In the '60s, more studies reported that microwaves could harm the gonads of animals and may lead to reproductive difficulties, and radio waves were also found to change brain activity in primates.

Although this initial research concerned some, many scientists concluded over the last few decades that for EMFs to truly affect one's health, exposure would need to be in excess, or in much larger amounts than one typically would experience during the day. (Sounds very similar to the story with toxins, doesn't it?)

The problem is that our exposure to EMFs is constantly increasing, with new technology more readily available than ever before. As a result of Wi-Fi and smartphones, we are constantly connected to the internet and carry it with us throughout the day. Children's schools are replacing books (and libraries) with computers; we rarely use CDs or tape recordings anymore; and Bluetooth technology is now operational in many people's cars. And really, who can blame us for using so much technology? It allows us to work from anywhere, Google our queries instantly, and turn on Netflix from the comfort of our bed.

After the initial studies in the '50s and '60s, research over the years has shown associations between exposure to extremely low frequency–electromagnetic fields (ELF–EMF) or radiofrequency radiation (RFR) and increased health risk (including cancer and fertility problems) in individuals working or living in environments exposing them to those fields. Not only have EMFs been shown to impact sperm levels, but women exposed to high amounts of EMFs during pregnancy may also have an increased risk of miscarriage. Other studies have raised concerns on cellular and hormonal changes with exposure over time to ELF–EMFs or RFR.

Sources of ELF–EMFs studied include power lines, electrical wiring, and electrical appliances, such as shavers, hair dryers, and electric blankets. The most common sources of RFRs are wireless telecommunication devices and equipment, including cell phones, smart meters, and portable wireless devices, such as tablets and laptop computers. Although hotly debated, several studies emerged that began to link cell phone radiation to tumors and cancerous growths in the brain and neck (i.e., close to the thyroid gland.)

In 2018, a massive study conducted by the US National Toxicology Program (NTP) looked at the effects of exposing rats and mice to cell phone radiation to help clarify potential health hazards, including cancer risk, from exposure to RFR like that used in 2G and 3G cell phones.

The results were astonishing.

- Clear evidence of tumors (malignant schwannomas) in the hearts of rats
- Some evidence of tumors (malignant gliomas) in the brains of rats
- Some evidence of tumors (benign, malignant, or complex combined pheochromocytoma) in the adrenal glands of rats

It is important to note that this research was conducted on the radiation from 2G and 3G phones. Since this research has been completed, many people are using even more powerful networks (4G and LTE) that arguably emit even more radiation than the 2G and 3G networks. There is mounting concern that the newest and strongest wireless network, 5G, will carry even greater health risks.

Currently at least 240 scientists from forty-one different nations with published peer-reviewed EMF papers are signatories to the International EMF Scientist Appeal, unified in the opinion that the body of research on EMF bioeffects is not only compelling, but urgent.

EMF SENSITIVITY

Electromagnetic hypersensitivity (EHS) is characterized by symptoms involved in the nervous or immune system that intensify when a person is exposed to EMFs. People who are overly sensitive to EMFs experience noticeable stress or illness associated with exposure or use of smartphones, laptops, microwaves, power lines, and other sources of EMFs. Some symptoms of EHS are similar to those of thyroid disease, including fatigue, memory troubles, and mood changes, such as anxiety and depression. Individuals with autoimmune diseases may be more likely to experience symptoms of electromagnetic hypersensitivity. Currently, EHS is not recognized as a medical diagnosis. However, it is accepted as a functional impairment in Sweden, and the Canadian Human Rights Commission identifies it as an environmental sensitivity and classifies it as a disability. Researcher and professor Dr. Magda Havas is an expert in the biological effects of non-ionizing frequencies. She is particularly interested in identifying and supporting people with EHS. Dr. Havas has developed a quiz to assess whether you are experiencing EHS:

- Does shopping in big box stores cause confusion and poor short-term memory? Do you go with a shopping list in hand just to spend as little time as possible because you become overwhelmed? yes/no
- Do you have difficulty finding your car after shopping at a mall or big box store? yes/no
- Do you experience a headache when shopping in big box stores or malls? yes/no
- Do you feel dizzy, nauseous, fatigued, anxious, or depressed after visiting a mall or big box store? yes/no
- Do you have problems with vision or hearing (buzzing in the ears) after shopping at a mall or big box store? yes/no

- Do you experience a feeling of warmth or have facial flushing on the side of the head where you hold your mobile phone? yes/no
- Do you experience tingling or numbness in the fingers on the same side where you hold the mobile phone? yes/no
- Do you get headaches that become increasingly worse with continued phone use? yes/no
- Do you have times when you cannot be in the same room as others who are using a mobile phone? yes/no
- Does being exposed to fluorescent lights cause you to experience a headache? yes/no
- Do you experience nausea, memory loss, or brain fog after being exposed to fluorescent lights? yes/no
- Do you experience eye strain, watery eyes, or problems with vision or hearing after being exposed to fluorescent lights? yes/no
- Do you experience skin rashes and itchiness when exposed to fluorescent lights? yes/no
- Do you feel depressed and moody when exposed to fluorescent lights? yes/no
- Do you experience brain fog or confusion that becomes worse when you are close to a computer or Wi-Fi? yes/no
- Do you experience rashes or skin problems when being close to a computer? yes/no
- Do you experience numbness or tingling of the hands or feet when you are close to a computer? yes/no
- Do you experience watery eyes or vision problems with computer use? yes/no

I also ask the question:

Do you have trouble sleeping and/or concentration issues especially after visiting a mall, being on the phone, working on the computer, or being exposed to fluorescent lights?

If you answered yes to three or more of these questions, you may be experiencing symptoms from exposure to EMFs or simply are exposed to too much EMFs. Nick Pineault, EMF expert and author of *The Non-Tinfoil Guide to EMFs*, suggests an "EMF challenge" if you believe you are experiencing EHS. He suggests, for three days, to:

- Shut down the circuit breakers to your bedroom at night (you would have to do this from your main circuit control box, often located in the basement of your home).
- Turn off or unplug your Wi-Fi router before going to bed.
- Ensure there are no EMF devices in your bedroom (laptops, electric blankets, alarm clocks, or cell phone docking stations that are connected to Bluetooth, etc.) and switch your phone to "airplane mode" before going to bed.

I also suggest removing TVs from the bedroom (if possible). Not only does it reduce EMF exposure, but it also reduces the temptation to watch television before bed, which inevitably interferes with restorative sleep!

If you feel better after three days of following the EMF challenge and particularly notice

- More energy
- Feeling refreshed after waking
- Reduction in headaches
- Reduction in brain fog or the ability to think more clearly
- Increased libido

Then you may want to consider consulting with a functional medical doctor, naturopathic doctor, or a doctor who specializes in environmental medicine. Make sure you are taking action and reducing your exposure to EMFs by following the tips found on page 75.

Even if we don't necessarily experience the EHS symptoms, we cannot deny that we now live in a world that is constantly plugged in. I believe this is partially to blame for the rise in anxiety and depression that we are seeing, especially in our youth.

WHAT DOES THIS ALL MEAN
FOR THE THYROID GLAND?

Cell phone radiation can affect thyroid gland metabolism as a part of its "nonthermal effects." These radio frequency (RF) waves emanate from the antenna, which is part of the body of a handheld cell phone. With the emergence of smartphones in the early 2000s, the antenna position is on the bottom of the smartphone, moving the concentration of the RF waves to right over the jaw and much closer to the thyroid gland. The waves are strongest at the antenna and lose energy quickly as they travel away from the phone. Studies have found body tissues closest to the phone, such as the thyroid and brain, absorb more energy than do tissues farther away.

- A 2005 study found that rats exposed to EMF from cell phones for 30 minutes a day, 5 days a week for 4 weeks, found that there was decreased serum TSH and thyroid hormone levels in their blood after exposure.
- In 2008, researchers found that chronic exposure to radiation from microwaves altered the levels of thyroid hormone in rats, and also changed the rats' emotional reactivity.
- Results from a 2016 study showed that computer workers who were exposed to computers for approximately 8 hours a day had lower levels of TSH, thyroid hormones, and zinc concentrations compared to the control group.
- A systematic review in 2014 suggests that in genetically predisposed subjects, the effects of EMFs may stimulate the onset and progression of autoimmune diseases (such as Hashimoto's hypothyroidism). Another 2016 review echoed this conclusion and stated that there is growing evidence of the potential role of EMFs in autoimmune activation and immune functions.
- A 2017 study found there was a significant correlation between total cell phone radiation exposure and increasing TSH values in the human study group.
- Research conducted by a group of scientists in 2018 reported that although they could not find any significant association between cell phone use and thyroid cancer, they did find an elevated risk of small cancerous tumors (microcarcinomas) in people who used a cell phone for more than 15 years, for more than 2 hours a day, or for a greater amount of lifetime hours. The researchers concluded more research was needed in looking into thyroid cancer and cell phone usage.

- In 2019, a review of 22 studies pertaining to EMFs and thyroid changes were examined by researchers. Of the 22 included studies, 11 reported changes in T3 and T4 levels (primarily decreases in T3 and T4, but a few found increases in these hormones). In 10 other studies, TSH alteration was reported. Seven studies examined cellular changes in the thyroid gland and found that the volume of thyroid cells could be reduced by EMF exposure. The authors of the study concluded, "Based on the evidence discussed above, the reduction in diameter of thyroid follicles is potentially linked with cell phone radiation. Exposure may negatively influence the iodine uptake in the thyroid gland or increases temperature effect on the thyroid gland . . . further research is necessary."

It is apparent that the evidence is not crystal clear when it comes to EMFs and health risks. However, studies have found some potential risks to the thyroid hormones and the tissue of the thyroid gland, and that they may also have some involvement with autoimmunity and immune system changes. This is especially true with increased exposure over time. Given that many of us continue to be exposed to more forms of EMFs and at potentially greater strengths, I have started to take precautions for myself and my family, and suggest that my patients do the same.

HOW EMFs MAY INHIBIT THYROID RECOVERY

Whether or not you choose to believe that EMFs may negatively affect your health, we cannot deny the impact technology is having on our sleep. Blue light emitted from smartphones, TVs, and laptops interferes with our natural circadian rhythm and hormonal balance. For the large number of Americans who keep their smartphone in their bedroom, this means access to the internet, text, or email at all hours of the night, and studies are showing that more and more people are on their phones at all hours of the night. Over the last fifty years, Americans are sleeping significantly fewer hours on a nightly basis (from eight to nine hours a night to only five to six hours a night on a regular basis!).

According to the National Institutes of Health (NIH), quality sleep, and getting enough of it at the right times, is as essential to survival as food and water. In fact, simply not getting enough sleep over time increases your risk of developing an autoimmune disease. The human immune system and sleep are both associated and influenced by each other. Not only is our ability to remain healthy dependent on adequate sleep, but our demand for sleep is increased when we are unwell. Lack of sleep or sleep deprivation can cause hormonal havoc. Individuals who were subjected to just six days of sleep restriction had changes in their TSH, T4, and leptin levels (leptin is one of the key hormones responsible for appetite). After the subjects recovered (by having twelve hours of sleep a night for a few days!), hormone balance was achieved again.

If you are on your phone into the late hours of the night, how will you ever get a good night's rest? Plus, you may be experiencing some form of EHS and not even know it, further contributing to the fatigue and other frustrating symptoms of hypothyroidism. Adults require between seven and nine hours of sleep a night for a healthy immune system and hormonal balance. Here are some tips for optimizing your sleep:

- Avoid looking at screens (smartphones, TVs, laptops) 45 minutes to one hour before bedtime. Although this tip may be the most difficult for many, I truly believe it is one of the most important factors to getting a good night's rest and achieving hormonal balance. The blue light emitted from screens interferes with our melatonin production, and it takes almost an hour after switching off screens for the brain to recalibrate and begin to produce adequate hormones for sleep. Blue light–blocking apps can help; however, screens are still stimulating. Reading a book (a physical book), hanging out with your bed partner, or practicing some deep breathing and/or meditation is much more relaxing than anything we would be doing with electronics.
- Keep your room dark. I use blackout curtains and do not keep any electronics in my room, as many of them emit some sort of light and EMFs.
- Reduce the temperature at night. Optimal temperature for sleep is approximately 61° to 65°F (16° to 18°C). Put on the AC, open the windows, or reduce the heat to keep your room closer to this temperature range.

- Keep quiet. Most of us sleep best noise-free. Consider the use of earplugs if you live in a noisy home or are easily awoken by sounds outside. I opt for white noise (my air filter provides some great white noise) but there are also some great white noise machines on the market (make sure they don't come with lights that glow overnight, interfering with your bedroom's darkness). Many apps, available on smartphones, can provide white noise or binaural beats. Just make sure to turn your phone to airplane mode!

- Create a routine—and stick to it. Go to bed and get up at the same time (within an hour) every day, even on weekends.

- Watch your caffeine intake. Many of us are slow metabolizers of coffee and other forms of caffeine. For some, it can take up to 12 hours for the caffeine to process and be eliminated from the body. This means that if we have a latte at 3 p.m., by 3 a.m. we still may have some caffeine lingering in our system, preventing us from getting into a good deep sleep.

- Avoid alcohol before bed or eliminate it altogether. Booze can make some people sleepy and is often associated with relaxation. Although alcohol may help us get to sleep, it can prevent us from having a rejuvenating slumber.

WHAT CAN WE DO TO PROTECT OURSELVES FROM EMFs?

Just like reducing our chemical load, small changes over time can make a big impact in reducing our exposure to EMFs. Simply by increasing our distance from the sources of EMFs we can limit our radiation.

EMF SAFETY TIPS FOR THE THYROID GLAND

- Avoid holding a cell phone close to your head/jaw and neck. Use speakerphone or a headset instead. Distance reduces the radiation exposure, so by keeping the cell phone away from your neck, the level of radiation decreases. Headphones can be helpful, but make sure they are not Bluetooth, as this technology also increases radiation to the head.

- Text more often (but not when you are driving!). Phones emit less radiation during texting compared to calling. Plus, it reduces the need for the cell phone to be close to your head and neck.
- Make your phone calls when the signal is strong. When the cell phone has fewer signal bars, research has shown that the phone emits more radiation when making the call. Hang up the phone if you are in an area with weak signals and call the person back when you have a stronger signal.

OTHER GENERAL EMF SAFETY TIPS

- Avoid storing your phone on or close to your body (including under the pillow or in your bed!). Even though the level of radiation is reduced when the cell phone is not actively making a call, it is still sending and receiving signals and connecting to cell phone towers (that is, radiation exposure is still taking place!). Instead, set your phone down on a table or desk. Some people have a special storage drawer or bowl that they keep on the counter for devices to not only keep them away from their body but also so they don't misplace their devices.
- Do not carry your phone in your pocket, bra, or anywhere else on your body. If you are using headphones to reduce your exposure to your head and neck, but you slip your phone in your bra or pocket, it just changes the area of your body that is experiencing the higher amount of radiation. Ideally your phone is on a table while you are talking, or if you need to carry the phone, it is best to hold it in your hand away from your body. If you must carry your phone in your pocket or bra (and hopefully you are not talking on it while you do so), consider switching it to airplane mode. By turning your phone to airplane mode, you disable the RF transmission, thereby significantly decreasing the radiation.
- Turn your Wi-Fi off at night. If you live in a home where people require the internet overnight, ensure that the Wi-Fi router is not in any of the bedrooms.
- Do not use your laptop on your lap. This seems counterintuitive, as the naming of the laptop clearly suggests the computer should

be used on your lap! But by setting your laptop over your body you are increasing the radiation to the pelvic area. Studies have shown that the heat and the radiation from Wi-Fi signals in the laptop can decrease sperm quality, impacting fertility.

- Consider using Wi-Fi less often and bring back the Ethernet cable. Do you remember when you had to plug into the internet? You can reduce your exposure to Wi-Fi by using an Ethernet cable attached to your computer and plugging it directly into the router. Make sure to turn off the Wi-Fi connection in the router; otherwise, it stays on even if unused.

- Switch your cell phone to airplane mode at night.

- Remove fluorescent lights and dimmer switches from the home (both contain higher levels of radiation). Plus, I have found many patients sleep better when they remove fluorescent lighting in the house and replace it with softer, dimmer light. This can also be true of bright lighting emitted from electronics. Reduce the intensity of light emitted from your smartphone and computer by going into their settings and dimming down the level of brightness.

- Smart meters (gadgets often attached to the side of buildings that track the use of utilities such as natural gas or water) emit the same type of RF waves as Wi-Fi and cell phones. Ideally, the bedrooms in your home should not be located on the same wall as the smart meter. People who are very sensitive to EMFs may consider calling the electrical company and requesting a manual meter for a higher cost.

- "Smart home" gadgets, such as security devices or items that start the oven and close the blinds, all link into Wi-Fi. The more signals that are continually being sent and received by these gadgets, the more EMF exposure. Some people may opt for the convenience as a trade-off for some increased exposure. But the benefit does not outweigh any potential risks for me; I will turn on the oven and close the blinds myself!

- Sit at least 6 feet away from TV screens and home entertainment systems.

SOME people may consider the use of certain products, such as cell phone cases and stickers, which are marketed to block EMFs from their phone. Although these items may reduce radiation exposure, ensure that the company has conducted third-party research confirming the case truly limits EMF exposure. Only a certain number of companies have evidence to support their claims. On the other hand, poorly designed cell phone cases can partially block a cell phone's antenna, making the device work harder to transmit signals and thus actually increasing EMF exposure. Cell phone cases that are known to increase the amount of EMF exposure include those that contain metal or aluminum parts or plastic cases designed to reduce impact if dropped. In theory, many cases may increase EMF exposure and users may be best to use no case at all.

CHAPTER 5

Genes

I f you have chronic disease in your family, you may be wondering whether you are destined to have that condition as well. This chapter looks at genes and genetics and what they mean—and do not mean!—for your thyroid and your health.

Home DNA testing kits are now readily available from many different companies. It's pretty easy: you request a test kit from a company, collect your spit in the provided plastic tube, and mail it back. Within three to eight weeks, you will receive a plethora of information that can include everything from how well you digest certain fats to your individual risk factors for heart disease or Alzheimer's. However, genetics are not always straightforward. Just because you may be at "risk" for a disease does not mean you will develop it! I hope in this chapter to shed some light on this somewhat complicated world of genetics. I will use some of my own genetic results to guide you through this complex topic.

GENES, EPIGENETICS, AND YOUR THYROID

Genes are contained within our DNA and provide instructions for our body to carry out certain functions. DNA is the genetic code that essentially determines all the characteristics of a living organism. We inherit our DNA from our parents; no one else in the world will have the same DNA as you unless you have an identical twin. Research has shown that certain genes *may* predispose an individual to develop an autoimmune or thyroid disease. The important term here is *may*, as both genes and environmental factors can contribute to the development of autoimmune disease. Epigenetics is the study of how biological and environmental factors turn genes on and off in our body. This aspect of genetics is huge: even if we have certain genes that predispose us to a disease, we can affect the outcome! Our lifestyle habits and food choices influence which genes are turned on and off. This is powerful: even if we have genes that predispose us to autoimmune disease or thyroid dysfunction, it doesn't mean that we will develop the disease. Simply put, our genes are not our destiny.

Although we are just beginning to scratch the surface in terms of research related to autoimmune disease and genetics, cancer has been extensively studied over the last few decades. A groundbreaking study in 2008 found that *only 5 to 10 percent of all cancer cases can be attributed to genetic defects, whereas the remaining 90 to 95 percent have their roots in the environment and lifestyle.*

The lifestyle factors that influenced the promotion of cancer include cigarette smoking, a diet high in conventional red meat and fried foods, heavy alcohol intake (approximately more than 2.25 ounces of distilled alcohol, 18 ounces of beer, or 7.5 ounces of wine a day), exposure to radiation (including UV radiation from sunlight), environmental pollutants, infections, stress, obesity, and physical inactivity.

Research has shown that there are some specific genetic markers, known as polymorphisms, for the development of autoimmune disease and/or Hashimoto's. **Polymorphism** is the ability of a genetic message to be displayed in more than one form. Polymorphism in genes that regulate the immune system (including HLA, CTLA4, PTPN22, CD40, CD25, and FCRL3) and thyroid-specific genes (TG and TSHR) are some examples of these genetic markers that may contribute to the development of Hashimoto's or other autoimmune diseases. That said, none of the polymorphisms in these genes are essential or necessary for disease development. The contributing genes for the development of autoimmune thyroid disease may differ from patient to patient and from population to population. This is even more evidence that environment (such as exposure to toxins or stress) plays a huge role in the development of the disease.

**Environmental & Lifestyle Risk Factors
for the Development of Hashimoto's**

1. Too much iodine consumption
2. Too little selenium consumption
3. Low vitamin D intake
4. Exposure to environmental pollutants such as PCBs and cigarette smoke
5. Viral and/or bacterial infections
6. Exposure to certain pharmaceutical medications, such as amiodarone and lithium
7. Stress
8. Exposure to radiation
9. Cytokine therapy (a treatment for some cancers and viruses)

GENETIC TESTING KITS

We now live in a world where genetic testing is readily available. Many companies offer genetic tests without ever having to go to a doctor for a requisition or visit. But there's something to keep in mind. Through my own research and speaking with Mansoor Mohammed, who has a PhD in molecular genetics and immunology, I have learned that testing individual genes is only nominally beneficial; it is much more powerful when you look at the genes in the context of pathways.

Two cellular pathways, the methylation pathway and the vitamin D synthesis pathway, have been implicated in the development of Hashimoto's. Over the last few years, many researchers and geneticists have studied variations in our genes known as single nucleotide polymorphisms (SNPs). Many of these SNPs do not result in any changes or medical outcomes, but some SNPs can make a considerable difference in our health. Understanding your own SNPs in the methylation pathway and the vitamin D pathway can shed light on how your body detoxifies, absorbs B_{12} and folate, and absorbs and processes vitamin D. Furthermore, if you identify that these pathways are not working optimally, you can modify the environment of the genes through supplementation to reduce certain risks that are associated with the SNPs. It can also provide you with information as to what form of supplementation may be best for you, and for how long. Testing and understanding genetic pathways can also provide personalized dietary guidelines. For example, genetic testing can shed light on how well you digest fats and dairy, and whether you are prone to weight gain with increased saturated fats. This can be valuable information, especially in a time when high–saturated fat diets are popular. If you are struggling with weight loss, understanding your own individual metabolism on a genetic level can be incredibly beneficial. I believe understanding these genetic pathways may be more important than identifying single genes that may put one at risk of autoimmune disease. For example, identifying that you are prone to low levels of vitamin D allows for the actionable step of supplementing this vitamin on a regular basis, opposed to the uncertainty of discovering you may be at risk of a certain disease.

METHYLATION AND AUTOIMMUNE DISEASE

DNA methylation is a natural process by which methyl groups are added to the DNA molecule.

Methylation is essential for important biochemical reactions, including:

- Making and repairing DNA and RNA
- Making neurotransmitters
- Making hormones
- Protein metabolism
- Cell division
- Regulation of detoxification and inflammation

From an autoimmune perspective, its ability to help us detoxify is key. When the methylation cycle is not functioning properly, inflammation in the body and our cells can increase. Long-term high levels of cellular inflammation can lead to autoimmune disease.

As noted on page 29, much attention has recently been given to one specific gene in the methylation cycle known as MTHFR. Research has shown that SNPs in the MTHFR gene seem to be more common in individuals with hypothyroidism. When there is a SNP in the MTHFR gene, it prevents the individual from proper methylation, reducing their ability to detoxify and also reducing the ability to use certain vitamins such as B_{12} and folic acid.

In his book *Dirty Genes*, Dr. Ben Lynch provides a questionnaire with a list of symptoms that may suggest that you have a SNP in the MTHFR or other genes. Some of the symptoms that he suggests are associated with MTHFR dysfunction include hypothyroidism, low white blood cell count, increased miscarriage or difficulty carrying to term, having children on the autism spectrum, menstrual cramping, difficulty tolerating certain medications, inability to tolerate alcohol, high levels of homocysteine, and feeling better after eating dark leafy vegetables. But, as always, note that while questionnaires may indicate a problem, they are not sufficient replacement for testing.

The MTHFR is only one gene of many that are responsible for the methylation pathway in the body. Methylation is a complex biological process and simply just testing for one of the many genes responsible may not show the whole picture. Just as testing only TSH when looking at thyroid disease, we only see a piece of the puzzle until we test for other blood markers of thyroid function, such as T4 hormone, T3 hormone, and thyroid antibodies (e.g., TPO and Tg). You may be asking, What's the point? If the environment is more important than genetics, why give this any more attention?

Understanding your genetic pathways can help personalize a health and wellness plan for you in a way that nothing else can. Does everyone need to test their genetics to be healthy? Absolutely not! However, for those who are ever so curious or have tried diet, supplement, and lifestyle changes and still have not had results, genomic testing can offer a final piece to the puzzle.

TESTING

Again, I don't believe testing is a necessity for all, but that it can be reserved as a last resort. Genetic testing isn't cheap, especially from companies that offer insight into the genetic pathways; it generally starts around US$400. Genetic testing is offered through multiple different labs. I used the DNA Company as it looks at the pathways and interactions between genes. The DNA Company also will destroy your genetic material and not use it for commercial purposes like some other companies.

Remember that 40 to 60 percent of the population has genetic mutations that impair the conversion of supplemental folic acid and B_{12} to its active form. Only about 10 percent of the population (including myself) has multiple SNPs that impair the ability to process the methylated forms of these vitamins. It is still generally thought that using methylcobalamin (a form of B_{12}) and methylfolate supplements is superior to cyanocobalamin (another form of B_{12}) and folic acid supplements. However, if you have always felt unwell, fatigued, or nauseous after taking methylcobalamin or methylfolate, it is better to supplement with lower doses of the inactive forms of cyanocobalamin and folic acid, and instead obtain these nutrients from your diet.

Tips for supplementation:

IF YOU HAVE . . .	HOW TO SUPPLEMENT . . .	AVOID . . .
SNP in some of the methylation genes, but not in SHMT1 or MTR	supplement with the methylated forms of folate and B_{12} (methylfolate and methylcobalamin)	cyanocobalamin
a SNP in the SHMT1 gene	obtain folate though the diet and/or with folinic acid	methylfolate
SNP in the MTR gene	add B_{12} through the diet or through supplementing with cyanocobalamin, or ideally adenosyl-cobalamin	methylcobalamin

Note: If you are taking any medications, be sure to consult with your health-care provider before taking any herbs or supplements.

VITAMIN D AND AUTOIMMUNE DISEASE

Vitamin D is an important and powerful immune regulator. As mentioned previously, vitamin D deficiency is a risk factor for the development of

Hashimoto's. This vitamin is primarily synthesized by the skin from exposure to UV light and to a lesser extent can be obtained through the diet. Not only is vitamin D deficiency linked to autoimmune disorders and Hashimoto's, but it also can promote cognitive decline and cardiovascular disorders.

Genes that are associated with the risk for low levels of vitamin D in the body include the VDR, CYP2R1, and GC genes.

- The VDR gene provides instructions for making a protein called vitamin D receptor (VDR), which lets the body respond to vitamin D.
- CYP2R1 encodes a key enzyme that activates the vitamin D that we obtain through sun exposure or diet and puts it into the bioavailable form.
- The GC gene encodes vitamin D–binding protein (VDBP).
- VDBP is the main transport protein in the blood for vitamin D. Essentially, VDBP is responsible for moving the vitamin D through your body and ensuring it gets to where it needs to go.

Although I have not tested my VDR gene, I have SNPs in both my CYP2R1 and my GC protein. The SNP in my CYP2R1 is unusual, as it is often found in people who are darker skinned and have a history of a high amount of sun exposure. In these populations, this SNP would be protective; by not converting too much of the vitamin D from the sun into its active form, it would protect against vitamin D deficiency. However, in my case, this SNP prevents me from maintaining enough vitamin D. As I currently reside in an area that is warm only a few months of the year, and I am fair skinned, I need to supplement year round to ensure I have adequate levels of vitamin D.

Most patients who have autoimmune disease benefit from vitamin D supplementation regardless of whether they have had genetic testing conducted, but it is important to test blood levels prior to starting supplementation and monitor blood levels to ensure they are in the optimal range. It is possible to supplement with too much vitamin D, which can cause adverse reactions (see page 269 for more info).

Tips for supplementation:

IF YOU HAVE . . .	SUGGESTIONS . . .	NOTES
SNPs in your genes that allow for proper vitamin D production and transport	you may need 5,000 IU of vitamin D or more a day	
a SNP in the CYP2R1 gene	it may be beneficial for you to separate the dosage into 2,500 IU taken twice daily	Because the SNP in the CYP2R1 results in slower transformation and processing of the vitamin D, 5,000 IU taken once a day may be too much to be properly absorbed and separating dosage may promote better uptake.

Note: If you are taking any medications, be sure to consult with your health-care provider before taking any herbs or supplements.

DETOXIFICATION, GENES, AND AUTOIMMUNE DISEASE

Genetic testing can also reveal how well you can detoxify chemicals, pharmaceutical drugs, and antibiotics from the body. If you recall from Chapter 2, chronic exposure to low levels of toxins and chemicals in our environment has been linked with autoimmune diseases, hormonal and fertility problems, chronic inflammation, developmental delays in children, Alzheimer's, and cancer. Therefore, if your genetics predispose you to having a reduced ability to process toxins, you may be at an increased risk for the development of autoimmune and hormonal issues due to a "higher body burden" of toxins and their substrates that could accumulate in the body.

Although genomic testing sheds light on this issue, many people can easily figure out on their own whether they are detoxifying well or not. The consumption of coffee and other caffeinated products is a perfect example. If you have ever eliminated caffeine from your diet for a few weeks and then added it back by having at least one large serving of your caffeinated beverage of choice (e.g., 1 large cup of coffee; however, 2 cups may provide a stronger response) and you noticed you were jittery, anxious, or felt as if you had high blood pressure—you are most likely a poor metabolizer of caffeine. This means that caffeine levels stay elevated in your system longer and overconsumption of caffeine may increase the risk of high blood pressure or could interfere with sleep.

My genetic profile for detoxification reveals that I have SNPs in the CYP1A2 gene, which means I am a slow processor of caffeine. However, I didn't need to go through genetic testing to figure this out. Even when I remove coffee or caffeinated tea from my diet for two to three days and then add it back, I feel the effects strongly. This doesn't mean I never drink coffee! I still enjoy a cup on most days, but I understand my body and I know I cannot tolerate multiple cups a day.

Other clues that you may have a reduced ability to detoxify include being sensitive to chemical smells and perfumes, not being able to tolerate certain antibiotics or pharmaceutical drugs, and feeling strong effects from alcohol.

Intestinal Permeability and Genetics

Research really began on leaky gut (intestinal permeability) in 2005. At this time, intestinal permeability was thought to have a possible genetic association. One study found that in healthy first-degree relatives, high mucosal permeability is associated with a genetic SNP in the CARD15 gene, suggesting that genetics may play a role in the development of intestinal permeability. Fast-forward and two studies in 2015 and 2019 revealed the contribution of genetics in intestinal permeability is modest at best. Yet again, environmental factors, such as smoking, were found to be much more likely to contribute to the onset of leaky gut.

Gut Microbiome and Genetics

Research is just starting to understand how our genetics influence our microbiome and the health of our gut bacteria. A recent study found that genetics had a stronger influence on the gut microbes in mice than exposure to beneficial bacterial during vaginal birth and/or supplementation of probiotics. Once more, however, the researchers concluded that although this study reveals that genetics are important, diet and lifestyle should be equally weighted.

Genetics and Thyroid Medication

For people who do not seem to respond well to T4-only medication (see Chapter 10), there could be a genetic link for the lack of response. Researchers have found at least one SNP in D2, a gene that helps maintain normal thyroid levels, reducing the ability to convert T4 into its active T3 form. The authors conclude that if you have a higher than normal ratio of T4 to T3 hormones upon blood testing, it could suggest that you have this SNP. People with this genetic change could be good candidates for natural desiccated thyroid (NDT) medication, or combination hormone therapy instead of just T4-only medication.

PERSONALIZED MEDICINE AND DIET

One of the most common reasons patients finally end up in my office, or book to see me online, is because of stubborn weight gain. Whether they are hypothyroid or not, weight seems to be one of the biggest motivators that can push someone to change their habits. Many people request I put them on the best diet to help them trim down. In the past few years, several of them have already tried, or would like to try, extremely high-fat diets, such as the ketogenic diet. Personally, I felt much worse when I tried a ketogenic diet. In fact, despite how well the ketogenic diet can help some people lose weight, after three weeks of the diet, I had gained 5 pounds. (I'm not alone; as you'll see in Chapter 8, my patient Bianca had a similar response.)

Genetic testing allows us to identify subtle (and not so subtle!) differences between us, including how we process fats, carbohydrates, and proteins.

Some of the interesting genes that have been identified that can play a role in metabolism and weight gain are:

- FTO gene: SNPs in this gene can reduce how full we feel after a meal and increase the risk of weight gain.
- MC4R gene: SNPs here are associated with changes in hunger cues and the desire for increased snacking and could increase the chance of weight gain.
- APOA2 gene: When someone has SNPs in this gene, it has been associated with increased weight gain and changes in hormone secretion after consumption of saturated fats.
- TCF7L2 gene: SNPs here can change how our body responds to sugar and increases the risk of type 2 diabetes.
- AMY1 gene: There is an increased association between consumption of starch and weight gain when SNPs exist in this gene.

I have SNPs in my APOA2 gene, so it is no wonder that I gained weight after trying the ketogenic diet!

In June 2019, results from an international team of scientists, including researchers from King's College London, Massachusetts General Hospital, and the nutritional science company ZOE, revealed that individual responses to the same foods are unique, even between identical twins. This means that even though understanding genetics can help guide us with personalized nutrition, it's not foolproof—even identical twins with the exact same genetic material still may react somewhat differently to different foods. This is another reason that I suggest food elimination and reintroduction as outlined in Phase 1 and Phase 2 of the Thyroid-Healing Diet (see Chapter 8). It allows us to tune in to how we feel after certain foods that may or may not be right for us.

It's a lot to take in, but when you begin to understand all the mechanisms at play in autoimmune hypothyroidism, my Thyroid-Healing Diet is like a personalized nutrition diet for those with Hashimoto's. It addresses the fact that we know individuals with Hashimoto's have intestinal permeability, they are more likely to have an MTHFR defect and therefore may require more folate from the diet, and they are also more likely to have a sensitivity to gluten and possibly other grains. For the vast majority of my patients, following my Thyroid-Healing Diet provided the results they were looking for: better energy, reduced skin irritation, better mood, improved digestion, and weight loss—without ever having to undergo genetic testing!

A FINAL NOTE ON GENETIC TESTING

The study of genetics is fascinating and can provide fantastic insights into your own unique makeup. However, I have seen firsthand some negative aspects of genetic testing. You see, when you test your genes and they provide knowledge that you have a SNP that could increase your risk of developing a disorder or a disease, it can cause significant stress to some people, even though it may be unlikely that the person ever develops the disease. For example, people who carry the gene for breast cancer (BRCA1 or BRCA2) have a higher risk of developing breast cancer compared to the rest of the population, but that doesn't actually mean they will develop it! In fact, the majority of people who develop breast cancer do not carry the BRCA1 or BRCA2 gene.

I will never forget how frustrated one of my patients was when he learned that he did not have SNPs in his FTO or MC4R gene. He had been struggling with weight loss for years and was convinced it was due to his genetics because his mother struggled with weight as well. He became very down on himself after testing his genes and became less interested in working on his diet and lifestyle habits for a period of time.

Additionally, some genetic companies may be providing third-party consumers with access to genetic results. Because a genetic test is uniquely yours, it identifies you only (unless you have an identical twin). Requests from courts or law enforcement for genetic data can happen, and the privacy guidelines of companies may be subject to change. If you are concerned about the handling of privacy around your genetic material, make sure you choose a company that will destroy your sample and your results after providing them to you.

CHAPTER 6

Infections

Certain infections and parasites (also referred to as pathogens) are known triggers for autoimmune diseases, including Hashimoto's. Some of these infections, such as human herpes virus 6 (HHV6) are extremely common. In fact, it is speculated that over 95 percent of Americans have been infected with HHV6! Not all Americans, however, develop an autoimmune disease because they have had an infection. So, why do some people develop an immune disease after an infection and others do not? Well, it depends on a few factors. Infections can be triggers for autoimmunity and Hashimoto's when a person has other contributing factors putting them at risk. If you remember from Chapter 1, autoimmunity is triggered when

- The person has a family history of autoimmune disease
- The person has a "leaky gut" or intestinal permeability
- The immune system is "triggered" by an inflammatory diet, medications, toxins, stress, and/or infections

There are a few ways pathogens can trigger an autoimmune response:

- Imitating your own cells: Commonly known as molecular mimicry, a pathogen essentially mimics your own cells. Processes in the body that are activated in response to the pathogen can cross-react and begin to attack your own tissues instead of just the pathogen. This can lead to damage of certain organs and cause activation and unwanted changes in the immune system.

- Bystander activation: A chronic infection can cause increased inflammation in the body that can cause harm and unwanted effects to other tissues in the body just as an innocent bystander can be hurt when they witness a crime. The increased inflammatory response may also trigger a domino effect, whereby activation of one aspect of the immune system can cause another aspect of the immune system to respond, further increasing inflammation in the body.

- Mysterious antigens: Commonly called cryptic antigens, the pathogen essentially tries to hide out in certain tissues of the body. However, the immune system is still able to detect the pathogen in the tissue, and ultimately begins to cause inflammation and direct an immune response to not only the pathogen, but to your own cells as well.

The primary infections that have been linked with Hashimoto's are small intestinal bacterial overgrowth (SIBO), *H. pylori, Yersinia enterocolitica, Blastocystis hominis*, Epstein-Barr virus (EBV), cytomegalovirus (CMV), candida, human herpes virus 6, parvovirus, and Lyme disease. However, it should be noted that this is not an exhaustive list—other infections may also increase risk of Hashimoto's in certain individuals.

If you are ready to tackle potential infections in your body, all the other potential triggers of autoimmunity should be addressed, such as dietary changes, stress reduction, and avoidance of toxins. The immune system needs to be strengthened by way of diet and lifestyle interventions to be able to effectively overcome the infection. I have witnessed amazing responses to chronic infections in both myself and my patients with the use of natural remedies. Since initially being diagnosed with Hashimoto's, I have tested positive for CMV, EBV, HHV6, and *Blastocystis hominis*. In my thyroid-healing journey, I did not address the infections right away; instead, I first and foremost adopted the Thyroid-Healing Diet, limited my toxin exposure, and worked on stress management. These factors improved my symptoms by 80 percent and effectively lowered my antibodies (with the help of natural supplements). Addressing infections, however, was the missing link to even further improve my energy and focus, and I know many other patients feel the same way.

GENERAL HERBAL AND NATURAL REMEDIES

I have found the combination of herbs, medicinal mushrooms, and/or n-acetyl cysteine (NAC) to be most effective for my patients and myself when addressing chronic infections.

Note: If you are taking any medications, be sure to consult with your health-care provider before taking any herbs or supplements.

Herbs: Certain herbal extracts have been used for thousands of years as antimicrobial, antibacterial, and antiviral treatments. Many of the herbs that are listed to treat infections may also provide support to the immune system and/or help repair intestinal permeability. Unlike conventional antibiotics, many herbs can be helpful, instead of harmful, to beneficial gut microbiota. Many of the herbs listed here are found only in tincture form and may require an herbalist or naturopathic doctor to prepare these tinctures for you.

Medicinal mushrooms: Extracts of specific mushrooms have been used medicinally since at least 3000 BCE. Studies have found that mushrooms strengthen the immune system and have antimicrobial, anti-inflammatory, antidiabetic, hepatoprotective (prevent damage to the liver), and anti-cancer properties.

N-acetyl cysteine (NAC): NAC is a supplement form of the amino acid cysteine. NAC helps make glutathione, a powerful antioxidant. NAC has been shown to help reduce chronic inflammation, particularly inflammation caused by viral infections. It has also been found effective at breaking down biofilms produced by bacteria, enabling antimicrobial herbs to be more effective at eradicating the infection. NAC can also help stop the replication of viruses.

Sometimes conventional medications may be necessary, with or without natural remedies to treat infections.

The following are the most common infections linked to Hashimoto's. Before we jump in, though, I'd like to offer a suggestion: When many people discuss these infections, they often discuss "killing" the said bacteria, virus, or parasite. It's true that we want to get rid of the pathogen in the body, but I've found that thinking about it in more positive terms can be much more powerful. Try to think about your own immune system *overcoming* the pathogen, and to *visualize* your immune system as a vital, balanced entity that is capable of removing these unwanted guests.

SIBO AND THYROID DISEASE

Small intestinal bacterial overgrowth (SIBO) is defined as an increase in the number of bacteria, and/or changes in the types of bacteria present in the small intestine. Typically, SIBO is caused by an overgrowth of bacteria in the small intestine that should normally only be found in the large intestine. This can be caused by a variety of reasons, including low stomach acid, long-term use of acid-suppressing medications, food poisoning, antibiotic use, and slowed digestive transit time (gastric motility).

SIBO can cause unwanted changes in the structure and the function of the small intestine. The bacterial overgrowth can damage the cells lining the small intestine and lead to intestinal permeability. Further, SIBO can interfere with the digestion and absorption of food and nutrients. Common nutrient deficiencies in patients with SIBO include reduced B_{12} and iron levels.

It is still unknown how common SIBO rates are in the general population; however, one study showed that 78 percent of individuals who had been given a diagnosis of irritable bowel syndrome (IBS) also tested positive for SIBO. This is not surprising, as many of the symptoms of SIBO and IBS are the same.

Symptoms of SIBO include:

- Bloating
- Stomach pain and/or discomfort
- Gas, nausea
- Heartburn
- Burping and changes in bowel habits (constipation and/or diarrhea)

People suffering from SIBO often notice that their stomach issues flare up when they consume probiotics and fermented or high-fiber foods (including cruciferous vegetables, such as cabbage). Many SIBO sufferers feel better when using antibiotics (or antimicrobial herbs, such as goldenseal), managing their symptoms through diet, and/or fasting or skipping meals.

Patients with SIBO have altered gut motility, meaning that time between when food is first ingested and when it exits the body is slower compared to that experienced by the rest of the population. This can lead to changes in the gut microbes (they have a longer time to feast on the food and its by-products!). Because hypothyroidism is also associated with constipation and slowed transit time, it can set the stage for SIBO. Both autoimmune hypothyroidism and autoimmune hyperthyroidism have been linked to SIBO and changes in small intestinal microbes. It is suspected that over 50 percent of patients with hypothyroidism also have SIBO. It is unknown whether SIBO leads to hypothyroidism because of the reduced transit time, changes in bacteria, and increased risk for intestinal permeability, or whether the slower transit time due to hypothyroidism leads to increased microbial growth that can cause SIBO. Either way, if you have symptoms of IBS (or SIBO), it is important to be tested for SIBO.

How to Test for SIBO

Testing for SIBO involves the use of an at-home lactulose breath test kit that can be ordered through your naturopathic or medical doctor. The test requires a 24-hour preparation phase during which only certain foods can be ingested, then breath samples are collected in test tubes before and after a lactulose substance is consumed. The test measures the amounts of hydrogen and methane contained in your breath. Large amounts of hydrogen and/or methane are produced by the bacteria causing SIBO and can be traceable in the breath. In my practice, I use the SIBO breath test from BioHealth Laboratories, however SIBO testing is also available from Genova Diagnostics labs.

JULIET, 23, was starting to wonder whether her strange symptoms were all in her head. She had freezing cold hands and feet (she used two or three pairs of socks to sleep!), she was always tired, and her bloating at night had gotten so bad that it "looked as if I was pregnant." She had been given the diagnosis of IBS years ago, but now her symptoms were worse than ever—she was also experiencing frequent loose bowel movements and very embarrassing gas. Her conventional doctor reported that her blood tests were normal. When I examined her blood results, her TSH was slightly over 3.0, but her T4, T3, and TPOAb appeared within the normal range. However, given her symptoms, I knew we had to dig a little deeper. I explained to Juliet that her gastrointestinal issues might be at the root cause of her thyroid symptoms and put her at risk of developing an autoimmune disease. Plus, the severity of her bloating and bowel habits could be an indication of an infection. Juliet ended up testing positive for SIBO. By changing her diet and using a combination of conventional and herbal medications, we were able to bring her gut back into balance. Once the infection had cleared, within weeks her symptoms resolved. When we tested her thyroid levels again, the TSH had decreased and was back into the optimal range. I am happy to report that Juliet no longer needs to wear any socks to bed!

Treatment for SIBO

Although SIBO is treatable, there can often be a long road to recovery. Natural and herbal options can work, but certain conventional antibiotics used for a short period of time may also significantly improve the rate of recovery. Successful treatment of SIBO requires liver support, eradication of the unwanted bacteria, and then prevention of recurrence.

Natural therapies. Supporting the liver with supplements, such as milk thistle, curcumin, schisandra, and NAC, helps reduce side effects of treatment and may also enhance the effectiveness of SIBO treatment.

Natural antimicrobials that have been shown to be effective in the treatment of SIBO include berberine, emulsified oil of oregano, allicin extract, barberry, goldenseal and other berberine-containing herbs, thyme, myrrh, neem, wormwood, horsetail, and cinnamon extract.

Pharmaceutical intervention includes the use of rifaxamine for hydrogen-producing bacteria, rifaxamine plus neomycin for methane-producing bacteria, and rifaxamine plus metronidazole for resistant/hard-to-treat cases. Rifaxamine is the cornerstone of pharmaceutical treatment of SIBO. Although a prescription-based pharmaceutical, rifaxamine is not a typical antibiotic. It has an affinity for the small intestine, and less than 1 percent of the antibiotic is actually absorbed into the bloodstream. It has been shown to increase beneficial bacteria in the gut, such as *Bifidobacteria* and *Lactobacilli*, plus it has an anti-inflammatory effect and also a very low side-effect profile.

DIETARY changes are vital for treatment and prevention of recurrence. The elemental diet, a liquid-only diet containing high amounts of amino acids and carbohydrates, is the primary diet that has been studied in regard to SIBO treatment. Studies have shown that 80 percent of people who follow an elemental diet have a resolution of symptoms within two weeks of following the diet. The elemental diet is used to treat chronic inflammatory conditions of the gut and is often supervised by a medical professional. This diet involves consuming nutritionally complete liquids or powders and avoiding all solid foods for a period of time. The elemental powders and formulas are predigested and easily absorbed by the gut. By avoiding solid foods and providing the body with all the nutrients it requires, this diet allows the digestive tract to rest and repair.

Although an elemental diet may be necessary for some patients with very difficult-to-treat SIBO, clinically I have found that for most cases, these SIBO symptoms improve when following a low-carb, low-FODMAP diet. The low-FODMAP diet has been found to help reduce symptoms in those suffering from SIBO and/or IBS. "FODMAP" stands for "fermentable oligosaccharides, disaccharides, monosaccharides, and polyols," which are elements found in certain carbohydrates. This diet restricts them primarily because they can feed unhealthy bacteria in our gut, causing gas, bloating, and changes in bowel habits.

Low-carb diets starve bacteria in the small intestine, helping reduce SIBO. In fact, research has shown that when people with autoimmune hypothyroidism follow a low-carb diet, their autoimmunity improves. If you have Hashimoto's and SIBO, I would suggest using the low-FODMAP diet (see page 167) during stages of SIBO treatment (low FODMAP can be good to use right after use of rifaxamine, but not necessarily during treatment of rifaxamine; it's best to consult your health-care provider as to whether this is right for you), and then consider adopting the Thyroid-Healing Diet.

H. PYLORI

Helicobacter pylori (*H. pylori*) is a common chronic bacterial infection in the stomach that affects almost half of the world's population. *H. pylori* infections are the most common cause of stomach ulcers (peptic ulcers). Studies have indicated that patients with autoimmune thyroid diseases are more susceptible to *H. pylori* infection. *H. pylori* strains share a highly identical sequence with thyroperoxidase (TPO). In this case, *H. pylori* could induce a form of molecular mimicry and an *H. pylori* infection could induce autoantibody damage to not just the stomach but also cause an antibody cross-reaction, resulting in thyroid tissue damage (increasing TPO antibodies). Research has also shown that pharmaceutical treatment and eradication of *H. pylori* infection reduced levels of thyroid autoantibodies in patients with both Graves' disease and Hashimoto's. Natural therapies for *H. pylori* are available; however, there aren't any studies indicating that using natural therapies, without the use of antibiotics, is as effective to lower thyroid antibodies in patients with autoimmune thyroid diseases.

Symptoms of *H. pylori* include:

- Burning in the stomach
- Nausea after eating
- Loss of appetite
- Frequent burping and/or bloating

Testing for *H. pylori* can be done by blood, breath, or stool testing. Breath or stool tests are much better at detecting active *H. pylori* infections.

Treatment: Although there are some natural methods for treating *H. pylori*, I generally find they are more effective at preventing a reoccurrence of *H. pylori* than completely eradicating an active infection. If you do test positive for an *H. pylori* infection, here are the general treatments:

- The use of the pharmaceutical "triple therapy" of amoxicillin, clarithromycin, and a proton pump inhibitor (such as omeprazole or pantoprazole) in addition to natural treatments is often the most effective to completely eradicate the bacteria. Triple-therapy treatment of *H. pylori* has been shown to be effective in 70 percent of cases.
- Combining triple therapy with zinc-carnosine, a natural supplement, has been shown to significantly increase eradication rates of *H. pylori* infection; some studies suggest it clears the infection in 100 percent of patients! Zinc-carnosine has also been shown to repair damaged stomach lining, reduce inflammation, and inhibit the grown of *H. pylori*.
- Probiotics is a key aspect of treating and preventing *H. pylori*. Probiotic treatment with *Lactobacillus reuteri* alone can eradicate the infection in about 32 percent of individuals, and when combined with triple therapy, the benefits of both the antibiotic and probiotic treatments are greater. Probiotics also help restore healthy gut function and prevent *H. pylori* reinfection. *Saccharomyces boulardii*, a yeastlike probiotic, can also significantly increase the eradication of *H. pylori* when used in combination with conventional therapies compared to conventional therapy alone.
- If you have struggled with eradicating *H. pylori*, or do not wish to use antibiotics, a combination of DGL, mastic gum, zinc-carnosine, and probiotics may be effective. Garlic, ginger, manuka honey, and marshmallow root may also hold benefit.

YERSINIA ENTEROCOLITICA

Yersinia bacteria are commonly found in undercooked pork, but also in meat, water, or milk. Antibodies to *Yersinia* (indicating a current or past infection with *Yersinia*) are much higher in patients with both Hashimoto's and Graves' disease compared to the rest of the population. Evidence has shown that there are TSH binding sites on *Y. enterocolitica*, and therefore thyroid autoimmunity may be triggered by bacterial infection via the molecular mimicry theory and with a cross-reactivity between *Yersina* and the TSH receptor. Symptoms of *Yersinia* are common food poisoning symptoms, including:

- Nausea
- Vomiting
- Diarrhea
- Fatigue
- Weight loss
- Abdominal pain

Most people can fight off *Yersinia* infections, but sometimes small amounts of the bacteria can stay in the gut and cause cross-reactivity due to the low-grade infection. If you have a history of food poisoning, *Yersinia* could be causing a low-grade infection.

Testing for *Yersinia* is done through comprehensive stool analysis kits, such as Diagnostics Solutions GI Map and Genova Diagnostics GI Effects gut pathogen profile. These can be ordered through your naturopathic or functional medical doctor.

Treatment of *Yersinia* involves a combination of strong antimicrobial herbs:

- In my practice, I use a combination of berberine, bearberry, black walnut, sweet wormwood, and tribulus, taken for 2 months. This herbal combination is sold by Designs for Health as GI Microb-X.
- Probiotics: Designs for Health ProbioMed: 50 billion cfu per day

If GI Microb-X does not treat the infection, using oil of oregano capsules in addition to GI Microb-X or the use of antibiotics may be necessary.

BLASTOCYSTIS HOMINIS

Blastocystis hominis is a parasite that can be picked up via contaminated food or water. Many conventional doctors believe that there is no need to treat *Blastocystis* and that it can live in the gut of healthy people without causing any symptoms or issues. However, research has shown that *Blastocystis* infection can cause injury in the gut and increase intestinal permeability, increasing the risk for the development of autoimmune disease. A case study has shown that eradication of *Blastocystis hominis* can prevent the development of both Hashimoto's thyroiditis and chronic hives. I have personally tested positive for *Blastocystis*, as have some patients and colleagues who have Hashimoto's and other autoimmune diseases. Symptoms include:

- Diarrhea
- Abdominal pain
- Loss of appetite
- Watery diarrhea
- Nausea
- Excessive gas

Many patients who have a chronic *Blastocystis* infection have no symptoms at all, aside from an autoimmune disease, such as Hashimoto's.

Testing for *Blastocystis* is done through comprehensive stool analysis kits, such as Diagnostics Solutions GI Map, Doctor's Data Parasitology, and Genova Diagnostics GI Effects gut pathogen profile. These can be ordered through your naturopathic or functional medical doctor.

Treatment of *Blastocystis* involves:

- A combination of berberine, bearberry, black walnut, sweet wormwood, and tribulus taken for 2 months. This herbal combination is sold by Designs for Health as GI Microb-X.
- *Saccharomyces boulardii*, a yeastlike probiotic, taken for 2 months. Not only has *S. boulardii* been shown to be effective in treating *Blastocystis*, it seems to be as effective as the antibiotic known as Flagyl (metronidazole) in killing off *Blastocystis*.

- Oil of oregano capsules can also be helpful in the treatment of *Blastocystis*.
- Prescription medication, such as Alinia (nitazoxanide), has been shown to be effective against *Blastocystis*, but can lead to yeast infections, so a low-yeast diet and probiotics are a must when using this medication.

CANDIDA ALBICANS

Candida is a fungus that is naturally occurring in small amounts in our gastrointestinal tract. Too much candida, or a candida overgrowth, can cause unwelcome symptoms and interferes with a healthy microbiome. Candida can cause damage to the intestinal wall and could lead to intestinal permeability. Candida overgrowth can be triggered by a diet very high in sugars and carbohydrates, frequent use of antibiotics, and/or long-term use of the oral birth control pill. Symptoms that suggest you may have a candida overgrowth include:

- Frequent vaginal yeast infections
- Frequent fungal infections, such as athlete's foot and/or ringworm
- Overgrowth of candida in the mouth, known as oral thrush
- Eczema and/or psoriasis
- Headaches
- Fatigue
- Intense cravings for sugar and starchy carbohydrates (white bread, white pasta, etc.)

Testing for candida is done through comprehensive stool analysis as listed for *Yersina* and *Blastocystis*.

Treatment for candida overgrowth includes:

- Probiotics: Designs for Health ProbioMed: 50 to 100 billion cfu per day, depending on the severity
- *Saccharomyces boulardii*, a yeastlike probiotic: 500 mg, twice daily
- Caprylic acid: 800 to 1,200 mg/day

- Goldenseal: 3 to 9 ml/day of a 1:1 liquid extract or equivalent in capsule form. For most products, this is typically equivalent to taking 400 to 500 mg/day.
- Astragalus: 5 ml/day of a 1:2 liquid extract, or equivalent in capsule form. For most products, this is typically 400 mg, 2 or 3 times per day.
- Oil of oregano and allicin are also very good treatment options.
- Diet: A diet restrictive in refined sugars and starches is nonnegotiable when addressing candida overgrowth, and often needs to be adhered to for anywhere from 6 weeks to 3 months.

INFECTIONS IN THE GUT AND ELSEWHERE

Lyme Disease

Just the mention of Lyme disease today can open a whole can of worms. Although it is undeniable that the incidence of Lyme disease has increased over the last decade, considerable controversy surrounds it. Many medical professionals do not agree it is a major issue, or that it is common; as a result, many patients cannot be properly diagnosed and treated. Lyme disease is also very often misdiagnosed as multiple sclerosis (MS), polymyalgia rheumatica (PMR), fibromyalgia, Parkinson's disease, chronic fatigue syndrome, and mononucleosis, just to name a few. To make matters more confusing, many patients who have Lyme disease do not have the same symptoms and many doctors are in disagreement in regard to defining the signs and symptoms of the disease.

Dr. Richard Horowitz, author of the book *Why Can't I Get Better? Solving the Mystery of Lyme and Chronic Disease*, has been treating Lyme and other tick-borne infections for twenty-eight years.

He has developed a screening questionnaire that has accurately differentiated those with Lyme disease from healthy individuals. The signs and symptoms of Lyme that are included in the Horowitz questionnaire are as follows:

- Fatigue
- Forgetfulness and poor short-term memory

- Joint pain and/or swelling (particularly pain or swelling that migrates or moves around the body from joint to joint)
- Tingling, numbness, and/or burning or stabbing sensations
- Disturbed sleep: too much, too little, and/or early wakening

Other questions that are important to consider for Lyme disease are:

- Have you ever had a tick bite? (Even so, many people who become diagnosed with Lyme disease do not recall being bitten by a tick as they are very small and can burrow in the folds of skin.)
- Have you ever had a bull's-eye rash with flulike symptoms? (Again, this used to be considered a defining feature of a tick bite and subsequent reaction; however, many people who are bitten by a tick never develop the classic bull's-eye rash.)
- Do you live in a Lyme-endemic area? (This is an emerging issue as many areas are not yet aware of, or only just discovering, the increased tick populations carrying Lyme disease.)

Many of my patients who have eventually tested positive for Lyme disease also have Hashimoto's. This is not surprising as the bacteria that causes Lyme disease, *Borrelia burgdorferi*, has been associated with the development of autoimmune thyroid disease.

If you are struggling with difficult-to-treat symptoms and you have a history of a tick bite, it is important to be tested for Lyme by a reputable lab.

Although many provinces and states offer ELISA testing, it can provide a false negative, especially in early stages of the disease. Many experts believe that ELISA misses many Lyme cases due to the fact that the ELISA test specifically detects the amount of antibodies that have been mounted against the bacteria causing Lyme, and these levels can vary from individual to individual depending on how long someone has been infected. Additionally, if a person has been treated with antibiotics for Lyme at the initial stages of the disease, the antibody levels may be blunted and not detectable with ELISA. Alternatively, ELIspot, Immunoblot, and Western blot are much more accurate ways to test for Lyme. IgeneX and Armin Labs offer good testing for Lyme disease and coinfections and may require your primary care physician, naturopath, or functional medicine doctor to write the requisition.

Treatment: Treatment of Lyme disease is a complex process and often involves the use of both pharmacological medicines, including antibiotics, and natural herbs and supplements. I recommend finding a doctor who is trained by the International Lyme and Associated Diseases Society (ILADS). ILADS is a nonprofit medical society dedicated to the accurate diagnosis and treatment of Lyme disease. Due to the complicated nature of Lyme disease, physicians and scientists came together to form ILADS to provide support for doctors and scientists in the quest for more effective treatment of tick-borne illnesses.

Epstein-Barr Virus, Cytomegalovirus, and Human Herpes Virus 6

The following viruses have been linked to the development of Hashimoto's. However, because these viruses are often chronic and low grade, exact signs and symptoms to point specifically to any one virus—say, Epstein-Barr virus (EBV)—are often not present, aside from the fact that many patients who are dealing with a low-grade infection report a "low immune system" or "chronic sore throat." Many people only learn that they have one of these low-grade infections, contributing to their autoimmune response, if they are tested for them. It can be tricky to navigate, as some people who have been infected with EBV and develop mononucleosis fight it off and never develop Hashimoto's. Other people, such as myself, developed Hashimoto's without ever being diagnosed with mononucleosis. It wasn't until testing that I discovered I had very high antibodies for EBV.

Epstein-Barr Virus (EBV)

Epstein-Barr virus is most likely the virus responsible for the development of mononucleosis (a.k.a. mono or the "kissing disease"), but most people who have an EBV infection have no symptoms at all. It is estimated that the incidence of EBV infection among adults is between 90 and 95 percent. EBV can activate, and latently persist in, some immune cells for the lifetime of the infected individual. Although many individuals can actively fight off EBV when they encounter it, others may not be able to fully clear the EBV infection. Chronic EBV infection has been found in the cells of the gastrointestinal tract and the thyroid gland. Research has shown that EBV can change the immune system in many ways and has been linked to the development of many autoimmune diseases, including systemic lupus erythematosus (SLE), multiple sclerosis, rheumatoid arthritis (RA), Sjögren's syndrome, and autoimmune hepatitis.

It is believed that in susceptible individuals, EBV gets into the cells of the thyroid gland and can cause the development of TPO antibodies. Vitamin D deficiency is believed to contribute to the susceptibility of the chronic EBV infection. Other studies have shown that EBV may also be involved in the development of Graves' disease. Personally, I have tested positive for EBV antibodies; it is very common in people suffering from Hashimoto's and other forms of autoimmune diseases.

Testing for reactivated EBV infections requires a blood draw to look at the immune response to EBV. Historically, this has been done by measuring the antibodies in the blood to EBV, via ELISA testing. These antibodies include:

- EBV-IGM/IGG VCA (viral capsid antigen)
- Anti-EBNA (Epstein-Barr nuclear antigen) antibodies

However, ELIspot testing (still collected via blood) is more sensitive than antibody testing, and is preferable if you have access to this test. EBV ELIspot can also help reveal whether EBV is actively replicating in the body or if it is lying dormant in the body. EBV ELIspot testing can be ordered through Armin Labs and may require your primary care physician, naturopath, or functional medicine doctor to write the requisition. The requested test would be:

- ELIspot EBV lytic antigen + EBV latent antigen

Treatment: Herbs are a key part of my treatment protocol for EBV. The suggested protocol using Chinese skullcap with licorice by master herbalist Stephen Buhner works wonders. He suggests adding the herb *Isatis*; however, I have had good results with Chinese skullcap and licorice alone, combined with Cordyceps and NAC. Due to the fact that a combination of herbs taken in tincture form may be needed, it is best to work with an herbalist or a naturopathic or functional doctor to obtain these herbal combinations.

- A tincture of Chinese skullcap with licorice in equal parts: ½ to 1 teaspoon, 3 to 6 times a day, for 3 months.
- Andrographis (*Andrographis paniculata*) capsules or tablets: 200 mg, 2 to 3 times a day, for 30 days, is also a good option.
- Cordyceps mushrooms (I recommend JHS): 3 to 4 tablets, twice daily, for 60 to 90 days.
- NAC: 1,500 to 1,800 mg/day.
- Goldenseal and other berberine-containing herbs are also a good choice for EBV as well as Saint-John's-wort (*Hypericum perforatum*).

Cytomegalovirus (CMV)

Cytomegalovirus (CMV) is a common virus that generally does not cause any symptoms, so many people will never know they have contracted this virus. Once infected, your body retains the virus for life. Research has shown that thyroid cells can become infected with CMV and can act as "antigen presenting cells" and therefore may be involved in autoimmunity. Although not as commonly discussed in the research, this is a virus that I have tested positive for, as well as other colleagues with autoimmune issues.

Testing for CMV is done in a similar fashion to EBV, either via testing for antibodies, or more precisely though ELIspot:

- CMV-IgM- and -IgG-antibodies

Or

- CMV ELIspot

Again, ELIspot testing is found through Armin Labs and may require your primary care physician, naturopath, or functional medicine doctor to write the requisition.

Treatment: Master herbalist and naturopathic doctor Tiffany Wyse suggests the following herbal protocol that I have found to be very effective for CMV and other viral infections. Again, due to the fact that a combination of herbs taken in tincture form may be needed, it is best to work with a naturopathic or functional doctor to obtain these herbal combinations.

- A tincture of equal parts *Houttuynia, Bidens pilosa,* and *Lomatium,* ¼ to ½ teaspoon of tincture combination taken 3 times a day
- A combination of medicinal mushrooms taken 2 to 3 times a day (in tincture form or in capsules). I often recommend 3 capsules of Reishi mushroom in combination with 2 capsules of Cordyceps mushroom, taken twice a day (I recommend JHS brand).
- NAC: 1,500 to 1,800 mg/day
- Goldenseal and other berberine-containing herbs are also a good choice for CMV as well as Saint-John's-wort (*Hypericum perforatum*).

Human Herpes Virus 6

Human herpes virus 6 (HHV6) has been associated with several chronic autoimmune inflammatory processes. Similar to EBV and CMV, HHV6 has been found to infect thyroid cells. Studies found that HHV6 is much more likely to be found in the thyroid tissue of Hashimoto's patients, and in higher amounts, compared to patients who do not have Hashimoto's.

Testing for HHV6 is collected via blood. The common test is:

- HHV6-antibodies

Treatment for HHV6 includes a combination of herbs taken in tincture form, and therefore working with a naturopathic or functional doctor is best.

- A tincture of Chinese skullcap with licorice in equal parts, ½ to 1 teaspoon, 3 to 6 times a day, for 3 months
- *Houttuynia*, elderberry, and *Isatis* also have antiviral action against HHV6 and could be added to the above formula.
- Reishi mushrooms (I recommend JHS brand): 4 capsules twice a day
- NAC: 1,500 to 1,800 mg/day

Although the infections outlined in this chapter are currently more commonly associated with Hashimoto's, multiple other infections could be linked to the onset of Hashimoto's, such as parvovirus B19, hepatitis C, *Toxoplasmosis gondii*, enterovirus, herpes viruses, and Coxsackie virus. I believe that we are really just beginning to scratch the surface in regard to the link between chronic infections and autoimmune diseases. Treating low-grade persistent infections may be the missing link for many people struggling with an autoimmune disease who have not yet found relief with other diet and lifestyle modifications.

CHAPTER 7

Special Considerations: Fertility, Pregnancy, and Postpartum

Many women are still not aware that there is a link between thyroid disease and infertility. This is true for Hashimoto's thyroiditis, Graves' disease, and both subclinical and overt hypothyroidism: all four conditions can reduce the ability to conceive and may increase the risk of miscarriage. I want to stress that despite the possibility of fertility problems, this is not the case for all women with thyroid issues! I was concerned that I may have trouble conceiving and it was not an issue for my husband and me. However, many women in my practice struggled for years to conceive without their thyroid being properly addressed. Once we improved thyroid function and optimized their TSH (very important for fertility), they were able to carry to term.

HOW DOES THE THYROID GLAND AFFECT FERTILITY?

To understand how the thyroid gland is connected to fertility, it is important to understand a woman's menstrual cycle. The menstrual cycle is a series of changes that a woman's body goes through every month to prepare for pregnancy. Each month or so, the uterus grows a new lining (called endometrium) to prepare for the chance of a fertilized egg. After the uterus has grown a new lining, an egg is released from the ovaries. If the egg is not fertilized by sperm, the uterus sheds its lining. This process is commonly referred to as a period, or menstrual bleeding. Most women bleed for five days on average, but bleeding for anywhere from three to seven days is considered normal. Women who have hypothyroidism can bleed more heavily compared to women who have normal thyroid functioning. Some women with hypothyroidism may stop bleeding altogether until their thyroid is properly treated.

A woman's cycle is defined from this first day of menstrual bleeding until the next time she bleeds. This is typically anywhere from twenty-five to thirty-one days in length. A woman's cycle can also be viewed as having four separate phases: the menstrual phase, the follicular phase, the ovulatory phase, and the luteal phase. Four primary hormones are involved in controlling the menstrual cycle:

1. **Estrogen.** This hormone is at its highest level in the first half of the follicular phase (which begins on the first day of bleeding and ends with ovulation). Estrogen helps the uterine lining and the egg to mature before ovulation.

2. **Follicle-stimulating hormone (FSH).** Released by the pituitary gland, this hormone stimulates a fluid-filled sac known as the ovarian follicle to mature and prepare to release an egg.

3. **Luteinizing hormone (LH).** Also released from the pituitary gland, this hormone is secreted mid-menstrual cycle, just before ovulation. Its job is to stimulate the matured ovarian follicle to release the egg.

4. **Progesterone.** Produced after ovulation by the ruptured follicle, progesterone is primarily secreted in the last part of the cycle (the luteal phase). Progesterone controls the buildup of the uterine lining and maintains this lining if pregnancy occurs. If there is no pregnancy, progesterone levels fall, the uterine lining begins to shed, and bleeding begins.

As mentioned earlier, hypothyroidism can affect a woman's menstrual cycle. Thyroid hormones act on almost every cell in the body. Thyroid hormone receptors have been found on women's ovaries. It appears that thyroid hormones can help a woman's ovary mature leading up to ovulation. One of the reasons hypothyroidism can interfere with a woman's ability to become pregnant is that insufficient thyroid hormones may inhibit the ovary from properly developing and releasing a healthy egg ready for fertilization. Hypothyroidism can also prevent normal amounts of luteinizing hormone and follicle-stimulating hormone from being secreted. Again, when there are lower levels of these hormones circulating in the body, it may prevent a woman's egg from being released, resulting in an "anovulatory cycle" (a menstrual cycle without an egg being released).

Women who are hypothyroid may also have lower levels of estrogen compared to individuals with balanced thyroid function. This may further impact the normal menstrual cycle and/or fertility. Thyroid-stimulating hormone can also be involved in the implantation process, and too little or too much may impact the ability for a fertilized egg to properly implant in the uterine lining.

WHAT ABOUT SUBCLINICAL HYPOTHYROIDISM?

Not only does overt hypothyroidism affect fertility, but subclinical hypothyroidism (SCH) also may reduce a woman's ability to conceive. As discussed in Chapter 1, SCH is when TSH levels are increased (sometimes only slightly increased) but T4 hormone levels remain normal. This is something I have commonly seen in my practice. Conventionally, SCH is often not addressed or treated with any intervention. There is a debate on whether women with subclinical hypothyroidism should be medicated (read more about this in Chapter 10). Although women suffering with SCH who are not trying to conceive may or may not find benefit with medication, thyroid medication may be a game changer in women with SCH wishing to conceive. In fact, the American Association of Clinical Endocrinologists (AACE) and the American Thyroid Association (ATA) recommend that treatment with levothyroxine (Synthroid) should be considered in women of childbearing age with SCH when they are planning a pregnancy. Studies have found that women with SCH undergoing in vitro fertilization (IVF) benefit from using thyroid medication (levothyroxine). Women who took thyroid medication had lower miscarriage rates and higher delivery rates compared to woman who had SCH and did not take thyroid medication.

HASHIMOTO'S AND INFERTILITY

The presence of thyroid antibodies can also impact fertility. A 2011 meta-analysis on the presence of thyroid antibodies showed an increased risk of unexplained subfertility (reduced fertility), miscarriage, recurrent miscarriage, preterm birth, and postpartum thyroid disease. The research reviewed in this meta-analysis looked at women with two antibodies: anti-TPO and anti-TG. The AACE recommends that antithyroid antibodies should be measured in women with subfertility or a history of miscarriage as well as SCH. Another very recent study showed that thyroid hormone supplementation is recommended for infertile women with SCH and/or have thyroid antibodies who are undergoing IVF.

Women who have a normal TSH and T4 hormone level, but have elevated antibodies, may still be at an increased risk for miscarriage, stillbirth, and preterm delivery.

Research in this area is still emerging, and there may be subtle differences when treating SCH and/or thyroid autoimmunity based on whether you are trying to conceive naturally or you are using assisted reproduction methods, such as IVF.

A recent 2019 study further found that levothyroxine supplementation (Synthroid) significantly decreased the risk of pregnancy loss in women with SCH. Furthermore, levothyroxine supplementation significantly decreased the risks of both pregnancy loss in women with positive thyroid antibodies. In women with SCH, levothyroxine supplementation reduced the risk of pregnancy loss in pregnancies achieved by assisted reproduction, but not in naturally conceived pregnancies.

If you are having difficulty conceiving and have not recently checked your TSH levels or your thyroid antibodies, I would highly suggest finding a naturopathic or medical doctor who can run these tests for you. If you do happen to have a TSH of over 2.5 mIU/L and/or thyroid antibodies, speak to your health-care provider about the use of levothyroxine and consider adopting Phase 2 of the Thyroid-Healing Diet.

SUPPLEMENTS FOR FERTILITY

I cannot stress enough how important diet is when planning for a baby. Nutrient-dense food and healthy diet alone can improve pregnancy outcomes. If you do have SCH and/or thyroid antibodies, following the Thyroid-Healing Diet until you conceive (or at the very least removing gluten from your diet) may be a game changer. Once a woman conceives, Phase 1 of the Thyroid-Healing Diet may be too restrictive through pregnancy and adopting Phase 2 of the Thyroid-Healing Diet or a modifaction of this phase can be helpful.

Aside from diet, and prenatal vitamins (with folic acid), supplements that have been shown to specifically improve pregnancy outcomes are as follows:

CoQ 10. Coenzyme Q10, also known as CoQ 10, has long been known for its fertility-boosting properties. CoQ 10 is an antioxidant that is naturally found in the body and can be taken in supplement form in either ubiquinol or ubiquinone form. CoQ 10 plays many important roles in the body, including energy production and protecting cells from oxidative damage (unwanted changes in cells that naturally occurs and increases with age). CoQ 10 is found in its highest concentration in the mitochondria of cells, also known as the cell's powerhouse, which manufactures much of a cell's energy.

As a woman (and a man) ages, all cells, including eggs (and sperm), are more prone to oxidative damage, which can affect the quality of the cells. Decreases in CoQ 10 levels are often observed in individuals as they age to co-occur with the age-related decline in fertility. Research has shown that supplementing with CoQ 10 can improve sperm and egg quality in both men and woman, respectively, and thus may lead to improved pregnancy outcomes.

Dosage: 100 to 600 mg per day may improve fertility outcomes. Recommended brands: Designs for Health Q-Evail or CanPrev Ubiquinol.

Fish oils (omega-3 fatty acids). Omega-3 fatty acids are a type of essential fatty acid, meaning your body does not make these fatty acids on its own and you must consume them via diet (or supplementation). A few different kinds of omega-3 fatty acids are found in foods; however, two specific omega-3 fatty acids, eicosapentaenoic acid (EPA) and docosahexaenoic acid (DHA), may be specifically beneficial for fertility and pregnancy.

Studies have shown that a diet high in omega-3 fatty acids specifically from fish may prolong age-related decline in reproductive function while also increasing egg quality. Omega-3 fatty acids from fish have also been shown to increase progesterone levels, which may improve fertility. Further, DHA consumption has been correlated with a decreased risk of anovulation. In other words, it reduced the risk of women having menstrual cycles where there is no egg released, therefore resulting in no chance of pregnancy for that cycle. Another study showed that women who were undergoing assisted reproduction were more likely to have live births if they had higher levels of omega-3 fatty acids in their blood. There have been no studies to date (that I am aware of) looking at vegan sources of omega-3 fatty acids and fertility. However, a 2008 study by Dr. James Greenberg and team, looking at omega-3 fatty acids in pregnancy, reported that "For those seeking to avoid seafood, there are few non-supplement options. Plant-based omega-3 fatty acids (i.e., α-linolenic acid [ALA]), like flaxseed oil, are poorly converted to the biologically active omega-3 fatty acid EPA, and converts even less to DHA." The study also reports that it is almost impossible to obtain the recommended omega-3 content from plant-based sources and that although meaningful vegetarian sources of DHA are found in algae-derived supplements, the EPA content of algae is much lower than what is found in fish.

Dosage: The International Society for the Study of Fatty Acids and Lipids (ISSFAL) recommends a minimum of 500 mg of combined EPA plus DHA for the general adult population. I typically recommend 1,000 to 2,000 mg of a combined EPA and DHA source daily. Many people are not meeting this recommendation with dietary intake and may want to consider the addition of a fish oil or algae supplement. If you do supplement, ensure you are purchasing a high-quality brand that tests for purity and heavy metals. This goes for dietary consumption of fish, too; refer to the chart on page 171 to help you select fish that are low in mercury and other contaminants. If you are vegan or vegetarian and choose to use algae over fish as a supplement, ensure you are eating a diet high in omega-3 fatty acids, such as chia seeds, flaxseeds, walnuts, and hemp seeds. Brands I recommend for omega-3 fatty acid supplementation include Designs for Health OmegaAvail Hi-Po capsules or liquid or Nordic Naturals Ultimate Omega.

Iron (if you have low ferritin levels or are iron deficient). Ferritin is the most reliable indicator of the body's iron stores. A clinical study found that an iron-containing supplement doubled pregnancy rates in women who had previously been unable to conceive. Although some argue that iron may not be important for fertility, evolutionary research shows that iron was a key nutrient for egg development. Historically, a woman's fertility may have naturally declined if her iron levels were low.

Clinically, I have also seen many women's energy levels skyrocket when iron supplementation is adequate and her ferritin levels improve. Plus, a woman's iron requirement increases in pregnancy for the developing fetus. If we can boost ferritin levels before conception, risk of iron deficient anemia in pregnancy may be reduced, resulting in better energy throughout pregnancy.

According to laboratory reference ranges, normal serum ferritin levels range from 12 to 150 ng/mL. However, if your ferritin level is under 30, talk to your health-care provider about the possibility of supplementing with iron.

Dosage: To prevent iron deficiency in pregnancy, take 80 to 100 mg of ferrous iron per day if you have a ferritin level of less or equal to 30 ng/mL; and 40 mg of ferrous iron per day if you have a ferritin level of 31 to 70 ng/mL. If you have had difficulties raising your ferritin levels in the past with iron supplements, heme iron seems to be more readily absorbed compared to other forms of iron. Liquid-based iron supplements may also enhance absorption of iron for some women and can be more gentle on the stomach. If you struggle with constipation when taking iron supplements, try taking your iron supplement with 1,000 mg of vitamin C and a good-quality probiotic.

Cordyceps. Cordyceps, also known as *Cordyceps sinensis* or caterpillar fungus, is a medicinal mushroom that has historically been used in Traditional Chinese Medicine. The benefits of Cordyceps are far reaching, due to its anti-inflammatory action ability to support the immune system. This mushroom has been known to modulate, or balance, the immune system. It also may have some immunosuppressant properties and therefore may particularly benefit women with Hashimoto's who are having difficulty conceiving, particularly if it is due to low-grade infections, such as CMV (which is also common in people with Hashimoto's; refer to page 107 for more on this subject). Cordyceps also helps cells produce energy (in the form of adenosine triphosphate, or ATP) and therefore may benefit egg quality.

Dosage: Immunity-balancing effects are seen at a dosage of 0.025 to 0.1 mg per day; however, Cordyceps is typically dosed at 400 mg, three to four times per day. Ensure the Cordyceps is from a Cs-4 *Cordyceps militaris* strain, and that it is hot water extracted and contains a minimum of 20 percent beta-glucans (also known as polysaccharides). See page 221 for more on Cordyceps.

Safety: The *American Herbal Products Association's Botanical Safety Handbook*, 2nd edition, classifies Cordyceps as a Safety Class 1A herb, meaning that it can be safely consumed when used appropriately, that it has a history of safe traditional use; no innately toxic substances have been identified in Cordyceps; and there have been no identified concerns for use during pregnancy or lactation. That said, as there have not been a large number of studies conducted around safety of Cordyceps used during pregnancy, I recommend Cordyceps be discontinued once the woman finds out she is pregnant.

Chaste tree (Vitex agnus-castus). Native to the Mediterranean region, chaste tree (also known as chasteberry) is an herb known to be of benefit to women's health, including promoting fertility. Studies have shown this herb to be particularly beneficial for women who have low progesterone or who have a luteal phase defect (a condition whereby the lining of the uterus does not grow properly in the luteal phase of the menstrual cycle and often also associated with low progesterone). Due to the hormone-balancing effects of chaste tree and its ability to increase progesterone, it may also be of particular benefit for women with hypothyroidism, since increasing progesterone has been shown to improve thyroid function.

Dosage: Herbal dosages range considerably for chaste tree; however, I typically start with a dose of 80 mg per day, taken in the morning.

Safety: The *American Herbal Products Association's Botanical Safety Handbook*, 2nd edition, classifies chaste tree as a Safety Class 1A herb, meaning that chaste tree can be safely consumed when used appropriately; it has a long history of safe and traditional use; no innately toxic constituents have been found in chaste tree; and there have been no identified concerns for use during pregnancy or lactation. Herbal practitioners have traditionally used chaste tree to prevent miscarriages in women with a history of miscarriage. If using chaste tree for this purpose, I usually keep the woman on the herb until approximately eight weeks' gestation. Otherwise, I suggest discontinuing the herb once she learns she is pregnant.

If you have SCH and/or elevated thyroid antibodies, certain herbs and supplements outlined on page 203, such as withania, may be beneficial to bring the thyroid back into balance prior to conception. However, there are no large clinical trials outlining safety and/or appropriate management of the thyroid with these herbs throughout pregnancy. Thyroid hormone is so vital throughout pregnancy, I do believe that women who have difficulty conceiving and have SCH and/or elevated thyroid antibodies may truly benefit from a small dose of thyroid hormones during pregnancy and often can discontinue the thyroid hormone after birth.

Please remember, always check with your health-care provider when taking any new supplements. Some herbs have contraindications or cautions that you might not be aware of and/or could cause an allergic response. The supplements listed here are intended to improve fertility rates, but may not be suitable to use throughout pregnancy.

THYROID DISEASE DURING PREGNANCY

Untreated thyroid disease in pregnancy is associated with a greater risk of complications, including blood pressure disorders, increased risk of miscarriage, growth restriction, and placental abruption. Childhood brain development also seems to be dependent on thyroid hormone regulation and impairment of school learning abilities have been seen in children whose mother had poorly controlled hypothyroidism during pregnancy. Regardless of whether a woman has thyroid disease, due to the hormonal changes of pregnancy and the requirements of the placenta, there is a 20 to 40 percent increase in the thyroid hormone requirement as early as the fourth week of gestation. If you have hypothyroidism and become pregnant, your thyroid levels will need to be closely monitored because of the increased demands on the thyroid. The American Academy of Family Physicians (AAFP) recommends that women who have balanced their thyroid hormone levels and are currently taking levothyroxine should notify their physician and then independently increase their dosage of levothyroxine by two additional doses per week after a positive pregnancy test.

If you have hypothyroidism, the upper limit of TSH throughout pregnancy should be equal or below 2.5 mIU/L. Serum TSH levels are the gold standard for assessing thyroid function in pregnancy and should be measured every 4 to 6 weeks until 20 weeks' gestation.

In the first trimester, a woman's TSH naturally drops lower because of the pregnancy hormone, HCG, stimulating the thyroid. Therefore, throughout pregnancy, women have lower TSH levels compared to before pregnancy, and a TSH below the nonpregnant lower limit of 0.4 mU/L is observed in as many as 15 percent of healthy women during the first trimester of pregnancy.

Monitoring every four to six weeks should continue, however, if the woman has not yet achieved balanced thyroid function and a stable medication dose. The TSH should then be measured again at 24 to 28 weeks' and 32 to 34 weeks' gestation.

The American Thyroid Association (ATA) recommends that if you become pregnant and your TSH and T4 levels are within the normal range, but you have tested positive for thyroid antibodies, you should have a measurement of your serum TSH concentration performed at the time of pregnancy confirmation and every four weeks until about 20 weeks' gestation.

Thyroid Medication Throughout Pregnancy

According to the 2012 report by the AACE and the ATA, and also the 2017 ATA report, levothyroxine (T4) is the only recommended treatment of hypothyroidism in pregnancy. Other thyroid preparations, such as T3 or desiccated thyroid, are not recommended.

An increasing amount of women are finding that they feel better and their symptoms are much improved when they take natural desiccated thyroid (NDT), a combination of T4 and T3. Prior to the manufacturing of synthetic levothyroxine in the 1960s, NDT was historically the treatment for hypothyroidism. Unfortunately, no studies have been done examining the safety of NDT in pregnancy. Some women still choose to use NDT throughout pregnancy if they have been using NDT with good results prior to conception. In the early '90s, a small study revealed that although women taking levothyroxine would need to increase their dosage to maintain thyroid balance in pregnancy, women using NDT did not need to increase their dosage to sustain normal thyroid function.

I personally chose to use NDT instead of levothyroxine during my pregnancy, as I had taken NDT for the past five years and my thyroid was well balanced. In my late twenties, when I first discovered I had hypothyroidism, I used levothyroxine with marginal improvement. I did not want my hypothyroid symptoms to return throughout my pregnancy if I switched back to T4-only medication. I monitored my thyroid closely and did not require an increase in NDT dosage throughout pregnancy.

In fact, per the prescribing information issued by Erfa (a Canadian company that makes a prescription NDT product), updated in 2016:

> Thyroid hormones do not readily cross the placental barrier. The clinical experience to date does not indicate any adverse effect on fetuses when the thyroid hormones are administered to pregnant women. On the basis of current knowledge, thyroid replacement therapy to hypothyroid women should be continued during pregnancy.

I will admit that despite close monitoring, and published current knowledge, my midwives still suggested I switch to levothyroxine. I also know many OB/GYNs would not be comfortable with their patients using NDT throughout pregnancy. Whether you choose to use NDT or T4-only medication throughout your pregnancy is a personal decision and should be discussed with your health-care team.

In my opinion, one of the main risks with using NDT is that it can be found on the internet or in health food stores—sold as a food supplement.

These preparations are not third-party tested for quality or purity. The strength could vary from batch to batch, which is not safe throughout pregnancy. Prescription-only NDT preparations, such as Nature-Throid, Armour, Westhroid (in the US), and Erfa (in Canada) are tested for purity and dosage. To my knowledge, these are not available online and must be prescribed by a health-care professional.

If you are currently taking NDT, become pregnant, and wish to stay on NDT it is **crucial** that you monitor your TSH and thyroid symptoms closely. If you have just been diagnosed with thyroid disease, or are only taking thyroid medication for fertility reasons, I do not see any value in using NDT over T4 throughout pregnancy. I would also not suggest switching from T4-only medication to NDT during pregnancy. Again, you should discuss this with your health-care provider.

Iodine During Pregnancy

Iodine is an element that is vital for proper thyroid functioning. When a woman becomes pregnant, her iodine requirements increase. If her iodine levels are adequate before she conceives, the body should be able to keep up with the increased demand and iodine levels in the body will remain stable throughout pregnancy. However, iodine levels decline steadily throughout pregnancy in women with mild to moderate iodine deficiency. Mild to moderate iodine deficiency may not result in any noticeable signs or symptoms; however, iodine is crucial for the developing fetus. Severe iodine deficiency in the mother has been associated with preterm delivery, miscarriage, stillbirth, and congenital abnormalities in their baby. Children of mothers with severe iodine deficiency during pregnancy can also have problems with growth, hearing, speech, and intellectual disabilities.

According to the American Thyroid Association, measuring iodine via urine is not an accurate way to assess iodine and iodine levels should be gauged on a population basis instead of an individual basis. However, there is an increasing amount of substances in our environment, such as fluorine and bromine, that compete with iodine and reduce iodine's uptake in the body—and some researchers are concerned that iodine sufficiency in humans is decreasing as a result. The National Health and

Nutrition Examination Survey (NHANES) has reported over the years that the iodine levels in humans in the US have been declining, especially in certain populations that do not eat foods high in iodine, such as seafood, dairy, eggs, and bread. Iodine may be even further reduced in those with Hashimoto's who intentionally avoid iodine in their diet because they have positive thyroid antibodies. During pregnancy, iodine requirements increase by 50 percent. Although I do recommend iodine restriction at times for patients with very high thyroid antibodies or those with Hashimoto's having difficulty reaching thyroid balance, I do not recommend avoiding iodine throughout pregnancy. I believe taking a prenatal supplement that contains iodine is important, as well as including iodine-rich foods in the diet before, during, and after pregnancy (if lactating). Some of my favorite iodine-rich foods include wild-caught cod, seaweeds, and shellfish.

Helpful Supplements for Pregnancy

Prenatal vitamins. Choosing a good prenatal supplement can be difficult, especially when there are so many options. Many vitamins and supplements on the market today contain the inactive form of folic acid and B_{12} and require the body to carry out the methylation process once ingested. Taking the bioavailable form of these vitamins guarantees that adequate amounts are being provided. Many people with Hashimoto's have a reduced capacity to carry out a biological process known as methylation, due to a MTHFR gene mutation (see more about this in Chapter 5). Methylation is a key biochemical process that is important for the proper functioning of all your body's systems. About 40 to 60 percent of the population has genetic mutations that impair the conversion of supplemental folic acid and B_{12} to their active form. It is important to note that some people have a reduced ability to also process the methylated forms of vitamins. If you have always felt unwell, fatigued, or nauseous after taking methylcobalamin or methylfolate, it is better to choose a prenatal vitamin with the inactive forms of these vitamins—cyanocobalamin and folic acid.

Dosage: If you feel nauseous when taking your prenatal vitamins (a common complaint among pregnant woman), take your prenatal partway through a meal and/or separate the dosage throughout the day; for example, take one capsule with breakfast and one capsule with dinner instead of two capsules with breakfast. Brands that I commonly recommend include Designs for Health Prenatal Pro, NFH Pre Natal SAP, MegaFood Prenatal (there is an option to purchase a methylcobalamin or cyanocobalamin form of this prenatal), or Mykind Organics Prenatal once a day.

Omega-3 fatty acids. (For additional information on omega-3s, please review the section on infertility supplements, pages 114–118.) Increasing omega-3 fatty acid consumption throughout pregnancy may reduce the risk of preterm birth and may also reduce the risk of having a baby with a low birth weight. Omega-3 fatty acids are anti-inflammatory and have been shown to be helpful in autoimmune disease treatment. Interestingly enough, consumption of DHA may reduce the risk of lupus and other immune diseases. A study of pregnant women revealed that fish consumers had lower rates of thyroid antibodies compared to meat consumers. The rates of thyroid antibodies were even lower in the woman who ate small oily fish compared to large fish (e.g., swordfish). Adequate consumption of omega-3 fatty acids, especially DHA, is also important because they act as vital building blocks for the baby's brain and retina. Omega-3 fatty acids also have been shown to help support healthy mood, and therefore may also be helpful to reduce the risk of anxiety and depression of the mother during pregnancy and after birth. I always suggest increasing the consumption of cold-water, low-mercury fish and seafood, such as sardines, anchovies, and scallops, during pregnancy (see pages 141–142 for more suggestions). That said, most woman still do not obtain enough omega-3 fatty acids through their diet and supplementing with a good-quality omega-3 product is key.

Dosage and safety: I recommend at least 450 mg of DHA daily throughout pregnancy, with a total of 1,000 mg of omega-3 fatty acids taken daily. Ensure you choose a supplement brand that tests for purity and heavy metals. Brands I recommend include Designs for Health OmegAvail Ultra DHA, or Nordic Naturals Prenatal DHA. Fish oil consumption is considered safe during pregnancy and lactation, as long as the product has been tested and guaranteed there are no heavy metals and contaminants in the product.

Probiotics. Although more research is needed to understand whether probiotic use in pregnancy can reduce the risk of autoimmune disease in the child, using probiotics can certainly have other additional benefits. Probiotics can help prevent and treat vaginal yeast infections, which can be more common during pregnancy. They have also been shown to be a safe and effective treatment for diarrhea, including traveler's or antibiotic-associated diarrhea. The World Health Organization recommends probiotics for pregnant women at high risk for having a child with allergies, as using probiotics in pregnancy may reduce the risk of the child having eczema or allergies.

Dosage and safety: Probiotics are considered safe to use during pregnancy. A daily dose of 10 to 30 billion cfu of a multistrain probiotic (a capsule containing many different strains) is recommended.

Vitamin D. Vitamin D is essential to the normal functioning of the human immune system. Although it is included in most prenatal vitamins, this is often not enough for most women. Optimizing vitamin D levels in pregnancy also reduces the risk of preeclampsia (characterized by high blood pressure and signs of damage to other organs, most often the kidneys and liver), preterm birth, and asthma in the child. Some researchers believe, based on the epidemiological data to date, it is likely that deficiencies of vitamin D, primarily due to our increased time spent indoors, is partially responsible for the epidemic of allergies, asthma, and autoimmune disease. It is extremely important to have your vitamin D levels checked and optimized during pregnancy. Because the majority of our vitamin D is obtained by exposing our skin to the sunlight, spending time outdoors in the sunshine for a few minutes daily (before the risk of burning) helps boost vitamin D levels and also helps boost mood! Most of the women I see in practice have low or insufficient levels of vitamin D, and supplementing with a good-quality vitamin D is a must.

Dosage and safety: Vitamin D is considered safe in pregnancy, as long as you are not oversupplementing, so test your vitamin D level. Dosage is dependent on your blood vitamin D level and ranges between 1,000 and 4,000 IU per day. Maintaining a circulating 25(OH)D concentration of at least 100 nmol/L (40 ng/mL) is recommended if you are pregnant; your health-care provider can assist you with monitoring this.

Selenium. If you have tested positive for TPO antibodies in pregnancy, taking selenium may reduce the risk of the development of hypothyroid during the postpartum period (known as postpartum thyroiditis; see page 126). Selenium supplementation may also help lower thyroid antibodies. Although some selenium may be included in your multivitamin, the dosage may not be enough to offer benefit for the thyroid and additional selenium supplementation may be necessary.

Dosage: Take 200 ucg of selenium daily (calculate the amount of selenium in your prenatal supplement and then take additional selenium if necessary). Brazil nuts also contain selenium; however, the dosage per nut is variable—there may be 68 to 91 ucg per nut. The maximum daily dosage of selenium is 400 ucg per day during pregnancy and lactation; selenium toxicity could occur if you exceed this daily dose over time. Symptoms of selenium toxicity include nausea; vomiting; nail discoloration, brittleness, and loss; hair loss; fatigue; irritability; and foul breath odor (often described as "garlic breath").

POSTPARTUM AND THYROID

Many women care for their body so well during pregnancy, but emphasis is not always placed on healing and recovery of their body after delivery, in the postpartum period. Traditional Chinese Medicine (TCM) suggests that a woman should rest and recover for forty days after childbirth. That time is also known as "the golden month." It is believed that if the mother takes time to rest during this period, she not only heals from childbirth, but can also heal from previous health issues or concerns. On the other hand, TCM holds that if a woman does not take time to recover during this time, she can do harm to her health. Here in the Western world, we encourage the busy, go-go-go lifestyle; many mothers feel as though they need to get back to their many tasks as soon as possible after giving birth. However, this belief may cause further anxieties and undue stress on new mothers. A 2015 study found that women lack an understanding of and preparation for the physical and emotional symptoms they may encounter following childbirth. Postpartum mothers also reported that they felt they lacked support from their health-care providers, including preparing them for the postpartum period and helping them cope with symptoms that occur. Alternatively, a 2007 paper reviewed common Chinese practices for the postpartum period. These practices are intended to help the mother regain her strength and protect her future health and include special dietary suggestions, staying inside the home, avoiding housework, and limiting visitors. The authors of the study concluded that many of these practices appear to be beneficial for the health of the mother. Although every woman is different, and some women really may be able to get "back to it" quickly, I believe most women, especially those with hypothyroidism and autoimmune conditions, need to rest. Many of my patients with hypothyroidism felt extremely fatigued after childbirth, and if there's ever a time to ask for help from your loved ones and support team, the postpartum period is it. My mother and mother-in-law were incredible after I gave birth, from cooking to cleaning or just holding the baby so I could take a shower and have a nap. I'm fortunate in that; I know many women do not have family help; however, there are many options for support. Postpartum doulas assist with newborn care and meal preparation and offer support, education, and companionship during the postpartum period. If you do not have access to a postpartum doula, consider hiring someone to clean your home for a month or two after birth or call a healthy meal-delivery service. These things can truly make a difference. If you have a partner, have real conversations about division of labor and support during these first months after delivery.

DEVELOPMENT OF AUTOIMMUNE THYROID DISEASE AFTER CHILDBIRTH

The year following childbirth is a critical time for the onset of autoimmune disease and/or the exacerbation of autoimmune diseases, including autoimmune thyroid disease. A condition known as postpartum thyroiditis (PPT) has a worldwide prevalence of somewhere between 1 and 22 percent. Approximately 50 percent of women who develop PPT will return to normal thyroid function without treatment, but the other 50 percent will have permanent hypothyroidism and require treatment. The vast majority of postpartum thyroid disease consists of PPT and the minority by Graves' disease and nonautoimmune thyroiditis. If you do not have hypothyroidism prior to pregnancy but test positive for TPO antibodies in the first trimester, you have about a 33 percent chance of developing PPT in the first year after childbirth. Additionally, if you have a preexisting auto-immune condition, such as lupus, rheumatoid arthritis, or type 1 diabetes, there is also an increased chance of developing PPT. As we are well aware of the link between stress and the onset of autoimmune disease, I cannot help but wonder whether the rate of PPT would decrease if women took more time to allow their body to rest and recover after childbirth.

Supplements, such as selenium and omega-3 fatty acids, may not only be helpful during pregnancy to prevent PPT, but may also help prevent the onset of thyroid autoimmunity during the postpartum period. Omega-3 fatty acids in the postpartum period are typically dosed at 1,000 mg per day with a combination of EPA and DHA. However, unlike during the pregnancy period where the DHA dosage is higher than the EPA dosage, the postpartum period requires a more equal ratio of DHA to EPA (a 1:1 ratio). A selenium dosage of 200 ucg per day can be maintained during the postpartum period.

Ultimately, having a thyroid condition during conception, pregnancy, and postpartum can present real challenges. The good news is that there are ways you can support your physical and emotional health for your well-being—and your baby's. Many of the other suggestions noted throughout this book, such as reducing toxins, stress, and EMFs, may also be very beneficial around the perinatal period. Discuss these options with your health-care provider.

PART 2

Natural Ways to Heal the Thyroid

CHAPTER 8

The Thyroid-Healing Diet

Hippocrates, the founder of medicine, said: "Let food be thy medicine and medicine be thy food." And he was right: food can be used as a powerful therapeutic intervention to heal the gut and reduce the inflammatory response in the body. But the way we eat has changed dramatically in the last sixty-five years. Many of us are no longer consuming whole, natural foods on a regular basis anymore. Factory-produced packaged foods, filled with additives, trans fats, pesticides, monosodium glutamate (MSG), and genetically modified (GMO) food ingredients are now normal parts of our diets. A typical Western diet that is high in refined sugars, trans fats, packaged foods, and artificial coloring and flavorings can increase inflammation in the digestive tract and can lead to disease. Not only are fast foods and junk foods devoid of nutrients, these items can cause irritation in the gut. And although it is common knowledge that fast foods are bad for our health, North Americans are still consuming high amounts of these products. Almost 40 percent of Canadians report they still eat out for meals one to three times per week and a recent study conducted by the US Centers for Disease Control and Prevention (CDC) found that 36.6 percent of American adults consumed fast food on a daily basis.

Even if we try to eat for our health, due to big bucks and crafty marketing, many packaged foods now have confusing health claims, such as low-fat, sugar-free, whole-grain, or high-fiber. Many of these so-called health claims may not actually be healthy at all. The development of National Food Guides, known as Food-Based Dietary Guidelines (FBDG), is known to be not only a scientific but also a political process, incorporating stakeholder perspectives into the suggestions provided for the masses. Both Canadian and American FBDGs have been suspected for many years to have been influenced by lobbyists to encourage the intake of meat and dairy. It is no wonder to me that autoimmune disease is on the rise. Our food, with industry influence, is making us sick! Nonetheless, change is on the horizon and 2019 marked the first year in Canada when dairy was not included as one of the main food groups to consume for a healthy diet.

So, what do we do and where do we start? Let us begin with the basics. Here are nine foods that you should avoid if you have thyroid or autoimmune disease.

1. **High-fructose corn syrup (HFCS):** Made from corn, this commonly used sweetener has been shown to adversely interact with the gut lining, promoting gaps in tight junctions and thus encouraging leaky gut! It is no wonder that excessive consumption of HFCS has been linked to multiple chronic inflammatory conditions. HFCS is also connected with other common problems seen in hypothyroid patients, such as elevated blood sugar and weight gain. Because HFCS is made from corn, it is almost always genetically modified. Packaged foods that typically contain HFCS include soda, salad dressings, sweetened yogurts, store-bought baked pastries and cookies, canned fruit, candy, breads, cereals, premade dinners, and granola bars.

2. **Chemically created trans fats:** There is no doubt: trans fats are bad for your health. Chemically created trans fats are different than the naturally occurring trans fats found in dairy, beef, lamb, and butterfat. The naturally occurring trans fats have not been found to have the same negative health outcomes as the chemically created trans fats. These chemically created fats, commonly found in margarine and other processed and packaged foods, have been shown to increase inflammatory markers in the body, such as CRP, and have been associated with chronic inflammatory conditions. In fact, over 540,000 deaths each year can be attributed to the intake of chemically created trans fats. These health risks have been well known for many years. Concerns over partially hydrogenated oils (PHO),

the main culprit of trans fat in our food, first arose in the 1970s. In the early '90s, large-scale studies, including one from Harvard, reported that chemical trans fats were harmful to the health. Despite this knowledge, it wasn't until 2015 that the FDA deemed PHOs unsafe for human consumption. Most recently, the FDA required all companies to have removed PHO from packaged and artificial foods by January 2020 (however, due to extensions that the FDA has granted companies in the marketplace, it is likely not until at least 2021 that PHOs will be effectively removed from the marketplace). Food sources of PHOs include margarine, frozen pizzas, crackers, cookies, store-bought pastries, and fast foods. PHOs likely will be replaced eventually with vegetable oils, which are also best to avoid.

3. **Vegetable and (some) seed oils:** Soybean, safflower, canola, corn, and sunflower oils were once promoted and encouraged, especially in place of the use of butter and lard. The theory was that these oils, high in omega-6 fatty acids, would reduce cholesterol levels in the body and were supposedly healthier than the use of animal fats. Over the last century, omega-6 fatty acid consumption has drastically increased compared to that of omega-3s, due to the frequent use of these vegetable oils. Unfortunately, the large intake of omega-6s results in increased inflammation in the body and has been linked with many chronic inflammatory conditions. Ongoing studies have revealed that "pro-inflammatory" vegetable oil could increase autoimmune disease by increasing free radical formation and decreasing protective enzymes, thereby increasing inflammation in the body. These oils are often found in chips, crackers, and other savory packaged goods. Since they are often inexpensive compared to other healthy oils, such as olive oil, they are also usually used for cooking at many restaurants and fast-food establishments.

4. **Genetically modified organisms or foods (GMOs or GM foods):** Genetically modified foods have been made from changing the DNA of other organisms via the methods of genetic engineering. Beginning in 1996, GMOs began appearing in many packaged foods. Since this time, they have become a big business. According to Fortune Business Insights, the global genetically modified seeds

market was valued at US$20.07 billion in 2018 and is expected to reach US$30.24 billion in 2026. Initially, GMOs were thought to be safe as well as a solution to improve food quality and quantity. Proponents of GMOs still believe that these organisms, with adequate research, can be safely consumed. However, various studies have highlighted potential health risks associated with creating and consuming GMOs. These concerns include allergies, inflammation, and digestive issues. Specially, a GMO corn known as "BT corn" has been shown to cause intestinal damage and may result in leaky gut. Genetically modified crops also require the use of extra toxins, such as pesticides and herbicides, which can also be a trigger for autoimmune disease. Unfortunately, many of our foods have become primarily genetically modified. In fact, over 90 percent of North American canola, soy, and corn are GMO crops. Sugar beet crops are also primarily GMO, and if you think you do not regularly consume beets, think again: most of the sugar found in packaged products, such as baked goods, sodas, soups, cereals, and yogurts, is derived from sugar beets. Other common foods that are also genetically modified, to a lesser degree, include zucchini, papaya, sweet corn, and summer squash.

If you are purchasing packaged foods, organic foods should not contain GMO products. The Non-GMO Project Verified seal verifies that the product does not have more than 0.9 percent genetically modified ingredients. Organic produce should also always be GMO-free.

5. **Artificial sweeteners:** Chemically made sweeteners, such as sucralose, aspartame, and saccharin, have been shown to negatively affect human health and lead to inflammatory diseases. Specifically, the sweetener sucralose has been shown to adversely affect the gut microbiome that plays a vital role in such processes as food digestion and fermentation, immune cell development, and nervous system regulation. Artificial sweeteners also have been linked to various other gastrointestinal problems and some studies show they may also increase the chance of diabetes, obesity, and even cancer. It is best to enjoy natural sweeteners, such as raw honey, pure maple syrup, and coconut sugar.

6. **Farmed fish:** Farmed fish can often contain high levels of toxic substances, such as PCBs, mercury, and dioxins. As previously discussed in Chapter 2, exposure to toxins and heavy metals can be a trigger for autoimmune disease. Certain chemicals, however, especially PCBs, have been associated with disrupting the thyroid gland. PCBs have been shown to harm the thyroid in many ways, including increasing antibodies and enlarging the thyroid. The manufacture of PCBs was stopped in the United States in 1977 because there was enough evidence that they accumulate in the environment and cause harmful health effects. However, PCBs persist in the environment and can accumulate in some foods, particularly in farmed salmon. A study in the scientific journal *Science* found that farmed salmon had *eight times more PCBs than wild salmon*! Additionally, farmed fish are fed myriad foods they shouldn't be eating, such as grains and soy. Wild-caught fish is best and can still be sustainable if you choose wisely. See page 171 for a guide on how to choose healthy, low-toxin fish.

7. **Conventionally raised and processed meat:** Red meat has long been thought to cause inflammation in the body; however, this response may be specific to the toxins found in conventionally raised and processed meats as opposed to grass-fed and organic meats. One of the main issues with conventionally raised meats is that they contain a known thyroid toxin called dioxin. Dioxins are a by-product of the manufacturing process and are found in pesticides and herbicides. Dioxin exposure has been linked with reduced thyroid function and reduced production of the T4 thyroid hormone and appears to affect females' thyroids more than males'. More than 90 percent of human exposure to dioxins is through the food supply, mainly meat and dairy products. Common types of processed meat, such as bacon, sausages, and hot dogs, contain molecules known as advanced glycation end products (AGEs) that can cause additional inflammation in the body. See page 172 for more details on how to choose your meat wisely.

8. **Soy:** Soy can offer some health benefits, but most soy is genetically modified and certain substances in soy may be undesirable for thyroid health. Goitrogens, substances found in soy (and some

other food groups), may block the synthesis of thyroid hormones and interfere with iodine metabolism. That said, studies do show conflicting information concerning the impact of soy on the thyroid. Although some molecules in soy inhibit an enzyme involved in thyroid hormone synthesis, it has not translated into poor thyroid function in otherwise healthy individuals with adequate iodine intake. This can be confusing because it is difficult to know what "adequate iodine intake" actually is (who knows how much iodine they are intaking? Plus, testing for iodine isn't always accurate). Additionally, consuming too much iodine can be a trigger for autoimmune disease. Soy also contains phytic acid. This molecule can bind to metal ions, inhibiting the absorption of certain minerals, such as calcium, magnesium, and zinc. Some of these minerals, especially zinc, are very important for optimal thyroid function. Zinc helps increase the conversion of the T4 hormone into the more active T3 hormone. As a general rule, it is best for thyroid sufferers to avoid soy, or at the very least choose organic, GMO-free soy and keep intake to a minimum, no more than 3 times per week.

9. **Dairy:** This may come as a surprise to many who were raised on milk and dairy products. We were led to believe that dairy was not only important but necessary for bone health. Dairy used to be one of the four food groups in both the American and Canadian food guides, with a recommendation of 2 to 3 cups a day. But over the last few years, many questions have been raised over the benefits of dairy. Many individuals report gastrointestinal upset due to the lactose in milk and others seem to be unable to tolerate casein, another protein found in milk. Dairy is now known as one of the most common triggers for irritable bowel syndrome (IBS) and is also one of the most common food sensitivities. The evidence is conflicting; I've outlined the pros and cons of eating dairy foods here, so you can make an informed decision about what's best for you.

The pros of dairy: Some studies have shown there to be no link to increasing inflammation in the body. Additionally, multiple studies have found that full-fat dairy was either inversely associated with obesity and metabolic disease, or not associated with them at all. In other words, people who ate the most high-fat dairy foods had the lowest risk for obesity, diabetes, and cardiovascular disease. Children and adolescents who consume calcium-rich foods, including dairy, may have stronger bones.

The cons of dairy: Other studies have linked dairy to inflammatory conditions, such as acne and digestive complaints. Interestingly, the research points to low-fat dairy having some of the most negative side effects. A study at the Harvard School of Public Health found that women who ate two or more servings of low-fat dairy foods per day, particularly skim milk and yogurt, increased their risk of infertility by more than 85 percent compared with women who ate less than one serving of low-fat dairy food per week. Questions have also been raised regarding a possible association between increased cancer risk and increased dairy consumption.

The most surprising part about the dairy debate? In the late 1990s, a study published in the *American Journal of Public Health* followed more than seventy-five thousand women for over twelve years and found no protective effect on certain bones (forearm and hip bones) due to increased milk consumption in adulthood. Another study focused on men found that greater milk consumption during teenage years was not associated with a lower risk of hip fracture in older adults, even though previous studies believed that increased milk consumption in adolescence would create stronger bones.

Although dairy does have a few benefits, I personally feel the side effects outweigh the benefits for frequent dairy consumption. This is especially true if you suffer from leaky gut, as dairy seems to upset many people's digestive tracts. I still enjoy some good-quality (raw) cheese from time to time, or some full-fat yogurt on occasion, but generally, I find patients' symptoms improve faster when they significantly reduce or avoid consumption of dairy and omit low-fat dairy completely.

10. **Carrageenan:** On initial thought, it may sound as if carrageenan is healthy; after all, it is derived from algae and added into many health food products (and even some baby formula!). However, it is a controversial food additive and I believe those with Hashimoto's should avoid it. In fact, in 1982, the International Agency for Research on Cancer identified that carrageenan posed a cancer risk

to humans. In the 1970s, the FDA considered removing it from the food supply, but the change was not made; and since this time, carrageenan has made its way into even more food products. Aside from the potential cancer-causing effect of this additive, carrageenan may also:

- Increase inflammation
- Increase leaky gut
- Cause gastric ulcers

Like many things in science, some research has shown that carrageenan shouldn't be a problem for human consumption and hence it has stayed in our food supply. Nonetheless, due to its potential for increased inflammation and leaky gut, I believe this additive is best to be avoided for those with Hashimoto's. Carrageenan is most commonly found in dairy alternatives, so it is best to select a brand that does not contain it or make your own homemade milks (for recipes, see pages 285–286).

Cruciferous Vegetables and Goitrogens

ONE of the commonly asked questions I receive is, *Can I eat cruciferous vegetables if I have hypothyroid disease?*

Cruciferous veggies, otherwise known as the Brassicaceae family of vegetables, include kale, broccoli, cabbage, cauliflower, bok choy, turnip tops, and Brussels sprouts. I don't know about you, but these are some of my all-time favorite vegetables to cook with! Plus, cruciferous vegetables have many health benefits, which include being a high source of fiber. They also have properties that may be effective at fighting cancer. These veggies contain indole-3-carbinol (I3C), which targets multiple aspects of cancer cell cycle regulation and helps benefit estrogen metabolism. This all sounds great, except that lately these veggies have been getting a really bad rep for harming the thyroid!

The claim is that the cruciferous vegetables contain goitrogens (goiter-producing substances) that could cause the thyroid to enlarge or slow down and reduce the absorption of iodine (important for thyroid function). Further, these vegetables also contain thiocyanate,

continues

continued

which may interfere with iodine absorption, further damaging the thyroid. Obviously, for all of us with hypothyroidism, this reads as a huge red flag and many of us may consider removing these delicious vegetables from our diet.

However, very few studies suggest that these claims are true. In fact, some studies show that the risk may be minimal at most.

Fact #1: Researchers at the University of California found that only certain types of cruciferous vegetables may actually reduce the amount of iodine uptake. These were collard greens, Brussels sprouts, and Russian kale. But other cruciferous vegetables, such as broccoli, kale, turnip tops, and broccoli rabe, contained less than 10 umol of goitrogenic chemicals per 100 g serving and *researchers concluded that these veggies therefore posed minimal risk to the thyroid.*

Fact #2: In another small study, researchers provided participants with 150 g of Brussels sprouts every day for four weeks. Remember, these Brussels sprouts are supposed to interfere with iodine uptake. And the Brussels sprouts used in the study did in fact contain a high amount of chemicals thought to harm the thyroid. However, the chemicals did not affect the thyroid function of the participants. Measurements of thyroid hormones were unchanged after the four weeks!

Fact #3: Other studies have shown that soaking, washing, boiling, and cooking can help reduce the goitrogens in these foods.

The bottom line is that cruciferous vegetables, including kale, broccoli, and cabbage, have many health benefits and do NOT seem to be as problematic to the thyroid as some are claiming. That said, if you have hypothyroidism, I recommend that you cook or lightly steam your crucifers more often, to ensure you are not being exposed to lots of goitrogens. Additionally, if you eat raw crucifers often, it would be a good idea to have your thyroid hormone levels checked via blood work to ensure that these vegetables are not interfering with your medication or affecting your thyroid in any way. Iodine deficiency can also impact how goitrogens affect the thyroid gland. If your antibodies are not high, or are no longer high, ensure you include iodine-rich foods in your diet if you love your cruciferous veggies! As is the case with many other vegetables, many cruciferous veggies are heavily sprayed with toxins that can affect the thyroid gland. Make sure that you are choosing organic.

Despite easy access to ample produce as a result of genetic engineering and pesticide use, I personally find the state of our food supply and the changes and modifications to our foods sad and angering. Even the quality of fruits and vegetables is not the same as it used to be. A study on the topic of nutritional quality of produce by Donald Davis and his team of researchers from the University of Texas–Austin studied US Department of Agriculture nutritional data from both 1950 and 1999 for forty-three different vegetables and fruits, finding "reliable declines" in the amount of protein, calcium, phosphorus, iron, riboflavin (vitamin B$_2$), and vitamin C over the past half century. The team of researchers believes this declining nutritional content is due to agriculture's focus on improving traits of produce, such as pest resistance, size, and growth instead of nutrition.

The good news is that we still have access to many healthy, nutrient-dense foods that can help reduce inflammation in the body. Some of these foods even have been shown to have specific anti-inflammatory properties and are especially important for anyone to consume if dealing with an autoimmune condition.

7 FOCUS FOODS FOR THYROID DISEASE

1. **Fruits and vegetables (organic as much as possible):** Everyone knows these foods are high in fiber, vitamins, and antioxidants, but *blueberries, apples, and dark leafy green vegetables* are especially good for aiding in reducing inflammation in the body. However, these are some of the most heavily sprayed fruits and veggies and contain loads of pesticides. Not only have toxins been linked to autoimmune disease, but specific chemicals found in pesticides have been linked to chronic inflammatory conditions and autoimmune disease. By making sure to choose organic foods, you not only reduce your exposure to harmful chemicals and help the environment, but you also increase your intake of healthy nutrients. Large studies have shown that organic produce contains higher levels of beneficial antioxidants compared to conventional produce. The Dirty Dozen of the Environmental Working Group (ewg.org) is a great resource to help understand what foods are best bought organic. See page 170 for more on the Dirty Dozen.

2. **Ginger and turmeric:** These spices have historically been used in many parts of the world to help reduce inflammation; now research backs that up with promising results showing that these spices help decrease inflammatory markers. You can typically find fresh ginger and turmeric at grocery stores or specialty health food stores. The dried spices can be used; however, fresh is always best, since the skin of the spice has additional health benefits. Ginger and turmeric can be taken in teas, added to salads, incorporated into cooking dishes, and even included in smoothies. It's important to note that these spices are best absorbed when combined with a little fat (think: coconut oil or coconut milk) and a sprinkle of freshly ground black pepper.

3. **Extra-virgin olive oil:** The main component of olive oil, oleic acid, has been shown to have anti-inflammatory effects when ingested in the diet. This acid can reduce the inflammatory marker CRP in the blood. Additionally, anti-inflammatory effects of olive oil are thought to be caused by the high amounts of antioxidants found in this oil. Olive oil is best used when cooked over low heat or poured cold on top of salad. This is because it has a low smoke point, meaning that at higher temperatures, it can change its molecular compensation and lose some of its health benefits. Unfortunately, many companies are mixing cheaper oils with olive oil to reduce the price, resulting in a diluted oil with weaker anti-inflammatory properties! This is essentially a "fake" olive oil. When choosing an olive oil, make sure to select "extra-virgin." This type is made from pure cold-pressed, unprocessed olive oil, whereas regular olive oil is a mixture of cold-pressed and processed olive oil and does not contain the same health benefit. To avoid purchasing a fake oil, look for a "pressed on" or "harvest date" stamp on the bottle; companies that provide these dates are often authentic. Last but not least, price matters. Good-quality oil is often more expensive—if the price is too good to be true, it's probably fake.

4. **Wild-caught fish:** Known to be beneficial in autoimmune diseases, due to the high omega-3 fatty acid content, fish can help reduce inflammation. Research has also shown that increasing consumption of omega-3 fatty acids may be helpful in metabolism.

Unfortunately, many of the fish that is available to us is either heavily contaminated with mercury or may have been pumped full of antibiotics and colorings if farmed. Top choices for fish that are low in mercury and high in omega-3s include wild caught salmon, trout, sardines, herring, and anchovies. The smaller fish listed are high in omega-3s and are generally more sustainable for our oceans as they are so plentiful and reproduce quickly. Refer to page 171 for more on choosing healthy and sustainable fish.

5. **Bone broth:** Bone broth is a liquid created by stewing or boiling the bones and connective tissues of animals in water for an extended period of time. Traditionally, bone broth has been consumed in many different cultures as a health-promoting food. The broth contains glycine, collagen, and gelatin, substances known to be healing for the gut and intestinal permeability. Bone broth can be made by using the stovetop, a slow cooker, or a pressure cooker, such as an Instant Pot. You can also purchase premade broth. Either way, make sure the base ingredients of the broth come from animals that are pasture raised and organic. Nutrition content of the broth varies depending on the quality of bones and connective tissue that have been used to create the broth. See page 295 for an easy recipe for homemade bone broth.

6. **Black cumin seeds (*Nigella sativa*):** Traditionally, these seeds have been used for everything from headaches to asthma and intestinal worms. It is a revered natural remedy in many parts of the world and has been reported to have been discovered in the tomb of King Tut. In a recent study, patients with Hashimoto's who took capsules containing these seeds lost weight, had a reduction in their antibody levels, and improved their TSH levels. Using a supplement containing black cumin seeds is discussed in the supplements section (page 212); however, these seeds can also be used in cooking. These seeds pair nicely with root vegetables and squash, may be a great addition to curries, and can be sprinkled on top of salads and soups.

7. **Nettle:** Also referred to as stinging nettle, this plant has been used in herbal medicine for hundreds of years. The leaves contain many nutrients, including high amounts of vitamins and minerals. Traditionally, nettle leaves, used in cooking or taken in a tea, have been

used to improve immune system function and reduce inflammation in the body. Nettles may be of particular benefit to those with autoimmune diseases. Many allergy sufferers also benefit from taking nettle leaves. See page 277 on how to make simple nettle tea.

A Note About Iodine-Rich Foods

AS iodine is a key nutrient required for thyroid hormone production, many people believe consuming iodine-rich foods will help their thyroid. It would make sense that hypothyroid patients eat foods high in iodine to make more thyroid hormones, but it's not that simple. Iodine is known as a "narrow therapeutic index nutrient," meaning that too little iodine can cause hypothyroidism, but too much iodine can also cause hypothyroidism. Although iodine deficiency has been linked to hypothyroidism, iodine excess has also been linked to autoimmune thyroid disease (Hashimoto's). Additionally, if someone has elevated thyroid antibodies, adding excess iodine to the diet can significantly increase antibodies. In fact, taking a high dose of iodine may not only aggravate Hashimoto's, but also increase thyroid cell destruction. The American Thyroid Association cautions against consuming more than 500 mcg per day, noting that doses above 1,100 mcg may cause thyroid dysfunction. These warnings are for the overall population, but studies have found that people with Hashimoto's may be sensitive to even smaller doses. If you have autoimmune thyroid disease, complete iodine restriction may be beneficial, even for a few months. Once the antibodies have significantly reduced, consuming foods with iodine and/or supplementation may be beneficial. See more on supplementing with iodine on page 204.

THE GLUTEN QUESTION

As research has shown, diet can be a powerful tool when addressing health and disease. If you are suffering from thyroid disease, and the only dietary changes you adopt are following recommendations listed in this chapter, you will likely notice a considerable improvement in your health. Aside from changes already discussed, opting to go gluten-free can be one of the most powerful dietary changes for individuals with hypothyroidism.

Gluten is a protein particle found in all forms of wheat, barley, and rye. It is also found in wheat additives, the most common additive used in American food products. Common sources of gluten include:

- Barley
- Beer
- Brewer's yeast
- Bulgur
- Farina
- Kamut
- Malt
- Rye
- Semolina
- Spelt
- Triticale
- Wheat

Removing gluten from the diet has certainly become a hot topic over the past few years due to many factors, including the large amount of people speaking out regarding the benefits they have experienced once they eliminate gluten from their diet. There still tends to be some confusion about the various reasons and conditions that cause individuals to adopt a gluten-free diet.

Individuals with celiac disease have a condition whereupon they become very ill when eating wheat and gluten products. In these people, even a tiny bite of something containing gluten can cause severe symptoms, such as vomiting, diarrhea, and extreme exhaustion. The gluten almost acts as a poison in their body. New research shows that people with celiac disease are actually four times more likely than the general population to have autoimmune thyroid disease!

Over the last few years, there have been reports from many people who do not have celiac disease but still feel sick after they eat gluten. Research has confirmed that gluten sensitivity or intolerance is on the rise. People with gluten sensitivities or intolerances experience such symptoms as bloating, headaches, fatigue, digestive changes, and acne when they consume gluten-containing products. These individuals report beneficial results from the removal of gluten and wheat, such as reduced bloating, improved energy, weight loss, and better bowel movements. In fact, a recent study reports that nonceliac gluten sensitivity (NCGS) can cause symptoms of IBS and inflammation in individuals who are not celiac and may be caused by other proteins found in wheat.

Although going gluten-free isn't necessary for everyone, if you have thyroid disease, especially autoimmune thyroid disease such as Hashimoto's or Graves' disease, I believe it should definitely be a consideration. Here's why:

- Several studies show a strong link between autoimmune thyroid disease (both Hashimoto's and Graves') and gluten intolerance.
- Individuals with these thyroid conditions may be more likely to be intolerant to gluten.
- In most patients who strictly followed a 1-year gluten-free diet, there was a normalization of subclinical hypothyroidism, suggesting that in distinct cases, gluten withdrawal may single-handedly reverse the abnormality.
- Additionally, some literature has suggested that microbial imbalance in the gut could affect thyroid hormone synthesis and metabolism. It has been suggested that so-called bad gut bacteria could even change thyroid hormones, thus affecting serum levels of these hormones in the body. Removing foods intolerances can help improve this.
- Gluten may play a role in the development of leaky gut. Gluten has been shown to be a key player in causing a large release of a substance known as zonulin to be released in the gastric tract. In turn, these elevated zonulin levels have been shown to cause intestinal permeability.

Gluten-free options include:

- Amaranth
- Arrowroot
- Beans
- Buckwheat

- Corn (non-GMO)
- Flax
- Gluten-free flours (bean, coconut, buckwheat, sorghum, nut, rice, corn, potato, quinoa, teff, etc.)
- Millet
- Quinoa
- Rice (brown, purple, wild, etc.)
- Sorghum
- Tapioca
- Teff

I honestly believe going gluten-free was one of the key dietary changes that helped not only myself, but many of my patients reach thyroid balance.

MAYA came to me with the primary complaint of weight gain, muscle pain, and fatigue. She was forty-two years old when she first ended up in my office and she was desperate to try anything. Her diet included lots of fruits and vegetables, but she also loved her Polish baked sweets (packed full of gluten and possibly many other undesirables such as high-fructose corn syrup and trans fats). When I tested her blood for her thyroid levels, her TSH, T3, and T4 hormones were all normal (and actually within the ideal ranges), but her TPO antibodies were elevated. I explained the possible link between autoimmune thyroid conditions and gluten consumption and suggested she adopt a gluten-free diet. Although she knew it would be a challenging task for her, she agreed. Within three weeks, she noticed she no longer had muscle pain and her energy had increased. Interestingly enough, she would treat herself to a pastry once in a while, and the day after, her muscle pain would return! After three months, she had lost 10 pounds with the help of a little extra gentle exercise. We didn't retest her antibodies again until eight months later. By this time, although they were still mildly elevated, they had decreased. Going gluten-free may have helped her avoid a continued increase and elevation of TPO antibodies that may have eventually attacked her thyroid and caused hypothyroidism. Better yet, Maya's symptoms were still improved and she felt empowered to use diet to improve her health!

For many people with Hashimoto's, however, removing gluten and the other ten foods listed below may not be enough. And that's where the Thyroid-Healing Diet comes in.

THE THYROID-HEALING DIET

Before delving into the specifics of the Thyroid-Healing Diet, remember that, as a general approach, the following foods should either be included or avoided if you have thyroid disease. Refer to page 150 for more. If you just want to make some basic changes to your diet, following these guidelines will be helpful.

THYROID-HEALING FOODS: EAT GENEROUSLY	THYROID-HARMING FOODS: AVOID TO IMPROVE THYROID FUNCTION
■ Wild-caught fish ■ Fruits and vegetables (organic as much as possible) ■ Fresh ginger and turmeric ■ Extra-virgin olive oil ■ Bone broth ■ Black cumin seed (*Nigella sativa*) ■ Nettle	■ High-fructose corn syrup (HFCS) ■ Chemically treated trans fats (anything that lists "partially hydrogenated vegetable oils) ■ Vegetable and some seed oils: soybean, safflower, canola, corn, and sunflower oil ■ Genetically modified foods (GMOs) ■ Artificial sweeteners ■ Farmed fish ■ Conventionally raised meat and processed meat ■ Soy ■ Dairy (especially conventional dairy) ■ Carrageenan ■ Gluten

HEALING TIP: Remember that food is medicine. When consuming nourishing, nutrient-dense healthy foods, think about how the nutrients in these foods are going to help your body, your immune system, and your thyroid gland.

The Thyroid-Healing Diet evolved from the principals of the auto-immune paleo (AIP) diet. Like the AIP diet, it has a specific focus on high nutrients and avoids foods that could cause inflammation or trigger leaky gut. Research has shown that other grains, not just gluten, can affect intestinal permeability as well as can sugars, alcohol, processed food, and substances known as lectins. Lectins are found in various foods, including beans, wheat, rice, spelt, and soy. Milk intolerance has also been shown to cause leaky gut. Clinically, autoimmune sufferers, including those with Hashimoto's and Graves' disease, have experienced benefit by removing these foods that can affect leaky gut and promote inflammation. In fact, a recent small study found that women with Hashimoto's had a significant improvement in quality of life and a reduction in thyroid symptoms after following the AIP diet for ten weeks. Although the AIP diet has helped many individuals with autoimmune diseases, the restrictive nature of the diet is not feasible for many people in the long term.

The Thyroid-Healing Diet differs from the traditional AIP diet in that it allows for seeds and spices, and encourages the reintroduction of certain food groups after an initial phase of the diet. The Thyroid-Healing Diet has helped me and many patients in the past, especially when thyroid symptoms are elevated or extreme. I generally find that following the Thyroid-Healing Diet for somewhere between six weeks and three months can make a huge difference in energy, weight, and overall symptom improvement. After following the diet for a period of time, I recommend slowly adding foods back into the diet while gauging your systems.

The Thyroid-Healing Diet occurs in three phases:

- Phase 1
- Reintroduction Phase
- Phase 2

Phase 1 incorporates the key aspects of the autoimmune paleo diet. The reintroduction phase is just that: when you slowly add foods back to see how you tolerate them. Phase 2 incorporates small amounts of legumes, nuts and seeds, alcohol, and nightshades, but still omits gluten and dairy.

Note: If you are not ready to embark on all the changes outlined in Phase 1, just start with Phase 2! Many of my patients have still experienced tremendous benefit from removing gluten and dairy alone. In fact, I experienced some of the greatest improvements in my symptoms when I solely followed the Phase 2 guidelines. If you are a vegetarian or a vegan, I would recommend following the Phase 2 diet and seriously consider having your food sensitivities tested.

Phase 1

I recommend my patients follow Phase 1 for anywhere from six weeks to three months. Removing certain foods for this period, especially when following other aspects of thyroid healing, allows the gut to heal and for inflammation to be reduced in the body. I personally followed Phase 1 for a total of three months. I then began to eat a small number of nuts. After one week, I reintroduced egg yolks to my diet. Following the egg reintroduction, I tried a few gluten-free grains in small amounts. From time to time, I now also consume some nightshade vegetables. However, when I eat beans, I often don't feel well and I tend to avoid them 100 percent of the time. What I have noticed with myself and with other autoimmune thyroid patients is that small amounts of these foods can be tolerated, but when one begins to incorporate too many foods outside those of Phase 1, symptoms can become aggravated.

Many followers of the traditional AIP diet remove butter, seeds, and certain spices. Aside from chile-based spices, I have found that many of my patients and myself have been able to tolerate these in small amounts. Black cumin seed (*Nigella sativa*) may also hold considerable benefit for those with Hashimoto's. Likewise, certain seeds (flax, chia, hemp, and pumpkin) and grass-fed butter are also often well tolerated. Although butter is dairy, it contains only trace amounts of lactose and casein, the proteins that are often responsible for causing inflammation and intolerances. Plus, butter provides a good alternative for those folks who are sensitive to coconut. The Thyroid-Healing Diet therefore incorporates these into Phase 1, but please note that this may not be for everyone. If you are struggling with serious symptoms and/or multiple forms of autoimmune disease, you may want to remove butter, seeds, and spices during Phase 1.

PHASE 1: EAT GENEROUSLY	
Animal proteins	Anchovies, beef, bison, bone broth, buffalo, chicken, cod, crab, duck, elk, fish, haddock, halibut, herring, lamb, pork, rabbit, salmon, sardines, scallops, turkey, venison, whitefish
Vegetables	Artichoke, arugula, asparagus, beet, bok choy, broccoli, Brussels sprouts, cabbage, carrot, cauliflower, celery, chard, chives, collard greens, cucumber, fennel, hearts of palm, kale, leek, lettuce, mushroom, onion, parsnip, pumpkin, radish, rhubarb, rutabaga, shallot, snap pea, spinach, squash, sweet potato, watercress, yam, zucchini
Fruit Fruit should be consumed in smaller quantities. Aim for no more than 1 or 2 servings a day. Berries, apples, and pears are also better options for lower glycemic/sugar impact.	Apple, apricot, avocado, banana, blackberry, blueberry, cantaloupe, cherry, clementine, coconut, date, fig, grape, grapefruit, guava, honeydew, huckleberry, kiwi, lemon, lime, mango, nectarine, orange, papaya, peach, pear, persimmon, pineapple, plum, pomegranate, raspberry, strawberry, tangerine, watermelon
Fats & oils	Animal fats (from pasture-raised sources), butter (grass-fed), lard, duck & goose fat Plant fats & oils: avocado oil, coconut oil (extra-virgin, organic), olive oil (extra-virgin, organic if possible)
Cooking & baking flours— all gluten-free	Arrowroot powder, coconut flour, tigernut flour, cassava flour (in moderation; no more than 5 servings per week)
Fermented foods Note: Some fermented foods may aggravate SIBO; pay attention to how these foods react in your body if you have or suspect you have SIBO and omit if necessary.	Fermented veggies, coconut aminos, coconut or water kefir, kombucha, sauerkraut, cider vinegar, other vinegars

continues

continued

Herbs and spices	Basil, bay leaf, cilantro, cinnamon, cloves, dill, garlic, ginger, lemongrass, marjoram, mint, oregano, paprika, parsley, peppermint, rosemary, saffron, sage, salt (Himalayan pink salt), spearmint, tarragon, thyme, turmeric
Beverages	Coconut milk, freshly pressed juices, herbal teas, kombucha, kefir (coconut or water kefir only), sparkling water, water
Other	Coconut milk (canned, full-fat), gelatin, grass-fed collagen
Dairy alternatives	Homemade Coconut Milk (page 285), coconut milk (canned, full-fat)

Cassava Flour and Thyroid Disease

CASSAVA flour is a wonderful gluten-free (and grain-free) baking substitute. It is made from the cassava root, which is found in many tropical places around the world. However, due to certain substances contained within cassava flour (a cyanogenic glucoside that can be metabolized to thiocyanate, to be exact), it was suspected to be a cause for thyroid swelling and goiter. Research thus far has not found this to hold true; nonetheless, I suggest eating cassava in moderation (no more than five servings a week).

PHASE 1: EAT IN MODERATION

Sweeteners	Agave, coconut sugar, dates, dried fruit, honey (raw, unpasteurized), pure maple syrup, molasses, stevia
Chocolate substitute	Carob
Seeds Note: If you are struggling with serious symptoms and/or multiple forms of autoimmune disease, omit these.	Black cumin, flax, chia, hemp, poppy, pumpkin, sesame, sunflower, including seed butter and seed milk
Seed-based spices Note: If you are struggling with serious symptoms and/or multiple forms of autoimmune disease, omit these.	Allspice, anise, annatto, caraway, cardamom, celery seeds, coriander, cumin, dill seeds, fennel seeds, fenugreek, juniper berry, mustard seeds, nutmeg, and vanilla bean
Dairy Note: If you are struggling with serious symptoms and/or multiple forms of autoimmune disease, omit these.	Grass-fed butter
Sweets	Sweets made with coconut sugar, dates, dried fruit, honey (raw, unpasteurized), pure maple syrup, molasses, stevia, grass-fed butter, and dairy alternatives

PHASE 1: FOODS TO AVOID

Grains (Including gluten-free grains)	Amaranth, barley, buckwheat, bulgur, corn, farro, Kamut, millet, oats, quinoa, rice, rye, sorghum, spelt, teff, triticale, wheat, wild rice
Dairy	Butter (conventional, non-grass-fed) & buttermilk, casein, cheese, condensed milk, cottage cheese, cream, cream cheese, dairy kefir milk (cow, goat, sheep, or buffalo), evaporated milk, frozen yogurt, ghee, goat cheese, ice cream, sour cream, whey, whey protein, whipped cream, yogurt
Eggs	Chicken eggs, duck eggs, goose eggs, quail eggs
Legumes	Adzuki beans, black beans, black-eyed peas, broad beans, chickpeas, fava beans, kidney beans, lentils, lima beans, mung beans, navy beans, peanuts, red beans, soybeans, white beans
Nuts	Almonds, Brazil nuts, cashews, chocolate, cocoa, coffee, hazelnuts, macadamias, pecans, pine nuts, pistachios, walnuts, nut butter, nut milks
Nightshades	All peppers (including cayenne pepper, chile pepper, red pepper, bell pepper, etc.), eggplant, potato (sweet potato and yams are okay), tomatillo
Fats & oils	Canola oil, corn oil, grapeseed oil, peanut oil, safflower oil, sesame oil, soybean oil, sunflower oil, vegetable oil, margarine
Other	Agave, alcoholic beverages, artificial sweeteners (aspartame, Splenda, Equal, sorbitol, mannitol), brown rice syrup, carrageenan, emulsifiers, food additives, packaged foods, refined sugars, stevia
Beverages	Beer, caffeinated tea and other beverages, coffee, dairy (conventional), fruit juices, iced tea, lemonade, packaged/store-bought juice blends, soda, spirits, wine
Sweets	Chocolate and any other candy or sweet treats made with refined sugar, grains, conventional dairy, etc.
Iodine-rich foods	Kelp noodles, seaweeds (kelp, nori, wakame, etc.)

FOOD ADDITIVES: These are often added to packaged foods to en-hance the texture, appearance, or flavor of the product or to increase its shelf life. Common additives that should be avoided include so-dium nitrate, food coloring (denoted as blue #2, red #3, etc.), MSG, artificial sweeteners and flavoring, carrageenan, polysorbate 60, and sodium benzoate.

Living Without Caffeine

OVER the years, I have found that eliminating coffee and caffeinated tea to be extremely difficult for some patients, especially if they expe-rience withdrawal symptoms (often headaches and fatigue). If this is the case for you, try substituting green tea (organic is best) for coffee or black tea. The caffeine content is much lower, and it is often much better tolerated than coffee or black tea for those living with auto-immune diseases.

Reintroduction Phase

As noted, I generally suggest sticking to Phase 1 for anywhere from six weeks to three months; whatever your amount of time is, you want to have symptom improvement *before* you begin to add back foods to your diet. During this time, you will reintroduce foods, one by one, and gauge your symptoms. I recommend waiting *three days between* each new food introduced, and making note of any symptoms you may feel. For some, this part can be very challenging, for a few reasons. Many people just want to start eating more foods again! And others may find it difficult to piece together whether a food is actually causing a symptom (for example, a headache that started the day of your period but also a day after coffee was introduced—was this due to the period or because of the coffee?). Therefore, it is extremely important to make note of the food you are in-troducing and the symptom you experienced. You may also want to grade how severe the symptom is on a scale from 1 to 10. Then, if you experience a headache again next month when your period arrives, or after reintroducing another food, you will have a little more data to help you navigate. I have created a worksheet that can be scanned or photocopied and used as a guide in Appendix A; please see pages 304–305. It is also available to print on my website: www.emilylipinski.com/resources.

Symptoms to monitor and make note of:

- Hashimoto's symptoms returning that had reduced/resolved since beginning the Thyroid-Healing Diet: fatigue, brain fog, feelings of anxiety and/depression that had lifted during Phase 1, constipation, bloating, feeling "puffy"
- Skin changes: rashes, acne, and/or redness (especially on face or ears)
- Cravings for sugar that had resolved in Phase 1
- Mood changes: irritability, racing heart
- Aches and pains (joint, muscle) that had resolved during Phase 1
- Digestive issues: diarrhea, stomach pains, bloating, gas, nausea
- Allergy-like symptoms: itchy mouth, throat, or ears; sneezing; runny nose; red or itchy eyes
- Other strange symptoms that started after the food was introduced (I always get nosebleeds when I eat artificial coloring or flavorings.)

Food Introduction Suggestions

While some people have an immediate reaction to foods, it can take anywhere from two to seventy-two hours for the reaction to present. Therefore, it is best to reintroduce one food at a time and wait three days before reintroducing the next food; otherwise, you will not know what food is causing what symptoms.

If you are terribly missing a particular food, introduce that food first. I know this is contrary to some AIP wisdom, but food is meant to be enjoyed, and if you are not sensitive to the food you love the most, you should enjoy it! Otherwise, I generally suggest reintroducing the following healthy, nutrient-dense foods first, then moving on to foods that are less nutritious and may be more likely to cause a reaction.

Try these foods in the first few weeks of reintroduction:

- Nuts
- Coffee/caffeinated tea
- Chocolate and cocoa
- Egg yolks (wait on the whites, as many people react to them)
- Legumes

Try these foods next:

- Gluten-free grains
- Alcohol
- Egg whites
- Nightshades
- Dairy

Quantity of Food for Reintroduction

Food quantity will vary, depending on the type of food that is reintroduced, but I generally suggest having one or two servings of each food upon reintroduction. For example, this would equate to 1 to 2 ounces of nuts, 1 to 2 cups of a beverage, 1 to 2 ounces of dark chocolate or 2 to 3 tablespoons of unsweetened cocoa powder, 1 or 2 egg yolks or whites, and at least ½ cup of cooked legumes, grains, or nightshades.

Depending on how many foods you would like to reintroduce back into your diet, the reintroduction phase can take anywhere from a few days to a few months. For example, if you feel great, but are missing out on almonds, then you may only wish to reintroduce these and then the reintroduction phase would only be four days (one day of eating the almonds and three of waiting and noting any symptom reactions). However, if you wish to reintroduce as many foods as possible, the reintroduction phase can take weeks to months because of the four-day cycle per food. Therefore, some people choose to reintroduce a few foods and then take a break and continue with the Thyroid-Healing Diet plus any foods that did not cause a reaction with the initial reintroduction.

Once you have experienced and noted your body's reactions to the potentially reactive food, you will have created your own, personalized Phase 2 Thyroid-Healing Diet. Everybody's version of Phase 2 may be slightly different. For example, I eat egg yolks a few times a week, eat gluten-free grains on occasion, and enjoy iodine-rich foods (now that my antibodies are so low). However, I avoid legumes and egg whites completely because I am quite sensitive to them. If I have a very stressful few weeks, and feel run down, I switch back to all the principles of Phase 1 to improve my symptoms and strengthen my immune system. You can use the worksheet on page 305 to help model this for yourself. Eventually, you won't need reminders, but it's good to keep track—especially at first.

PHASE 2: EAT GENEROUSLY	
Animal proteins	Anchovies, beef, bison, bone broth, buffalo, chicken, cod, crab, duck, elk, fish, haddock, halibut, herring, lamb, pork, rabbit, salmon, sardines, scallops, turkey, venison, whitefish
Vegetables	Artichoke, arugula, asparagus, beet, bok choy, broccoli, Brussels sprouts, cabbage, carrot, cauliflower, celery, chard, chives, collard greens, cucumber, fennel, heart of palm, kale, leek, lettuce, mushroom, onion, parsnip, pumpkin, radish, rhubarb, rutabaga, shallot, snap pea, spinach, squash, sweet potato, watercress, yam, zucchini
Fruit Note that fruit should be consumed in smaller quantities. Aim for no more than 1 to 2 servings a day. Berries, apples, and pears are also better options for lower glycemic/sugar impact.	Apple, apricot, avocado, banana, blackberry, blueberry, cantaloupe, cherry, clementine, coconut, date, fig, grape, grapefruit, guava, honeydew, huckleberry, kiwi, lemon, lime, mango, nectarine, orange, papaya, peach, pear, persimmon, pineapple, plum, pomegranate, raspberry, strawberry, tangerine, watermelon

continues

continued

Fats & oils	Animal fats (from pasture-raised sources), butter (grass-fed), lard, duck & goose fat Plant fats & oils: avocado oil, coconut oil (extra-virgin, organic), olive oil (extra-virgin, organic if possible)
Cooking & baking flours (all gluten-free)	Arrowroot powder, coconut flour, tigernut flour, cassava flour (in moderation; no more than 5 servings per week)
Fermented foods Note: Some fermented foods may aggravate SIBO; pay attention to how these foods react in your body if you have or suspect you have SIBO and omit if necessary.	Fermented veggies, coconut aminos, coconut or water kefir, kombucha, sauerkraut, cider vinegar, other vinegars
Herbs and spices	Basil, bay leaf, cilantro, cinnamon, cloves, dill, garlic, ginger, lemongrass, marjoram, mint, oregano, paprika, parsley, peppermint, rosemary, saffron, sage, salt (Himalayan pink salt), spearmint, tarragon, thyme, turmeric
Beverages	Coconut milk, freshly pressed juices, herbal teas, kefir (coconut or water kefir only), kombucha, sparkling water, water
Other	Coconut milk (canned, full-fat), gelatin, grass-fed collagen
Dairy alternatives	Homemade Coconut Milk (page 285), coconut milk (canned, full-fat)

PHASE 2: EAT IN MODERATION, AND ONLY IF TOLERATED

Gluten-free grains	Amaranth, buckwheat, bulgur, non-GMO corn, oats, quinoa, rice, sorghum, wild rice
Dairy	Grass-fed butter; raw cheese and other products made from grass-fed cow's, goat's, or sheep's milk; kefir from cow's, goat's, or sheep's milk
Eggs Note: Many people with autoimmune disease will have a strong response to egg whites, but may tolerate the egg yolk. You may need to avoid eggs completely for an extended period of time or only eat the egg yolk once in a while.	Chicken eggs, duck eggs, goose eggs, quail eggs
Legumes	Adzuki beans, black beans, black-eyed peas, broad beans, chickpeas, fava beans, kidney beans, lentils, lima beans, mung beans, navy beans, peanuts, red beans, soybeans, white beans
Nuts	Almonds, Brazil nuts, cashews, chocolate, cocoa, coffee, hazelnuts, macadamias, pecans, pine nuts, pistachios, walnuts, nut butter & nut milks
Seeds	Black cumin seed; chia, flax, hemp, poppy, pumpkin, sesame, and sunflower seeds, including seed butter & seed milks
Seed-based spices	Allspice, anise, annatto, caraway, cardamom, celery seeds, coriander, cumin, dill seeds, fennel seeds, fenugreek, juniper berry, mustard seeds, nutmeg, and vanilla bean

continues

continued

Nightshades	All peppers (including cayenne pepper, chile pepper, red pepper, bell pepper, etc.), eggplant, potato (sweet potato and yams are okay), tomatillo
Sweeteners	Agave brown rice syrup, coconut sugar, dates, dried fruit, honey (raw, unpasteurized), pure maple syrup, molasses, stevia
Other	Alcohol
Beverages	Caffeinated teas, coffee, beer, wine, spirits
Sweets	Dark chocolate and any other sweets made with agave, brown rice syrup, coconut sugar, dates, dried fruit, honey (raw, unpasteurized), pure maple syrup, molasses, stevia, grass-fed butter and dairy alternatives
Chocolate & chocolate substitute	Carob, dark chocolate
Iodine-rich foods Note: Iodine-rich foods should only be introduced if your antibodies are negative or significantly reduced.	Kelp noodles, seaweeds (kelp, nori, wakame, etc.)
Dairy alternatives	Almond milk, cashew milk, flax milk, hemp milk, macadamia nut milk, oat milk

A Note on Dairy Alternatives

MANY dairy alternatives found at grocery and health food stores contain fillers, binders, preservatives, and added flavors. When used in small amounts in moderation (e.g., a splash in your morning tea or used in a shake once a week), they are often okay for people with Hashimoto's and other autoimmune diseases. However, if you are using dairy alternatives in large amounts and daily, you may want to consider making your own dairy alternatives (see recipes on pages 285–286) to avoid the additives in the store-bought products. Remember that if you do purchase commercially made milk alternatives, always avoid carrageenan, added sugars, and artificial flavors and colors.

PHASE 2: FOODS TO AVOID	
Gluten-containing grains	Wheat, barley, bulgur, farro, Kamut, millet, rye, spelt, teff, triticale
Some dairy	Non-grass-fed butter, processed cheeses made from cow's milk that is not grass-fed, buttermilk, casein, condensed milk, cream, evaporated milk, frozen yogurt, ice cream, non-grass-fed ghee, sour cream, whey, whey protein, whipped cream, yogurt
Fats & oils	Canola oil, corn oil, grapeseed oil, peanut oil, safflower oil, sesame oil, soybean oil, sunflower oil, vegetable oil, margarine
Other	Artificial sweeteners (aspartame, Splenda, Equal, sorbitol, mannitol), brown rice syrup, carrageenan, emulsifiers, food additives, packaged foods, refined sugars
Beverages	Dairy (conventional), fruit juices, iced tea, lemonade, packaged/store-bought juice blends, soda
Sweets	Candy or sweet treats made with white sugar, grains, sweets made with conventional dairy

IF PART OF YOUR GOAL IS WEIGHT LOSS . . .

Opting for a **lower-carbohydrate diet** has been shown to be effective for reducing weight in patients with Hashimoto's. However, too few carbs can reduce T3, so if you are counting macronutrients (carbs, fats, and proteins) aiming for 80 to 120 grams of carbs per day is a good starting target for most people. If you don't track macronutrients (and honestly, you do not have to!), try removing starches completely for one or two meals a day and most snacks. For example, if you had cereal (a starch) for breakfast, have only vegetables and an animal protein for lunch or dinner.

Blood sugar control is also helpful for weight loss, cravings, and improving symptoms of hypothyroidism. Tips for improving blood sugar control:

- Consume some form of protein with each meal (e.g., a piece of chicken or a handful of hemp seeds). As a general rule, aim for a daily intake of at least 0.8 g of **protein per kilogram of body weight**, or 0.36 g **per pound**. For example, if you are a woman weighing 150 pounds, your protein intake should be at least 54 g (150 x 0.36 = 54). If you are an athlete, pregnant or breastfeeding, or a very active person, the recommended daily intake is slightly higher. To put this in perspective, here are a few examples:

FOOD	SERVING SIZE	PROTEIN CONTENT
Chicken, beef, or pork	3 oz (85 g)	20 to 23 g
Beans	3 oz (85 g)	16 to 20 g
Fish	3 oz (85 g)	15 to 17 g
Spirulina	2 tbsp (14 g)	8 g
Egg	1	7 g
Cheese	1 oz (28 g)	7 g
Nuts	1 oz (28 g)	5 to 7 g
Seeds	1 oz (28 g)	4 g

- Ensure you are eating fiber! (This includes flax/chia seeds or beans if tolerated, and lots and lots of vegetables.) Ideally, daily fiber intake for most adults should be at 25 to 30 g. Here are some examples:

FOOD	SERVING SIZE	FIBER CONTENT
Beans	3 oz (85 g)	8 to 15 g (depending on the type of bean)
Chia seeds	2 tbsp	10 g
Flax seeds	2 tbsp	6 g
Cauliflower	⅓ head	6 g
Apple (skin on)	1 medium	4.5 g
Sweet potato	1 medium	4 g
Carrots	2 medium	3.5 g
Berries	½ cup	2 to 4 g
Buckwheat groats (cooked)	½ cup	2.5 g
Oatmeal (cooked)	½ cup	2 g
Salad greens	2 cups	1.5 g
Celery	3 medium stalks	1.5 g

- Aim for 12 hours of "overnight fasting" (wait 12 hours from your last meal at dinner before you consume your first breakfast meal).
- Be mindful of your sugar intake, including natural sugars, such as fruit and sweeteners. The World Health Organization (WHO) recommends that "free sugar" intake for adults be no more than 50 g per day, but ideally less than 25 g per day. "Free sugars" are all sugars added to foods and drinks, including sugars present in syrups, fruit juices, and honey and other natural sweeteners. With tricky

marketing tactics and health claims, sugar consumption can easily exceed the recommended intake. For example, if you have a cup of orange juice with a serving of store-bought granola for breakfast and have ½ cup of vanilla yogurt as a morning snack, you would have already consumed over 50 g of sugar. Not to mention any chocolate, candies, mints, etc., that may sneak into your diet throughout the day! Even if you are purchasing gluten-free, dairy-free, non-GMO "health food," make sure to check the label.

- Eating whole, fresh fruit is the best option for a sweet snack or after-dinner treat; however, too much fruit can also impact sugar consumption. I generally recommend aiming for no more than 2 cups of fresh fruit a day. Choosing fruits that are naturally lower in sugar, such as blueberries and raspberries, instead of high-sugar fruits, such as bananas, melons, and pineapple, may also be beneficial if weight loss is a goal.

The following chart lists the sugar content of some common foods and sweeteners:

FOOD	SERVING SIZE	SUGAR CONTENT
Coca-Cola	1 (15-oz) can	39 g
Orange juice (Tropicana)	1 cup	21 g
Store-bought granola (Kellogg's)	⅔ cup	17.4 g
Honey	1 tbsp	17 g
Vanilla yogurt (Activia)	½ cup	13 g
Vanilla almond milk (Silk, sweetened)	1 cup	13 g
Pure maple syrup	1 tbsp	12 g
Coconut sugar	1 tbsp	12 g
Granola bar (Nature Valley Oats and Honey)	2 bars	11 g

IS THE THYROID-HEALING DIET VEGAN-AND VEGETARIAN-FRIENDLY?

If you are vegan or vegetarian, I am sure you either cursed or laughed out loud when reading the guidelines for the Thyroid-Healing Diet! If you do not eat animal products, following this diet can be challenging and becomes a diet heavily based on seeds and algae protein powders (spirulina and chlorella) to ensure optimal protein intake.

That said, there are some aspects of the diet that vegans and vegetarians can follow, including the elimination of alcohol, gluten, dairy, refined sugars, and packaged foods. Additionally, if you are following a vegan or vegetarian diet, testing for food sensitivities may be even more imperative to help identify whether certain nuts, seeds, or legumes are causing inflammation in your system (see page 176). If these foods are causing a pro-inflammatory response in your body, it will be up to you if you are willing to add a small amount of high-quality, clean fish, chicken, or beef to your diet. I understand the many reasons that one chooses a vegetarian or vegan diet. Much of our meat and fish supply is not raised humanely and is fed terrible, nutrient-poor food. I have no doubt that some people have developed difficulty digesting animal proteins because of the poor quality of factory-farmed and conventional meat. The way industrial animal farms raise cattle and poultry is also not beneficial for the environment. Plus, although I have yet to see a hypothyroid patient truly improve on a vegetarian or vegan diet, I have seen other forms of autoimmune disease (specifically eczema, psoriasis, and fibromyalgia) improve with a vegan diet.

If you are open to including a small amount of fish or other animal proteins in your diet, refer to page 170 for a guide to choosing animal proteins wisely.

A note on meat alternatives. With new, heavily marketed vegan meats available, many people are confused as to whether these products are healthy. Vegetarian and vegan burgers, hot dogs, and other meat alternatives have been around for a while, but they have recently surged in popularity. But vegan does not automatically equal healthy. First, these products are processed foods; second, some of these products contain GMOs, which are best avoided altogether. And finally, the increase in intake of meat-substitute products has increased consumption of pea and other legume concentrates than in traditional diets. This may, and already has, caused allergic reactions in people who had never had problems with plant proteins in the past. As always, I highly suggest skipping the packaged, processed foods and focusing on whole, real foods for optimal health.

OTHER DIETS THAT MAY BE BENEFICIAL TO THYROID HEALTH

Although I primarily use the Thyroid-Healing Diet in practice, other diets may be helpful to those living with thyroid disease.

DIET NAME: AUTOIMMUNE PALEO (AIP) DIET			
Who It's For	What It Is	Pros	Cons
Autoimmune disease (including Hashimoto's and Graves')	Similar to the Thyroid-Healing Diet, the AIP diet focuses on nutrient-rich food and avoids foods that can cause inflammation or trigger leaky gut. Most of the foods that are excluded in the Thyroid-Healing Diet are excluded in the AIP diet, with the addition of many spices and seeds.	■ Beneficial to reduce an autoimmune response ■ May help reduce inflammation ■ May help with weight loss ■ Eliminates processed and refined foods	■ Very restrictive ■ May be difficult to adhere to long term
DIET NAME: PALEO DIET			
Who It's For	What It Is	Pros	Cons
■ Reduction of inflammation ■ Weight loss	Based on the principles of the hunter-gatherer diet, the paleo diet eliminates many food groups that our Paleolithic ancestors would have not consumed, such as dairy, grains, beans, processed foods, and sugars.	■ May help reduce inflammation ■ May help with weight loss ■ Eliminates processed and refined foods	■ Still restrictive for some ■ May be difficult to adhere to long term

continues

continued

DIET NAME: LOW-FODMAP DIET

Who It's For	What It Is	Pros	Cons
■ IBS ■ SIBO	FODMAP stands for fermentable oligosaccharides, disaccharides, monosaccharides, and polyols. The low-FODMAP diet restricts these elements found in certain carbohydrates, primarily because they can feed unhealthy bacteria in our gut. When these types of carbohydrates feed the unhealthy gut bacteria, it causes gas, bloating, and changes in bowel habits.	■ Has been shown to offer relief to people with IBS ■ May be of particular benefit to those suffering from SIBO	■ Can be difficult to calibrate, as many foods contain these types of carbohydrates in varying amounts ■ Restrictive ■ Not a long-term solution for many

DIET NAME: SPECIFIC CARBOHYDRATE DIET (SCD)

Who It's For	What It Is	Pros	Cons
Inflammatory bowel disease (IBD)	The specific carbohydrate diet is a grain-free diet, low in sugar and lactose. First developed in the 1920s as treatment for celiac disease, it came into favor in the late '80s as a treatment for inflammatory bowel disease. The allowed carbohydrates are monosaccharides and have a structure that allow them to be easily absorbed by the intestine wall	■ May help reduce inflammation in the body ■ May help promote the growth of beneficial bacteria in the gut ■ Eliminates processed and refined foods	■ Similar to the low-FODMAP diet, this diet can be hard to navigate ■ Restrictive ■ Not a long-term solution for many ■ Eggs and some beans are allowed, which may be problematic for individuals with autoimmune disease

continues

continued

DIET NAME: GUT AND PSYCHOLOGY SYNDROME (GAPS) DIET			
Who It's For	*What It Is*	*Pros*	*Cons*
■ Leaky gut ■ Mood disorders that may be related or exacerbated by leaky gut (anxiety, depression) ■ Behavioral issues (autism, ADD/ADHD)	Similar to the SCD diet, the GAPS diet also promotes a high intake of fermented foods. The diet comprises many phases, with the first phase being the most restrictive.	■ May help reduce inflammation in the body ■ May help promote the growth of beneficial bacteria in the gut ■ Many proponents claim this diet to be beneficial for children suffering from autism or ADD/ADHD ■ Eliminates processed and refined foods	■ The multiple phases of the diet causes a high drop-off rate of people adhering to the guidelines ■ Restrictive ■ Not a long-term solution for many

Caution: The Ketogenic Diet and Thyroid Disease

The keto diet is having a major moment right now, and to be fair, it has great health benefits for some individuals. High in fat and low in carbohydrates, it mimics the metabolic state of starvation and has historically been used therapeutically for epilepsy that does not respond to medication. The keto diet has recently been found to help cause significant weight loss, especially in patients with diabetes or prediabetes. However, the thyroid hormones are known to decrease in people during times of starvation (this makes sense as it is best to conserve energy if there is actually no food available). Thyroid malfunction has been shown in one study that looked at children who had adopted a ketogenic diet and suggested that treatment with levothyroxine may be necessary. Another study has shown that there is a reduction of T3 in the body when carbohydrates and calories are too restricted. Although the ketogenic diet may be helpful for some, I caution patients with thyroid disease for putting their body through ketosis for long periods of time.

BIANCA had just turned 40 years old when I first met her in my office. She had recently been diagnosed with autoimmune thyroid disease and she was scared—she did not want to be on lifelong medication. Although she felt tired and anxious, she did not have many of the other common symptoms. We discussed diet changes and stress reduction at length, but Bianca wasn't truly ready to give up her lifestyle yet. She stopped coming to her appointments, and decided she could manage her symptoms herself. Bianca continued to work long hours at her high-powered job and to spend evenings and weekends training hard at the gym. She thought that if she worked hard enough in the gym, the weight would come off. She also put herself on a ketogenic diet after her friend lost 30 pounds by going keto herself. After one week, Bianca felt more fatigued than ever before, but she continued to push through. After diligently sticking to the ketogenic diet for one month, she had gained 7 pounds and felt as though she could hardly get out of bed. Clearly, keto was not working. Bianca ended up back in my office ready to make a change. When we tested her antibodies, they were sky-high, and her T3 hormone was slightly lowered. Bianca agreed to adhere to the Thyroid-Healing Diet. During the reintroduction phase, she became aware that she reacted to dairy, eggs, and soy. She now follows her own version of the second phase of the Thyroid-Healing Diet. Eight months after Bianca discontinued the keto diet and began the Thyroid-Healing Diet, we retested her thyroid. Her antibodies had dropped by over 50 percent and her T3 levels had elevated! Since this time, I am happy to report that Bianca started coming for regular visits again, changed jobs, started yoga, and stopped obsessing at the gym. She is slowly losing weight and regaining energy, one week at a time.

GROCERY GUIDE

Produce (fruits and vegetables): Every year, the Environmental Working Group (EWG; ewg.org) releases a guide of the Dirty Dozen (the twelve foods most sprayed with pesticides) and the Clean Fifteen (the top fifteen conventionally grown produce items that are not heavily sprayed). The list is based on reports from the US Department of Agriculture's Pesticide Data Program. I highly suggest purchasing organic for the produce listed on the Dirty Dozen list. Here's the list for 2020:

DIRTY DOZEN* (BUY ORGANIC)	CLEAN FIFTEEN (NOT AS CRUCIAL TO BUY ORGANIC)
1. Strawberries	1. Avocados
2. Spinach	2. Sweet corn**
3. Kale	3. Pineapples
4. Nectarines	4. Onions
5. Apples	5. Papayas
6. Grapes	6. Sweet peas (frozen)
7. Peaches	7. Eggplants
8. Cherries	8. Asparagus
9. Pears	9. Cauliflower
10. Tomatoes	10. Cantaloupe
11. Celery	11. Broccoli
12. Potatoes	12. Mushrooms
* hot peppers are also dirty, per EWG	13. Cabbage
	14. Honeydew Melon
	15. Kiwi
	** sweet corn, papaya, and summer squash sold in the United States can be produced from genetically modified seeds. Buy organic varieties of these crops if you want to avoid genetically modified produce.

Healthy and Sustainable Fish. When selecting fish, you want to ensure it is low in mercury and other heavy metals. Shopping for fish can become very confusing, but sustainability can still be achieved, especially if you select small fishes (e.g., sardines and anchovies) that have a very short reproductive cycle (meaning there is continually lots of these fishes reproducing in the ocean) and do not require invasive fishing methods (such as trawling).

The following is a guide created by the National Resources Defense Council (NRDC). An environmental advocacy group, it has also collected research on the levels of mercury and other chemicals in common fish.

LOW MERCURY Choose these fish first	MODERATE MERCURY Do not exceed more than 6 servings of these fish a month	HIGH MERCURY Do not exceed more than 3 servings of these fish a month	VERY HIGH MERCURY It is best to not eat these fish
Anchovies	Bass (striped, black)	Croaker	Bluefish
Butterfish	Buffalo fish	Halibut (Atlantic)*	Grouper*
Catfish	Carp	Halibut (Pacific)	Mackerel (king)
Clam	Cod (Alaskan)	Mackerel (Spanish, Gulf)	Marlin*
Crab (domestic)	Jacksmelt (silverside)	Perch (ocean)	Orange roughy*
Crawfish/crayfish	Lobster	Sablefish	Shark*
Croaker (Atlantic)	Mahimahi	Sea Bass (Chilean)*	Swordfish*
Flounder*	Monkfish*	Tuna (canned albacore)	Tuna (bigeye, ahi)*
Haddock (Atlantic)*	Perch (freshwater)	Tuna (yellowfin)*	
Hake	Sheepshead		
Herring	Skate*		
Jacksmelt (silverside)	Snapper*		
Mackerel (N. Atlantic, chub)	Tilefish*		
Mullet	Tuna (canned chunk light)		
Oyster	Tuna (skipjack)*		
Plaice			
Pollock			
Salmon (canned)**			
Salmon (fresh)**			
Sardines			
Scallops*			
Shrimp*			
Sole (Pacific)			
Squid (calamari)			
Tilapia			
Trout (freshwater)			
Whitefish			
Whiting			

* These fish are in trouble! They are either being caught using methods that are destructive to the environment or the fish populations are in very low numbers.

** These fish may contain high levels of PCBs! These chemicals can lead to serious long-term health effects.

Meat. Ideally, your beef, lamb, bison, and goat should be grass-fed and raised without hormones and antibiotics. It is important to clarify with your butcher, farmer, or natural grocer that the meat has not only been raised grass-fed, but finished with grass or hay. Some companies now make claims that their animals are grass-fed; however, they fail to report that they feed the animals corn or grains to "finish" them. Most grass-fed animals are also not fed antibiotics or hormones and are typically treated much better than conventionally raised animals. They are allowed to graze on grass and not forced into tiny, harsh, cramped spaces.

If you do not have access to grass-fed meat, always choose organic. To be certified organic, the animals cannot be in confined spaces for a long period of time, cannot be given antibiotics and hormones, and must be fed animal feed that is organic and not genetically modified.

A Reminder About Pesticides

CHEMICALS found in pesticides can also be found in animal feed; these can be harmful to the thyroid. Additionally, consuming meat that has been given hormones can wreak havoc on our hormonal system. Plus, as mentioned in previous chapters, overconsumption of antibiotics can cause leaky gut. Although we often think of antibiotic exposure as times when we have orally taken antibiotics ourselves, exposure to antibiotics can also come from meat we consume that has previously been fed antibiotics.

Chicken and Eggs. As much as possible, choose pasture-raised, organic chicken and eggs. This means the chickens are outside, feeding on their natural diet of grasses, dirt, grubs, and bugs. These chickens and eggs are not only more nutritious, but also likely to have had a much better life than chickens that are indoors and fed a diet that consists only of soy and grains. Beware of claims such as "free range" and "vegetarian diet." Free range, although better than other possible living conditions, doesn't necessarily mean the chickens are outdoors that often and doesn't address what the animals are being fed. "Vegetarian diet" sounds healthy, but it doesn't mean the chickens have had good living conditions, nor does it indicate a healthy diet—the chickens could still be fed processed, genetically modified soy and other grains.

You'll find more information on personalizing the Thyroid-Healing Diet, as well as delicious recipes, in Part 3!

CHAPTER 9

Keep Your Microbiome Happy

Every one of us is composed of about 37 trillion cells, but we carry approximately 100 trillion microbes in and on our body. In fact, we are made up of more microbes than cells! The human microbiome is the assortment of organisms, such as bacteria, viruses, and fungi that live in and on us. They reside on our skin; in our nose, mouth, and ears; in the gastrointestinal (GI) tract; and on virtually every other surface of the body. If this is news to you, you may be alarmed, but know that these microbes are critical to our health and wellness. Although many of us think of sickness when we hear about bacteria, viruses, and fungi, many of these microbes are vital for our health and well-being. Gut microbiota have evolved with humans through an advantageous relationship, providing many benefits for humans. We now know that the health of our gut, and the array of microbes that it contains, affects virtually every system in our body and regulates the inflammatory response, the immune response, and nutrient absorption. Undesirable changes in these gut microbes may affect gut permeability and lead to low-grade inflammation in the body.

The microbiome is established in early life and differs between infants born by caesarean delivery and by vaginal birth. The development of the microbiome begins in utero; during vaginal delivery, the bacteria found in the mother's vaginal canal "seeds" the newborn's gastrointestinal tract. Children born via caesarean miss out on the "seeding" process during vaginal delivery. Studies show that due to this lack of exposure to healthy bacteria, these children may be more likely to develop immunity-related disorders, such as asthma and allergies, inflammatory bowel disease, and are more prone to be obese. Additionally, evidence has shown that breast milk microbes can directly seed an infant's gut microbiota; the effects of breast milk on infant gut microbiota are dose-dependent and therefore the longer the infant is breastfed, the longer he or she will be exposed to more of the mother's microbes via breast milk. After this period of early life, the microbiome is primarily affected by diet, exercise, exposure to probiotics, prebiotics, medications, and antibiotics.

When we talk about the gut microbiome, we are essentially referring to the entire digestive tract, including the mouth and esophagus, stomach, small intestine, liver, gallbladder, pancreas, large intestine (colon), and rectum. In healthy individuals, relatively few microbes exist in the stomach and small intestine. The large intestine, on the other hand, teems with bacteria that is important for our health. However, the amount and type of bacteria in the large intestine is important, as some bacteria are better than others for our health. Additionally, infections in the stomach and small intestine can be a trigger to autoimmunity.

HOW THE GUT REGULATES THE IMMUNE SYSTEM

The small intestine makes up over 50 percent of our intestinal tract. And this organ really isn't so small—uncoiled and spread out, it measures about 16 feet! Not only is the small intestine a major part of the digestive tract, it also is incredibly important for the immune system: it contains the largest number of immune cells in the entire body. The small intestine has a plethora of lymphoid cells (specialized cells that help fight off infections and regulate the immune system). The walls of the intestines act as barriers, regulating what enters the bloodstream to be transported to the organs, while certain receptors in the walls of the intestines help differentiate what bacteria is helpful versus harmful to the body.

Intestinal permeability, also known as leaky gut, is more common in the small intestine. As we know, intestinal permeability is a key factor in the development of autoimmune disease. Leaky gut takes place when tight junctions (tiny gaps in your intestinal wall) become loose. Instead of allowing solely nutrients and water to pass through, bacteria and toxins begin to pass from the gut into the bloodstream. Over time, food particles (known as antigens) can also pass through the permeable intestinal wall and create immune complexes in the bloodstream, leading to food sensitivities, inflammation, and changes to immunity. Not only does intestinal permeability lead to autoimmune disease development and progression, but healing and repairing leaky gut can help reverse autoimmune disease. Well-known gastroenterologist Dr. Alessio Fasano reports that the autoimmune process can be stopped when we reestablish intestinal barrier function, which is essentially when we reestablish a healthy gut.

Several studies suggest that there is an interaction between the gut microbiota and the immune system, and that adverse changes in gut microbiota may contribute to chronic inflammation. Part of a healthy functioning gut-immune system interaction involves short-chain fatty acids (SCFAs). These are produced when beneficial bacteria ferment fiber in the gut. There are three main types of SCFAs: butyrate, acetate, and propionate. SCFAs, in particular butyrate, are used as energy by intestinal cells to help strengthen intestinal barrier integrity. A strong intestinal barrier helps limit the number of microbial molecules that pass through the intestines and stimulate the immune system, therefore inducing inflammation. The underlying mechanisms that account for this microbiota–immune system interaction are not completely understood, but SCFAs are known to play a large role.

FOOD SENSITIVITIES

Food sensitivities, or intolerances, are a common result of intestinal permeability. Remember that when leaky gut is present, partially digested food particles can enter into the blood system. When this happens, immune complexes can form and the immune system can begin to react against an otherwise innocuous food. Food sensitivities are not true allergies. Food *allergies*, mediated by an **IgE** immune response, cause an immediate response to a food ingested and often result in hives, itching, and swelling, and may lead to a life-threatening anaphylactic reaction. Food *sensitivities*, on the other hand, are mediated by an **IgG** immune response and cause a reaction anywhere from twenty minutes to two days after the ingestion of food. Symptoms of food sensitivities include bloating, diarrhea, headaches, acne, mood changes, fatigue, and eczema.

Up to 13 percent of the general population could have a food sensitivity to gluten, and this number is most likely higher for those who have an autoimmune thyroid condition. Remember from Chapter 8 that several studies show a strong link between autoimmune thyroid disease (both Hashimoto's and Graves') and gluten intolerance. Having a sensitivity, or intolerance, to gluten is different from having celiac disease. Celiac disease is an autoimmune condition; people who have it are unable to ingest even small amounts of gluten as the gluten causes damage to their intestinal tract and considerable inflammation (you'll read more on celiac disease in just a bit). Wheat allergies are yet another type of reaction that can be possible and involve an immune (rather than an autoimmune) response. However, a growing number of people have neither celiac disease nor a wheat allergy, but feel much better when they remove gluten from their diet. This is known as nonceliac gluten sensitivity (NCGS). In people who suffer from NCGS, ingestion of gluten can still cause an inflammatory response in their body and result in unwanted symptoms.

Other common food sensitivities include dairy, soy, eggs, nuts, and corn. Beans and the nightshade family of vegetables (tomatoes, peppers, eggplant, potatoes, etc.) may also be problematic for many.

People with food allergies, celiac disease, and other food sensitivities have different gut microbes compared to individuals who do not have these food reactions. Eliminating these foods also helps reduce inflammation in the gut and thereby promotes a healthier microbiome.

Testing for food sensitivities via blood (IgG food sensitivity testing) used to be a big part of my practice. However, after years of running tests with different patients, I realized that most people were suffering from the most common food sensitivities listed here. Rather than going through the testing, simply removing some of those sensitivities from their diet made a huge difference. Known as an elimination diet, this can help identify what foods are causing symptoms. Phase 1 of the Thyroid-Healing Diet, pages 250–252, encompasses the aspects of an elimination diet. (The exception is for celiac disease; I talk more about that in a bit.) After the elimination of the most common food sensitivities, you can gradually reintroduce some of the foods. Once you address intestinal permeability and heal your gut, you likely will not experience as many food sensitivities. That said, it doesn't necessarily mean you can freely eat all the previously sensitive foods again, though many people can enjoy these foods again from time to time.

If you are a vegetarian or vegan, running a food sensitivity test may be very helpful as an elimination diet can be quite protein deficient when you remove legumes, nuts, seeds, eggs, and dairy.

Vegetarian or not, if you notice that you have multiple food sensitivities (via testing or food elimination), it is likely you have small intestinal bacterial overgrowth (SIBO) and/or an intestinal infection and further testing should be considered.

CELIAC DISEASE

People with Hashimoto's are more likely to be sensitive to gluten and they are also more likely to have celiac disease. In fact, one study has shown that the prevalence of celiac disease in patients with autoimmune thyroid disease is 8.6 percent (other studies have shown it to be slightly less, between 3 and 4 percent). Common symptoms of celiac disease can not only be similar to the symptoms of hypothyroidism but may also be similar to other problems in the gut. They include:

1. Diarrhea and/or constipation
2. Bloating and gas
3. Fatigue
4. Iron-deficiency anemia
5. Mood changes, especially depression
6. Weight loss
7. Joint pain

Given the fact that the prevalence of celiac disease is so high among patients with Hashimoto's, if you have Hashimoto's and experience gastric symptoms, such as diarrhea, constipation, bloating, and/or gas, I suggest you test for celiac disease—especially if it runs in your family!

Testing for celiac disease can be done via a blood sample. Testing should consist of two tests:

- Anti–tTG IgA
- Anti–deamidated gliadin IgG

Although IgA is the primary antibody produced in people with celiac disease, some people have IgA deficiency and therefore can produce a false negative. This is why both tests should be examined. **Do not eliminate gluten from your diet before testing!** Please make sure that when you test for celiac disease, you consume gluten, on multiple occasions, within two weeks before the test, including the days leading up to the blood draw. I have had many patients over the years who made this common mistake when they initially tested, yielding a false negative. If your antibody results are positive, your doctor may request an endoscopy and possible biopsy (sample of skin tissue from the walls of the intestine).

CHRONIC AUTOIMMUNE GASTRITIS (CAG)

Autoimmune gastritis is a chronic inflammatory disease resulting in destruction of certain cells in the stomach responsible for stomach acid secretion and the absorption of B_{12}. It has been reported that 40 percent of patients with chronic autoimmune gastritis (CAG) also have Hashimoto's. Not only do individuals with CAG develop a vitamin B_{12} deficiency, known as pernicious anemia, but the destruction of the stomach cells can lead to reduced iron absorption, which can cause low iron stores or iron-deficiency anemia. The lower stomach acid resulting from autoimmune gastritis is also a risk factor for the development of SIBO.

If your vitamin B_{12} tests consistently come back in the lower range, especially if you are supplementing with B_{12}, consider further testing. Vitamin B_{12} levels lower than 300 ng/mL should be retested and investigated. If you do have autoimmune gastritis, vitamin B_{12} injections may be necessary to maintain normal B_{12} levels in the body.

Gut Infections

Certain infections and parasites are known triggers for autoimmune diseases, including Hashimoto's. SIBO, *H. pylori, Yersina entercolitica,*

Blastocystis hominis, and *Candida albicans* can all disrupt a healthy microbiome and can also act as triggers for autoimmune disease. Please refer to Chapter 6 for more on the gut and infections.

Low Stomach Acid

Changes in gut function and infections, such as SIBO, can lead to a reduced amount of stomach acid in people with Hashimoto's. Conditions related to low stomach acid are more common in Hashimoto's (low B_{12}, reduced iron absorption, and gastritis). Many people report improvements in thyroid symptoms, especially improvements in energy, when using supplements to increase the stomach acid in the body and/or improve digestion.

Medications, Antibiotics, and the Birth Control Pill

Medications can adversely alter the microbiome. We now know that the microbiome is altered by antibiotic exposure. After stopping antibiotics, the antibiotic "footprint" remains, meaning that the microbiome does not fully return to its preantibiotic state for a prolonged period of time. NSAIDs (ibuprofen, aspirin, naproxen, etc.) can also disrupt the microbiome, resulting in leaky gut and associated immune responses. Further, recent research has shown modification in the gut microbiome from oral contraceptives (the birth control pill) could influence the development of autoimmune diseases.

If you frequently use antibiotics, NSAIDS, and/or take the birth control pill and have Hashimoto's, I would encourage you to consider other alternatives. Finding a good naturopathic or functional medical doctor can provide natural, evidence-based alternatives to antibiotics that may be helpful in certain situations. If you chronically suffer from pain (period cramps, headaches, etc.) for which you are using an NSAID, working with an ND or functional doctor could help you get to the root cause of the issue. Other effective alternatives to the birth control pill could be considered.

CREATING A HEALTHY GUT

I hope that, by now, you agree that creating a healthy gut, low in inflammation and thriving with beneficial bacteria, is so important to health and the prevention and treatment of autoimmune disease. A healthy gut starts with diet. In fact, diet is arguably the most important factor in building and maintaining a healthy microbiome. If you create a healthy environment in the gut, healthy bacteria will take residence and thrive, fostering a healthier and more balanced immune system. On the other hand, if you consume a diet filled with processed foods, high in sugars and trans fats, unhealthy bacteria will flourish.

The Thyroid-Healing Diet is an ideal diet for creating a healthy microbiome. It inherently follows the same general principals as suggested by such gut experts as Dr. Raphael Kellman and Dr. Michael Ruscio. In *The Microbiome Diet*, Dr. Kellman explains that a microbiome diet consists of removing toxins and chemicals that are harmful to good bacteria, repairing the gut by eating healthy, anti-inflammatory foods, and then replenishing and reinoculating the gut with foods (and possibly supplements) that promote the growth and maintenance of healthy gut microbes. In *Healthy Gut, Healthy You*, Dr. Ruscio outlines that whole foods must be a focus of diet for a healthy gut, and that a paleo or low-FODMAP diet supports healthy gut bacteria. Key aspects of a diet focused on gut health include eating to reduce inflammation and balance blood sugar, and avoiding food allergies and/or intolerances. Reducing carbohydrates not only helps increase healthy bacteria but also may reduce thyroid autoimmunity.

7 KEY FACTORS IN CREATING A HEALTHY GUT

1. **Reduce inflammation.** Inflammation in the gastric tract is tightly correlated to our diet. As mentioned earlier, food sensitivities can cause unwanted changes in our gut bacteria and increase inflammation in the body. By eliminating the most common food sensitivities and then reintroducing them to our diet, we can gain a lot of knowledge about what foods produce an inflammatory response in the body. Inflammation is also linked to infections and undiagnosed conditions, such as celiac disease.

2. **Reduce toxins.** Toxins include pesticides, cigarettes, refined/processed foods, etc. High amounts of alcohol (binge drinking more than 4 or 5 times a month and/or more than 8 drinks per week for women or more than 15 drinks per week for men) can also kill off the beneficial bugs. Reducing your exposure to toxins not only helps the thyroid, but the microbes like it too!

3. **Increase your fiber intake.** Studies have shown that consuming fiber boosts the amount of healthy bacteria species, such as *Lactobacilli* and *Bifidobacteria*. Fiber also increases the diversity of species in the gut. Remember, short-chain fatty acids (SCFA) are produced when beneficial bacteria ferment fiber in the gut. By eating more fiber, we can increase our SCFA levels. These SCFAs help heal the intestinal barrier. Plus, SCFA help reduce the growth of salmonella and *E. coli*. See page 163 for a chart outlining high fiber foods.

4. **Supplement with probiotics.** Taking probiotics supplements can help ensure you are getting sufficient amounts of the right type of bacteria known to be beneficial for gut health. Probiotics are essentially microorganisms, like bacteria and yeasts, that need to be consumed. Research has shown that when a person takes a probiotic, it helps balance and increase the amount of different types of microbes in the gut, decrease pathogens and their toxins, and encourage restoration of healthy bacteria after antibiotic use. Probiotics also help protect and restore the intestinal barrier, reducing intestinal permeability, therefore making them a key element in the treatment of such diseases as Hashimoto's. In both animal and human trials, probiotics have been found to be beneficial for many inflammatory and autoimmune diseases.

What is the best type of probiotic?

If you have ever taken a look at the probiotic section in the natural health food store you may have been overwhelmed with how many different types and options there are! I suggest starting with a combination of ten of the most highly researched probiotic strains. Belonging to the *Lactobacillus* and *Bifidobacterium* species of probiotics, these strains include:

Bifidobacterium animalis subsp. Lactis (UABla-12)

Lactobacillus plantarum (UALp-05)

Lactobacillus acidophilus (DDS-1)

Bifidobacterium breve (UABbr-11)

Lactrobacillus casei (UALc-03)

Lactobacillus paracasei (UALpc-04)

Lactobacillus rhamnosus (GG)

Lactobacillus salivarius (UALs-07)

Bifidobacterium bifidum (UABb-10)

Bifidobacterium longum subsp. Longum (UABI-14)

I have tried many different types and combinations of probiotics over the years and have consistently had the best results with this combination of probiotic species.

Saccharomyces boulardii, a yeastlike probiotic, has been found to be effective in treating *Blastocystis hominis* and *H. pylori* (as discussed on pages 101 and 99, respectively) and may also be particularly helpful for those who struggle with diarrhea.

5. **Consider other forms of supplementation.** Many supplements can also be helpful for gut health, especially in the case of healing intestinal permeability. See page 214 for supplement options.

6. **Eat fermented foods.** Fermented foods are another great way to increase healthy gut microbes. During the process of fermentation, beneficial bacteria break down the food and make it rich in enzymes and nutrients. Additionally, these bacteria are beneficial to our gastrointestinal tract and have been shown to be helpful to a variety of gastrointestinal disorders, including IBS.

Historically, fermenting vegetables has been common practice in many countries all over the world. However, today North Americans consume much less fermented foods than did our ancestors before us. Fermented vegetables, such as carrots, beets, and cabbage (think: kimchi and sauerkraut), as well as kombucha and kefir, are excellent and tasty options to include in your diet.

Fermented foods are helpful only when they contain active, live cultures of beneficial bacteria. Some fermented foods are heated and so no longer contain these healthy microbes once they are on the store shelves, or only contain a very small amount of them that is not enough to really affect the gut. This is why it is best to ensure that you purchase fermented foods found in the refrigerated section of the store (not in the unrefrigerated store aisle). You can also look for "raw" or "live enzymes" on the label. If you suffer from SIBO, fermented foods may aggravate your symptoms and are best avoided until SIBO has been treated.

7. **Reassess your medication.** As mentioned earlier, many medications can be bad news for the gut. Have a discussion with your health-care provider about the best options for you. The next chapter takes an in-depth look at medications.

CHAPTER 10

What You Need to Know About Medications

I will never forget how I felt when I was first told I required medication for the rest of my life because of my slow thyroid. I was angry, disappointed, and afraid. Wasn't there another option? Although addressing other aspects of thyroid healing through diet and lifestyle is crucial, restoring thyroid hormone levels is vital in the treatment of hypothyroidism and for the improvement of symptoms—and many patients will still require some type of medication and/or supplementation. The key here is finding the right medication that works for you, with or without a combination of vitamins and supplements that can help both the medications and thyroid function more optimally. In more recent history, T4-only medication (levothyroxine) has been the sole thyroid hormone prescribed. Most of my patients have been told that levothyroxine was their one option to manage their hypothyroid. However, this is simply not the case. Natural desiccated thyroid (NDT) contains both T3 and T4 hormones and may be more helpful in managing some patients' symptoms. Herbs and supplements may not only be helpful for thyroid symptoms, but may help medications work better and improve thyroid function. Here is a detailed look at your options for medication.

T4-ONLY MEDICATION

The go-to medication for Hashimoto's and hypothyroidism is T4-only medication (levothyroxine). It is most commonly sold as Synthroid,

Levothyroid, Levoxyl, Unithroid, or Eltroxin in North America. Tirosint is a newer "gel cap" T4 medication that does not contain some of the fillers that the other commonly sold brands include, and some patients seem to have a better response to this formulation. T4-only medication is the recommended standard of treatment by the American Thyroid Association (ATA). However, research has shown that about 15 percent of the ten to twelve million people in the US with hypothyroidism continue to feel sick and have symptoms despite following the standard of care recommended by the ATA. Even more frustrating is that the patient's blood work may show normal levels of TSH and T4 hormones while taking the T4 medication, but they still have symptoms of hypothyroidism and feel unwell.

Medical professor and past president of the American Thyroid Association Antonio Bianco, MD, reports that some patients still complain of being depressed, having a foggy mind, having difficulty losing weight, and having less energy despite being on T4-only medication and having a normal TSH level. And despite these symptoms, doctors continue to tell them that they are on the right medication, their blood work is normal, and therefore they should feel fine.

Although this conventional approach helps replace thyroid hormones in the body, this medication does not address the number one reason why people have hypothyroidism (autoimmune disease), nor does it do anything to reduce inflammation. As we know, Hashimoto's is a complex disease; medication is just one piece of the puzzle. I have found that for some patients, once they adopt the Thyroid-Healing Diet, address gut health, improve stress levels, and reduce toxins, symptoms resolve without the need to change medication (sometimes we even have to lower the medication dosage as their thyroid health begins to improve!).

For other patients, however, switching to a combination medication of T4 and T3 thyroid hormones may be best for them, even if they address all the other aspects of thyroid healing. Research has shown that individuals taking T4-only medication have lower amounts of T3 hormone compared to individuals without thyroid disease. This is because some people have difficulty changing the inactive T4 hormone into the active T3 hormone and therefore their symptoms of hypothyroid persist because, despite taking thyroid hormones, the hormones are not fully active in the body. When a patient uses NDT or combination therapy, the active T3 hormone is provided within the medication and this can be a game changer.

Reasons that you may want to continue with T4-only medication:

- T4-only medication is prescribed by most conventional doctors and is dispensed by most pharmacies; essentially it may be easier to obtain than NDT.
- T4-only medication comes in a variety of dosages and is easy to titrate up and down.
- People who suffer from palpitations, abnormal heart rhythms, and/or significant anxiety may tolerate T4-only medication better than using a medication that contains T3.
- Some patients respond very well to T4-only medication.

Reasons that you may want to consider NDT or combination hormone medication:

1. You are still experiencing, or have begun to experience, hypothyroid symptoms again, despite have a "normal" TSH.
2. You have not experienced any weight loss, or are continuing to gain weight, since using T4-only medication, despite adhering to a healthy diet and exercise regimen.
3. Since using T4-only medication, your TSH and T4 levels have improved, but your T3 levels are low.

NATURAL DESICCATED THYROID (NDT)

Combination therapy of T4 hormone and T3 hormone can be prescribed as natural desiccated thyroid (NDT) and is extracted from a porcine (pig) source. It used to be available in a synthetic combination tablet (sold as Liotrix or Thyrolar), but is now no longer available. Combination thyroid medications contain T4 and T3 hormones in a 4:1 ratio. NDT, unlike synthetic T3 and T4 medications, also contains small amounts of the lesser-known inactive thyroid hormones T1 and T2. New research is showing that these hormones may have added benefit for the thyroid gland.

Natural thyroid preparations, such as NDT, were the first pharmacologic treatments available and historically have been the primary way hypothyroidism has been treated. Instead of doctors looking at TSH levels in the blood, they would use natural thyroid remedies until the patient's symptoms resolved, their basal metabolic rate returned to normal, and/or iodine levels improved. Adverse effects from natural thyroid medications were uncommon. However, concerns about the potencies of NDT began to arise, and upon testing, it was revealed that some tablets contained high amounts of thyroid and others contained very little. In the 1970s, monitoring the thyroid gland by way of measuring TSH in the blood led to the discovery that some of these patients were overmedicated. Further, the scientific discovery that T4 hormone naturally converted to T3 in the body led to the decision to provide patients with T4-only therapy, assuming their body would naturally convert the hormone into the active T3 form. In 1985, stable potency of NDT was achieved, but by then the reputation of natural thyroid products was tarnished for some conventionally trained doctors. Today, manufacturers of desiccated thyroid take the proper steps to ensure potency before the products are shipped to pharmacies and analytical tests are performed on the hormones to ensure potency and correct dosage.

Combination therapy remains a heavily debated topic in medicine. Some research has shown it to be beneficial and other research has not; however, as previously discussed, without addressing the root cause of hypothyroidism, many people may not feel better on any form of medication!

In 2013, a study published in the *Journal of Clinical Endocrinology and Metabolism* revealed almost half of patients preferred NDT compared to levothyroxine. Plus, patients were more likely to lose weight when using NDT. A more recent study, in 2018, found that patients using NDT for just over two years had a 92.7 percent improvement of symptoms and quality of life. When I first made the switch from T4-only medication to NDT, I did not yet have the information I have now, regarding addressing the root cause of hypothyroidism with diet, gut healing, and removal of toxins. Even so, when I changed to NDT, I felt better within three days and I lost approximately 5 pounds after two weeks of making the switch. I have predominately prescribed NDT in my practice and have found it to be very effective. NDT medications are most commonly sold under the brand names of Armour, Nature-Throid, Bio-throid, WP Thyroid, or Erfa. Note that all NDT and compounded thyroid medications currently approved for use by the FDA are from a porcine source. Bovine-source thyroid medications are available online, but as of this writing have not yet been approved for use by the FDA.

STARTING NDT OR SWITCHING FROM T4-ONLY MEDICATION TO NDT

If you have never taken thyroid hormones before, the starting dose of NDT is usually 30 mg (1 grain). Dosages are typically increased, if needed, every six weeks after blood testing has been done to assess how the hormones are working in the body.

When switching from T4-only medication to NDT, some individuals can do a straight switch and others may require a slightly lower NDT dosage compared to their T4-only medication dosage, due to the added T3. I also suggest that patients who take NDT make note of the equal dose of Synthroid for their given dose. In the case of an emergency, if you don't have access to NDT (e.g., in a hospital setting if you don't have your medication with you, or if you forget your medication while traveling to another country) it is important to know what dose of Synthroid would replace your NDT for a duration of time. Synthroid is readily available in the hospital and worldwide; however, this is often not the case with NDT.

While you would switch to NDT under a doctor's supervision, this chart is still helpful for you to have. I have found that many MDs do not know the conversion dosages (I actually brought this chart into my MD's office when I was first diagnosed). It is also good for you to know your NDT dose conversions for levothyroxine for certain situations, as discussed.

SYNTHROID	ARMOUR	NATURE-THROID	WP THYROID
25 mcg (0.025 mg)	¼ grain (15 mg)	¼ grain (16.25 mg)	¼ grain (16.25 mg)
50 mcg (0.05 mg)	½ grain (30 mg)	½ grain (32.5 mg)	½ grain (32.5 mg)
75 mcg (0.075 mg)		¾ grain (48.75 mg)	¾ grain (48.75 mg)
88 mcg (0.088 mg)			
100 mcg (0.1 mg)	1 grain (60 mg)	1 grain (65 mg)	1 grain (65 mg)
112 mcg (0.112 mg)			
125 mcg (0.125 mg)		1.25 grains (81.25 mg)	1.25 grains (81.25 mg)
137 mcg (0.137 mg)			
150 mcg (0.150 mg)	1.5 grains (90 mg)	1.5 grains (97.5 mg)	1.5 grains (97.5 mg)
175 mcg (0.175 mg)		1.75 grains (113.75 mg)	1.75 grains (113.75 mg)
200 mcg (0.2 mg)	2 grains (120 mg)	2 grains (130 mg)	2 grains (130 mg)
		2.25 grains (146.25 mg)	
		2.5 grains (162.5 mg)	
300 mcg (0.3 mg)	3 grains (180 mg)	3 grains (195 mg)	
	4 grains (240 mg)	4 grains (260 mg)	
	5 grains (300 mg)	5 grains (325 mg)	

(Source: WP Thyroid and Nature-Throid Conversion Guide. https://getrealthyroid
.com/conversion-guide.html, accessed August 19, 2019.)

COMPOUNDED T4/T3

Natural combination medication of T4 and T3 can also be made from scratch by a compounding pharmacist. This can be beneficial when patients do not tolerate the 4:1 ratio of thyroid hormones contained in natural tablets and require a custom ratio. Humans naturally produce the T4 and T3 hormones in a 14:1 ratio (compared to the 4:1 ratio found in NDT) and therefore some patients have a higher than normal T3 level when taking NDT. This was the case for me, and having the thyroid medication made in a customized dosage was a great solution. Others find benefit when taking compounded T4-only medication with NDT medication to achieve the right dosage. Another advantage of compounding can be if the patient requires a more tailored dosage. For example, NDT tablets are available in standard dosages of 15 mg, 30 mg, 60 mg, and so on. If a patient requires a 20 mg dosage, it may be easier to compound the medication instead of splitting up the medication with a pill cutter to try to achieve the correct dosage. Compounded formulas are typically made without any fillers or binders and therefore may be beneficial for individuals who cannot tolerate these additives. However, compounded formulas are often very expensive and require a specially trained pharmacist to prepare the formula. Many of the NDT formulas (Nature-Throid, WP Throid) have very small amounts of fillers and are good hypoallergenic options.

SYNTHETIC T3-ONLY MEDICATION

A synthetic T3 medication, liothyronine (commonly sold as Cytomel), can also be added to T4-only medication, or in some cases, to NDT medication. Using T3 medication can be an option when a patient requires a customized dosage of T3. However, compared to NDT and compounded thyroid, liothyronine is quick release, meaning that the thyroid hormone will only be active in the body for a certain period. Patients will typically have to dose liothyronine two or three times daily to achieve a steady hormone state in the body.

Concerns About T3

Many conventional clinicians feel uncomfortable prescribing T3 hormone alone or in a combination formula, due to the concern that high blood T3 concentration can cause osteoporosis, as well as a rapid and irregular heartbeat. When patients are given too much T3 hormone, undesirable symptoms can arise, such as too much weight loss, diarrhea, and anxiety.

Although these are all possible side effects from *overmedication* of T3 hormone, proper symptom and lab monitoring can significantly reduce these risks. (I have only had one patient in the last few years experience palpitations from NDT medication and these symptoms quickly disappeared after lowering her medication dosage.)

LOW-T3 SYNDROME AND MEDICATION

Recently, more patients have requested T3-only medication when they have low T3 levels show up on blood work, without having a previous diagnosis of hypothyroidism. If the patient also has elevated TSH levels, paired with hypothyroid symptoms, we need to dig a little deeper, address potential thyroid conversion issues, and consider medication. However, more commonly I have seen what is referred to as low-T3 syndrome, also called euthyroid sick syndrome or nonthyroidal illness syndrome (NTIS). Here, T3 levels are often low because of changes that are happening in the body and not because of thyroid disease itself. In these patients, TSH levels are often normal, or may even be a little low, and reverse T3 levels are often high. Some of the more common reasons this can happen are caloric restriction (including fasting); the patient is under high amounts of stress; or the patient is exposed to chemicals and heavy metals, such as bromine, fluoride, mercury, and/or cadmium. Chronic illness and diabetes can be another reason a patient may experience low-T3 syndrome. It may seem logical to use T3 medication when T3 levels are low in the blood; however, studies have shown that many patients experience adverse effects when using T3 or thyroid medication for low T3 if the other markers of thyroid health are otherwise normal. If you have had low T3 levels show up on blood work, check your reverse T3 levels, consider the amount of stress you are currently under, address your diet, and ensure you have reduced your exposure to chemicals and heavy metals.

BEST MEDICATION FOR REVERSE T3 SYNDROME

As it is common to have low T3 hormone levels when someone has high reverse T3 (RT3) levels, the question is raised again as to whether to use T3 medication for high RT3 levels. The same underlying root causes are often responsible for high RT3 as for low T3: fasting, calorie restriction, stress, exposure to toxins, diabetes, and chronic illness. I believe the best treatment for RT3 is to first address the underlying cause and then support the proper conversion of T4 to T3 (see pages 209–211 on supplements), instead of providing medication that could cause side effects.

TESTING AND MONITORING WHEN USING THYROID HORMONES

When I start a patient on thyroid hormone medication, I test TSH, T3, and T4 every four to six months until hormone balance is achieved and hypothyroid symptoms have resolved. I continue to monitor the patient's thyroid levels every six to eight months, or if symptoms return. Taking a medication that contains T3 hormone (natural or synthetic) can alter your blood results when you consume the medication close to the time of the blood draw. If you take your medication at night, this is often not an issue; however, if you do it first thing in the morning and then have the blood test soon after, your T3 levels may look abnormally high. If you are using a thyroid medication that contains T3 and you consume it during the daytime, I suggest waiting to take the medication until after your blood draw on the day of testing, or at the very least waiting six to eight hours after medication to have the blood draw. Either way, it is important to be consistent with testing. If you test your blood levels eight hours after taking your medication one month, make sure to do the same for the next time of testing. Although it does not replace the need for blood testing, tracking your basal metabolic temperature can also be a good method to assess how a medication change is impacting your body. See page 306 for more on charting your temperature.

MONITORING ANTIBODIES

Monitoring thyroid antibodies can be a great way to help identify whether diet and lifestyle interventions are having a beneficial effect, but reduction of antibodies can take time! Many conventional doctors do not typically retest thyroid antibodies, as many believe that once you test positive, you will be positive for life. However, this is not the case for me or many of my patients and I have found that checking antibodies can be helpful to guide treatment. That said, because antibodies are slow to shift, I generally only suggest retesting them anywhere from three to six months later, depending on the diet and lifestyle intervention. For example, if you were to change nothing else but adopt the Thyroid-Healing Diet for three months, you could test your antibodies before and after starting the diet and note the change in addition to any changes in your symptoms.

TSH SUPPRESSION

A fair number of patients who use NDT or a medication containing T3 hormones experience TSH suppression, meaning their TSH levels in the blood are below normal and recommended values. On top of this, their T3 hormone on blood testing may be slightly elevated, but their T4 level is normal. Some of these patients with suppressed TSH feel great, and if we do lower their medication dose, some of their symptoms return. However, a suppressed TSH could also indicate that the person is being overdosed on medication and the dosage should be reduced. (From personal experience, being overdosed on medication felt horrible. I also experienced a mix of both hyperthyroid and hypothyroid symptoms when my medication was too high. I felt anxious and had a higher-than-normal heartbeat, but I was freezing cold and my muscles felt slow and sluggish.) Suppressed TSH has also been shown to increase the rate of bone loss and may put the person at risk of osteoporosis. This is especially important to consider if you have gone through menopause as your risk of osteoporosis is greater. Factors to consider if you have a suppressed TSH:

- NDT medications contain T4:T3 in a 4:1 ratio and T3 is much more effective at lowering TSH. Especially if your T3 is slightly higher on blood work, you may want to consider having your thyroid medication specially compounded in a ratio with less T3 hormone.
- If you take your medication in the morning and you have a suppressed TSH and an elevated T3 level, test your hormones again, making sure to wait until after the blood draw to take your medication. If your TSH is still significantly suppressed, you most likely need less medication.
- You need to consider how greatly your TSH is suppressed. Less than 0.4 mIU/L is typically considered a suppressed TSH. You are at greater risk of side effects if your TSH is 0.1 compared to 0.3. That said, a study published in 2009 found that patients with a suppressed TSH of only 0.03 or less had an increased risk of cardiovascular disease, abnormal heartbeat, and fractures.
- Does osteoporosis run in your family? Osteoporosis has a strong genetic component, and if you have a family history, you also may be at greater risk of developing loss of bone with a suppressed TSH.

If you do have a suppressed TSH but continue your current dosage, you must monitor your symptoms and address any signs of hyperthyroidism (anxiety, palpitations, racing heart, high blood pressure, weight loss) or hypothyroidism (especially weak muscles or cold intolerances) with your doctor ASAP. Please remember that more medication is not always best. In my experience, many patients are nervous their metabolism will slow down and they will gain weight if they reduce medication (even though this is almost never the case). I have had patients resist lowering thyroid medication or increasing their thyroid medication dosage on their own. It is important to seriously consider the side effects of overmedication.

CONSIDERATIONS WHEN USING THYROID HORMONES

Birth control pills. Birth control pills contain a combination of both estrogen and progesterone hormones. Estrogens seem to increase a protein in the body known as serum thyroxine-binding globulin (TBG). In a patient with hypothyroidism, T4 hormone may be decreased when the birth control pill is started, due to the effects on TBG. This may or may not increase the need for thyroid hormone medication. If the patient does not have hypothyroidism and starts to take the birth control pill, the T4 hormone will naturally compensate and would not require any thyroid medication, but medication change may be necessary if the patient is currently taking thyroid meds. If you are currently taking the birth control pill, or have just started to take it and are also taking thyroid medication, make sure to have your thyroid blood tests run, especially if you are experiencing hypothyroid symptoms—you may need a dosage change.

Best practices for taking your thyroid hormones. Whether you are taking synthetic or natural thyroid hormones, here are some rules that will make them more effective.

1. It is imperative that you take your thyroid medication on an empty stomach, at least 1 hour away from food and ideally 2 to 4 hours away from caffeine, dairy, or iron-containing food and supplements. I cannot tell you how many of my patients experienced a huge improvement in symptoms when they began to adhere to these guidelines. Caffeine, dairy, and iron can all significantly interfere with the absorption of the thyroid medication, resulting in reduced thyroid hormone levels in the body and/or variations from day to day in hormone levels.

2. To achieve consistent levels of thyroid hormones it is also best to take your thyroid medication at the same time (or around the same time) daily. It is commonplace to suggest taking thyroid medication in the morning; however, some patients feel better taking their medication at nighttime. The improved results from nighttime dosing could partially be due to the fact that the digestive tract slows down at night and the slower transit time allows for greater medication absorption. I imagine this could also be a result of increased absorption due to the reduced chance of interactions with foods and caffeine.

MEDICATING SUBCLINICAL HYPOTHYROIDISM

Not unlike the use of NDT and T3 medication, treating subclinical hypothyroidism (SCH) remains a hotly debated topic in medicine. Remember from Chapter 1, subclinical hypothyroidism is often considered a "mild" form of hypothyroidism whereby the TSH becomes elevated but the T3 and T4 thyroid hormones are still within normal levels. Usually, if the TSH is only slightly elevated, patients are told they will be monitored but medical invention is not necessary. Usually, medical doctors wait to prescribe medication until the patient is "overtly hypothyroid" (increased TSH and decreased thyroid hormones). Subclinical hypothyroidism is also referred to in medicine as "mild thyroid failure," which is an early stage of thyroid disease and can progress to overt hypothyroidism. Progression to overt hypothyroidism is more common if the patient is positive for thyroid antibodies. In some people, there is a spontaneous recovery from subclinical hypothyroidism without any intervention. Although a person may have no symptoms when they have subclinical hypothyroidism, the vast majority of patients I see with this condition have persistent and frustrating symptoms of low thyroid function—it's why they ended up booking an appointment with me in the first place! This is my approach to treating subclinical hypothyroidism:

1. Run a full thyroid panel to understand whether the patient has positive antibodies and/or high levels of RT3.
2. Test for any nutrient deficiencies and correct them if present.
3. Use the Thyroid-Healing Diet, reduce toxins and stress and EMFs, address gut health, and consider supplementation to either help lower antibodies, reduce the stress response on the body, and/or improve thyroid function. Supplements that directly support the thyroid gland can also help; I have had a lot of success in my practice with the use of ashwagandha (withania) to improve thyroid function in subclinical hypothyroidism. The use of ancient therapies, such as acupuncture, may also be helpful (see page 228 for more information).
4. If the patient is positive for thyroid antibodies, I consider other reasons for autoimmunity, such as infection.

5. Rerun blood tests in 3 months.

6. If after 3 months, despite dietary changes and the use of supplements, the patient is still experiencing symptoms and the TSH level has not shifted into, or close to, the optimal range of 0.5 to 2.5 mIU/L, we will discuss thyroid medication.

An Experimental New Therapy: LDN

LOW-DOSE naltrexone (LDN) is a very small dose of naltrexone. Naltrexone is a pharmaceutical medication that is approved for the use of helping people ween off opioid drugs at a dose of 50 to 100 mg per day. At this dosage, naltrexone is an opioid antagonist, blocking the opioid receptors in the brain, preventing opioid drugs from causing their effects. In the 1980s, Dr. Bernard Bihari discovered that when he gave AIDS and cancer patients a very low dose of naltrexone (around 3 mg) it helped their immune system. Since that time, there has been a grassroots movement of both patients and clinicians who have used LDN, raising awareness about the benefits of this medication and urging for more research.

Doses between 1.5 and 4.5 mg per day have been found to help the immune system in people with such autoimmune diseases as fibromyalgia, Crohn's disease, and multiple sclerosis. It appears to be particularly helpful for patients with autoimmune disease who are suffering from pain. At this low dose, the medication transiently blocks the opioid receptors in the brain, causing a natural "opioid rebound" increase of endorphins in the body. This elevated level of endorphins has been shown to benefit the immune system and can have anti-inflammatory effects.

At this time, there have been no clinical trials looking at the effectiveness for LDN and Hashimoto's. However, there are countless patient testimonials reporting that LDN significantly improved or reduced their thyroid antibodies, and some reporting a reduced need for thyroid medication after LDN usage.

continues

continued

LDN is still considered an "off-label medication" and is not easily available at the low dosages. A compounding pharmacist must custom make these lower dosages. Unlike compounded thyroid medication, LDN is a relatively low-cost medication. Little to no side effects of LDN therapy have been reported, except for some users experiencing very unusual and vivid dreams. However, I tried LDN for just over one month and experienced nosebleeds, especially after switching from 1 mg to 2 mg, and therefore I discontinued this therapy.

If you are interested in trying LDN therapy, you need to find a functional medical doctor or naturopathic doctor who is well versed in LDN therapy.

CHAPTER 11

Natural Herbs and Supplements

Using herbs, supplements, and vitamins to improve health and treat disease is probably more common today than ever. My mom was an early adopter of natural remedies; taking supplements or herbs with breakfast, dinner, before bed, and even in between is second nature to me. For others, swallowing pills, making teas, and taking tinctures can feel like a hassle. Yet I have not only seen incredible results in my patients from the use of natural remedies, but we now also have some great research to support their use. The number of studies looking at natural therapies will never be as robust as the studies pertaining to pharmaceutical medications; simply put, pharmaceutical companies have a lot more money to fund tests and experiments. Nonetheless, many natural remedies, especially herbal remedies, have historically been used with success over hundreds of years for certain aliments and diseases. Here are some important things to remember with herbs and supplements:

- Just as with diet and exercise, results are often not overnight or immediate. Many effective natural remedies can take upward of 3 weeks for people to start to notice a difference; some may need to be taken long term for results to continue.
- Check with your health-care provider when taking any new supplements. Some herbs have contraindications or cautions that you might not be aware of and/or could cause an allergic response.

- If you are currently taking thyroid medication, and begin a new supplement to improve thyroid function, **it is important that you are under the care of a health-care provider who can monitor blood levels and thyroid symptoms. The use of some supplements may change the amount of thyroid medication required.**

- Quality is crucial when using natural remedies. In a world where herbs and supplements can be found just about anywhere, you need to use a product that has been tested for quality and potency. The researched benefit of many herbs comes from the extract of certain parts of the plant. For example, echinacea is well known for its ability to reduce the duration and severity of the common cold and has been shown to enhance the immune system. These health benefits come from specific derivatives and components primarily found in high amounts in the root of the plant. To obtain these components, they need to be extracted, often with alcohol. I cannot tell you how many herbal products I have seen that contain the "dried flower tops" of the echinacea plant put into a capsule. These capsules may not actually have any, or very little, therapeutic results. So, it is no wonder that some people take cheap forms of echinacea and see no benefit in cold and flu symptoms!

I have had numerous patients over the years choose an herb or supplement from brands that I typically don't recommend or a brand that doesn't third-party test its products. Usually patients opt for these brands because they are much more affordable. However, you really do get what you pay for, and this is so true with natural remedies. Many of these patients who opted for the more affordable brand of herb or supplement ultimately did not experience the expected results with the product and eventually switched to the higher-quality product and noticed a difference. Most of them were frustrated that they even wasted money on the cheaper version of the supplement in the first place.

When choosing a natural or herbal supplement, here are some factors that should be considered.

- Ensure the product has been tested for pesticides, heavy metals, toxins, and microbes.
- Ensure the product has been third-party tested for purity, strength, and composition. Look for the label "GMP certified" or "NSF certified"; both indicate the product has been sufficiently tested.
- Ensure the product DOES NOT contain added sugars or artificial colorings or flavorings. Sometimes, the label will clearly state that the product also does not contain any coatings or binders. This is ideal.
- If the recommended herb has a standardized extract percentage or dose recommended, make sure the label notes that the herb contains the necessary standardization.

Unfortunately, sometimes the label doesn't clearly state whether any of these requirements have been followed for the product. It may be necessary to visit the company website to gather more information.*

Although using supplements can be an important factor when healing the thyroid, it should never be the first or only step you take for thyroid health. I always suggest adopting the Thyroid-Healing Diet prior to, or at the same time as, using herbs and supplements. Addressing the health of the gut and other potential triggers of autoimmune disease and inflammation is equally as important (see the following steps). Then, I typically suggest supplements are first used to correct any deficiencies in the body that may be leading to exaggerated symptoms of hypothyroidism. After monitoring the benefits of correcting deficiencies and further reducing your exposure to environmental factors that could harm the thyroid, other supplements could be added.

---

* It should also be noted that some of the most important North American healing herbs are now unfortunately endangered. This includes goldenseal, slippery elm, and echinacea. The United Plant Savers is a group of plant enthusiasts committed to raising public awareness of our wild medicinal plants and to protect these plants and encourage the regrowth of them in our natural habitat. If you are interested in learning more, or would like to donate, please visit https://unitedplantsavers.org/join-ups/. Their goal is to ensure that these valuable medicinal plants will be preserved for our grandchildren and our grandchildrens' grandchildren.

HOW TO USE HERBS AND SUPPLEMENTS TO SUPPORT THYROID HEALING

Natural thyroid healing requires individualized healing, and the best herbs and supplements for one person with Hashimoto's may be different for another person with Hashimoto's. However, if you like it super simple, here is my general Hashimoto's herb and supplement protocol:

1. Once you have been tested for potential nutrient deficiencies (B_{12}, vitamin D, and iron), begin proper B_{12}, vitamin D, and/or iron supplementation, dosage dependent on your determined deficiency.
2. Selenium: 200 ucg a day, for reducing antibodies
3. Ashwagandha (*Withania somnifera*): 600 mg a day in tablet form, or 2.5 ml twice daily of a 1:1 liquid extract
4. Probiotics: multistrain formula 50 to 100 billion cfu per day
5. L-glutamine: 5 g upon waking
6. Digestive enzymes: with any meal that contains a protein and a fat
7. If stress or sleep is an issue and has not been corrected with ashwagandha, choose an herb that is best suited to your needs (see "Herbs/ Supplements for Managing Stress," page 217). If SIBO or other infections are present, use herbals and/or antibiotics (discussed in Chapter 6).

I want to stress that I *start* with this formula and it can do the trick for many patients. Ashwagandha (*Withania somnifera*) is my go-to herb for Hashimoto's and hypothyroidism as it helps improve T3 and T4 levels in the body as well as helps the body react to stress. It can also be beneficial for mood and sleep. I have also had many patients with subclinical hypothyroidism use withania along with the Thyroid-Healing Diet, and avoid using medication. Likewise, some patients will require a medication adjustment once they begin this supplement regime and therefore it is absolutely crucial you are working with a health-care provider and regularly monitoring your thyroid blood levels.

Many patients may need much more than my recommended protocol, or they don't respond well to some of the suggested herbs or supplements. Some patients have tried all of them, yet they need other options.

A Note on Iodine and Tyrosine: The Building Blocks for Thyroid Hormones

IODINE and tyrosine are ingredients that are commonly added to natural thyroid supplements; as you may remember from Chapter 1, these nutrients are essential to thyroid function and hormone production. However, both iodine and tyrosine may be better used *after* thyroid antibody levels have been reduced, as they may not necessarily help people suffering from Hashimoto's when inflammation and antibodies are high.

Iodine

Iodine is a key element needed to make thyroid hormones. Both iodine deficiency and iodine excess has been linked to hypothyroidism—which makes the topic of iodine and hypothyroidism a bit confusing!

Historically, in places where people were iodine deficient, levels of hypothyroidism were much more prevalent, so industrialized nations began to add iodine to table salt. However, it seems that this may have increased the rate of autoimmune hypothyroidism. People with Hashimoto's may be more sensitive to iodine. When the body is exposed to high levels of iodine, perhaps especially when the iodine levels are not typically that high in the diet, the thyroid gland reduces its production of thyroid hormones. This is referred to as the Wolff-Chaikoff effect. In most people, this decreased production of thyroid hormones is transient, and regular production resumes in a few weeks. However, in people who have preexisting thyroid disease, excess iodine can induce further thyroid dysfunction, which may be transient or permanent.

I only recommend someone with hypothyroidism take iodine in three instances:

1. During pregnancy, iodine is included in the prenatal vitamin and is important for fetal development. Unless antibodies are sky-high, I also generally suggest including healthy foods that contain iodine (e.g., cod) during pregnancy.

continues

continued

2. If a patient is hypothyroid, with negative antibodies (the patient does not have Hashimoto's).
3. If a patient has Hashimoto's but antibodies have significantly decreased and/or are now negative.

It is also important to mention that certain chemicals can reduce how our thyroid gland is able to use iodine. The chemicals fluorine, chlorine, and bromine can be especially problematic. These chemicals act to "displace" iodine binding and can reduce thyroid hormone production in the thyroid gland. Unfortunately, most of these chemicals are found in our water. Whether you have Hashimoto's or not, I recommend a good-quality water filter to reduce the levels of these chemicals in your drinking water.

Don't get me wrong, I believe iodine is an incredibly important nutrient, not only for the thyroid gland but for other tissues in the body. I am also well aware that iodine deficiency may increase cystic tissue in the body (fibrocystic breasts, uterine cysts, etc.) and may also be correlated with a higher risk of breast cancer. However, I just don't think it is worth it to use iodine when you have high levels of antibodies. Once the antibodies are lowered, iodine can be taken, in supplement form or increased in the diet.

Dosage: As a general rule, 2 mcg/kg (0.9 mcg/lb) of body weight is recommended when using iodine; however, pregnant and breastfeeding woman will require slightly more than this. The American Thyroid Association cautions against using doses of more than 500 mcg per day (for nonpregnant individuals) and notes that doses above 1,100 mcg may cause thyroid dysfunction.

Tyrosine

The use of tyrosine is also controversial in Hashimoto's. Just like iodine, tyrosine is necessary for thyroid hormone production and therefore it seems logical to believe that taking more tyrosine can increase thyroid hormone production. L-tyrosine is a synthetic version of the amino acid tyrosine found in your body. Although some studies have shown that L-tyrosine may be helpful to improve cognition, especially during times

continues

continued

of stress, studies have not necessarily shown thyroid improvements when supplementing with tyrosine. But, by the same logic that we understand iodine can increase antibodies, we can assume supplementing with tyrosine may also elevate antibodies (as both iodine and tyrosine are the building blocks for the thyroid gland). Tyrosine also requires iodine for thyroid hormone production, and if you are limiting iodine in your diet and/or avoiding iodine supplements, it doesn't necessarily make sense to use increased tyrosine at the same time.

As with iodine, I generally wait until antibodies are low to use L-tyrosine. Adding more protein to the diet can help naturally boost levels of tyrosine.

Dosage: If you do try using L-tyrosine (once antibodies have lowered), the dosage is 500 to 2,000 mg per day, generally taken in the morning or before exercise.

In this chapter, you will find multiple natural supplements and herbs for healing your thyroid.

Again, be sure to check with your health-care provider before starting any supplements.

SUPPLEMENTS TO CORRECT NUTRIENT DEFICIENCIES

Vitamin B_{12}. Many people with hypothyroidism have been shown to have low B_{12} levels upon blood testing. As this vitamin is important for energy production, deficiencies in B_{12} can compound symptoms of fatigue, mood changes, and brain fog. Approximately 40 to 60 percent of the American population has genetic mutations that impair the conversion of supplemental folic acid and B_{12} to its active form. It is therefore generally thought that using the active forms of vitamin B_{12}, known as methylcobalamin, is superior to cyanocobalamin, the inactive form of vitamin B_{12}.

Normal levels of B_{12}: 200 to 900 pg/mL

Deficiency: less than 200 pg/mL; however, I typically suggest supplementation if levels are less than 400 pg/mL

Dosage for nutrient replenishing: 1,000 to 5,000 ucg of methylcobalamin sublingually (taken under the tongue in liquid form) daily (if
you feel more fatigued or generally feel unwell when you use methylcobalamin, switch to cyanocobalamin and notice whether you feel
any improvement. A small number of individuals process cyanocobalamin better than methylcobalamin).

Iron. A 2019 study reports that autoimmune thyroid patients are frequently iron-deficient due to their higher incidence of autoimmune gastritis and celiac disease (both of which cause iron loss). In two-thirds of
women with persistent symptoms of hypothyroidism, despite appropriate
levothyroxine therapy, restoration of serum ferritin (the blood marker for
iron stores) above 100 ng/ml reduced the persistent symptoms that were
not improving with levothyroxine medication alone. This is huge—so
many of thyroid patients I see have ferritin levels of 30 ng/ml or less. Often, they have been told that because they do not have anemia, just lower
iron stores, iron supplementation isn't necessary. Iron supplementation
can be a game changer for symptoms of fatigue and cold intolerance, but
it is important to find an absorbable form of iron.

Note: If you have tested positive for SIBO, I suggest treating the bacteria first before increasing iron levels. Iron can feed pathogens and it can
be difficult to raise iron levels until gut health and bacteria are addressed.

Normal levels of serum ferritin for women: 11 to 307 ng/ml
Normal levels of serum ferritin for men: 20 to 336 ng/ml
Deficiencies: As you may notice, the normal range is very wide for
both women and men. Iron-deficiency anemia is often diagnosed
at levels under 11 ng/ml in women or under 20 ng/ml in men in
addition to the presence of a low hematocrit or hemoglobin level.
However, serum ferritin levels of less than 30 ng/ml can represent
low iron stores and less than 100 ng/ml can hinder optimal thyroid
function.
Dosage for nutrient replenishing: Iron supplements can often cause
gastrointestinal problems and constipation. I recommend supplementing with lower amounts of bioavailable forms of iron for

greater absorption and generally fewer gastrointestinal issues (heme iron for nonvegetarians and iron bisglycinate for vegetarians/vegans). Although 200 to 300 mg a day is a common conventional dosage of iron, I suggest starting at 20 to 30 mg, taken twice daily. Take your iron with vitamin C and take it four hours away from thyroid medication, calcium supplements, or food containing high amounts of calcium, for optimal absorption.

Vitamin D. Vitamin D deficiency is a risk factor for the development of Hashimoto's; it is also frequent in Hashimoto's thyroiditis. Treatment of Hashimoto's patients with vitamin D may slow down the course of development of hypothyroidism and may also decrease cardiovascular risks associated with hypothyroidism.

> Deficiencies: The US laboratory reference range for adequate vitamin D levels (blood marker: 25(OH)D) is 30 to 74 ng/mL; however, the Vitamin D Council suggests a higher range of 40 to 80 ng/mL, with a target of 50 ng/mL. I aim for a target between 40 and 60 ng/mL. If your 25(OH)D is less than 35 ng/mL, I recommend supplementation.
>
> Dosage: Depending on the level of deficiency, dosage is typically 1,000 to 5,000 IU per day. Taking vitamin D in an oil form and/or with vitamin K_2 enhances the absorption. Designs for Health and Seroyal make a great liquid vitamin D. Cod liver oil also contains vitamin D and can be a great way to get vitamin D in a more natural form. As always, look for a brand of fish oil that is third-party tested for quality.

HERBS/SUPPLEMENTS TO DIRECTLY IMPROVE THYROID FUNCTION

Ashwagandha (*Withania somnifera*). A 2018 randomized trial reported improvements in thyroid hormone levels among participants with subclinical hypothyroidism who supplemented daily with withania. I have witnessed this phenomenon countless times with my patients.

Dosage: 500 to 600 mg per day in tablet form, standardized to contain 2.5 percent withanolides, or 5 ml of a 1:1 or 1:2 liquid tincture, ideally standardized to contain 2.0 mg/mL of withanolides. Standard Process Ashwagandha 1:1 liquid is my go-to, 2.5 ml taken twice daily to start. (Note that the liquid form can have an incredibly strong taste.)

Remember that small amounts of iodine and/or L-tyrosine, only once antibodies are lowered, can be very helpful for thyroid function. See box on page 204 for more information.

HERBS/SUPPLEMENTS TO IMPROVE CONVERSION FROM T4 TO T3

If you are having difficulty converting T4 to T3, whether you are taking medication or not, using a few key supplements can help improve conversion relatively quickly and may significantly reduce some symptoms.

Remember that conversion of T4 to T3 is reduced when a person is under stress, undergoing fasting, and/or has exposure to a high amount of chemicals (e.g., fluorine and bromine) and heavy metals (e.g., mercury and cadmium). Make sure that you take steps to address diet and reduce your exposure to toxins.

Zinc. This trace element is necessary for the proper conversion of T4 to T3 hormones. Zinc deficiency is more common in individuals with hypothyroidism. Low zinc and hypothyroidism can result in a cycle when the thyroid isn't optimized, as thyroid hormones are also necessary for the proper absorption of zinc from the diet. Studies have shown that supplementing with zinc helps improve T3 levels in the body. As a bonus, many thyroid sufferers who experience hair loss notice improvements in hair growth once they begin to supplement with zinc. Zinc is also beneficial for the immune system and can help fight off colds and flu.

Dosage: 30 mg per day. If you do begin to supplement with zinc and you are also taking a multivitamin, make sure you check the dosage of zinc in the multivitamin. Higher levels of zinc long term (usually over 50 to 70 mg) can lead to copper deficiency.

Selenium. This micronutrient is also important for thyroid hormone production. In adults, the thyroid is the organ with the highest amount of selenium per gram of tissue. Selenium can also help improve thyroid conversion, and may also help lower thyroid antibodies (see "Herbs/Supplements to Reduce Antibodies," page 211).

> Dosage: Selenium methionine, 200 ucg per day. High amounts of selenium over time can result in selenium toxicity. Symptoms of toxicity include nausea, vomiting, abdominal pain, diarrhea, hair loss, brittle nails, peripheral neuropathy, and the smell of garlic in sweat and breath. Toxicity is typically seen when someone is taking a dosage of over 400 ucg for a long period of time along with a diet that is high in selenium.

Iron. Iron can help improve thyroid function and has been shown to improve T3 levels in the body. Low iron levels may reduce the ability of T4 to be converted to T3. Remember that a serum ferritin level under 100 ug/l could be contributing to thyroid symptoms. Again, if you have tested positive for SIBO, treat gut bacteria before starting to increase iron levels.

> Dosage: see page 207.

Guggul (*Commiphora mukul*). This traditional Ayurvedic medicinal herb is used to improve metabolism and may have benefits for weight loss. It also has thyroid-stimulating effects and may improve T3 levels. Guggul can also help lower cholesterol in the body and is a great option for individuals wishing to improve their blood lipid levels.

> Dosage: A standard dose of guggul (standardization should be 2.5 percent) of 400 to 500 mg taken 3 times a day with meals, totaling 1,200 to 1,500 mg a day. I recommend Pure Encapsulations guggul extract capsules, 1 capsule taken at each meal.

Bacopa (*Bacopa monnieri*). Bacopa, another Ayurvedic herb, has traditionally been used to improve memory, focus, and cognitive function. Bacopa has also been shown to improve T3 hormone levels in the body.

Dosage: A standardized extract of Bacopa (standardized to contain 20 percent bacosides) of 200 mg taken 3 times a day with meals. Pure Encapsulations carries this product and dosage.

Ashwagandha (*Withania somnifera*). Yet another herb historically used in Ayurvedic medicine, withania is traditionally used to treat stress, but is one of my go-to herbs for thyroid function. Withania can help improve both T3 and T4 levels in the body and seems to have a direct effect on the thyroid gland. I find withania to be of particular benefit in patients with anxiety and/or sleeping issues.

Dosage: 500 to 600 mg per day in tablet form, standardized to contain 2.5 percent withanolides, or 5 ml of a 1:1 or 1:2 liquid tincture, ideally standardized to contain 2.0 mg/mL of withanolides. Standard Process Ashwagandha 1:1 liquid is my go-to, 2.5 ml, taken twice daily to start.

HERBS/SUPPLEMENTS TO REDUCE ANTIBODIES

Selenium. Not only can selenium improve T3 levels in the body, but studies suggest that selenium supplementation of Hashimoto's patients results in reduction in TPO antibodies, improved thyroid ultrasound results, and improved quality of life.

Dosage: Selenium methionine, 200 ucg per day. Please remember not to overdose, as selenium toxicity can result when high amounts of selenium are taken long term. Toxicity is typically seen when someone is taking a dosage of over 400 ucg for a long period of time along with a diet that is high in selenium.

Myo-inositol. Selenium alone can help reduce antibodies, but a combination of selenium plus myo-inositol is even better. Inositol is a naturally occurring substance found in some foods and plants. In a recent study, patients diagnosed with Hashimoto's and with a TSH between 3 and 6 IU/ml were randomized into two groups: one received 600 mg of myo-inositol daily plus 83 mcg of selenium; the other group received just the

83 mcg of selenium per day. After six months, both groups had decreases in TSH, TPOAb, and TgAb levels and improvements in symptoms and T4 levels. Although the improvements were seen in the group taking selenium alone, they were greater in those who took myo-inositol with selenium. (It should be noted here that the selenium dosage is much less than I typically use to lower antibodies and it is unknown whether a higher dosage of selenium compared to the combination of myo-inositol would yield a different result.)

Dosage: 600 mg daily for 6 months

Black cumin seeds (*Nigella sativa*). Traditionally, this seed has been used for everything from headaches to asthma and intestinal worms. It is a revered natural remedy in many parts of the world and has been reported to have been discovered in the tomb of King Tut. In a recent study, patients with Hashimoto's took 2 g of powdered black cumin seed capsules or placebo immediately before lunch and dinner for eight weeks. Significant reductions in body weight, TSH, and TPO were seen in the group that took the black cumin seeds. This seed has also been found to be very beneficial for the immune system; I find when I take ½ teaspoon of this oil over the winter months, it keeps colds and flu at bay.

Dosage: Black cumin seeds can be taken in seed, ground, or oil form. Some people add the seeds to salads or sprinkle them on top of soups, stews, and curries.

Wobenzym. This is a specially formulated product containing the following clinically studied enzymes: pancreatin, papain, bromelain, trypsin, and chymotrypsin, all well known for their anti-inflammatory effect in the body. They help balance the inflammatory process and have been extremely helpful to many of my patients suffering from aches and pains, particularly those suffering from arthritis and polymyalgia rheumatica (PMR). Due to their anti-inflammatory effects, it is not surprising that some clinicians have used wobenzym with success to reduce inflammatory markers, including thyroid antibodies, in Hashimoto's patients. I have yet to have a patient require a reduction in thyroid medication due to the use of wobenzym alone; however, I have seen markers of inflammation decrease dramatically after the use of wobenzym. This product has also helped many of my patients reduce their dosage of pain medications.

Dosage: 3 tablets taken 2 or 3 times a day on an empty stomach (20 minutes before or 2 hours after meals). If wobenzym is taken with meals, it will not be as helpful to lower inflammation in the body.

Rosmarinic acid. Rosmarinic acid is a derivative found in the mint family of herbs and can be powerful in reducing inflammation in autoimmune disease. Rosmarinic acid has been found to help promote healthy gut bacteria as well as to be very beneficial for reducing allergy symptoms, such as hay fever and asthma.

Dosage: 500 mg per day is a suggested dosage; however, there is not ample research in regard to dosage. A tea made from rosemary leaves and/or using rosemary in cooking would also be helpful.

Fish oil. Omega-3 fatty acids found in fish oils are well known for their anti-inflammatory effects. A number of clinical trials have looked at the benefits of dietary supplementation with fish oils in many inflammatory and autoimmune diseases in humans, including psoriasis, multiple sclerosis, rheumatoid arthritis, Crohn's disease, ulcerative colitis, and lupus erythematosus. Many of the placebo-controlled trials of fish oil in chronic inflammatory diseases showed significant benefit, including decreased disease activity and a lowered use of anti-inflammatory medications. There has been limited research looking into how fish oils help lower antibodies in thyroid disease, aside from one study showing that women who consumed higher amounts of omega-3 fatty acids in pregnancy had lowered thyroid antibodies compared to those who consumed lower amounts of fish oils. Nonetheless, fish oil can be a tremendous help for those with inflammation and autoimmune diseases.

Dosage: 1,000 mg 1 to 3 times per day of high-quality, third-party-tested fish oils taken with meals. I often use Designs for Health Hi-Po fish oil. Nordic Naturals also makes a good product.

HERBS/SUPPLEMENTS FOR HEALING THE GUT

If you have SIBO and/or other infections, please refer to pages 96–98.

Digestive enzymes/HCl. The use of digestive enzymes in not a new phenomenon; they have been reported to help people with digestive symptoms, such as bloating, gas, and the feeling of being "too full," for the last seventy years. When addressing the gut and working on restoring both a healthy microbiome and a healthy lining, I suggest the use of digestive enzymes.

Remember from Chapter 9, people with Hashimoto's are more likely to have lower stomach acid and reduced digestive function. Additionally, food sensitivities are more common in people with Hashimoto's, due to the increased incidence of leaky gut. Digestive enzymes can help with all of these issues. Some people report tremendous results in symptoms with just the addition of digestive enzymes!

> Dosage: Digestive enzymes are typically dosed as 1 tablet with each meal. I suggest finding a brand that contains amylase, pepsin, lactase, protease, and betaine HCl. Ox bile, another potential ingredient in digestive enzyme formulations, may be of added benefit, especially if you suffer from gallbladder issues. Designs for Health Digestzymes or Pure Encapsulations digestive enzymes with betaine HCl are good options. If you experience a burning sensation behind your ribs or in the upper stomach upon using a digestive enzyme, you may want to try a brand that does not contain betaine HCl and/or use the digestive enzyme only when eating larger, richer meals.

Probiotics. Probiotics help increase the diversity of beneficial bacteria in the gut, decrease pathogens and toxins, and aid in restoring healthy gut function. They also help restore intestinal barrier function, reduce intestinal permeability, and improve immune functioning.

> Dosage: I suggest finding a probiotic that is dairy-free and contains most of the following strains:

Bifidobacterium animalis subsp. *Lactis* (UABla-12)

Lactobacillus plantarum (UALp-05)

Lactobacillus acidophilus (DDS-1)

Bifidobacterium breve (UABbr-11)

Lactrobacillus casei (UALc-03)

Lactobacillus paracasei (UALpc-04)

Lactobacillus rhamnosus (GG)

Lactobacillus salivarius (UALs-07)

Bifidobacterium bifidum (UABb-10)

Bifidobacterium longum subsp. *Longum* (UABI-14)

I have tried many different types and combinations of probiotics over the years and I have consistently had the best results with this combination. This combination is sold by Designs for Health as ProbioMed and comes in two strengths, either 50 or 100 billion cfu.

Zinc. Not only does zinc support thyroid hormone conversion, it also improves intestinal barrier function and can be a key nutrient for healing intestinal permeability.

Dosage: Zinc picolinate, 30 mg per day. (I have seen multiple brands and forms of zinc to be effective in clinical practice; however, zinc picolinate is thought to be the most absorbable form and is sold by Pure Encapsulations.)

L-glutamine. The amino acid L-glutamine has been shown to be effective in healing intestinal permeability. Research has shown that this specific amino acid can help improve the growth of intestinal cells and support the health of the intestinal lining during times of stress.

Dosage: Designs for Health L-glutamine powder (or comparable brand), 5 g of powder mixed into water and taken 1 to 3 times per day on an empty stomach (20 minutes before or 2 hours after meals).

Licorice *(Glycyrrhiza glabra)*. Licorice extract has been used historically for its ability to help heal gastric ulcers and gastritis and improve digestive symptoms. Licorice extract is also a great therapy to reduce inflammation in the body. Licorice can be found in its pure extracted form, or in another form called DGL (deglycyrrhizinated licorice). I recommend DGL if you have high blood pressure or if you are currently taking blood pressure medication, as licorice extract can increase blood pressure. Otherwise, licorice extract in its pure form can have added benefits, such as helping to improve the stress response and increasing energy.

> Dosage: I opt for a high-quality, strong liquid licorice extract, a 1:1 product that has a minimum of 30 mg/mL of glycyrrhizin. This product is Standard Process licorice high grade 1:1, and I suggest 2.5 ml taken once daily, or another high-quality licorice extract tincture. If you have high blood pressure, or do not like the idea of liquid, many companies sell DGL. The recommended dosage is 500 to 1,000 mg of DGL with meals. Designs for Health DGL Synergy, 1 capsule before each meal, is a good option.

Cabbage juice. This is an old-school remedy for helping to heal ulcers and improve stomach function. Studies have shown that cabbage juice can rapidly heal ulcers. I have found cabbage juice to be very helpful for patients who are suffering from gastric symptoms and are up for juicing cabbage at home. And yes, cabbage is in the Brassicaceae family of vegetables and many people are concerned about such veggies reducing thyroid function. Research has shown that this really isn't a problem unless at high doses; please see page 138 for more information.

> Dosage: ⅓ cup of fresh juice taken for 7 to 10 days on an empty stomach upon waking.

Herbs and supplements for gut infections. Please see pages 214–216.

Herbs and supplements for other infections. Please see pages 103–109 for herbs for Epstein-Barr virus (EBV), cytomegalovirus (CMV), and other infections.

HERBS/SUPPLEMENTS FOR MANAGING STRESS

Many different herbs have been either proven to be effective, or historically used, to manage stress. The following are just the ones that I more commonly use in practice and have found to be effective with my patients. These herbs are referred to as adaptogens, as they help the body adapt to stress. Countless formulas on the market contain a mix of "adaptogenic" herbs. Although I do love one formula in particular (Restorative Formulations Adaptogen), many formulas may contain certain herbs that may not agree with the individual and I often find using single herbs at a time to be helpful, especially if you are using other herbs and supplements to address other areas of thyroid healing or well-being.

Ashwagandha (*Withania somnifera*). As previously mentioned, ashwagandha is an herb that can help improve thyroid hormone conversion and thyroid function. This herb is also used for its ability to help improve the stress response in the body. Other benefits of ashwagandha include improving libido.

> Dosage: 500 to 600 mg per day in tablet form, standardized to contain 2.5 percent withanolides, or 5 ml of a 1:1 or 1:2 liquid tincture, ideally standardized to contain 2.0 mg/mL of withanolides. Standard Process Ashwagandha 1:1 liquid is my go-to, 2.5 ml taken twice daily to start.

Siberian ginseng (*Eleutherococcus senticosus*). It is thought that Siberian ginseng has been used for over two thousand years in China. In Traditional Chinese Medicine (TCM), eleuthero root is used to invigorate qi (chi, or energy) and restore vital energy and is used as a warming herb. Siberian ginseng has been found to reduce effects of stress, as well as improve physical strength in athletes. It can also boost immune function. I find this herb to be particularly beneficial for those who are struggling with fatigue.

> Dosage: 250 mg (standardized to at least 0.8 eleutheroside content), taken 1 to 3 times per day. Pure Encapsulations Eleuthero 0.8

percent E & B is a good option, taken once daily. Restorative Formulations Adaptogen is also a good product for stress reduction that contains Siberian ginseng.

Passionflower (*Passiflora incarnata*). This herb has been historically used throughout the world for its many different benefits. Native Americans have used passionflower to treat boils, wounds, earaches, and liver problems. In Europe, passionflower has traditionally been used to reduce restlessness and agitation. I have found passionflower to be extremely helpful for patients (Hashimoto's and otherwise) who have anxiety as a result of stress. Passionflower can also help improve sleep. Many formulas that contain passionflower are marketed as sleep formulas, but don't let this fool you. I have had countless patients use passionflower with great benefits aside from improved sleep. Additionally, many formulas that contain passionflower may also be combined with valerian and other herbs commonly associated with reducing anxiety and acting as a mild sedative.

Dosage: Often found in capsule form, standardized to contain 3.5 percent vitexin and dosed 100 mg, 2 to 4 times per day. Frequently, passionflower can be found in tincture form alone; however, often it is available in tablet form in a combination formula. Pure Encapsulations muscle cramp/tension formula or Restorative Formulations sleep formula are good combination products to help alleviate stress and promote a more restful sleep.

Rhodiola (*Rhodiola rosea*). With a long history of use in both Asian and Eastern European traditional medicine, rhodiola can help support mental and physical performance, improve concentration, and also decrease cortisol (the stress hormone) levels in the body. It also may be beneficial for fatigue and fertility. If I know a patient has higher cortisol levels, and/or reports reduced endurance during workouts and physical exercise, this herb is at the top of my list.

Dosage 200 mg (standardized to contain 3 percent total rosavins and 1 percent salidroside) taken 1 or 2 times per day. I recommend Pure Encapsulations rhodiola, 2 tablets twice daily.

Schisandra (*Schisandra chinensis*). This is another herb that has been used in TCM. It is commonly called "five-flavor fruit" as Schisandra is thought in TCM to be extremely balancing because of its five tastes: sweet, salty, bitter, pungent, and sour. Traditionally, it has also been used in TCM to treat autoimmune conditions by improving yin deficiency. Schisandra can be helpful to boost energy levels and may also reduce some symptoms of menopause, including hot flashes. Schisandra may also benefit the liver and appears to be helpful for damaged tissue in the liver. It is no surprise that traditional Chinese use for this herb included "liver qi stagnation," and it was said to improve the flow of "life force" through the liver.

> Dosage: Liquid: 5 ml of a 1:2 extract tincture taken daily. Standard Process carries this product in this formulation. Wise Woman Herbals also makes a good product, but in a weaker strength of 1:3.4, and therefore the dosage would be 20 to 30 drops taken twice daily. In capsule form, the dose is typically 500 mg twice daily. Vital Nutrients Schisandra is a good option.

Licorice (*Glycyrrhiza glabra*). Licorice extract has been used historically for its ability to help endurance and stress response. Licorice extract is also a great therapy to reduce inflammation in the body. Be aware that licorice extract can increase blood pressure. Otherwise, licorice extract in its pure form can have added benefits, especially for the gastric tract.

> Dosage: I use a strong liquid licorice extract, a 1:1 product that has a minimum of 30 mg/mL of glycyrrhizin. This product is Standard Process licorice high-grade 1:1, and I suggest taking 2.5 ml once daily, or another high-quality licorice extract tincture. If you have high blood pressure, or do not like the idea of liquid, many companies sell DGL. The recommended dosage is 500 to 1,000 mg of DGL with meals. Designs for Health DGL Synergy, 1 capsule before each meal, is a good option.

American ginseng (*Panax quinquefolius*). This herb is different from Siberian ginseng. It can be very helpful to boost energy levels and is often found in many formulas targeted at managing stress, also known as adaptogenic formulas. However, over the years many of my patients, especially those prone to anxiety, have experienced increased anxiousness and a "racing mind" with this herb, so if you are prone to anxiety, proceed with caution if using American ginseng.

> Dosage: Most high-quality brands standardize to at least 10 percent ginsenosides, and 200 to 400 mg is taken per day, if you tolerate this herb.

Magnesium. This important mineral is involved in the energy production for your body. It also helps relax the nervous system, encourage a deeper sleep, may improve bone density, can help lower blood pressure, and also may aid in promoting a healthy mood. Many different types of magnesium are currently available in the marketplace. I generally recommend magnesium bisglycinate due to the fact that it is the most bioavailable form of magnesium and also less likely to cause diarrhea compared to other forms. Magnesium citrate is a cheaper form of magnesium and can be good to help promote relaxation; however, it is much more likely to cause diarrhea or loose bowel.

> Dosage: 200 to 400 mg daily of magnesium bisglycinate

OTHER HERBS THAT COULD HELP THE THYROID

Certain herbs such as blue flag root (*Iris versicolor*), coleus (*Coleus forskohlii*), and gotu kola (*Centella asiatica*) have been traditionally used to treat the thyroid gland. Blue flag root has reportedly been used to treat goiters and thyroid enlargements. However, studies are lacking for these herbs. Nonetheless, these herbs could offer potential benefit and may be more commonly used in the future.

HERBS/SUPPLEMENTS FOR CHRONIC FATIGUE

CoQ 10. Some individuals who are very fatigued, especially if they have been struggling with symptoms of Hashimoto's for a long period of time and/or have had chronic infections long term, may benefit from CoQ 10 supplementation to support mitochondrial function (the energy factories of our cells). CoQ 10 is an important antioxidant that has shown to be lower in people with chronic fatigue syndrome. CoQ 10 also helps reduce inflammation in the body.

> Dosage: CoQ 10: ubiquinol, 100 to 200 mg taken 1 or 2 times a day. I recommend Designs for Health CoQnol.

MEDICINAL MUSHROOMS

A discussion on natural remedies to heal the thyroid would not be complete without the mention of medicinal mushrooms. Medicinal mushrooms have been used for hundreds of years in such places as Japan and China to treat almost every type of aliment you can think of. Recently, due to the ample scientific studies supporting their use, medicinal mushrooms are now becoming popular in the West. When we talk about medicinal mushrooms, we aren't speaking about the typical grocery store variety. Although these common mushrooms, such as portobello, button, and cremini, are tasty and provide antioxidants, they have not been historically used as medicines. Common medicinal mushrooms include Cordyceps, Reishi, and Maitake (just to name a few) and were primarily used in teas and tonics. Hot water extracts are the main type of mushroom supplements studied in the scientific research and the method of preparation used in traditional herbal practice. Mushroom extracts preserved in tinctures of alcohol or prepared in mycelium powders have not been extensively studied and therefore I generally recommend using only "hot water–extracted" mushroom formulations.

Multiple therapeutic benefits of mushrooms have been reported, such as anticancer activity, suppression of autoimmune diseases, and reduction of allergies. Mushrooms can also be very helpful in treating chronic infections, such as Epstein-Barr virus (EBV) and cytomegalovirus (CMV).

Although there are many different types of mushrooms, I use Cordyceps (*Cordyceps sinensis*) and Reishi (*Ganoderma lucidum*) most often in practice. Cordyceps, also known as caterpillar fungus due to its caterpillar-like appearance, has traditionally been used in Chinese and Tibetan medicine. This mushroom is highly regarded for its ability to enhance performance, boosting energy, endurance, and stamina. It has been shown in Chinese studies to reduce thyroid antibodies. Due to its increase in popularity, wild harvested Cordyceps has become incredibly expensive and has been sold for as high as US$11,300 per pound. Therefore, other comparable extracts, known as Cs-4 and *Cordyceps militaris*, are commonly sold in supplement form.

Reishi mushroom has a long history of use in many Asian countries for promoting health and longevity. Historically, it has been used to improve the functioning of the immune system and has been shown to have anticancer properties. A recent study found that after testing nineteen different Reishi mushroom supplements, only 5 percent passed their test for quality. Just as with other supplements, it is important to choose a Reishi supplement that has been tested for its content and purity.

Both Cordyceps and Reishi have shown benefit in balancing the immune system and therefore can be very helpful in such autoimmune diseases as Hashimoto's.

Dosage: Cordyceps: The Cs-4 strain of Cordyceps mycelium provides all the active compounds found in the wild harvested Cordyceps mushrooms. The Cs-4 strain is also the extract that has been extensively studied in research. Therefore, I generally recommend using the Cs-4 strain at a dose of 400 mg, 3 or 4 times per day.

More recently, the *Cordyceps militaris* strain of Cordyceps has become available; this strain provides high amounts of the beneficial properties of Cordyceps and therefore could also be an option. However, please keep in mind that the majority of studies with Cordyceps have been conducted using the Cs-4 strain.

Regardless of whether you choose a Cs-4 strain or *Cordyceps militaris*, ensure the product is hot water extracted and contains a minimum of 20 percent beta-glucans (also known as polysaccharides).

I typically use JHS Cordyceps (Cs-4), 2 to 4 tablets twice daily.

Dosage: Reishi: As mentioned earlier, ensure you choose a quality Reishi supplement. This can be done by checking that the product contains at least 12 percent polysaccharides and 4 percent triterpenes. The common dosage is 400 mg, 3 to 4 times a day. I typically use JHS Reishi Gano 161, 2 to 4 tablets twice daily.

Again, be sure to check with your health-care provider when taking any new supplements. Some herbs have contraindications or cautions that you might not be aware of and/or may cause an allergic reaction.

CHAPTER 12

Ancient and Emerging Therapies

M any of the following therapies have deep roots in traditional forms of healing. Some of these therapies may have little to no clinical research to support their use; however, many of them have been used with success in different cultures around the world. As it is with most natural remedies, the type of therapy is based on the individual's needs and preferences. What works for one person may not work for another. Although some of the therapies listed here may seem new, many are rooted in ancient tradition. Several of these therapies listed are also not typically recommended as a stand-alone treatment, but may be a great complementary therapy.

In this chapter, you will find more detailed information on cannabis and CBD, acupuncture, qigong, tai chi, yoga, breathwork, mindfulness meditation, Reiki, chakra balancing, contrast hydrotherapy, osteopathy, essential oils, aromatherapy, homeopathy, and bee venom therapy. A newer technology, based on measuring tendon reflexes (one of the original ways thyroid disease was diagnosed and monitored) will also be discussed.

CANNABIS AND CBD

Although cannabis currently has a lot of media attention, it has been used as a recreational drug for over five thousand years. Over the last few years, it has become apparent to me that patients are using medical marijuana (or cannabis) for a variety of health reasons. As this use was prior to legalization, many patients would feel shy about admitting their usage of marijuana. Some asked me whether I judged them for their choice to experiment with CBD or THC. Countless patients also requested I not share their use of marijuana with their children, parents, spouse, or other health-care practitioners. But these patients were using marijuana because they truly felt it offered tremendous benefit in either reduction of inflammation, pain, or anxiety.

In Canada, cannabis became legalized in 2018. In the US, eleven states have legal recreational and medical cannabis and multiple other states allow for medicinal cannabis use (as of May 2020). In the UK, medical cannabis is legal when prescribed by a doctor, but otherwise cannabis is currently illegal.

Before delving any further into the benefits of CBD, I would like to clarify a few terms as it appears that there is still a lot of confusion with regard to cannabis and its usage.

- **Cannabis,** also known as marijuana, pot, or weed, is a drug originating from the cannabis plant.
- **Medical cannabis,** or medical marijuana, refers to the use of cannabis and/or its cannabinoids (typically THC and CBD) to treat a disease or address symptoms.
- **Cannabinoids** are natural compounds found in cannabis (phytocannabinoids) and also the human body (endocannabinoids).
- **THC** is a phytocannabinoid that has known health benefits and strong psychoactive effects and intoxicating effects in large amounts. In other words, this molecule is the reason someone becomes high from cannabis consumption.
- **CBD** is a phytocannabinoid that has known health benefits without the intoxicating effects of THC (however, even small amounts of THC may enhance CBD's benefits).

Cannabis. For both recreational and medical usage, cannabis can be consumed in a number of ways including smoking, vaping, cannabis tea, edibles, capsules, and oil. Although originally cultivated in South America and the Kush regions of Asia, it is now grown all over the world. Documented references of the health benefits of cannabis date back to over four thousand years and have also been published in some of the top scientific journals in the world, including *Nature*, *Science*, the *Lancet*, and *Journal of the American Medical Association.* Recent investigation has found over one hundred natural compounds in cannabis that are known as phytocannabinoids. Cannabidiol (CBD) and tetrahydrocannabinol (THC) are the two well-known cannabinoids. Although both have documented health benefits, CBD is *not* intoxicating like THC and therefore does not make someone feel high.

Researchers have now found that human beings (all mammals, to be exact, and many other animals) have a built-in system that can receive, process, and use the phytocannabinoid compounds found in cannabis, such as CBD and THC. This special system within our body is called the endocannabinoid system, also known as the endogenous cannabinoid system (ECS), and is an extensive network of neurons, receptors, enzymes, and pathways that work to maintain a state of homeostasis, or balance, in our body. The ECS is involved in regulating a variety of processes, including fertility, embryo development, pregnancy, fetal development, appetite, pain sensation, mood, and memory, as well as processing the pharmacological effects of cannabis. Amazingly, this system not only produces its own cannabinoid-like compounds known as *endo*cannabinoids, but it also interacts and processes the *phyto*cannabinoids (THC and CBD) found in cannabis.

Humans have endocannabinoid receptors (sites where both endocannabinoids and phytocannabinoids can be received and processed) all throughout the body, including the brain, eyes, heart, digestive tract, liver, bone, adrenal glands, and even the thyroid gland. Even immune cells have been found to express both CB1 and CB2 receptors (where cannabinoids can be received), secrete endocannabinoids, and have functional cannabinoid transport and breakdown mechanisms.

Of the 111 phytocannabinoids currently identified, THC and CBD have been the most extensively studied for their health benefits. Some of the beneficial pharmacological effects of these cannabinoids are the following:

THC: Anticancer, anti-inflammatory, antioxidant, analgesic (reduces pain), anxiolytic (reduces anxiety), anxiogenic (increases anxiety), antiepileptic (reduces seizures), antiemetic (reduces nausea and vomiting), neuroprotective, sleep promoting

CBD: Anticancer, antiemetic (reduces nausea and vomiting), anti-inflammatory, antibacterial, antidiabetic, antipsoriatic (helps with psoriasis), antidiarrheal, analgesic (reduces pain), bone stimulant, immunosuppressive, antispasmotic, neuroprotective, antiepileptic, antipsychotic, anxiolytic (reduces anxiety), transforms white fat into brown fat (may be helpful for weight loss)

Although THC and CBD have been found to be beneficial on their own, in an isolated form, it appears that some conditions respond better to the synergistic and combined use of CBD and THC.

Multiple studies have suggested that cannabidiol may benefit a number of human diseases and disorders, including rheumatoid arthritis, diabetes types 1 and 2, atherosclerosis, Alzheimer's disease, hypertension, metabolic syndrome, ischemia-reperfusion injury, depression, and neuropathic pain. It is believed that cannabidiol may help these conditions and diseases because of its positive effect on the immune system and its ability to reduce inflammation. In fact, a 2019 study concluded that the data overwhelmingly demonstrate that CBD is immune suppressive and anti-inflammatory. The authors, however, determined that more research is needed.

This knowledge is fascinating, as we know that most thyroid disease sufferers have an immune system that is out of balance. The question has to be raised, can such cannabinoids as THC or CBD help balance the immune system in people with Hashimoto's (or Graves') and thus help heal thyroid disease? A 2017 analysis of data from 2007 to 2012 found that recent marijuana use had no impact on thyroid antibody levels, but appeared to be associated with a lower TSH (less than 5.6 mIU/L). Nonetheless, lack of clinical data in this emerging field prevents a definitive conclusion. Cannabis could be a potential therapy in the future, but it is not without side effects.

First and foremost, I believe cannabis addiction is one of the main adverse effects of chronic cannabis use. Although once believed that cannabis was not addictive, recent research shows that cannabis users can develop a physiological addiction or dependency to cannabis. In the US, 30 percent of adults who use marijuana will develop marijuana use disorder, a diagnosis that includes addiction and other related problems. People who begin using marijuana before the age of eighteen are four to seven times more likely to develop a marijuana use disorder compared to adults. Part of the risk for dependency could be due to the fact that marijuana potency, as detected in confiscated samples, has steadily increased over the past few years. In the early 1990s, the average THC content in confiscated marijuana samples was roughly 3.8 percent. However, in 2014, this number jumped to 12.2 percent. The National Institute on Drug Abuse (NIDA) reports that the average marijuana extract now contains more than 50 percent THC, with some samples exceeding 80 percent. I have seen addiction to cannabis in clinical practice many times, especially in younger users, and like any form of addiction, it can be difficult to treat and overcome. Addiction with CBD use may or may not be an issue; however, most CBD does contain THC and in theory could also cause a dependency.

Additionally, cannabis consumption can result in brain changes, such as reduction of gray matter. Other adverse effects include anxiety, hallucinations, racing heart, and stimulation of appetite (for those not wishing to increase appetite). Due to these potential side effects, especially the risk of addictions, I suggest using other natural remedies before trying cannabis, especially due to the lack of evidence in terms of cannabis pertaining to Hashimoto's and hypothyroidism. Just like every other system in your body, the ECS is affected by dietary and lifestyle interventions. A diet rich in greens, onions, mushrooms, beans, berries, and seeds is known to benefit the ECS. Lifestyle practices that benefit the ECS are acupuncture, meditation, and deep breathing. Moderate to high-intensity exercises also increase endocannabinoid levels in the body.

ACUPUNCTURE

In this Traditional Chinese Medicine (TCM) practice, specific points on the body are stimulated by inserting small needles into the skin. Acupuncture is one of the oldest forms of medicine; in fact, it was first mentioned in documents dating from a few hundred years leading up to the Common Era. Some people feel uncomfortable at the thought of acupuncture, but the needles are very thin and most patients report that they hardly feel anything at all when the needles are inserted.

According to TCM, acupuncture balances the complementary extremes of yin and yang of the "life force" known as qi (pronounced "chi"). Qi is believed to flow through pathways, known as meridians, in the body. Inserting needles into specific points along the meridians is thought to bring the flow of energy back into balance in the body. You may be wondering, how exactly does inserting needles into the body and improving the flow of qi improve health? Although researchers are just starting to understand how acupuncture works (from a Western perspective), it appears that inserting acupuncture needles may result in changes in natural opioid substances and changes in cell signaling; it can affect the nervous immune network, and may also benefit the immune system. The nervous immune network, also known as neuro-endocrine-immune (NEI) network (involving the nervous, endocrine, and immune systems), is the basis to sustain the body's homeostasis (the ability for the body to maintain a stable internal balance). This network, a recently discovered interconnection, may be a key reason as to how acupuncture provides benefit. What this essentially means is that trauma to the nervous system can result in immune or hormonal changes, and vice versa. To put this in perspective, a 2017 study highlights that injuries to the brain or spinal cord, such as those caused by stroke or brain trauma, result in a considerable weakening of the immune system. This often leads to severe infections, such as pneumonia or urinary tract infections, which reduce nervous tissue regeneration as well as rehabilitation in affected patients. We also know that emotional trauma and stressors, causing a nervous system activation, can also weaken the immune system, resulting in more frequent viral and bacterial infections. Studies have now found that acupuncture can help balance this NEI network and therefore be beneficial for the nervous, hormonal, and immune systems. As we have reviewed in earlier chapters, stress can negatively affect the thyroid gland. Acupuncture therefore may be very helpful for some individuals in helping not only alleviate stress but balance the connection between the nervous system and the thyroid hormones.

According to TCM, improper diet, poor constitution, and overexertion lead to hypothyroidism; whereas self-care and rest are vital for improving hypothyroidism. Acupuncture can help promote relaxation and healing. Current studies are only just beginning to understand the benefits and clinical potential of this ancient practice. Results from numerous studies show that acupuncture can help ease many different types of pain, including back pain, headaches, and pain from osteoarthritis. There are specific points on the body that may help stimulate thyroid gland functioning, which I have used as a complementary therapy in patients with hypothyroidism. I have found acupuncture excellent in helping patients manage stress and relax. I have personally seen many patients who struggle with anxiety and depression benefit from acupuncture. Some studies have indicated that patients with hypothyroidism had improvements in symptoms and lab values where acupuncture was used alone or in combination therapy.

Acupressure

FOR individuals who cannot fathom the thought of tiny needles being inserted in the body, acupressure may be an option. Acupressure practitioners typically use their fingers and palms but may also use elbows, feet, or special devices to apply pressure to acupoints on the body's meridians. During an acupressure session, patients typically lie, wearing clothes, on a massage table. The practitioner presses on acupressure points on their body instead of inserting needles into these points.

There are a few acupuncture protocols listed in research papers that may be helpful for those with Hashimoto's or hypothyroidism. If you are interested in using acupuncture to help treat symptoms, you may want to discuss the following protocols with your acupuncturist, Chinese Medicine practitioner or naturopathic doctor:

- I have used CV 22, a point that matches the location of the throat chakra, as a key point for thyroid gland simulation. This point is traditionally used for all things related to the throat, including trouble swallowing, sore throat, and thyroid problems.

- In the review article "Traditional Chinese Medicine Approach to Hypothyroidism," Damir Malikov suggests the following nine acupuncture points for the treatment of hypothyroidism: Du4, Ren4, Ren6, St36, Sp6, UB17, UB23, Li4, and P6.
- Another study reports that a balance of both immunostimulating and immunosuppressing points should be used to balance the immune system in the case of autoimmune disease: Immunostimulant points include LI-4, LI-11, ST-36, GB-39, SP-6, GV-14, BL-11, BL-20, BL-23, BL-24, BL-25, BL-26, BL-27, BL-28, and CV-12. Needling of BL-47 is suggested to be immunosuppressive.

Note that acupuncture points for hypothyroidism will be personalized; based on each individual's symptoms and general characteristics (e.g., Are they hot or cold? Do they have dry skin? Do they suffer with anxiety? Do they have particular cravings or difficulty sleeping at night?), other points would be added in addition or in favor of the points noted here.

Energy Healing Acupuncture: Tong Ren Therapy

Tong Ren Therapy, a form of acupuncture that can be described as "acupuncture at a distance," combines qigong, acupuncture, and the focused intention of the patient and practitioner. Typically, the Tong Ren practitioner uses a lightweight, magnetic hammer to tap specific points on a small anatomical model of the human body, which serves as an energetic representation of the patient. The practitioner and patient direct qi to blockage points corresponding to the patient's condition and focus on healing. There is very little research on this therapy; however, a 2009 study survey reported that anxiety, depression, cancer, and autoimmune disorders appeared to have the greatest treatment responses to Tong Ren Therapy, with 63.8, 61.0, 60.3, and 58.1 percent of participants with these respective conditions reporting substantial improvements. This study concluded that self-reported effects of Tong Ren Therapy were high, with no adverse effects reported, and that more research is warranted. I have never tried this therapy myself, nor have my patients; however, I believe it is still worth noting. I must admit, the tapping of points on the acupuncture dolls does look a little strange at first, but this therapy may be a very good option for people wishing to explore energy medicine. It also does not require needles to be inserted in the body and therefore may be helpful for those wishing to experience acupuncture but nervous about needles (acupressure is also an option).

There are specific acupuncture points that Tong Ren has outlined as beneficial for Hashimoto's. These points may be used for a Tong Ren healing session or may be used for a typical acupuncture or acupressure session.

> Main Points: T1 huatuo, T2 huatuo, T3 huatuo, C6 huatuo, C7 huatuo, SI 16, KD 26. Secondary Points: T7 huatuo, KD 3, ST 9, ST 10, GV 22

If you are interested in Tong Ren Therapy, look for a certified provider close to you.

QIGONG AND TAI CHI

Qigong and tai chi have been proposed, along with yoga and breathwork (pranayama), to constitute a unique category or type of exercise referred to as "meditative movement." Qigong, an ancient Chinese tradition that focuses on cultivating and harmonizing qi in the body, is a series of movements performed in a slow and focused manner, without pausing, so the body is in constant motion. Likewise, tai chi involves coordinating slow-flowing postures and stretching, deep rhythmic breathing, and a calm, meditative state of mind. Tai chi was originally developed as a form of martial arts and is believed to make one fit and strong with good posture and a focused mind. Both qigong and tai chi have been found to improve bone health and heart health, improve quality of life, reduce anxiety and depression, and benefit immunity. Although there have been no studies of these practices as specifically pertaining to hypothyroidism and Hashimoto's, both qigong and tai chi have shown a benefit in improving the immune response and lowering markers of inflammation in the body. Other studies have shown that qigong can increase energy levels in those suffering from chronic fatigue. Both qigong and tai chi are considered low-impact exercises and require no equipment. You can view videos on-line to practice at home, or most towns and cities offer classes. The book *How to Heal Hashimoto's*, by Marc Ryan, offers some good qigong exercises that are specifically targeted to the thyroid gland.

YOGA AND BREATHWORK (PRANAYAMA)

Yoga, a discipline that originated in India, is a combination of physical, mental, and spiritual practices. It is thought that the origins of yoga in India date as far back as the sixth and fifth centuries BCE. Today, there are many different types of yoga schools throughout the world. The reported benefits of regularly practicing yoga are far reaching and include a reduction in anxiety and depression, balancing hormones, improvements in immune functioning, and a reduction of stress levels. Many studies report that individuals who regularly practice yoga report an elevated state of well-being. Case reports and small studies have suggested that yoga can improve thyroid functioning; however, as it is clear that stress impacts the thyroid gland, choosing any healthy therapy that can reduce the impact of stress could inevitably be beneficial for the thyroid and immune system. A review article found the following combination of poses to be beneficial to thyroid function:

1. Sarvangasana (Shoulder stand)
2. Matsyasana (Fish pose)
3. Marjarasana (Cat pose)
4. Halasana (Plow pose)
5. Bhujangasana (Cobra pose)

Certain forms of pranayama (controlled breathing) are also suggested to accompany these poses and bring benefit to the thyroid gland. These practices include Bhramari (Hummingbird) pranayama and Ujjayi (Ocean Breath) pranayama. The controlled breathing enables both the rhythm of performing yoga poses and relaxing the mind for meditation.

If you are not familiar with these practices, find a yoga instructor close to you who can help guide you through the poses and breathwork.

Generally speaking, the poses that are often reported to benefit the thyroid gland are considered throat-stimulating. These poses are thought to improve circulation and energy flow around the thyroid as well as strengthening and stretching the neck.

Similar to tai chi and qigong, yoga can be practiced alone at home or in a group setting. Most cities and towns, big and small, now offer some form of yoga classes, even if it is in a church basement. If you are interested in the thyroid-healing poses listed here, speak to a yoga teacher to help guide you through the postures.

MINDFULNESS MEDITATION

A discussion on mind body interventions would not be complete without addressing mindfulness meditation. Mindfulness meditation is the act of simply being present in the moment and observing, but not judging, our thoughts and feelings. Mindfulness has been used for centuries as a part of Buddhist and other spiritual practices. However, it has only been since the late 1970s that the application of mindfulness in Western medical and mental health has taken place. During this time, mindfulness-based stress reduction (MBSR) programs were developed by Jon Kabat-Zinn and became the first standardized mindfulness-based intervention (MBI).

A 2016 review study, looking at data from 1,600 participants, found that practicing mindfulness meditation may be beneficial for the immune system and was shown to reduce blood levels of CRP, a marker of systemic inflammation. Many other research studies over the years have shown that mindfulness meditation can be a powerful tool to help reduce stress, decrease anxiety, and boost mood. Additionally, another study found that mindfulness meditation, as well as other mind-body interventions, such as qigong and tai chi, can positively influence our genes and may reduce the risk of inflammatory diseases (e.g., Hashimoto's).

Jon Kabat-Zinn, PhD, is the founding executive director of the Center for Mindfulness in Medicine, Health Care, and Society at the University of Massachusetts Medical School. He has written numerous books on mindfulness meditation that have helped many of my patients over the years learn and understand the techniques of MBSR. *The Miracle of Mindfulness: An Introduction to the Practice of Meditation*, by Thich Nhat Hanh, is also a wonderful introduction to mindfulness.

As discussed on page 59, there are many different apps (including three designed by Jon Kabat-Zinn) that can be purchased on your smartphone or tablet to help guide you through meditations. Thousands of resources are available online, and most cities offer classes and workshops on meditation.

REIKI

Reiki, another form of energy medicine, was developed by Mikao Usui in Japan in the 1920s. It is a form of healing therapy that is applied through noninvasive, nonmanipulative gentle touch. Reiki involves gently laying of hands just above or on the clothed body, moving over the front and back in a slow progression of hand positions. The word *Reiki* stems from the Japanese words *rei*, which means "universal life," and *ki*, which means "energy." Reiki is not affiliated with any particular religion or religious practice; its practitioners believe that everyone has the ability to connect with their own healing energy and that connecting with energy can help heal disease. Similar to Chinese theory, it is believed that optimal health exists when the ki, or energy life force, is strong and flowing. Reiki is reported to be a safe, gentle, and profoundly relaxing healing modality that can be practiced by anyone who has received an "attunement" from a Reiki master. A recent review study reports that Reiki is better than placebo in activating the parasympathetic nervous system (the part of the nervous system that is responsible for resting, relaxing, and digesting). It has also been found to be more effective than placebo for reducing anxiety, depression, and pain in patients with chronic health conditions. In fact, because of the reported benefits of Reiki, multiple US hospitals, including many UCLA hospitals, now offer Reiki.

To experience Reiki, you will need to find a Reiki master, which may or may not be an option in your area. However, as Reiki is a form of energy medicine, it is believed that it can be practiced at a distance, such as over the phone or via video conferencing.

CHAKRA BALANCING

Some practitioners of Reiki practice the art of "chakra balancing." *Chakra* is a Sanskrit word that means "wheel of life"; chakras are energy points along the body. There are seven main chakras. The position of each of the major chakras corresponds with an endocrine gland and thus is believed to control hormonal balance. These chakras are located at the base of the spine (root chakra), between the genitals and naval (sacral chakra), a couple of inches above the naval (solar plexus chakra), the center of the chest (heart chakra), middle of the neck (throat chakra), just above the brow area (third-eye chakra), and the top of the head (crown chakra). In a healthy individual, the seven chakras provide the right balance of energy to every part of your body, mind, and spirit. I have not been able to find any specific studies or research pertaining to chakras per se; however, as mentioned, many practitioners of Reiki use these chakras as a guide for Reiki treatment.

For thyroid health, the throat chakra may be an area of energetic focus for healing. The fifth chakra, also known as the throat chakra, is believed to govern the anatomical regions of the thyroid, parathyroid, jaw, neck, mouth, tongue, and larynx. To be balanced in the fifth chakra is to speak, listen, and express yourself freely. The throat chakra helps us speak our truth. A blocked or unbalanced throat chakra is thought to cause insecurities and anxieties about speaking our truth or being judged for doing so, and inhibits the ability to express our dreams and desires. A blocked or unbalanced throat chakra is believed to lead to physical ailments, including dental problems, laryngitis, thyroid disease, TMJ and neck pain, and compulsive eating.

A Reiki master can help balance the throat chakra, but it can also be done by focusing on incorporating the elements of chakra balancing in meditation, yoga poses, chanting, humming, or singing.

CONTRAST HYDROTHERAPY

The use of water as a healing treatment (hydrotherapy) is one of the oldest therapies known to humankind. The specific use of both hot (or warm) and cold water is called contrast hydrotherapy. Ancient Greek physicians, such as Galen and Hippocrates, used hydrotherapy as an integral part of

Care for Self and Care for Others

MANY of these ancient therapies focus on bringing balance to self, which brings balance to our relationships with others. Speaking and listening with compassion are important aspects to bring balance to the throat chakra.

According to board certified neurologist and expert in mind-body medicine David Simon, MD, there are three gateways you should cross before speaking.

1. First, ask yourself, "Is what I am about to say true?"
2. If so, proceed to the second gateway and ask, "Is what I am about to say necessary?"
3. If the answer is yes, go to the third gateway and ask yourself, "Is what I am about to say kind?"

Speaking your highest truth doesn't mean you're allowed to be hurtful or critical. The truth from your spiritual essence will come across as kind and compassionate.

treatment. It is a treatment modality that has been used widely in ancient cultures, including India, Egypt, and China. In the early nineteenth century, Sebastian Kneipp, a Bavarian priest, began treating his parishioners with cold water applications after he cured himself from tuberculosis through hydrotherapy. Kneipp wrote many papers on the subject, and opened hydrotherapy clinics known as the Kneipp clinics. Today, Kneipp still has a large following, especially in Europe. A research paper published in 2014 looked at all the evidence documented from 1986 to 2012 and found that hydrotherapy has been widely used worldwide for a plethora of health reasons, including to improve immunity, fatigue, anxiety, and obesity. Contrast hydrotherapy may have benefit in stimulating thyroid gland function. You may be wondering, how can using hot and cold water help improve thyroid function? The reason that hydrotherapy works is thought to be attributed to a pumping action caused by the change in blood flow during treatment. By applying warm water to an area on the body, it increases blood flow to the region, also known as vasodialation. Applying cold water causes vasoconstriction, reducing blood flow. This continued back-and-forth between vasodilation and vasoconstriction creates the pumping action. The alterations in tissue temperature and blood flow may also help reduce inflammation.

THYROID HYDROTHERAPY

To prepare for thyroid hydrotherapy, you will need:

- 2 bowls, pots, or buckets that have the capacity to be filled with at least 1 to 2 gallons of water
- 2 hand towels
- 1 timer (you can simply use the timer on your phone)

Fill one container with very warm water and the other with cold water. Generally, the water temperature does not need to be tested with a thermometer, but you want the warm water to be warm to hot (make sure it is not burning; you should be able to hold your hand comfortably in the water) and the cold water should feel quite cold. It is best to run the tap for a few seconds to try to make the water as cool as possible. Next, find a comfortable place to sit. Some people choose to bring a chair into the bathroom, others prefer to set up in their living room on the couch. Then, put each towel in one of the containers. Beginning with the warm water, take the towel out of the warm water container, wring it out into the container (again, make sure the temperature is not too hot!), fold it over a few times, and place it over your neck. Set your timer for 3 minutes and wait. Then, put the towel back in the warm water. Switch to the cold towel, wringing it out first into its container, then fold it over and place it over your neck (if the towel is too cold, remove it and warm the water slightly, then try again). Set the timer for 3 minutes and wait. Repeat this cycle three times (hot, cold, hot, cold, hot, cold, always ending on cold) per set. For maximum benefit, hydrotherapy should become part of your routine that is practiced daily or a few times a week. Some practitioners have noted that thyroid medication needs to be reduced after patients begin using hydrotherapy. Please ensure that you are working with your health-care provider to run thyroid blood tests regularly when implementing thyroid hydrotherapy.

OSTEOPATHY

Osteopathy is a noninvasive manual type of therapy. An osteopathic practitioner aims to improve the body's nervous system, circulatory system, and lymphatic system by primarily focusing the manual treatment on the muscles, joints and spine. Typically, many people think of osteopathic manual treatment (OMT) as being beneficial for aches and pains such as arthritis and low back issues. Although this is true, it may hold value for many other health conditions, especially due to its focus on the lymphatic and nervous system. Plus, the improvement in circulation may also increase blood flow to the thyroid gland. Not to mention, some studies have demonstrated that OMT helps to lower the inflammatory response in the body. Lymphatic pump techniques have been shown to strengthen the immune response. As one strengthens the immunity by way of the lymphatic system, it may also help to clear chronic infections (and therefore may be ideal for those living with chronic EBV, CMV, etc.).

Depending on the health issues at hand, some people may require more treatments to feel benefits, while others may only need treatment every few months or a few times a year. Personally, I felt the shift in my body after just one treatment. Overall, I find OMT to be extremely relaxing and can also really help to promote more restful and rejuvenating sleep. As OMT is a manual therapy, in order to experience and explore this complimentary therapy you will need to find a qualified osteopathic practitioner close to your home.

ESSENTIAL OILS AND AROMATHERAPY

Essential oils are extracts from aromatic plants that may have medicinal benefits. Ancient Egyptians were reported to use aromatic oils, such as cedar, myrrh, and anise, in cosmetic preparations and ointments as early as 4500 BCE. The use of other aromatic oils, such as cinnamon, sandalwood, and ginger, was also recorded in Chinese and Indian medicine around 3000 to 2000 BCE. Greek history documented the use of the essential oils of thyme, saffron, cumin, peppermint, and marjoram around 500 to 400 BCE. Essential oils differ from herbal extracts, such as the ones discussed in the previous chapter. Essential oils are extracted by pressing or steam distilling the leaves, stems, roots, or flowers of a plant to obtain the volatile oils (medicinal properties). Herbal extracts, on the other hand, are often extracted with alcohol and contain different medicinal properties. Unlike herbal extracts, essential oils, for the most part, are made to be used topically or to diffuse into the air.

Essential oils have become very popular over the last few years; personally, I have always loved the smell of lavender and other oils and can understand why so many people have adopted the use of these aromatic extracts. Research has identified medicinal properties of many different essential oils. The reported benefits differ depending on the oil; although there are no studies to suggest targeted thyroid benefit, some oils have been proven to be very effective at reducing inflammation and thus may benefit patients with Hashimoto's. Here are some popular and beneficial oils:

Myrrh. Until the Europeans discovered morphine, myrrh was a common analgesic and was used to clean wounds and sores for over two thousand years. Myrrh has been used for centuries as an anti-inflammatory agent. This is the essential oil of the herb discussed in Chapter 11: guggul (*Commiphora mukul*), a traditional Ayurvedic medicinal herb used to improve metabolism, and which may have benefits for weight loss, has shown to have thyroid-stimulating effects and improve T3 levels, when taken in its herbal extracted form. A study looking at the benefits of the essential oil of myrrh found that when mixed with the essential oil of frankincense, it created a potent anti-inflammatory mixture (used topically).

Frankincense. Originating from Africa, India, and the Middle East, frankincense oil has been important as an ingredient in incense and perfumes for thousands of years. Similar to myrrh, frankincense oil is prepared from aromatic hardened gum resins. One of the main components of frankincense oil is boswellic acid, a component known to have anti-inflammatory and anticancer properties. Frankincense is also well known for its benefit to the immune system.

Rose geranium. This scented geranium has been used in folk medicine as an antibacterial and antifungal agent as well as a food preservative. Recent research has proven it to be an anti-inflammatory agent in clinical trials.

Lemongrass. Although commonly thought of as an insect repellent due to its citronella-like smell, this oil has been found to have antifungal and anti-inflammatory properties. Interestingly, there is growing evidence that lemongrass essential oil, in its diffused, or vapor, form, is an effective and potent antifungal. Some researchers are even suggesting that diffused lemongrass oil should be used as an air decontaminant in hospitals!

Lavender. This essential oil has been extensively studied for its relaxing and calming benefits. Lavender essential oil has long been known as a remedy to reduce anxiety and this use has now been supported by multiple clinical trials.

Essential oils can be diffused into the air or used topically on your body. Some people choose to dab the oil on their wrists or make a diluted mixture with water in a spray bottle and use it like a perfume. A drop of oil can also be diluted with a few drops of a carrier oil, such as almond oil or olive oil, and applied directly over the thyroid gland. I mix rose geranium oil with argan oil and apply it topically over my thyroid gland. I keep a lavender spray beside my bed to help with sleep and have personally used myrrh topically with good results for eczema, cuts, and scrapes; I've also diluted myrrh to make a mouthwash when I had inflamed gums.

Robert Tisserand is an international speaker and educator on the science, safety, and benefits of essential oils and has written numerous books on essential oils. *The Complete Book of Essential Oils and Aromatherapy*, by Valerie Ann Worwood, is a well-regarded book on essential oils, providing easy-to-follow essential oil recipes.

HOMEOPATHY

Dating back to the late 1700s, homeopathy is "the treatment of disease by extremely minute doses of natural substances that in a healthy person would produce symptoms of disease." According to a bulletin posted by the World Health Organization (WHO)

> Homoeopathy is one of the most widespread non-conventional ap-
> proaches to treatment known to the world, along with traditional Chi-
> nese medicine, herbal medicine and osteopathy. Homoeopathy forms
> part of our overall common heritage because of its low costs, because
> prescriptions are safe so long as they form part of a diagnostic ap-
> proach, and because of the simple technology employed in its prepara-
> tion, albeit requiring high levels of experience and knowledge.

A 2018 study found that individuals who took the homeopathic remedy Thyroidinum 3x in addition to levothyroxine reported improved
symptomatic relief and weight loss compared to taking levothyroxine
alone. In another study, 72 of 86 children with subclinical hypothyroidism had reductions in both TSH levels and thyroid antibodies after using
homeopathic remedies. The homeopathic remedies used as treatment in
this study were dependent on individual symptoms and patient history.
Some patients only took the prescribed homeopathic remedy once, some
patients took the remedy a few times, and some patients required a different homeopathic remedy than the one initially prescribed. The study
outlined that the most effective remedies for the treatment of hypothyroidism included Phosphorus 200CH, Calcarea carb 200CH, Silicea
200CH, Sulfur 200CH, Lycopodium 200CH, and Pulsatilla 200CH.
Bromium 6CH has also been reported to be helpful in the treatment of
hypothyroidism.

As homeopathic remedies are recommended on a very individual basis,
it is ideal to find a homeopathic or naturopathic doctor well versed in thyroid health if you are interested in using homeopathic remedies. Note that
many homeopathic practitioners believe the correct homeopathic remedy
for a person should not be based on a certain diagnosis (such as hypothyroidism), but a careful and lengthy assessment of the person (sometimes
lasting 3 hours) taking into consideration all the symptoms and characteristics of the individual, after which the homeopathic remedy is then cho-
sen. Therefore, the dosing of homeopathic remedies is very patient specific
and can range from only using the medicine once to a series of times.

GEMMOTHERAPY, herbal medicines that are made from the buds or shoots of young plants and then diluted in a similar manner to homeopathic remedies, have also been reported to be helpful in healing the thyroid gland. The gemmotherapy remedies that are thought to provide benefit to the thyroid gland include *Cornus sanguinaria* and *Prunus amygdalus*.

BEE VENOM THERAPY

This is a therapy I have not tried, however there is certainly some "buzz" about this potential treatment! Bee venom (BV) therapy is a form of medicine that is believed to have originated from Greece and China, and anti-inflammatory benefits of BV have been published for over a hundred years. BV is a colorless, acidic liquid; bees excrete it through their stingers into a target when they feel threatened. It contains both anti-inflammatory and inflammatory compounds, including enzymes, sugars, minerals, and amino acids. The main component of BV is an amino acid compound called melittin that has been reported to have antibacterial and antiviral effects as well as being a potent anti-inflammatory agent.

Today, multiple scientific reports suggest that BV is beneficial to reduce inflammation and can offer relief to those who have inflammatory pain conditions, such as rheumatoid arthritis. Although studies are suggesting BV may carry potential for treatment for those with anti-inflammatory effects and chronic infections, such as Lyme disease, the treatment is not without side effects. There has been one case report of BV precipitating the onset of lupus in a patient, and many people can have a strong allergic response to BV.

I believe this therapy holds potential, but more research is needed. Due to the potential of some serious side effects, if you do wish to try this therapy, make sure you seek out a qualified trained professional.

EMERGING TESTS FOR THYROID FUNCTION

Thyroflex. One of the oldest known tests for hypothyroidism was the Achilles tendon reflex test. In the nineteenth century, during a physical examination, the doctor would test the rate of relaxation of the Achilles tendon. It was well known that the rate of relaxation was visibly delayed in people with hypothyroidism. The Thyroflex machine, designed by Daryl Turner, PhD, is based on these findings when doctors observed that patients with hypothyroidism had very slow or absent tendon reflexes. Tendon reflex speed is an indicator of cellular energy and function, and cellular function is controlled by the T3 hormone. The Thyroflex machine is a noninvasive form of testing to determine an individual's thyroid status based upon the measurement of conduction velocity through a tendon reflex and can help understand how well thyroid hormones are entering the cells. Unlike a thyroid blood draw, the test is performed by the patient placing a sensor over their finger and connecting to the Thyroflex computer. A tendon in the forearm is then stimulated and will make the finger move involuntarily. The time between the stimulation of the tendon and the movement of the finger is measured by the computer and the average speed of nerve conduction is calculated, indicating the level of intracellular thyroid function. Thyroflex providers can now be found worldwide. To find one close to you, visit the Thyroflex website.

PART 3
Putting It All Together

CHAPTER 13

Your Thyroid-Healing Plan

Whether you are only ready to take a few small steps toward natural thyroid healing, or willing to go all in, in this chapter I outline the steps I take with my patients when addressing thyroid health. Please note that the order of these steps is the most common plan I follow with patients. Of course, if they are currently experiencing terrible digestive symptoms or have a known chronic infection, we also address that from the beginning. Additionally, some patients get blood testing and adopt only the Thyroid-Healing Diet, and their symptoms improve to a level they are happy with and they don't want to address other aspects of thyroid health. If this is you and you feel great—awesome! However, many patients need to address many of the thyroid-healing steps to truly feel their best. For many, this can take months (or years, as for me); however, the more you feel better, the more encouraging it is to continue on the journey. I always start with basic blood tests to gain a more in-depth look at the thyroid gland function as well as check for any nutrient deficiencies that could be contributing to symptoms or reducing the optimal function of the thyroid. I recommend you start here as well. If you are found to be deficient in iron, vitamin B_{12}, or D, use supplements to correct these deficiencies. Next, diet needs to be addressed, as it really is the foundation of our health: *ultimately, we are what we eat.* Then, you can begin to address environmental and emotional aspects that can contribute to thyroid health. This can also be a good time to explore ancient and emerging therapies that may resonate with you. Supplements are added to the regimen based on the individual's blood tests and symptoms. Then, we focus on healing the gut and finally address infections.

1. First, have blood work tests performed:
   - Have a complete thyroid panel blood test run to understand whether you are positive for thyroid antibodies and/or have low T3 or high RT3.* If you already know you have Hashimoto's, retesting your hormones and your antibodies before starting the program can give you a baseline for you to track your improvement in addition to tracking your symptoms.
   - Ask your health-care provider to test for the following potential nutrient deficiencies: vitamins B$_{12}$ and D, and iron. If you have deficiencies, use supplements to correct them.
2. Adopt the Thyroid-Healing Diet. If you are not ready to take on this diet in its entirety, focus on increasing thyroid-healing foods and reducing thyroid-harming foods (see chart, page 147).
3. Address stress and environmental triggers, including toxins and electromagnetic fields. Take some time to explore ancient and emerging therapies.
4. Use supplements tailored to your needs. If you are having issues converting T4 to T3, or have positive antibodies, use supplements to help increase this conversion or reduce the antibody response (see the following box).
5. Heal your gut and keep your microbiome happy.
6. Address potential chronic infections that could be contributing to an autoimmune response.

If you are currently taking medication and begin to take supplements to support thyroid hormone conversion, support the adrenal glands, and/or stimulate the thyroid gland, it is important that you monitor thyroid hormone levels in your blood, ideally every six to eight weeks, until stable, especially if you have a change in symptoms.

---

* If you are unable to test all your markers of thyroid health, that is okay! Just start with adopting the Thyroid-Healing Diet.

AS discussed in Chapter 11, supplements are ideally used on an individual and case-by-case basis. Natural thyroid healing requires individualized care. The best herbs and supplements for one person with Hashimoto's may be different for another person with Hashimoto's. However, if you like it super simple, here is my general Hashimoto's herb and supplement protocol:

1. Once you have been tested for potential nutrient deficiencies (vitamins B_{12} and D, and iron), begin proper vitamin B_{12}, D, and/or iron supplementation, dosage dependent on your determined deficiency
2. Selenium: 200 ucg a day for reducing antibodies
3. Ashwagandha (*Withania somnifera*): 500 to 600 mg a day in tablet form, or 2.5 ml twice daily of a 1:1 liquid extract
4. Probiotics, multistrain formula: 50 to 100 billion cfu per day
5. L-glutamine: 5 g upon waking
6. Digestive enzymes with any meal that contains protein and fat
7. If stress or sleep is an issue and has not been corrected with the use of ashwagandha, choose an herb that is best suited to your needs (see "Herbs/Supplements for Managing Stress," page 217).
8. If SIBO or other infections are present, use herbals and/or antibiotics discussed in Chapter 6.

Many patients need much more than this protocol, or they don't respond well to some of the suggested herbs or supplements. Please remember the importance of working with a knowledgeable healthcare provider. For an overview of supplements, please refer to Chapter 11.

SAMPLE WEEK OF THE THYROID-HEALING DIET WITH SUPPLEMENTS AND RECIPES

PHASE 1

	SUNDAY	MONDAY	TUESDAY	WEDNESDAY	THURSDAY	FRIDAY	SATURDAY
Morning supplement (upon waking but at least 1 hour after thyroid medication, if currently taking)	5 g L-glutamine in water	5 g L-glutamine in water	5 g L-glutamine in water	5 g L-glutamine in water	5 g L-glutamine in water	5 g L-glutamine in water	5 g L-glutamine in water
Breakfast	Grain-Free Pancakes, Nettle Tea	My Favorite Green Shake with Arrowroot Biscuit and Honey Butter, 1 cup Basic Bone Broth	Simplest Green Smoothie and Pumpkin Spice Muffin, Nettle Tea	My Favorite Green Shake with Arrowroot Biscuit and Honey Butter	Arrowroot Biscuit with avocado, olive oil, and salt, Nettle Tea	Simplest Green Smoothie and Pumpkin Spice Muffin	Grass-Fed Beef Breakfast Patties, Sweet Potato "Fries" with or without Simplest Green Smoothie, Nettle Tea

continues

	SUNDAY	MONDAY	TUESDAY	WEDNESDAY	THURSDAY	FRIDAY	SATURDAY
Morning supplements (with breakfast)	500–600 mg ashwagandha 200 ucg selenium Digestive enzyme B₁₂ if deficient Vitamin D if deficient	500–600 mg ashwagandha 200 ucg selenium Digestive enzyme B₁₂ if deficient Vitamin D if deficient	500–600 mg ashwagandha 200 ucg selenium Digestive enzyme B₁₂ if deficient Vitamin D if deficient	500–600 mg ashwagandha 200 ucg selenium Digestive enzyme B₁₂ if deficient Vitamin D if deficient	500–600 mg ashwagandha 200 ucg selenium Digestive enzyme B₁₂ if deficient Vitamin D if deficient	500–600 mg ashwagandha 200 ucg selenium Digestive enzyme B₁₂ if deficient Vitamin D if deficient	500–600 mg ashwagandha 200 ucg selenium Digestive enzyme B₁₂ if deficient Vitamin D if deficient
Lunch	Simple Greens Salad with Baked Fish	Leftover Lamb Roast and Cauliflower Mash with Mushroom Gravy	Arrowroot Biscuit or cassava/raw wrap with sliced turkey (nitrate- and hormone-free) or leftover meat and avocado	Leftover Baked Fish and roasted vegetables, 1 cup Basic Bone Broth	Arrowroot Biscuit(s) or cassava/raw wrap with sliced turkey or Grass-Fed Beef Patty (if you have some stored in the fridge) with avocado and olive oil	Leftover Shepherd's Pie	Simple Greens Salad, 1 cup Basic Bone Broth
Afternoon supplement (with lunch)	Digestive enzyme	Digestive enzyme	Digestive enzyme	Digestive enzyme	Digestive enzyme	Digestive enzyme	Digestive enzyme

continues

continued

	SUNDAY	MONDAY	TUESDAY	WEDNESDAY	THURSDAY	FRIDAY	SATURDAY
Midafternoon supplement (2 hours after lunch)	Iron (bisgylcinate or heme iron) if deficient	Iron (bisglycinate or heme iron) if deficient	Iron (bisglycinate or heme iron) if deficient	Iron (bisgylcinate or heme iron) if deficient	Iron (bisglycinate or heme iron) if deficient	Iron (bisglycinate or heme iron) if deficient	Iron (bisglycinate or heme iron) if deficient
Dinner	Lamb Roast and Cauliflower Mash and with Mushroom Gravy and Chocolate Cake for dessert	Basil Ginger Chicken with Cauliflower Rice and Simple Greens Salad	Simple Greens Salad with Baked Fish and roasted vegetables	Bibimbap with Cauliflower Rice	Shepherd's Pie with Simple Greens Salad	Baked Fish with roasted veggies and Sweet Potato "Fries"	Turkey Tacos with homemade tortillas or cassava/raw wraps
Dinner supplements	Digestive enzyme Probiotics, multistrain, 50–100 billion cfu	Digestive enzyme Probiotics, multistrain, 50–100 billion cfu	Digestive enzyme Probiotics, multistrain, 50–100 billion cfu	Digestive enzyme Probiotics, multistrain, 50–100 billion cfu	Digestive enzyme Probiotics, multistrain, 50–100 billion cfu	Digestive enzyme Probiotics, multistrain, 50–100 billion cfu	Digestive enzyme Probiotics, multistrain, 50–100 billion cfu
Snacks	Homemade Applesauce, Golden Turmeric Latte	Celery and carrot sticks with Cauliflower Hummus, Nettle Tea	Raw Lemon Date Bites	Apple Peach Crisp or a fresh apple, Nettle Tea	My Favorite Green Shake	Kale Chips or berries, Nettle Tea	Pumpkin Spice Muffin, Golden Turmeric Latte

PHASE 2: MY PERSONAL THYROID-HEALING DIET

Remember, everyone's version of Phase 2 will be slightly different once the various foods have been tested during the reintroduction phase. I can tolerate egg yolks (but not egg whites) and gluten-free grains well. I cannot tolerate beans and therefore do not include them in my diet. Dairy is only taken raw, in small amounts. Your own version of Phase 2 may look quite different from mine. Once you complete the reintroduction phase, you will have your own custom Phase 2.

For simplicity's sake, I have outlined the same supplement regimen for Phase 1 and Phase 2. Again, however, you may require another specific supplement (e.g., for stress or gut health) or may no longer require a supplement that you had been taking in Phase 1. Please review the thyroid healing steps carefully and make sure to check with your health-care provider.

I know it may seem overwhelming—and let's face it, one change is hard enough, let alone revamping your diet and detoxing your whole life! The following pages have some practical ideas that have worked for my patients and me.

Week 1: Focus on Reducing Toxins

Day 1: If you haven't done so already, assess whether you have a high toxic body burden by taking the quiz on page 30. If you do score high on this test, ensuring you are working to reduce toxins in your life is key.

Day 2: Filter your home water. Water is one of the main sources of chemicals that can reduce thyroid function, and by purchasing a water filter (be it a simple countertop filter or a whole-house filtration system), we can reduce our body's exposure to some of these chemicals. If you haven't done so already, commit to not drinking water from plastic water bottles—it's bad for your thyroid and the planet.

Day 3: Review the EWG's Dirty Dozen and begin to purchase the organic options for these fruits and vegetables. While you're at the supermarket, start to get in the habit of either not taking a receipt, or not handling

continues on page 257

PHASE 2

	SUNDAY	MONDAY	TUESDAY	WEDNESDAY	THURSDAY	FRIDAY	SATURDAY
Morning supplement (upon waking but at least 1 hour after thyroid medication, if currently taking)	5 g L-glutamine in water	5 g L-glutamine in water	5 g L-glutamine in water	5 g L-glutamine in water	5 g L-glutamine in water	5 g L-glutamine in water	5 g L-glutamine in water
Breakfast	Grain-Free Pancakes, Nettle Tea	Cooked buckwheat with berries, flax seeds, and maple syrup	My Favorite Green Shake, Nettle Tea	Arrowroot Biscuit or cassava/raw wrap with egg yolk and avocado	Simplest Green Smoothie and Carrot Raisin Breakfast Muffin, Nettle Tea	My Favorite Green Shake	Egg yolk and Arrowroot Biscuit and Sweet Potato "Fries"
Morning supplements (with breakfast)	500–600 mg ashwagandha 200 ucg selenium Digestive enzyme B$_{12}$ if deficient Vitamin D if deficient	500–600 mg ashwagandha 200 ucg selenium Digestive enzyme B$_{12}$ if deficient Vitamin D if deficient	500–600 mg ashwagandha 200 ucg selenium Digestive enzyme B1$_2$ if deficient Vitamin D if deficient	500–600 mg ashwagandha 200 ucg selenium Digestive enzyme B$_{12}$ if deficient Vitamin D if deficient	500–600 mg ashwagandha 200 ucg selenium Digestive enzyme B$_{12}$ if deficient Vitamin D if deficient	500–600 mg ashwagandha 200 ucg selenium Digestive enzyme B$_{12}$ if deficient Vitamin D if deficient	500–600 mg ashwagandha 200 ucg selenium Digestive enzyme B$_{12}$ if deficient Vitamin D if deficient

continues

	SUNDAY	MONDAY	TUESDAY	WEDNESDAY	THURSDAY	FRIDAY	SATURDAY
Lunch	Simple Greens Salad with Baked Fish	Leftover Lamb Roast and Cauliflower Mash	Arrowroot Biscuit or cassava/raw wrap with sliced turkey (nitrate- and hormone-free) and avocado	Leftover Black Cumin Seed Chicken and roasted vegetables	Arrowroot Biscuit(s) or cassava/raw wrap with sliced turkey or Grass-Fed Beef Patty (if you have some stored in the fridge) with avocado and olive oil	Leftover Shepherd's Pie	Simple Greens Salad
Afternoon supplement (with lunch)	Digestive enzyme	Digestive enzyme	Digestive enzyme	Digestive enzyme	Digestive enzyme	Digestive enzyme	Digestive enzyme
Midafternoon supplement (2 hours after lunch)	Iron (bisglycinate or heme iron) if deficient	Iron (bisglycinate or heme iron) if deficient	Iron (bisglycinate or heme iron) if deficient	Iron (bisglycinate or heme iron) if deficient	Iron (bisglycinate or heme iron) if deficient	Iron (bisglycinate or heme iron) if deficient	Iron (bisglycinate or heme iron) if deficient

continues

continued

	SUNDAY	MONDAY	TUESDAY	WEDNESDAY	THURSDAY	FRIDAY	SATURDAY
Dinner	Lamb Roast and Cauliflower Mash with Mushroom Gravy	Basil Ginger Chicken with Cauliflower Rice and Simple Greens Salad	Simple Greens Salad with Black Cumin Seed Chicken and baked vegetable	Bibimbap with Cauliflower Rice or brown rice/quinoa	Shepherd's Pie with Simple Greens Salad	Baked Fish with roasted veggies and Sweet Potato "Fries"	Turkey Tacos with homemade tortillas or cassava/raw wraps
Dinner supplements	Digestive enzyme Probiotics, multistrain, 50–100 billion cfu	Digestive enzyme Probiotics, multistrain 50–100 billion cfu	Digestive enzyme Probiotics, multistrain, 50–100billion cfu	Digestive enzyme Probiotics, multistrain, 50–100 billion cfu	Digestive enzyme Probiotics, multistrain, 50–100 billion cfu	Digestive enzyme Probiotics, multistrain, 50–100 billion cfu	Digestive enzyme Probiotics, multistrain, 50–100 billion cfu
Snacks	Homemade Applesauce, Golden Turmeric Latte	Celery and carrot sticks with a handful of raw nuts, Nettle Tea	Raw Lemon Date Bites	Apple Peach Crisp or a fresh apple, Nettle Tea	My Favorite Green shake	Kale Chips or berries, Nettle Tea	Pumpkin Spice Muffin, Golden Turmeric Latte

continued from page 253

the receipt or paper money for long. Most of these receipts (and all paper money) now have chemicals that are not great for the thyroid gland.

Day 4: Try dry brushing (find out how on page 34). If you think you can easily incorporate this into your weekly routine, aim to dry brush before your shower at least 2 to 3 times per week.

Day 5: Check your deodorant, shampoos, creams, and cosmetics for fragrances and other thyroid-harming chemicals outlined in Chapter 2. Even if it's a slow transition, begin to make a switch to more natural alternatives.

Day 6: Ditch your conventional household cleaning chemicals and opt for natural alternatives or make your own. You can find my favorite DIY cleaning recipes on my website, www.emilylipinski.com/resources.

Day 7: Check your home and personal care products for antibacterial chemicals, such as triclosan, and toss them. Choose natural antibacterial products or essential oil mixes for cleaning and hand sanitizing. These can be found in natural health food stores or online and I also share some of my favorite DIY natural hand-sanitizing and cleaning recipes on my website.

Please refer to Chapter 2 for more tips on reducing your exposure to toxins on a daily basis.

Week 2: Focus on Reducing Stress

Day 1: Determine whether you are experiencing adrenal fatigue by taking the quiz on page 52. This will provide you with a baseline and help determine how much stress may be impacting your health.

Day 2: Assess your daily routine. Take a day to become mindful of your actions, thoughts, and stress levels throughout the day. For an in-depth review of this exercise, refer to page 55. Pinpoint some times of day, or situations, that are bringing you stress. Is there something that can be done to make these incidences less stressful? Some of the techniques that will be explored over the next few days may be helpful.

Day 3: Mindfully meditate for at least 3 minutes. If you are new to meditation, check out an app (Calm, Headspace, or Jon Kabat-Zinn, just to name a few) or find a mindful meditation CD at your closest library or bookstore.

Day 4: Try diaphragmatic breathing (see page 59).

Day 5: Spend time in nature. Whether it is a walk outside after work, a bike ride on the weekend, or just sitting out on a park bench for 15 minutes over your lunch hour—take in the sounds and smells of the outdoors. Focus on really seeing all of nature's beauty—the fluffy clouds, the beautiful trees, and the diversity of birds, mammals, and other wildlife.

Day 6: Try a low-intensity, gentle exercise, such as yoga, tai chi, Pilates, walking, or swimming.

Day 7: Choose a relaxation technique that you tried over the past 6 days and commit to incorporating it into your lifestyle at least 1 or 2 times a week. Can any of these techniques (such as deep breathing) be incorporated into your day when you are stressed? Think about small changes that you are willing to commit to that will make each day a little less stressful.

Week 3: Focus on Reducing EMFs

Day 1: Assess whether you are experiencing electromagnetic hypersensitivity by taking the quiz on page 69. If you are, it will be even more important that you focus on implementing these EMF-reducing solutions.

Day 2: Avoid holding your cell phone close to your jaw, head, or neck. Use the speakerphone or a headset, but avoid using Bluetooth.

Day 3: Find another place to store your cell phone instead of in your pocket or inside your bra. The farther away your phone is from your body, the better.

Day 4: Get in the habit of turning your Wi-Fi off at night before you go to bed.

Day 5: Start turning your cell phone to airplane mode at night, and/or keep your cell phone outside of the bedroom.

Day 6: Avoid looking at all screens, including smartphones, laptops, and TVs, at least 45 minutes prior to going to bed.

Day 7: Ensure that there are no EMF devices in your bedroom (laptops, electric blankets, devices connected to Bluetooth).

For more tips on how to reduce EMF exposure, refer to Chapter 4.

Week 4: Explore Ancient Remedies

For this week, consider trying one of the ancient remedies discussed in Chapter 12 that you haven't tried before. Many of them do require working with an experienced provider, so make sure to take the time in finding someone who is right for you.

MONITORING THYROID FUNCTION AT HOME

Monitoring thyroid function by way of measuring body temperature (basal metabolic temperature monitoring) is also a wonderful tool to help gauge how well the body is responding to a new intervention, be it the Thyroid-Healing Diet, a change in medication, or a new supplement.

In 1976, Dr. Broda Barnes first wrote about how important it is to use body temperature as a guide to monitor thyroid treatment in the book *Hypothyroidism: The Unsuspected Illness*. Over the past twenty years, Dr. Denis Wilson, a pioneer in complementary treatment of thyroid disease, has treated thousands of patients with thyroid disease and reports monitoring of temperature to be very important, especially after the initiation of natural desiccated thyroid (NDT). Many studies have cited that basal body temperature (BBT) is very responsive to thyroid hormones. Thyroid hormones influence BBT by regulating available energy in the body, and by tracking BBT, we can gather more information to understand whether natural or conventional interventions are helping the thyroid function and/or can often show an early sign of overmedication. For instance, a BBT that is consistently low throughout the month, paired with symptoms of hypothyroidism, may be an indicator that a person is hypothyroid, or that the medication dosage is too low. A higher-than-normal BBT plus symptoms of hyperthyroidism could be indicative of overmedication. BBT is usually the lowest point that your temperature will be throughout the day, and is easily measured by taking your temperature first thing in the morning, prior to getting out of bed, drinking a glass of water, or taking any medications.

Dr. Wilson reports that thyroid function is optimal around a BBT of 98.6°F (37°C). However, conventional medical wisdom believes average BBT to be slightly lower, and in women, it also fluctuates with the menstrual cycle. Before ovulation, a woman's BBT averages between 97°F (36.1°C) and 97.5°F (36.4°C). After ovulation, it rises to 97.6°F (36.4°C) to 98.6°F (37°C). Regardless, over the course of a month, a woman's temperature should be reaching close to 98.6°F (37°C), especially after ovulation. Dr. Wilson suggests that temperature should be measured three times a day and then averaged for an accurate result; however, I believe simply taking a daily morning reading over the course of one month can provide a good deal of information.

Oral temperature can be measured at home by using a store-bought thermometer. Digital thermometers, although convenient, can yield inaccurate results. Mercury thermometers provided a more accurate reading but are no longer sold, due to environmental and health concerns. New liquid thermometers (now using a substance known as Galinstan) are thought to be most accurate. These thermometers are available online, such as at Amazon, and may also be available at your local drugstore.

I've included a BBT chart on page 308 that you can photocopy and use to track your own temperature. You can also find this chart on my website at www.emilylipinski.com/resources.

Supplements

For easy reference, here is a chart detailing supplements I have discussed throughout this book.

As mentioned earlier, please keep the following in mind:

1. Check with your health-care provider when taking any new supplements. Some herbs have contraindications or cautions that you might not be aware of and/or could cause an allergic response.
2. If you are currently taking thyroid medication, and begin a new supplement to improve thyroid function, it is important that you are under the care of a health-care provider who can monitor blood levels and thyroid symptoms. The use of some supplements may change the amount of thyroid medication required.
3. Just as for diet and exercise, results are often not overnight or immediate. Many effective natural remedies can take upward of 3 weeks for people to start to notice a difference; some may need to be taken long term for results to continue.

HERB/N. S.*	REASON	DOSAGE	CAUTIONS/CONTRAINDICATIONS
American ginseng (*Panax quinquefolius*)	Helps improve energy levels, can help the body adapt to stress	200–400 mg per day, standardized to 10% ginsenosides	May cause palpitations, nausea, agitation, and restless thoughts.
Andrographis (*Andrographis paniculata*)	Can be helpful in treating chronic infections, including EBV	200 mg, 2–3 times per day	High doses can cause nausea and vomiting; not to be taken if there is a known allergy to the daisy family.
Ashwagandha (*Withania somnifera*)	May improve T3, T4; reduces symptoms of hypothyroidism; improves sleep; may increase libido	500–600 mg/day in tablet form, standardized to 2.5% withanolides, or 5 ml/day of a 1:1 or 1:2 tincture standardized to 2.0 mg/mL withanolides	High doses can cause gastric upset, diarrhea, and vomiting. Thyroid labs should be monitored on a regular basis as this herb may change the need for thyroid medication.
Astralagus (*Astralagus membranaceus*)	Can be helpful in treating chronic infections and improving immune system function	5 ml of a 1:2 liquid extract or 400–500 mg per day in capsule form	Not to be used in acute infections. May cause gastric upset.
Bacopa (*Bacopa monnieri*)	May improve T3 levels; can help with focus and memory	200 ucg, taken 3 times per day in a tablet standardized to contain 20% bacosides	May cause gastric upset. Thyroid labs should be monitored on a regular basis as this herb may change the need for thyroid medication.
Black cumin seed (*Nigella sativa*) oil	May improve weight loss, reduce thyroid antibodies, and improve overall thyroid function	½ tsp of oil daily	May cause gastric upset, nausea, vomiting and/or skin irritation. Thyroid labs should be monitored on a regular basis as this herb may change the need for thyroid medication.
Caprylic acid	Can be helpful in eradicating *Candida albicans* (yeast infections)	800–1,200 mg daily	Can cause gastric upset and nausea.

*N. S. = Natural Supplement

continues

continued

HERB/N. S.*	REASON	DOSAGE	CAUTIONS/CONTRAINDICATIONS
Chaste tree (*Vitex agnus-castus*)	Can promote fertility, improve progesterone levels, and help regulate the menstrual cycle	80 mg a day	May reduce the effectiveness of the oral contraceptive pill, may cause gastric upset.
Chinese skullcap (*Scutellaria baicalensis*)	Helpful in treating infections, including EBV and HHV-6	Equal parts of licorice and Chinese skullcap are mixed together and ½–1 tsp is taken 3–6 times a day for 3 months	May cause gastric upset. Can lower blood sugar levels and therefore may have an additive effect with blood sugar-lowering medications.
CoQ 10	Helps improve energy, especially in those who have been struggling with chronic infections, such as EBV, may help reduce inflammation in the body, can promote fertility	CoQ 10 (ubiquinol) 100–200 mg per day	Gastric upset; may lower blood pressure and therefore could cause an additive effect with blood pressure-lowering medication.
Cordyceps	Helps balance the immune system, may enhance stamina and exercise performance, may improve fertility	400 mg, Cs-4 strain of Cordyceps or *militaris* strain, hot water extracted and contains a minimum of 20% beta-glucans (also known as polysaccharides), taken 2–4 times a day	May cause a reduction in blood sugar levels and therefore may have an additive effect with blood sugar-lowering medications, may interact with blood-thinning medications. Could cause gastric upset.
DGL	Helps reduce symptoms of gastritis and heartburn, may aid in improving digestive symptoms	500–1,000 mg with meals	May cause gastric upset.

continues

continued

HERB/N. S.*	REASON	DOSAGE	CAUTIONS/CONTRAINDICATIONS
Digestive enzymes with HCl	May help restore healthy digestive functioning, can be helpful in those with food sensitivities, can help improve nutrients and may increase energy	100–200 mg with meals	Nausea, diarrhea. HCl can cause a burning sensation in the stomach.
Fish oil (omega-3 fatty acids)	Has anti-inflammatory properties, known to be of benefit for those with autoimmune diseases	1,000–3,000 mg, taken 1–3 times a day with meals	May cause gastric upset, diarrhea, or cause a fishy aftertaste.
GI Microb-X (berberine, bearberry, black walnut, sweet wormwood, and tribulus)	The herbs contained in this formula have been shown to be helpful in eradicating many different pathogens that contribute to gut infections and helps promote healthy gut bacteria balance	2–4 tablets daily	Can cause stomach pain, diarrhea, nausea, and bloating.
Goldenseal	Has been shown to be helpful in treating infections (including Candida albicans) and may improve digestion	3–9 ml per day of a 1:1 liquid extract, or 400–500 mg per day in capsule form	Can cause stomach pain, diarrhea, nausea, and bloating.
Guggul (Commiphora mukul)	May aid in weight loss, improve T3 levels, and help lower cholesterol levels	400–500 mg, taken 3 times per day with meals in a tablet standardized to 2.5% guggulsterones	May cause gastric upset, diarrhea, or a skin rash. Thyroid labs should be monitored on a regular basis as this herb may change the need for thyroid medication.

continues

continued

HERB/N. S.*	REASON	DOSAGE	CAUTIONS/CONTRAINDICATIONS
Iodine	Key nutrient for the thyroid gland, necessary building block to make thyroid hormones, may help reduce symptoms of hypothyroidism	2 ug/kg (0.9 ug/lb) of body weight; increased dosage required in pregnancy and lactation	May increase antibodies in Hashimoto's. Too much iodine can cause symptoms of hyperthyroidism. Thyroid labs should be monitored on a regular basis as this herb may change the need for thyroid medication.
Iron	Used to correct deficiency or used to improve low ferritin levels; increasing ferritin levels may improve thyroid function and improve symptoms of hypothyroidism	20–30 mg of iron bisglycinate or heme iron taken 1–3 times per day	Constipation and gastric upset are the primary concerns when supplementing with iron of any kind. Ensure to take iron 4 hours away from other medications.
L-glutamine	Helps heal intestinal permeability	5 g taken 1–3 times per day on an empty stomach	Could cause nausea, joint pain, or rash.
Licorice (Glycyrrhiza glabra)	Helps improve digestive symptoms, can help reduce inflammation in the body, can help the body adapt to stress; can be mixed with Chinese skullcap to help treat EBV and HHV-6.	2.5 ml of a 1:1 extract standardized to contain 30 mg/ml of glycyrrhizin. When treating infections, equal parts of licorice and Chinese skullcap are mixed together and ½–1 tsp is taken 3–6 times a day for 3 months	May increase blood pressure, fluid retention, and headache. May cause gastric upset. If you are using licorice for over 6 weeks, it is best to monitor potassium levels in the blood.
Magnesium	Helps relax the nervous system, may help regulate mood, improve sleep, lower blood pressure, and improve bone density	Magnesium bisglycinate, 200–400 mg per day	Diarrhea with high amounts.

continues

continued

HERB/N. S.*	REASON	DOSAGE	CAUTIONS/CONTRAINDICATIONS
Myo-inositol	Improves selenium's ability to lower thyroid antibodies when used in combination with selenium	600 mg per day for 6 months	May cause mild gastric discomfort. This supplement may also lower blood sugar levels; use caution if taking other blood sugar–lowering medication.
NAC (N-acetyl-cysteine)	Can help reduce chronic inflammation, particularly if caused by viral infections. Also can break down biofilms produced by bacteria, enabling antimicrobial herbs to be more effective at eradicating infection. Can also help stop the replication of viruses.	1,500–1,800 mg per day	May cause gastric upset.
Oil of oregano	Can be helpful in treating infections, including *Blastocystis* and *Candida albicans*	50–60 mg of emulsified oil of oregano, taken 1–4 times a day	Can cause stomach upset, nausea, and diarrhea.
Passionflower (*Passiflora incarnata*)	May help the body adapt to stress, reduce anxiety and restlessness, and promote a better night's sleep	100 mg standardized to 3.5% vitexin, taken 2–4 times a day	May cause dizziness or drowsiness.
Probiotics	Helps restore healthy gut function, can aid in repairing intestinal permeability, helps regulate immune function. Can also help prevent the reoccurrence of *H. pylori*	50–100 billion cfu of a multistrain formula, 1–2 times per day	Nausea, diarrhea, bloating, gas, constipation.

continues

continued

HERB/N. S.*	REASON	DOSAGE	CAUTIONS/CONTRAINDICATIONS
Reishi (*Ganoderma lucidum*)	Improves immune function, may have anticancer properties	400 mg, 2–3 times a day, hot water extract formula and standardized to 12% polysaccharides and 4% triterpenes	May cause gastric upset.
Rhodiola (*Rhodiola rosea*)	May help the body adapt to stress, known to improve exercise performance, can boost energy levels and reduce cortisol levels	200 mg standardized to 3% total rosavins, 1% salidroside, taken 1–2 times a day	May reduce effectiveness of the oral contraceptive pill, may cause gastric upset, drowsiness, or dizziness.
Rosmarinic acid	Can help reduce inflammation in autoimmune diseases, may help contribute to healthy gut bacteria, can help reduce such allergy symptoms as hay fever and asthma	150–500 mg twice per day	Gastric upset, rash.
Saccharomyces boulardii	A yeastlike probiotic, has beneficial effects on altered intestinal microbiota and can help restore leaky gut. Has also been found to be effective in treating *Blastocystis*.	500 mg, or 10 billion cells daily	May cause gas, bloating, or constipation.
Schisandra (*Schisandra chinensis*)	May help improve fatigue, traditionally used in TCM to treat autoimmune conditions, may increase libido	5 ml of a 1:2 liquid extract, or 500 mg tablets taken twice daily	May cause agitation, heartburn, reduced appetite, rash; may increase clearance of prescribed medications or increase levels of immunosuppressant medications at high dosages.

continues

continued

HERB/N. S.*	REASON	DOSAGE	CAUTIONS/CONTRAINDICATIONS
Selenium	Important thyroid gland nutrient. May lower thyroid antibodies, improve thyroid hormone conversion.	200 ucg per day	High amounts of selenium over time can result in selenium toxicity. Symptoms of toxicity include nausea, vomiting, abdominal pain, diarrhea, hair loss, brittle nails, peripheral neuropathy, and the smell of garlic in sweat and breath. Toxicity is typically seen when someone is taking a dosage of over 400 ucg for a long period of time along with a diet that is high in selenium.
Siberian ginseng (*Eleutherococcus senticosus*)	Helps the body adapt to stress, helps improve fatigue	250 mg, standardized to 0.8–1% eleutherosides	May be contraindicated when taking blood-thinning medication; may cause fatigue, palpitations, or breast pain.
Tyrosine	Key nutrient for the thyroid gland, necessary building block to make thyroid hormones, may help reduce symptoms of hypothyroidism	500–2,000 mg per day	May increase antibodies in those with Hashimoto's (in theory). May cause gastric upset, drowsiness, and agitation. Thyroid labs should be monitored on a regular basis as this herb may change the need for thyroid medication.
Vitamin B$_{12}$	Used to correct deficiency or low B$_{12}$ levels seen in blood. May improve energy and cognitive functioning.	1,000–5,000 ucg per day taken sublingually (under the tongue) in liquid or tablet form	None known.

continues

continued

HERB/N. S.*	REASON	DOSAGE	CAUTIONS/CONTRAINDICATIONS
Vitamin D	Used to correct insufficiency or deficiency. Using vitamin D may slow down the progression of hypothyroidism and may reduce the risk of cardiovascular disease associated with hypothyroidism	1,000–5,000 IU per day in liquid, emulsified form. Using vitamin D with K$_2$ improves absorption.	Too much vitamin D supplementation can cause vitamin D toxicity. If you are supplementing with vitamin D, ensure you are monitoring your blood levels every 3–6 months.
Wobenzym	Helps reduce inflammation in the body, may help improve thyroid function and reduce thyroid antibodies, may also reduce pain	3 tablets, 2–3 times daily on an empty stomach	May cause gastric upset, nausea, and vomiting.
Zinc	May improve conversion of T4 to T3, may help improve immunity and may slow hair loss	30 mg per day	Excess zinc can cause copper deficiency when taken long term. Zinc, especially when taken on an empty stomach, can cause nausea.
Zinc-carnosine	Combining triple therapy with zinc-carnosine has been shown to eradicate H. pylori infection in 100% of patients. Zinc-carnosine also helps repair damaged stomach lining, reduce inflammation, and inhibit the grown of H. pylori.	75 mg taken twice daily for 3–6 weeks	Zinc-carnosine is generally considered safe until 8 weeks. Taking zinc long term can cause a copper deficiency. If zinc-carnosine is required long term, then supplementing with 2 mg of copper daily is suggested.

continues

Recipes

As you know, I believe nutrition is the backbone of healing. These recipes are some of my favorites—they are easy to prepare, delicious, and incorporate key ingredients from the Thyroid-Healing Diet. For the most part, they are also family-friendly, making it easier when cooking for the entire family. Morning muffins and grain-free pancakes are often a hit with kids. Most children love tacos or putting together their own version of a cassava flour wrap or raw wrap. I am also always surprised how many little ones like sweet potato fries and roasted veggies. And for those who love their sweets as much as I do, you will be pleased to know you will not have to give them up! The Thyroid-Healing Diet allows for sweet treats and desserts, if desired. Anyone who has ever tried a new way of eating before knows that there is always a bit of a learning curve when adhering to a different type of diet. Planning ahead will be key for success, especially when you first start out. Leftovers from dinner are often an easy lunch, however some people plan for two cooking days a week (often a Sunday and Wednesday night) and prepare their meals for the next three to four days.

Before we get to the recipes, here are a few basics.

INGREDIENTS

Some of the ingredients may be unfamiliar to you; here's a quick rundown:

Arrowroot flour (also referred to as arrowroot starch or powder): Commonly used in many paleo and gluten-free recipes, Arrowroot powder is extracted from the root of a tropical plant known as *Maranta arundinacea*. Arrowroot is a good source of folates and other B vitamins and may also be beneficial for the immune system.

You can purchase this at such stores as Whole Foods, natural health stores, online, and in some major grocery chains.

Avocado oil: A natural oil pressed from the pulp of an avocado that is high in oleic acid, a fatty acid that is known for its numerous health benefits, such as reducing inflammation in the body.

You can purchase this at most major grocery stores, as well as Trader Joe's, Whole Foods, natural health stores, and online.

Black cumin seeds: Also known as nigella seeds (*Nigella sativa*), these flavorful seeds have proved to be quite helpful to the thyroid gland.

You can purchase this at such stores as Whole Foods, natural health stores, online, and in some major grocery chains.

Bone broth: A broth made from slow cooking the bones (and connective tissues) of animals, commonly beef or chicken. This food is high in collagen and therefore great for gut healing. It has also traditionally been used in many cultures all over the world for improving immunity.

You can make your own (page 295) or you can purchase premade broth at most grocery stores, as well as Trader Joe's, Whole Foods, and natural health stores.

Buckwheat groats: Buckwheat groats are the hulled seeds of the buckwheat plant and somewhat resemble steel-cut oats. Despite what the name may suggest, buckwheat is not part of the wheat family, but is a seed that is related to the rhubarb family. Buckwheat is high in many minerals and antioxidants and makes a great breakfast porridge. Please note that although it is technically a seed, the body may metabolize it like a grain due to its high carb content. Therefore, this seed is best enjoyed in Phase 2.

You can find buckwheat groats packaged and in the bulk section of Whole Foods or other large health food stores and online.

Carob powder: This powder comes from the carob tree (*Ceratonia siliqua*). Carob is naturally sweet and has a chocolate-like flavor, but unlike chocolate, it is caffeine-free. It is also high in fiber, minerals, and vitamins, making it a nutritious additive to foods. Although carob is technically a legume, it is very well tolerated by most people (note that you will want to avoid or curtail it if you suffer with IBS, as it is a high-FODMAP food).

You can purchase this at such stores as Whole Foods, natural health stores, online, and in some major grocery chains.

Cassava flour: This flour comes from cassava root, commonly found in South America, parts of Africa, and Asia. Its consistency is very similar to wheat flour and also has a very neutral and mild taste. However, I have found that all brands are not created equal when it comes to the quality of cassava flour. Using cheaper forms of cassava flour, especially when I have bought this flour in bulk, has led to less than optimal baking results. If you want to use cassava flour for any of the following recipes, it may be worthwhile to purchase a flour that is slightly more expensive, for a better final product. Cassava flour does contain a substance that in large amounts, could (in theory) increase thyroid goiter or swelling. This, however, has not been found to be true in research. Nonetheless, I suggest limiting intake to five servings a week.

Tapioca flour is the starch from the cassava plant and can also be used in gluten-free baking. However, whereas cassava flour is made from the whole root, peeled and dried, tapioca solely contains the starch. For this reason, the consistency of each flour is different, and they cannot necessarily be substituted for each other.

You can purchase this at such stores as Whole Foods, natural health stores, online, and in some major grocery chains.

Cassava wraps: A few companies now make cassava flour wraps. They are a great gluten- and grain-free, Thyroid-Healing Diet–friendly option to have on hand, or if you simply do not like the idea of baking your own grain-free bread alternative.

You can purchase this at such stores as Whole Foods, natural health stores, online, and in some major grocery chains.

Coconut (shredded, unsweetened): I use shredded coconut to make homemade coconut milk—a creamy preservative-free version of what is found at the store. Coconuts are a high-fat fruit that are packed with nutrients, and are especially high in manganese, a mineral that is essential for many important reactions in the body, especially fat and sugar metabolism. Unsweetened shredded coconut can be found in bulk at such stores as Whole Foods and natural health stores, in some grocery chains, and also online.

Coconut aminos: Similar to soy sauce but made from coconut. I also find it less salty than soy sauce and much more tasty (FYI—it is also much more expensive).

You can purchase this at such stores as Whole Foods, Trader Joe's, natural health stores, online, and in some major grocery chains.

Coconut flour: Flour made from coconuts; coconut flour is commonly used in gluten-free and paleo baking. I have found this flour to be tricky when used alone in recipes, but it combines very nicely with arrowroot or cassava flour.

You can purchase this at such stores as Whole Foods, natural health stores, online, and in some major grocery chains.

Coconut manna: This is not to be confused with coconut oil. Coconut manna (also referred to as coconut butter) is pureed dried coconut meat, made from whole coconuts with the water removed. It does contain coconut oil that can separate to the top, so make sure to soften and mix the coconut manna before using it in recipes.

You can purchase this at such stores as Trader Joe's, Whole Foods, natural health stores, online, and in some major grocery chains.

Coconut milk (canned, full-fat): Although coconut milk is now found in a diluted form in Tetra Paks (often where almond milk is found), my recipes call for full-fat, canned coconut milk. It is richer and has fewer additives. Products containing coconut fat, such as coconut milk and coconut oil, contain MCT, a type of fat that may help with cognitive functioning (memory, focus, and more).

You can purchase this at most major grocery chains (check the ethnic foods aisle) and such stores as Trader Joe's, Whole Foods, natural health stores, and online.

You can also make your own homemade Coconut Milk (page 285).

Coconut sugar: Also called coconut palm sugar, this is a sweet alternative to regular granulated or brown sugar. Coconut sugar is made from coconut sap. Unlike regular granulated sugar, coconut sugar is less processed and retains more minerals, nutrients, and fiber. It is still sweet, however, so for those wishing to lose weight, or with blood sugar issues or diabetes, coconut sugar should be used sparingly.

You can purchase this at such stores as Whole Foods, natural health stores, online, and in some major grocery chains.

Collagen peptides (hydrolyzed collagen powder): Collagen is a protein that forms connective tissue in your body. Although your body makes its own collagen every day, collagen production slows down as we age. When collagen is broken down or hydrolyzed into its peptide form, it becomes much more bioavailable and becomes more easily absorbed into the body. Collagen peptides taken orally have been shown to prevent further damage to the intestinal lining and improve intestinal barrier function. This is key for those suffering from leaky gut! Collagen peptides have also been shown to help joint function and improve skin elasticity, reduce wrinkles, and increase skin hydration.

You can purchase this at such stores as Whole Foods, natural health stores, online, and in some major grocery chains.

Flaxseeds: These nutty-tasting seeds are rich in fiber, fat, and antioxidants and are a good source of omega-3s. Their bioavailability is increased when they are ground; you can purchase whole flaxseeds and grind them in a coffee grinder.

I use these in my egg substitute (see page 280).

You can purchase this at such stores as Trader Joe's, Whole Foods, natural health stores, online, and in most major grocery chains.

Gelatin powder: This powder is rich in protein and amino acids. Like collagen peptides, gelatin may be helpful for healing leaky gut. I use this in my egg substitute (see page 280).

You can purchase this in most major grocery chains and at such stores as Whole Foods, natural health stores, and online.

Ginger (fresh, unpeeled): For most people, ginger will not be a novel ingredient. However, many of the thyroid-healing recipes call for ginger root with the skin on. This is due to the fact that the skin of the ginger is where most of the antioxidants are contained. Although peeled ginger absolutely has benefit, it is ideal to keep the skin on. Better yet, it is less prep work!

Grass-fed butter: Unlike typical butter that is from conventionally raised cows, grass-fed butter has been found to be more nutritious and contain higher amounts of omega-3 fatty acids and beta-carotene.

Himalayan pink salt: This natural salt is unprocessed and contains trace minerals, including magnesium. Commonly found table salt, on the other hand, is highly processed, contains anticaking agents, and is devoid of many trace minerals due to its processing. Additionally, pink salt does not have added iodine (unlike common table salt), and therefore may be of added benefit for those avoiding iodine due to their autoimmune thyroid conditions.

You can purchase this in some major grocery chains and at such stores as Whole Foods, natural health stores, and online.

Nettles: I use dried nettle leaves to make nettle tea, known to be high in nutrients and which may have particular benefit for those suffering from autoimmune disease and inflammation. These dried leaves are often found at health food stores and can also be found "prebagged" in packaged tea.

You can purchase this at such stores as Whole Foods, natural health stores, and online.

Raw food wraps: These food wraps, sold by a variety of different companies nationwide, are made with a combination of dehydrated vegetables and seeds. They are gluten-free, packed with nutrients, and quite delicious. A number of brands make raw wraps; most of them freeze well and can be used in place of sandwich bread or tacos in a pinch.

You can purchase this in some major grocery chains and at such stores as Whole Foods, natural health stores, and online.

Turmeric (fresh, unpeeled): Similar to ginger, turmeric contains powerful anti-inflammatory properties and also belongs to the same plant family, Zingiberaceae. Scientists have discovered that many of ginger's beneficial properties are found in the skin of the ginger. As turmeric is part of the same family and also looks similar, some herbalists and researchers also assume that we gain benefit from leaving the turmeric skin on when cooking and eating this special root. The major active compound in turmeric, called curcumin, is known to be beneficial for inflammation, cancer, and diabetes. The catch is that curcumin is not easily absorbed into the bloodstream. However, its absorption is increased by heating up turmeric and combining it with pepper and a fat (olive oil or coconut oil, etc.).

You can purchase this at such stores as Whole Foods.

Breakfasts

NETTLE TEA

SERVES 1
PHASE 1 & PHASE 2

I always have dried nettles on hand and encourage a daily cup of nettle tea, especially during Phase 1 of the Thyroid-Healing Diet. I think they taste great (especially with a little raw honey) and are always helpful in allergy season. Nettles have traditionally been used for allergic responses and hay fever. The nutrients contained in the plant can help fight inflammation and may be helpful in balancing the immune system. Research has shown that nettles may be of particular benefit to those with autoimmune disease because of their beneficial impact on the immune system. The tea has a mild, mellow, herbaceous taste and is naturally caffeine-free.

1 to 2 cups boiling water
1 to 2 tablespoons dried nettle leaves
Honey

> Steep dried nettle leaves in boiled water. Let stand for 3 minutes, then add honey to taste. Enjoy!

MY FAVORITE GREEN SHAKE

SERVES 1 TO 2
PHASE 1 & PHASE 2

I make this drink most mornings, and sometimes for an afternoon snack. The coconut milk adds fat, which gives this shake a rich and satisfying flavor. Making this shake is also a great way to get greens into your day. You can swap in other mild greens (such as baby kale, beet greens, or Swiss chard) or berries, to your liking.

⅓ to ½ (16-ounce) can coconut milk (make sure to stir it up so the top cream mixes with the watery part, if separated), or 1 cup Coconut Milk (page 285)
1 banana
3 to 4 heaping handfuls spinach
½ cup frozen strawberries
A few ice cubes
3 tablespoons grass-fed collagen peptides
Water (optional, if you like a less creamy smoothie)
⅓ avocado, peeled and pitted (optional, if you like an extra-creamy smoothie)

➤ Place all ingredients in a blender, including water to taste or avocado, if desired, blend, and serve.

SIMPLEST GREEN SMOOTHIE

SERVES 2
PHASE 1 & PHASE 2

This is an easy way to get in your greens in the morning with very minimal effort!

2 cups coconut water
2 cups spinach or any other mild greens (baby kale, beet greens, or Swiss chard)
Pinch of Himalayan pink salt
4 ice cubes

➤ Place all ingredients in a high-speed blender and blend until smooth, about 1 minute. Serve and drink!

PUMPKIN SPICE MUFFINS

MAKES 18 TO 20 MUFFINS
PHASE 1 & PHASE 2

These muffins are so satisfying and tasty! Pumpkin puree makes these muffins moist, while also providing antioxidants and vitamins A and C. They are great for breakfast on the go, an afternoon snack, or even an after-dinner treat. I make up a batch (or two) and keep some in the freezer, so I can always pull one out when I am in a hurry or having a sweet craving!

1 cup avocado oil, plus more for muffin tin
1 (16-ounce) can pure pumpkin puree
½ cup unsweetened applesauce
4 gelatin or 5 flax eggs (see box, page 280)
1¾ cups coconut sugar
1 cup coconut flour
2 cups arrowroot flour
2 teaspoons baking soda
2 teaspoons baking powder
1 teaspoon sea salt
2 teaspoons ground cinnamon
1 tablespoon ground ginger

> Preheat oven to 350°F.
> Grease 18 to 20 muffin tin wells with avocado oil.
> In a medium-size bowl, mix together pumpkin puree, applesauce, and gelatin or flax eggs.
> In a large bowl, mix together coconut sugar, coconut flour, arrowroot flour, baking soda, baking powder, salt, cinnamon, and ginger.
> Add wet ingredients to dry ingredients and stir until just incorporated; batter will be a bit lumpy.
> Scoop mixture into prepared muffin wells.
> Bake for 20 to 30 minutes, or until they are just starting to slightly brown on top. You may notice that when they are still warm out of the oven, they may appear a little "uncooked" inside. After they cool, they will firm up with a better consistency.

CARROT RAISIN BREAKFAST MUFFINS

MAKES 12 MUFFINS
PHASE 2 ONLY

These muffins are for those who have completed the reintroduction phase and have learned that they tolerate some gluten-free grains, white potatoes, and nuts. They are moist, nutritious, and delicious and keep well in the fridge for four to five days or can be frozen for up to six weeks.

⅔ cup extra-virgin, organic coconut oil or avocado oil, plus more for pan (optional)
½ (16-ounce) can pure pumpkin puree (can store the rest in a glass jar in the fridge for a few days or freeze for 2 months)

¼ cup honey

1 teaspoon pure vanilla extract

3 flax or gelatin eggs (see box below)

1½ cups brown rice flour

½ cup almond flour

⅓ cup coconut flour

⅔ cup coconut sugar

Heaping ¼ cup potato flour, if tolerated. If not tolerated,
    add an extra ¼ cup almond flour

4 teaspoons ground cinnamon

3½ teaspoons baking soda

Pinch of salt

½ cup raisins

3 large carrots, shredded

1 banana, mashed

- Preheat oven to 350°F.
- In a high-powered blender or with an electric hand mixer, blend or mix to-gether oil, pumpkin puree, honey, vanilla, and flax eggs. Set aside.
- Mix together brown rice flour, almond flour, coconut flour, coconut sugar, potato flour, cinnamon, baking soda, and salt in a large bowl.
- Add wet ingredients to dry ingredients. Then, add raisins, shredded carrots, and mashed banana and stir well.
- Scoop into 12 oiled or lined muffin tin wells. I find the trick with these muffins is to press batter down into each well, which helps muffins stick together and bind.
- Bake for 25 minutes, or until slightly browned on top.

Gelatin and Flax Eggs

Gelatin Eggs: For each egg you are replacing, combine 1 tablespoon of grass-fed gelatin with ¼ cup of water in a small saucepan, let "blossom" for a few minutes until all the gelatin has absorbed (typically this takes about 5 minutes). Then, stir over low heat until liquidy, 1 to 2 minutes. Let cool before using in a recipe; you'll want to make sure that your ingredients are at room temperature if using a gelatin egg. If they are really cold, it may affect the recipe.

Flax Eggs: For each egg you are replacing, combine 1 tablespoon of ground flaxseeds with 1½ tablespoons of cold water in a small bowl or cup. Let sit for 5 minutes and then stir vigorously for 30 seconds to 1 minute, or until the mixture is thick and somewhat jellylike. Alternatively, you can use ground chia seeds to make an egg replacement with the exact same method as you would to make the flax egg.

GRAIN-FREE PANCAKES

SERVES 2 TO 4
PHASE 1 & PHASE 2

I *love* pancakes. I love them for breakfasts, for snacks, and I even like the leftovers for dessert. These are not your typical "fluffy" pancake; the grain-free flours and coconut milk make them a bit heartier—which means they really are a filling meal. I especially like them topped with pure maple syrup and berries!

1 cup arrowroot flour
½ cup coconut flour
1 teaspoon baking soda
1 teaspoon ground cinnamon
Pinch of salt
2 flax or gelatin eggs (see box, page 280)
1 tablespoon extra-virgin, organic coconut oil, plus more for pan
1 cup canned full-fat coconut milk (for homemade, see page 285)
1 cup water

> Preheat a large skillet on medium-high heat.
> In a large bowl, combine arrowroot flour, coconut flour, baking soda, cinnamon, and salt.
> Mix together flax or gelatin eggs, coconut oil, coconut milk, and water in a medium bowl and then stir into dry ingredients until fully combined.
> Add a little coconut oil to pan and let heat, then scoop batter into pancake-shaped disks, approximately 5 inches in diameter. Cook on one side until browned and bubbles form on top, 2 to 3 minutes. Flip and cook on other side.
> Serve with your favorite sweet or savory toppings.

GRASS-FED BEEF BREAKFAST PATTIES

SERVES 4
PHASE 1 & PHASE 2

These delicious patties are packed with nutrients, such as vitamins B_{12} and B_6, iron, selenium, and zinc. Adding turmeric provides flavor and can be of added benefit to the thyroid given its anti-inflammatory nature. The patties are quick and easy to make, and can be prepared and cooked in advance and then stored in the freezer. Then, just take them out of the freezer in the morning and reheat in a skillet! These patties are also tasty with ground chicken or turkey!

1 pound grass-fed beef
2 teaspoons fresh sage, or ½ teaspoon dried
1 or 2 pinches of Himalayan pink salt

1 garlic clove, chopped or pressed
1 teaspoon ground turmeric (optional)
1 to 2 tablespoons coconut oil or avocado oil, for pan

➤ Place all ingredients, except oil, in a medium-size bowl and mix thoroughly. Divide into eight to ten portions and flatten each into a thin patty.

➤ Heat oil in a medium-size sauté pan over medium-high heat. Working in batches, add patties and cook for about 3 minutes, or until they begin to brown on bottom, then flip and cook for another 1 to 2 minutes, or until there is no pink in the middle.

➤ The patties can be stored in the fridge for 3 to 4 days or for much longer in the freezer. Serve with Sweet Potato "Fries," sautéed greens, and/or fermented veggies.

SWEET POTATO "FRIES"

SERVES 4
PHASE 1 & PHASE 2

Sweet potatoes are rich in vitamins A and C. The orange and purple varieties are also high in antioxidants. I make large batches of these "fries" regularly and add them to breakfast, lunch, or dinner meals. They keep well in the fridge for a few days and can also make a great quick snack.

2 large sweet potatoes, washed, unpeeled
1 tablespoon extra-virgin, organic coconut oil
Leaves from 6 rosemary sprigs, or 2 teaspoons dried
1 teaspoon Himalayan pink salt

➤ Preheat oven to 400°F.

➤ Slice sweet potatoes thinly, either lengthwise or widthwise; just make sure pieces are uniform.

➤ Coat a roasting pan or baking sheet with coconut oil (I use a large Pyrex baking dish). Place potatoes in pan in a single layer and sprinkle with rosemary and salt.

➤ Bake for 30 to 45 minutes, or until crispy on bottom and soft on inside.

BUCKWHEAT GROATS PORRIDGE

PHASE 2 ONLY
MAKES 4 SERVINGS

Buckwheat, contrary to what its name suggests, is not part of the wheat family at all; it is actually a seed that is consumed like a grain and thus is referred to as a "pseudocereal." Buckwheat is high in minerals and antioxidants. The cooked groats have a mild, nutty taste. Due to the fact that the body may still process buckwheat like a grain, it is best to reserve this recipe for Phase 2.

    2 cups water
    1 cup buckwheat groats
    1 heaping tablespoon extra-virgin, organic coconut oil
    A few pinches of Himalayan pink salt
    Suggested toppings: pure maple syrup, cinnamon, hemp hearts, almond milk,
        fruit, or any other topping of your choice

> Combine water, groats, coconut oil, and salt in a medium-size saucepan. Bring to a boil and then lower heat to a simmer, cover, and let cook until water is absorbed, 10 to 12 minutes. Fluff with a fork and transfer to bowls. Add your topping(s) of choice.
> Cooked buckwheat groats can be kept in the fridge and reheated with a little water for up to 3 days.

Bread Alternatives

ARROWROOT BISCUITS

PHASE 1 & PHASE 2
MAKES 6 LARGE OR 8 MEDIUM-SIZE BISCUITS

When I first began the Thyroid-Healing Diet, not having any bread at all was a challenge for me. I hadn't yet created this recipe and just simply learned to live without biscuits, buns, and sandwiches. However, now I make these once a week and keep them around to have at breakfast (especially with honey butter [recipe follows] or a meat patty) or with a little avocado and leftover meat as a "mini sandwich." I know many of my patients feel like these are a lifesaver when they adopt Phase 1 of the Thyroid-Healing Diet.

    ¼ cup avocado oil, plus more for pan
    1½ cups arrowroot flour
    ½ cup coconut flour
    1 tablespoon baking powder
    1 tablespoon honey
    1 cup canned full-fat coconut milk or homemade Almond Milk (page 286)

> Preheat oven to 450°F. Oil 6 large or 8 medium-size muffin tin wells with avocado oil.

> In a large bowl, mix together arrowroot flour, coconut flour, and baking powder. Add avocado oil and honey and blend with an electric mixer until combined (alternatively, you can do this by hand or in a food processor). Add coconut milk. Scoop mixture into prepared muffin wells and bake for 7 to 9 minutes, or until lightly browned on top.

HONEY BUTTER

MAKES ¾ CUP HONEY BUTTER
PHASE 1 & PHASE 2

This was introduced to me by our sweet Waldorf teacher Miss Judi and now I cannot imagine having muffins or biscuits without it! Grass-fed butter, opposed to regular butter from cows fed grains, has a higher amount of unsaturated fats and beta-carotene. On average, grass-fed also provides over 20 percent more anti-inflammatory omega-3 fatty acids compared to regular butter.

¾ cup unsalted grass-fed butter, at room temperature
¼ cup raw honey

> Mix both ingredients together in a bowl until smooth. Store in the fridge for up to 1 month; bring to room temperature before use.

TORTILLAS

MAKES TWELVE 6-INCH TORTILLAS
PHASE 1 & PHASE 2

Most traditional tortillas are made from flour or corn; these rely on grain-free flour. These simple tortillas can be cooked up for breakfast, lunch, or dinner, but can also be made in advance and stored in the fridge throughout the week. I typically use them for an evening meal of tacos, but they are also great wrapped around a breakfast patty.

⅔ cup coconut flour
⅔ cup arrowroot flour or cassava flour
1 teaspoon Himalayan pink salt
¼ teaspoon baking soda
1 pinch ground black pepper
⅓ cup avocado oil
⅓ cup water
¼ teaspoon cider vinegar
2 gelatin or flax eggs (see box, page 280)

> Preheat oven to 350°F. Line two cookie sheets with parchment paper. In a large bowl, mix together coconut flour, arrowroot flour, salt, baking soda, and

pepper. Then, add avocado oil, water, vinegar, and gelatin or flax eggs and blend, using an electric mixer (alternatively, you can blend by hand or with a food processor), until completely combined. Make twelve equal-size balls of dough from mixture, and with a rolling pin (or by just using your hands) flatten each ball into a 6-inch circle on a prepared baking sheet. I often bake three or four on a baking sheet at a time. Bake for 5 to 7 minutes, or until lightly browning.

Dairy Alternatives

Making your own homemade dairy milk alternatives is simple and only requires a high-speed blender and a nut milk bag: this is a fabric bag that is used to strain blended homemade coconut milk, almond milk, and other nut milk to remove any fiber or pulp.

You can purchase nut milk bags at such stores as Whole Foods, natural health stores, and online.

COCONUT MILK

MAKES 3 CUPS COCONUT MILK
PHASE 1 & PHASE 2

As mentioned previously, most store-bought dairy alternatives contain additives and preservatives that you may want to avoid (e.g., carrageenan). This homemade milk is creamy and delicious and can be prepared in minutes. As it does not contain any preservatives (aside from a pinch of salt that helps keep it fresh for a few days), it needs to be consumed within five days of preparing—but it can be made ahead of time and stored in the freezer!

3 cups filtered water
2 cups shredded unsweetened coconut
Pinch of Himalayan pink salt
1 to 2 pitted dates (optional, for sweetness)
½ teaspoon pure vanilla extract (optional, for flavor)

> Combine water, coconut, salt, and any optional ingredients in a high-speed blender. Blend for 2 to 3 minutes, or until mixture is well combined. Then, strain mixture through a nut milk bag into a large bowl. Transfer coconut milk to a tightly lidded container (quart-size or 32–fluid-ounce mason jars work very well, or repurpose 1-liter glass kombucha containers). Store in the fridge for up to 5 days; shake before use. This milk can also be frozen for up to 1 month.

ALMOND MILK

MAKES 4 CUPS ALMOND MILK
PHASE 2 ONLY

This recipe can be put together in minutes, but does require a bit of prep work as you will need to soak the almonds beforehand (ideally overnight). The result is a creamy and slightly sweet milk that is extremely versatile. Nuts are removed from Phase 1 of the Thyroid-Healing Diet, so this milk is reserved for Phase 2 and to be taken only if you do not react to almonds during the reintroduction phase.

   4 cups filtered water (for thinner almond milk, add more water)
   1 cup raw almonds (soaked overnight in filtered water)
   Pinch of Himalayan pink salt
   1 to 2 pitted dates (optional, for sweetness)
   1 teaspoon pure vanilla extract (optional, for flavor)

➤ Combine water, almonds, salt, and any optional ingredients in a high-powered blender. Blend for about 2 minutes, or until well blended. Then, strain mixture through a nut milk bag into a large bowl. Transfer almond milk to a tightly lidded container (quart-size or 32–fluid-ounce mason jars work very well, or re-purpose 1-liter glass kombucha containers). Store in the fridge for up to 4 days; shake before use. This milk can also be frozen for up to 1 month.

Vegetarian Mains and Sides

SIMPLE GREENS SALAD

SERVES 2
PHASE 1 & PHASE 2

This salad can be prepared in minutes, is packed full of nutrients, and is so delicious. Beets are sweet, add a beautiful color, and also contain folate, fiber, and vitamin C. Carrots, on the other hand, are an excellent source of vitamin A and also contain vitamins B_6 and C. Raw onion contains allicin, a substance that can help keep colds and the flu at bay. That said, the ingredients in this salad are extremely flexible. If you just aren't up to putting together a salad, buy prewashed greens, add a few slices of avocado, and drizzle some Simply Delicious Salad Dressing (recipe follows) on top. I must admit, I probably eat this salad with at least one meal, seven days a week. Add a protein, and it can be a meal unto itself.

5 to 6 large lettuce leaves (romaine, green or red, etc.)
2 large kale leaves, stemmed
1 medium-size carrot, washed
½ medium-size beet, washed
¼ red onion, thinly sliced
½ avocado, peeled and pitted
Fresh herbs of your choice, such as dill, basil, chives, etc. (optional)
Simply Delicious Salad Dressing (recipe follows)
Black cumin seeds, for garnish (optional)

➤ Tear or chop lettuce leaves and place in a large bowl. Rip kale leaves into smaller pieces and add to bowl. Shred carrot and beet (often I keep a lidded glass container full of preshredded beets and carrots in the fridge to keep them "salad ready"; however, it is quick and easy to shred carrots and beets on the spot, using a cheese grater) and add to bowl. Add red onion to salad.

➤ Slice avocado half into multiple pieces and add to bowl.

➤ Add herbs (if using). Toss with Simply Delicious Salad Dressing and black cumin seeds (if using) and serve.

SIMPLY DELICIOUS SALAD DRESSING

SERVES 2
PHASE 1 & PHASE 2

This salad dressing is essentially all I ever use at home. Simple yet tasty, it is beneficial for the gastrointestinal tract due to the fermented vinegar, and is anti-inflammatory, as it contains olive oil. It can be prepared ahead of time in larger quantities and kept for weeks in a cool, dark cupboard. I often prepare it on the spot.

¼ cup extra-virgin olive oil
2 to 3 tablespoons cider vinegar
Pinch of Himalayan pink salt
Fresh herbs, such as dill, rosemary, basil, chives, etc. (optional), finely chopped

➤ Mix together all ingredients in a small bowl or cup until blended.

CAULIFLOWER RICE

SERVES 2 TO 4
PHASE 1 & PHASE 2

This recipe makes cauliflower rice in its most basic form. It is great as a side, or added to a curry dish. There are really so many ways to flavor this! Don't be afraid to add spices and vegetables to make the rice much more flavorful!

1 cauliflower head, leaves removed
2 teaspoons avocado oil
Himalayan pink salt and/or black cumin seeds

> Break cauliflower into large chunks and place in a food processor. Pulse until coarsely chopped. Alternatively, cauliflower can be grated into ricelike shreds by using a cheese grater.
> Heat avocado oil in large skillet over medium-high heat. Add cauliflower and cook until softened, about 5 minutes. Sprinkle with salt and/or black cumin seeds to taste.

FENNEL RICELESS RISOTTO

SERVES 4
PHASE 1 & PHASE 2

A dish created by my husband, this is a unique and tasty take on the classic. Fennel bulbs, which look like a cross between celery and white onion, provide a light, aniselike taste. Fennel bulb is also high in fiber and is a source of selenium, a mineral that may help lower antibodies in those with Hashimoto's.

1 head of cauliflower
2 tablespoons unsalted grass-fed butter
1 medium-size yellow onion, diced
2 large sweet potatoes, peeled and chopped into cubes
3 golden or red beets, peeled and chopped into cubes
2 large fennel bulbs, root sliced into thin strips; leaves finely chopped
2½ cups cremini mushrooms, sliced
½ cup bone broth or vegetable stock
2 handfuls spinach
½ cup fresh dill, chopped, or 8 teaspoons dried
Himalayan pink salt

> Create cauliflower rice: Cut or break cauliflower into large chunks or florets and place in food processor. Pulse until coarsely chopped. Alternatively, cauliflower can be grated into ricelike shreds by using a cheese grater. Set aside.
> Heat butter in a large saucepan over medium heat to coat surface of pot. Add onion and sauté until cooked, about 5 minutes.
> Add sweet potatoes, beets, fennel root (reserving chopped leaves), and mushrooms. Stir, and then slowly add broth, stirring occasionally. Cook until broth has almost fully evaporated and vegetables are fully cooked, about 30 minutes. If broth has evaporated but vegetables have not fully cooked, add another ¼ cup of broth or water, as you will need a small amount of liquid for cauliflower rice to cook. Add cauliflower rice and cook until it becomes tender, another 5 to 8 minutes. Remove from heat and mix in spinach, dill, and fennel leaves. Add salt to taste.

ROASTED BRUSSELS SPROUTS

SERVES 4
PHASE 1 & PHASE 2

Brussels sprouts, part of the Brassicaceae family, are packed with nutrients. As discussed on page 138, cruciferous veggies have not actually proved harmful to the thyroid gland in reasonable amounts, and contain certain nutrients that may help fight cancer. If you have memories of boiled sprouts and have sworn off ever having them again, these will convert you! I often make larger batches of these in advance and have them with my meals throughout the week or even as a snack—they are that good!

    4 cups Brussels sprouts
    1 tablespoon extra-virgin, organic coconut oil
    1 teaspoon Himalayan pink salt

> Preheat oven to 400°F.
> Rinse Brussels sprouts, cut off and discard ends, and halve lengthwise.
> Rub a glass baking dish with coconut oil and then add Brussels sprouts. Sprinkle with salt. Roast for 30 to 40 minutes, or until slightly browned and a little crispy on outside.

Meat Mains

BAKED FISH

SERVES 2
PHASE 1 & PHASE 2

Fish is loaded with anti-inflammatory omega-3 fatty acids and is also a source of vitamin D, a nutrient that many people with autoimmune disease are lacking. This simple recipe is a go-to for me. Although my favorite fish is salmon, this basic formula can be applied to most other fish fillets of your liking. Refer to page 171 for more information on choosing fish that are low in mercury.

    1 tablespoon avocado oil or extra-virgin, organic coconut oil
    1 pound wild-caught salmon fillets
    Juice of 1 lemon
    Pinch of Himalayan pink salt

> Preheat oven to 350°F.
> Coat a baking sheet or Pyrex baking dish with oil. Place fish in prepared pan.
> Squeeze lemon juice over fish; sprinkle with salt. Bake for 13 to 15 minutes, or until fish is cooked through. Serve with vegetables, Simple Greens Salad (page 286), Sweet Potato "Fries" (page 282), or Cauliflower Rice (page 287).

BASIL GINGER CHICKEN

SERVES 4
PHASE 1 & PHASE 2

Ginger is a wonderful anti-inflammatory herb and brings so much flavor. This recipe can be made with ground ginger, but fresh ginger really tastes best.

2 to 3 tablespoons chopped fresh basil, or ½ to 1 tablespoon dried
¼ cup fresh ginger, finely chopped with skin on
2 to 3 tablespoons avocado oil
Himalayan pink salt
4 boneless chicken breasts
2 to 3 tablespoons extra-virgin, organic coconut oil

> In a large bowl, combine basil, ginger, avocado oil, and salt to taste. Stir this mixture well. Add chicken breasts, ensuring each breast has been coated well with the mixture. Heat coconut oil in a large skillet over medium-high heat. Add chicken to skillet and brown for about 3 minutes on each side, then turn again, and cook on medium-low heat, or until done and no longer pink inside. You may need to cover with a lid to ensure chicken cooks through. This dish pairs very well with Cauliflower Rice (page 287), broccoli, and asparagus.

VARIATION: Cut chicken breasts into cubes or strips and marinate in the basil ginger mixture for a few hours in the fridge. Then, cook on the skillet until done and serve with asparagus, broccoli, and Cauliflower Rice (page 287).

BLACK CUMIN SEED CHICKEN

SERVES 4
PHASE 1 & PHASE 2

This is such a tasty dish that contains black cumin seeds, a revered spice that may not only ward off colds and the flu, but also has shown to be beneficial for those with Hashimoto's.

6 to 8 skinless chicken thighs, bone in or boneless
1 teaspoon salt
Juice of ½ lemon
1 teaspoon chopped fresh turmeric, or ⅓ teaspoon ground
Pinch of chili powder
2 teaspoons coconut or avocado oil
1 large onion, diced
5 garlic cloves, crushed or finely diced
2 tablespoons grated fresh ginger
1 teaspoon ground allspice
1 teaspoon black cumin seeds
¼ cup chopped fresh cilantro leaves, for garnish

> Rub chicken thighs with salt, place in a bowl, then add lemon juice, turmeric, and chili powder. Let marinate in fridge for 10 to 20 minutes.

> Heat oil in a large skillet over medium heat. Add onion and cook for 2 to 3 minutes, or until translucent. Next, add garlic, ginger, allspice, and black cumin seeds. Stir well. Add chicken and coat well with onion and spices. Cook over medium-low heat for about 15 minutes, turning chicken regularly. If chicken begins to stick to bottom of pan, add a few tablespoons of water and continue to cook, stirring. Once chicken is cooked and is no longer pink throughout, serve garnished with cilantro.

BIBIMBAP

SERVES 6
PHASE 1 & PHASE 2

Bibimbap is a lovely Korean dish that is full of vegetables. Unfortunately, many of the common sauces used to make this dish contain preservatives, colorings, and additives. This is my take on a healthier yet still delicious bibimbap. Omit the egg if you are on Phase 1, or sensitive to eggs or egg whites. Omit beef for a vegetarian version.

2½ to 3 tablespoons extra-virgin, organic coconut oil
1 tablespoon grated, unpeeled fresh ginger
1 garlic clove, crushed
1 pound grass-fed ground beef (omit to keep this a vegetarian meal)
1½ cups fresh spinach
1 cup sliced mushrooms (I often use shiitake, but whatever mushrooms you like will work here)
1 large carrot, shredded
1 large zucchini, unpeeled, shredded
6 large eggs (optional)

2 cups prepared Cauliflower Rice (for Phase 1; page 287)
   or prepared brown rice (if on Phase 2 and only if tolerated)
6 or more tablespoons coconut aminos
Kimchi, to serve

➤ Set aside a large platter onto which you'll place all your cooked ingredients.
➤ Heat 1½ teaspoons of coconut oil in a large skillet over medium-high heat. Add ginger and garlic and sauté until fragrant, 1 to 2 minutes. Add ground beef and cover. Cook, stirring occasionally, until fully cooked through, 7 to 10 minutes. You can prepare other ingredients while beef cooks.
➤ Heat 1½ teaspoons coconut oil in a separate large skillet, add spinach and cook until wilted, 2 to 3 minutes. Transfer to platter and set it in an unheated oven to keep warm.
➤ Repeat this with mushrooms, carrots and zucchini, cooking each vegetable separately in a further 1½ teaspoons of same oil until they are soft: mushrooms require about 2 minutes of cooking; carrot, about 4 minutes; and zucchini, about 2 minutes. Add them to platter once cooked.
➤ When you've finished cooking vegetables, heat 1½ teaspoons of oil in pan and crack in eggs, keeping them all separate (work in batches if necessary). Cook on one side until its bottom has turned white, 2 to 3 minutes, then quickly flip to cook other side. You want the eggs to cook, but keep their yolk runny. Remove eggs from heat.
➤ Fill six bowls with about ⅓ cup of cauliflower rice. Then, bring out platter and top will all your cooked ingredients. Add eggs last (if using), placing one on top of each bowl of goodness!
➤ Add a tablespoons or more of coconut aminos to each bowl, along with kimchi (if using), and serve.

SHEPHERD'S PIE

SERVES 8
PHASE 1 & PHASE 2

This is my husband's take on the classic comfort food dish. Swapping in sweet potatoes for regular white potatoes adds some extra flavor and nutrients while keeping the recipe in line with the Thyroid-Healing Diet's guidelines.

   3 large sweet potatoes, unpeeled
   3 tablespoons extra-virgin, organic coconut oil
   2 garlic cloves, crushed
   1 medium-size onion, finely chopped
   3 medium-size carrots, finely chopped
   2 broccoli heads, chopped into small florets
   2 pounds grass-fed ground beef or pastured ground chicken or turkey

1 teaspoon dried thyme
1 to 2 teaspoons Himalayan pink salt

> Boil sweet potatoes until soft, 15 to 20 minutes, drain, and set aside to cool.
> Preheat oven to 350°F.
> Heat 1 tablespoon coconut oil in a large skillet over medium heat. Add garlic and onion. Lower heat to medium-low, cover, and cook until onion becomes translucent, 3 to 5 minutes. Add carrots and broccoli and cook until they have softened somewhat, 5 to 6 minutes.
> Remove veggies from pan and set aside. Add another tablespoon of oil to skillet, increase temperature to medium and add beef, thyme, and salt. Mixing well and often in pan, cook until beef is no longer pink, 7 to 10 minutes.
> Coat large baking pan (I use a 9 x 13-inch Pyrex pan) with remaining tablespoon of oil. Mix beef and vegetables together and transfer in an even layer to prepared pan.
> Mash sweet potatoes (I keep the skin on, but you can remove it if you wish), then top beef mixture with mashed potatoes.
> Bake until flavors have blended well together, about 20 minutes.

LAMB ROAST

SERVES 2 TO 4
PHASE 1 & PHASE 2

Cooking lamb used to be intimidating to me, until I realized all you have to do is prep it and pop it in the oven. It's actually supersimple and makes great leftovers.

2 lamb shanks
¼ cup avocado oil
Leaves from 6 rosemary sprigs, or 2 teaspoons dried
Himalayan pink salt and freshly ground black pepper
2 onions, chopped
1 cup bone broth
5 medium-size carrots, peeled and cut lengthwise into quarters
Mushroom Gravy (page 294), for serving

> Preheat oven to 275°F.
> Coat lamb shanks with 2 tablespoons of oil, rosemary, and salt and pepper as desired and set aside.
> Heat remaining 2 tablespoons of oil in a large cast-iron skillet over medium-high heat. Add onions and cook for about 5 minutes, or until lightly browned. Transfer onions to a roasting pan.
> In same skillet, sear each side of each lamb shank, starting with fatty side, for 2 minutes per side, or until browned.

> Transfer lamb to roasting pan, add bone broth, and cover. Roast in oven for 90 minutes. Remove from oven, add carrots, and then place back in oven and roast, covered, for an additional 30 minutes. Remove lamb and vegetables from roasting pan and cover. Pour juice from roasting pan into a saucepan to use for Mushroom Gravy. Make sure to scrape the browned bits from the bottom of the roasting pan into the saucepan.
> Lamb goes very well with Cauliflower Mash with Mushroom Gravy, Fennel Riceless Risotto (page 288), or Roasted Brussels Sprouts (page 289).

CAULIFLOWER MASH WITH MUSHROOM GRAVY

SERVES 3 TO 4
PHASE 1 & PHASE 2

Lamb just isn't the same without the addition of a tasty gravy. Cauliflower mash is a great, low-carb alternative to potatoes and pairs so nicely with the rich flavors of lamb and garlic.

    1 cauliflower head, leaves and core removed
    4 garlic cloves, crushed
    Cooked juice from lamb shank (page 293)
    2½ cups chicken or vegetable stock or Basic Bone Broth (page 295)
    8 ounces cremini mushrooms, sliced
    3 tablespoons arrowroot flour (optional)
    2 green onions, green part only, chopped

> Bring a pot of water to a boil. Cut cauliflower into small pieces and place in boiling water. Lower heat and simmer for about 10 minutes, or until fully cooked. Drain water, add crushed garlic, and mash.
> Prepare mushroom gravy: Heat saucepan of lamb juice over high heat and add stock and mushrooms. If a thicker consistency gravy is desired, add arrowroot flour to mixture. Cook, stirring constantly, until broth reduces and thickens, 7 to 9 minutes. Remove from heat and let gravy cool for 5 minutes.
> Serve gravy directly on cauliflower mash and lamb, or in a gravy boat. Top with chopped green onion.

TURKEY TACOS

SERVES 4
PHASE 1 & PHASE 2

I could eat this meal three times a week, and sometimes we do! It's easy to prepare and works great for leftovers too! The slightly bitter flavor of the turmeric pairs so well with the slightly sweet flavor of the sautéed onions. The mushrooms also provide a nice texture and add some bulk to the dish. Turkey meat makes for a lighter-tasting taco filling; however, other meats can be used for a richer flavor.

1 tablespoon butter or extra-virgin, organic coconut oil
½ onion, peeled and thinly sliced
1 cup mushrooms, washed and thinly sliced (I like cremini or shiitake, but any type will work)
1 pound ground turkey meat, or ground chicken, beef, or lamb
1 tablespoon dried turmeric, or 3 tablespoons grated fresh
¼ teaspoon freshly ground black pepper
Himalayan pink salt
To serve: tortillas (page 284); shredded romaine lettuce or other greens, fermented veggies (optional), sauerkraut (optional), black cumin seeds (optional)

> Melt butter or coconut oil in a large skillet over medium heat. Add onion and cook until softened, about 3 minutes. Add mushrooms, cover, and let cook for another 2 minutes. Add ground turkey and turmeric and cook, stirring often, until fully cooked, 5 to 8 minutes, or when no pink color is seen throughout the meat. Add pepper, then salt to taste.
> Serve with tortillas and shredded greens. Fermented veggies, sauerkraut, or a few pinches of black cumin seeds can also be used for flavor.

BASIC BONE BROTH

MAKES 14 TO 16 CUPS BROTH
PHASE 1 & PHASE 2

Bone broth is surprisingly easy to prepare. It can be made with a variety of different types of bones. Although traditionally beef marrow and knuckle bones are used, other bones work well too, such as a chicken carcass (which can be obtained from a trusted butcher or left over from cooking a chicken).

Bone broth can be prepared on the stovetop, in a slow cooker, or in a pressure cooker. This recipe provides directions for stovetop or slow cooker; however, recipes using a pressure cooker are easy to find online.

16 cups filtered water
2 pounds bones (see headnote)
3 tablespoons cider vinegar
1 bay leaf
1 teaspoon Himalayan pink salt

> Combine all ingredients in a large stockpot or slow cooker and bring to a boil. Lower heat to a simmer and cover. While broth cooks, check mixture

periodically to make sure it is still simmering. You can also skim any scum (white froth) off top if you wish when checking broth, although this is not necessary.

➤ Cook for at least 8 hours; however, ideally bone broth is cooked for 24 hours to increase its nutrient value.

➤ Let mixture cool, then strain broth. Bone broth keeps for a few days in the fridge; however, I often store some in the freezer. Bone broth can be enjoyed warm in a mug at any time of the day, or makes a fantastic base for a soup or other recipes that call for broth or stock.

Simple Snacks

HOMEMADE APPLESAUCE

MAKES 12 CUPS APPLESAUCE
PHASE 1 & PHASE 2

Applesauce is so effortless to make—and you can have it without any preservatives or added sugar. It's great eaten as a snack, added to sweet breakfasts, or served with pancakes (page 281) or even a savory meat. This recipe, although often thought of in fall, is delicious all year round.

12 to 16 apples, unpeeled, cored, and chopped
1 to 2 teaspoons cinnamon
1½ cups filtered water

➤ Put chopped apples in a large pot, such as a stockpot, ideally one that is at least 12 inches in diameter. Add ground cinnamon and cover apples with filtered water. Bring water to a boil over medium-high heat, then lower heat to a simmer and cook, covered, for 20 to 25 minutes, or until apples are soft enough to easily mash.

➤ Once cooked, mash apples in pot. (Sometimes I leave applesauce as is, with a bit of chunky fruit and skin.) You can also transfer mixture, in batches, to a blender and blend until smooth.

➤ Pour into storage containers. Homemade applesauce will keep for a few days in the fridge or store in the freezer for a later date!

KALE CHIPS

MAKES 4 TO 6 SERVINGS
PHASE 1 & PHASE 2

Kale chips are a crowd-pleaser (even with many kids). They are easily found at most health food stores but are often prepared with nuts and therefore not ideal for Phase 1. This is a simple way to prepare kale chips that is ideal for Phase 1 or Phase 2.

1 bunch kale, stemmed and rinsed
2 tablespoons avocado oil
1 teaspoon Himalayan pink salt

- Tear kale leaves into chip-size pieces. Place in a salad spinner and spin thoroughly (you want to make sure to get leaves as dry as possible).
- Spread out leaves on clean kitchen towels to air dry for at least 1 hour (Don't rush this part! If they are not really dry, you won't have nice and crispy chips).
- When leaves feel dry, preheat oven to 350°F and line two cookie sheets with parchment paper.
- Place dry leaves in a bowl and add avocado oil and salt. Rub oil and salt into leaves. Place on prepared cookie sheets, ensuring that the kale pieces are not touching one another; this will allow them to crisp up nicely.
- Bake for 10 to 12 minutes. Make sure to check on kale chips while they bake, as you do not want them to burn (and they can burn swiftly!).
- Store in an airtight container (or eat immediately!). The chips will last in a container for 1 to 2 days.

CAULIFLOWER HUMMUS

MAKES 4 SERVINGS
PHASE 1 & PHASE 2

A slightly different texture than the original hummus made with legumes, but equally as yummy. This is another recipe that can be made in advance, stored in the fridge, and used throughout the week for a snack with veggies or even an Arrowroot Biscuit (page 283).

1 tablespoon avocado oil
1 garlic head, peeled (6 to 8 cloves), papery skin removed
1 cauliflower head, cut into florets
½ teaspoon salt, or more to taste
Juice of 1 lemon
½ cup + 2 tablespoons extra-virgin olive oil

½ teaspoon ground cumin (optional)
¼ cup fresh parsley, for garnish
Pitted olives, for garnish
A sprinkle of smoked paprika, for garnish (optional)

> Preheat oven to 400°F.
> Drizzle a baking sheet with avocado oil and then place garlic and cauliflower on prepared pan. Sprinkle with salt.
> Bake for about 35 minutes, then stir and leave in oven for an additional 20 minutes, or until mixture begins to brown. Transfer mixture to a high-speed blender and blend for 1 minute. Stop machine and add lemon juice and olive oil, and cumin, if you wish. You may need to stop blender, scrape down sides, and blend a few times until oil is smoothly incorporated and hummus becomes creamy. Taste the hummus and add more salt, if desired.
> Transfer to a bowl, top with parsley and olives, plus smoked paprika (if using), and serve with freshly cut veggies.

GOLDEN TURMERIC LATTE

SERVES 1
PHASE 1 & PHASE 2

I love this caffeine-free latte after a meal or as a midafternoon pick-me-up. The turmeric and ginger are wonderful anti-inflammatory spices, and adding a pinch of ginger helps with the bioavailability of their anti-inflammatory properties.

1 cup canned full-fat or homemade Coconut Milk (page 285)
½ teaspoon ground ginger, or 1½ teaspoons grated fresh
1½ teaspoons ground turmeric powder, or 1½ tablespoons grated fresh
Pinch of ground cinnamon
Pinch of freshly ground black pepper
3 to 4 tablespoons pure maple syrup

> Place all ingredients except maple syrup in a small saucepan and bring to almost boiling while stirring/whisking constantly. You can also use a handheld milk frother to mix. Once it is just about to boil, lower heat, add maple syrup, and let simmer for about a minute. Remove from heat, pour into a mug, and enjoy!

Sweets and Desserts

RAW LEMON DATE BITES

MAKES 10 OR 11 BITES
PHASE 1 & PHASE 2

These little raw bites are great for dessert or a snack. Typically, raw snack bars and balls are made with nuts and therefore are not Phase 1–friendly! This nut-free version is sweet and lemony, thanks to the lemon zest!

½ cup dates, pitted
⅓ cup coconut manna (a.k.a. coconut butter)
½ cup shredded unsweetened coconut
1 teaspoon lemon zest

➤ Place all ingredients in a food processor and blend until well combined. The dates should be well processed and mixture should stick together and almost look "shiny" when pressed between your fingers. Transfer mixture to a piece of parchment paper. Roll mixture into a log and then wrap the parchment paper around it. Once wrapped, press and roll mixture a little more to ensure it is an evenly shaped and firm log. Chill the log in the fridge for 1 hour and then cut into ten or eleven bite-size pieces. These raw bites are best kept cool in the fridge and can also be frozen.

CHOCOLATE CAKE

SERVES 8
PHASE 1 & PHASE 2

In all honesty, this is one of the tastiest cakes I have ever had. It is nice and moist, has lots of flavor, and is not too sweet. You can use carob if you are currently on Phase 1, or use chocolate if you are on Phase 2 (again, assuming you can tolerate chocolate). If you like chocolate cake with whipped cream, make sure you try this cake with the Coconut Whipped Cream (page 300)!

2 to 3 tablespoons avocado oil, for pan
1 cup arrowroot flour
1 cup coconut flour
¾ cup carob powder (Phase 1) or unsweetened cocoa powder (Phase 2, if tolerated)
1 teaspoon baking powder

2 teaspoons baking soda
½ teaspoon Himalayan pink salt
2 cups coconut sugar
2 gelatin eggs or flax eggs (see box, page 280)
1 cup canned full-fat coconut milk
1 cup avocado oil
1 cup hot water
1 teaspoon pure vanilla extract
Coconut Whipped Cream, for serving (optional)

> Preheat oven to 350°F. Prepare two 8-inch square pans or one 9 x 13-inch pan with avocado oil.
> Mix together arrowroot flour, coconut flour, carob powder, baking powder, baking soda, salt, and coconut sugar in a large bowl.
> Stir in gelatin or flax eggs, coconut milk, oil, hot water, and vanilla.
> Beat well with an electric mixer for about 1 minute (alternatively, you can hand mix or use a food processor).
> Pour into prepared pan(s).
> Bake for 30 to 40 minutes, or until a knife or toothpick inserted into center comes out clean and cake is slightly springy when touched.
> Remove from oven and let cool. Serve plain or with coconut whipped cream.

COCONUT WHIPPED CREAM

SERVES 4 TO 6
PHASE 1 & PHASE 2

Depending on how many people you will be serving, you may need to double or triple this recipe; each can serves four to six people.

1 (16-ounce) can full-fat coconut milk
½ cup coconut sugar
Dash of pure vanilla extract

> Place can of coconut milk in fridge overnight to make sure top and bottom layer separate and cream rises to top.
> Scoop out cream (you can save "watery" milk for a smoothie) and add coconut sugar and vanilla. Blend with an electric mixer until well combined. Put in fridge and serve on the side with cake or other desserts.

APPLE PEACH CRISP

MAKES 8 TO 10 SERVINGS
PHASE 1 & PHASE 2

Nothing beats a warm fruit crisp right out of the oven. This dish also pairs very well with Coconut Whipped Cream (page 300).

    ½ cup extra-virgin, organic coconut oil, plus more for pan
    4 apples, unpeeled, cored, and sliced
    3 peaches, pitted and sliced
    ½ cup arrowroot flour
    ½ cup coconut flour
    2 teaspoons ground cinnamon
    1 teaspoon ground nutmeg
    ½ cup shredded unsweetened coconut
    ½ cup coconut sugar
    Pinch of salt
    ¼ cup cold water

> Preheat oven to 350°F. Coat a 9 x 13-inch baking dish with coconut oil.
> Place sliced apples and peaches in the prepared pan.
> Combine arrowroot flour, coconut flour, cinnamon, nutmeg, shredded coconut, coconut sugar, and salt in a medium-size bowl. Add coconut oil and cold water and mix well. Either sprinkle mixture over fruit or pat it into a thin "crust" on top of fruit.
> Bake for 30 to 40 minutes, or until lightly browned on top.

LEMONY COCONUT COOKIES

MAKES 8 COOKIES
PHASE 1 & PHASE 2

These cookies are a big hit with my family. Please note these cookies will not be what a normal "cookie" looks or feels like—they are not crispy and have a light and airy texture. But they are definitely delicious and healthier than packaged cookies!

    ⅓ cup coconut flour
    ⅓ cup arrowroot flour
    ⅓ cup shredded unsweetened coconut
    ¾ teaspoon baking soda
    ¼ teaspoon sea salt
    1 tablespoon lemon zest
    ¼ cup freshly squeezed lemon juice
    ¼ cup applesauce (for homemade, see page 296)

¼ cup coconut manna (a.k.a. coconut butter), softened
2 tablespoons pure maple syrup
2 tablespoons extra-virgin, organic coconut oil
1 teaspoon pure vanilla extract
2 gelatin or flax eggs (see box, page 280)

➤ Preheat oven to 325°F. Line two cookie sheets with parchment paper.
➤ Mix together coconut flour, arrowroot flour, shredded coconut, baking soda, and salt in a medium-size bowl.
➤ Mix together lemon zest and juice, applesauce, coconut manna, maple syrup, oil, vanilla, and gelatin or flax eggs in a large bowl, using an electric mixer (alternatively, you can mix by hand or in a food processor). Add dry ingredients to wet ingredients while still beating mixture and combine well.
➤ Scoop out dough with a dinner spoon and flatten cookies on prepared baking sheets to make 2-inch circles.
➤ Bake for 18 to 20 minutes, or until cookies are lightly browned on top. Remove from oven and let cool completely before eating (otherwise they may fall apart!). These cookies can be frozen up to 1 month.

CHOCOLATE AVOCADO PUDDING

SERVES 3 TO 4
PHASE 1 & PHASE 2

Creamy, delicious, and filled with healthy fats, this dessert is so satisfying! And, yes, avocados do really make a yummy pudding! You can use carob or chocolate, depending on whether you are on Phase 1 or Phase 2. The pudding is best served cold and should be consumed the same day (or one day after) it is prepared.

2 avocados, peeled and pitted
1 banana
1½ cups canned full-fat coconut milk
¼ cup carob (Phase 1) or unsweetened cocoa powder (Phase 2, if tolerated)
1 tablespoon pure maple syrup
1 teaspoon pure vanilla extract (if tolerated)

➤ Place all ingredients in a high-powered blender and blend until nice and smooth. Refrigerate until ready to serve.

Acknowledgments

I'd like to thank the following people: My husband, Kevin, for his patience, never-ending support, and countless home-cooked (thyroid-friendly) meals. My parents, Marti and Steve, for introducing me to both natural and conventional medicine; teaching me the values of being disciplined, open-minded, and compassionate; and your constant support in so many ways. My other set of parents, Kathy and Rick, thank you for your incredible support, kindness, and hours of your time helping our family. My brother Jon, your drive, success, and talent is a continuous source of inspiration. Marie, I am so grateful for your help with photos and design, you have the best eye! To my patients, thank you for trusting me with your care. I learn so much from you all. Renée Sedliar, your edits, knowledge, and attention to detail have made this book come alive. To the rest of the HBG team, I am so grateful for your patience and expertise. Sam Hiyate, I wouldn't have been able to do this without you! Katie C., thank you for all your help with the initial thyroid diet plan and helping me get it out to the world. My other friends and colleagues, thank you for your encouragement, insights, and inspiration. To my mentors, including Dr. T—your knowledge, support, and insights have been invaluable. The indigenous peoples of the world, you were the first to understand, value, and cherish the healing properties of plants, food, and our body's innate ability to heal naturally—thank you for all your wisdom. To all the other natural and conventional medicine practitioners who have dedicated their time and efforts to furthering the advancement of thyroid health, healing, and medicine—thank you for paving the way for improving our ability to understand and treat the thyroid gland.

APPENDIX A

Reintroduction Chart and Symptom Tracker Worksheet

In the following chart, rate your symptom score on a scale from 0 to 10 on each of the three days of the food reintroduction. Remember, each food you reintroduce to your diet will require three days of observation.

Day 1: Eat the food—1 (generous) to 2 servings—you would like to reintroduce, observe, and rate symptoms.

Day 2: Return to Phase 1 of the diet and observe and rate symptoms.

Day 3: Follow Phase 1 diet guidelines and observe and rate symptoms.

Day 4: Follow Phase 1 diet guidelines and observe and rate symptoms.

On the fifth day, it will be time to reintroduce another food.

Monitor and note whether you experience any of the symptoms in column 1 of the following chart.

Food/beverage: (e.g., coffee, gluten, dairy, etc.) _____ _____ Amount/serving size: _____				
Symptom	Date Day 1	Date Day 2	Date Day 3	Date Day 4
Hashimoto's symptoms returning that had reduced/resolved since beginning the Thyroid-Healing Diet: fatigue, brain fog, feelings of anxiety and/or depression that had lifted during Phase 1, constipation, bloating, feeling "puffy"				
Skin changes: rashes, acne, and/or redness (especially on face or ears)				
Cravings for sugar that had resolved during Phase 1				
Mood changes: irritability, racing heart				
Aches and pains (joint, muscle) that had resolved during Phase 1				
Digestive issues: diarrhea, stomach pains, bloating, gas, nausea				
"Allergy-like" symptoms: itchy mouth, throat, or ears; sneezing; runny nose; red or itchy eyes				
Other strange symptoms that started after the food was introduced (I always get nosebleeds when I eat artificial coloring or flavorings.)				

APPENDIX B

Basal Metabolic Temperature Monitoring

Monitoring thyroid function by way of measuring basal body temperature (also referred to as BBT, or basal metabolic temperature monitoring), is also a tool to not only assess baseline thyroid function, but to help gauge how well the body is responding to a new intervention, be it the Thyroid-Healing Diet, a change in medication, or a new supplement. Many studies have cited that BBT is very responsive to thyroid hormones. Thyroid hormones influence BBT by regulating available energy in the body, and by tracking BBT, we can gather more information to understand whether natural or conventional interventions are helping the thyroid function and/or can often show an early sign of overmedication.

For instance, a BBT that is consistently low throughout the month, paired with symptoms of hypothyroidism, may be an indicator that a person is hypothyroid, or that the medication dosage is too low.

It appears that thyroid function is optimal around a BBT of 98.6°F (37°C). However, conventional medical wisdom believes average BBT to be slightly lower, and in women it also fluctuates with the menstrual cycle. Before ovulation, a woman's BBT averages between 97°F (36.1°C) and 97.5°F (36.4°C). After ovulation, it rises to 97.6°F (36.4°C) to 98.6°F (37°C). Regardless, over the course of a month, a woman's temperature should be reaching close to 98.6°F, especially after ovulation. If your temperature is consistently lower than these numbers, talk to your doctor—especially if you are experiencing other symptoms of hypothyroidism.

It is best to track BBT, by way of taking your oral temperature—as soon as you wake in the morning, and ideally around the same time every day (within an hour). Digital thermometers, although convenient, can yield inaccurate results. Mercury thermometers provided a more accurate reading but are no longer sold, due to environmental and health concerns. New liquid thermometers (now using a substance known as Galinstan) are thought to be most accurate. These thermometers are available online, such as at Amazon, and may also be available at your local drugstore.

I suggest printing out this page and keeping it on your bedside table so it is easily accessible for daily morning tracking.

BASAL METABOLIC TEMPERATURE MONITORING

Here is a BBT chart that you can photocopy and use to track your own temperature.
You can also find this chart on my website at www.emilylipinski.com.

Month: .

Medication & Dosage:

Supplements:

99.9	37.72
99.8	37.67
99.7	37.61
99.6	37.56
99.5	37.5
99.4	37.44
99.3	37.39
99.2	37.33
99.1	37.28
99	37.22
98.9	37.17
98.8	37.11
98.7	37.06
98.6	37
98.5	36.94
98.4	36.89
98.3	36.83

°C	°F	1	2	3	4	5	6	7	8	9	10	11	12	13	14	15	16	17	18	19	20	21	22	23	24	25	26	27	28	29	30	31
36.78	98.2																																
36.72	98.1																																
36.67	98																																
36.61	97.9																																
36.56	97.8																																
36.5	97.7																																
36.44	97.6																																
36.39	97.5																																
36.33	97.4																																
36.28	97.3																																
36.22	97.2																																
36.17	97.1																																
36.11	97																																
36.06	96.9																																
36	96.8																																
35.94	96.7																																
35.89	96.6																																
35.83	96.5																																
35.78	96.4																																
35.72	96.3																																
35.67	96.2																																
35.61	96.1																																
35.56	96																																

Notes

INTRODUCTION: A Journey to Thyroid Health and Healing

When I first finished this book, my references formed almost a fifth of the book! I paired them down and left the ones that are ultimately the most important. However, for the ever-curious and fellow science lovers, you can find the entire list of references on my website at www.emilylipinski.com/resources.

American Academy of Allergy, Asthma and Immunology. 2017. https://www .aaaai.org/global/latest-research-summaries/Current-JACI-Research /autoimmune-disease.

Cunningham, M. W. "Post-Streptococcal Autoimmune Sequelae: Rheumatic Fever and Beyond." In *Streptococcus pyogenes: Basic Biology to Clinical Manifestations*, edited by J. J. Ferretti, D. L. Stevens, and V. A. Fischetti. Oklahoma City: University of Oklahoma Health Sciences Center, 2016. https:// www.ncbi.nlm.nih.gov/books/NBK333434/.

Müssig, Karsten, Andreas Künle, Anna-Laura Säuberlich, et al. "Thyroid Peroxidase Antibody Positivity Is Associated with Symptomatic Distress in Patients with Hashimoto's Thyroiditis." *Brain, Behavior, and Immunity* 26 (2012): 559–563. https://doi.org/10.1016/j.bbi.2012.01.006.

Roychoudhuri, R., K. Hirahara, K. Mousavi, et al. "BACH2 Represses Effector Programmes to Stabilize Treg-Mediated Immune Homeostasis." *Nature* 498 (2013): 506–510. https://doi.org/10.1038/nature12199.

CHAPTER 1: Thyroid 101

American Association of Clinical Endocrinologists (AACE). "Hashimoto's Thyroiditis: Information for Patients." 2005. http://www.aace.com/pub/thyroid brochures/pdfs/Hashimoto.pdf.

American Thyroid Association. 2019. https://www.thyroid.org/media-main /press-room/.

Arango, M. T., Y. Shoenfeld, R. Cervera, et al. "Infection and Autoimmune Diseases." In *Autoimmunity: From Bench to Bedside*, edited by J. M. Anaya, Y. Shoenfeld, A. Rojas-Villarraga, et al. Bogota, Colombia: El Rosario University Press, 2013. https://www.ncbi.nlm.nih.gov/books/NBK459437/.

Armstrong, M., E. Asuka, and A. Fingeret. "Physiology, Thyroid Function." Updated 2019. In StatPearls [internet]. Treasure Island, FL: StatPearls Publishing, 2019. https://www.ncbi.nlm.nih.gov/books/NBK537039/.

Baloch, Z., P. Carayon, B. Conte-Devolx, et al. Guidelines Committee, National Academy of Clinical Biochemistry Laboratory Medicine Practice Guidelines. "Laboratory Support for the Diagnosis and Monitoring of Thyroid Disease." *Thyroid* 13, no. 1 (2003): 3–126.

Cai, Y. J., F. Wang, Z. X. Chen, et al. "Hashimoto's Thyroiditis Induces Neuroinflammation and Emotional Alterations in Euthyroid Mice." *J Neuroinflammation* 15, no. 1 (October 29, 2018): 299. https://doi.org/10.1186/s12974-018-1341-z.

Collet, T. H., D. C. Bauer, A. R. Cappola, et al. "Thyroid Antibody Status, Subclinical Hypothyroidism, and the Risk of Coronary Heart Disease: An Individual Participant Data Analysis." *J Clin Endocrinol Metab* 99, no. 9 (20149): 3353–3362. https://doi.org/10.1210/jc.2014-1250.

Davies, T. F. "Pathogeneis of Hashimoto's Thyroiditis (Chronic Autoimmune Thyroiditis)." Accessed May 5, 2019. https://www.uptodate.com/contents/pathogenesis-of-hashimotos-thyroiditis-chronic-autoimmune-thyroiditis.

De Santis, S., E. Cavalcanti, M. Mastronardi, E. Jirillo, and M. Chieppa. "Nutritional Keys for Intestinal Barrier Modulation." *Front Immunol* 6 (December 7, 2015): 612. https://doi.org/10.3389/fimmu.2015.00612.

Endocrine Society. "Underactive Thyroid Within Normal Range May Affect Woman's Ability to Conceive." 2017. https://www.endocrine.org/news-and-advocacy/news-room/2017/underactive-thyroid-within-normal-range-may-affect-womans-ability-to-conceive.

Fasano, Alessio. "Leaky Gut and Autoimmune Diseases." *Clinical Reviews in Allergy & Immunology* 42 (2011): 71–78. https://doi.org/10.1007/s12016-011-8291-x.

Foley, Thomas. "The Relationship Between Autoimmune Thyroid Disease and Iodine Intake: A Review." *Endokrynologia Polska* 43 Suppl 1 (1992): 53–69.

Franco, J. S., J. Amaya-Amaya, and J. M. Anaya. "Thyroid Disease and Autoimmune Diseases." In *Autoimmunity: From Bench to Bedside*, edited by J. M. Anaya, Y. Shoenfeld, and A. Rojas-Villarraga. Bogota, Colombia: El Rosario University Press, 2013. https://www.ncbi.nlm.nih.gov/books/NBK459466/.

Friedman, M. Thyroid Masterclass: Session 1. HealthMastersLive.com Thyroid Masterclass 2015 course content.

Fröhlich, E., and R. Wahl. "Thyroid Autoimmunity: Role of Anti-thyroid Antibodies in Thyroid and Extra-thyroidal Diseases." *Front Immunol* 8 (May 9, 2017): 521. https://doi.org/10.3389/fimmu.2017.00521.

Hollowell, J. G., N. W. Staehling, W. D. Flanders, et al. "Serum TSH, T4, and Thyroid Antibodies in the United States Population (1988 to 1994): National Health and Nutrition Examination Survey (NHANES II)." *J Clin Endocrinol Metab* 87 (2002): 489–499.

InformedHealth.org. "How Does the Thyroid Gland Work?" Cologne, Germany: Institute for Quality and Efficiency in Health Care, 2006. Online November 17, 2010; updated April 19, 2018. https://www.ncbi.nlm.nih.gov /books/NBK279388/.

Janeway, C. A. Jr., P. Travers, M. Walport, et al. *Immunobiology: The Immune System in Health and Disease.* 5th ed. New York: Garland Science, 2001. https://www.ncbi.nlm.nih.gov/books/NBK27155/.

Kumar, H. K. V., and K. D. Modi. "Twins and Endocrinology." *Indian J Endocrinol Metab.* 2014; 18(Suppl 1): S48-S52. doi:10.4103/2230-8210.145074.

Lerner, A., and T. Matthias. "Changes in Intestinal Tight Junction Permeability Associated with Industrial Food Additives Explain the Rising Incidence of Autoimmune Disease." *Autoimmun Rev* 14, no. 6 (2015): 479–489. https:// doi.org/10.1016/j.autrev.2015.01.009.

Manzel, A., D. N. Muller, D. A. Hafler, S. E. Erdman, R. A. Linker, and M. Kleinewietfeld. "Role of 'Western Diet' in Inflammatory Autoimmune Diseases." *Curr Allergy Asthma Rep* 14, no. 1 (2014): 404. https://doi.org/10.1007 /s11882-013-0404-6.

Medline Plus Medical Encyclopedia. "Chronic Thyroiditis (Hashimoto's Disease)." February 22, 2018. http://www.nlm.nih.gov/medlineplus/ency/article /000371.htm.

Mincer, D. L., and I. Jialal. *Hashimoto Thyroiditis.* Updated 2018. In StatPearls [internet]. Treasure Island, FL: StatPearls Publishing, 2019. https://www .ncbi.nlm.nih.gov/books/NBK459262/.

Mu, Q., J. Kirby, C. M. Reilly, and X. M. Luo. "Leaky Gut as a Danger Signal for Autoimmune Diseases." *Front Immunol* 8 (May 23, 2017): 598. http:// doi/10.3389/fimmu.2017.00598.

Nana, R., and J. R. Wall. "Remission of Hashimoto's Thyroiditis in a 12 Year Old Girl with Thyroid Changes Documented by Ultrasonography." *Thyroid* 20, no. 10 (2010).

Nussey, S., and S. Whitehead. "The Thyroid Gland." In *Endocrinology: An Integrated Approach.* Oxford, England: BIOS Scientific Publishers, 2001. https:// www.ncbi.nlm.nih.gov/books/NBK28/.

Savas, E., A. Sakin, S. Aksoy, et al. "Serum Levels of Inflammation Markers in Patients with Thyroid Dysfunction and Their Associated Autoimmune Status." *Int J Clin Exp Med* 9, no. 2 (2016): 4485–4490. www.ijcem.com /ISSN:1940-5901/IJCEM0012422.

Stasiolek, M. "Neurological Symptoms and Signs in Thyroid Disease." *Thyroid Res* 8 Suppl. 1 (June 22, 2015): A25. http://doi.org/10.1186/1756-6614 -8-S1-A25.

Stojanovich, Ljudmila, and Dragomir Marisavljevich. "Stress as a Trigger of Autoimmune Disease." *Autoimmun Rev* 7 (2008): 209–213. http://doi.org /10.1016/j.autrev.2007.11.007.

Takasu, N., I. Komiya, T. Asawa, Y. Nagasawa, and T. Yamada. "Test for Recovery from Hypothyroidism During Thyroxine Therapy in Hashimoto's Thyroiditis." *Lancet* 336 (November 3, 1990): 1084–1086.

Thyroid Foundation of Canada. 2018. "About Thyroid Disease." https://thyroid .ca/thyroid-disease/.

University of Rochester Medical Center. "Free and Bound T4." Accessed May 4, 2019. https://www.urmc.rochester.edu/encyclopedia/content.aspx?content typeid=167&contentid=t4_free_and_bound_blood.

Vojdani, A., K. M. Pollard, and A. W. Campbell. "Environmental Triggers and Autoimmunity." *Autoimmune Dis* 2014 (2014): 798029. http://doi.org /10.1155/2014/798029.

Wartofsky, L., and R. A. Dickey. "The Evidence for a Narrower Thyrotropin Reference Range Is Compelling." *J Clin Endocrinol Metab* 90, no. 9 (2005): 5483–5488.

Wentz, Izabella. *Hashimoto's Protocol: A 90-Day Plan for Reversing Thyroid Symptoms and Getting Your Life Back.* New York: HarperOne, 2017.

Yahyapour, R., P. Amini, S. Rezapour, et al. "Radiation-Induced Inflammation and Autoimmune Diseases." *Mil Med Res* 5, no. 1 (March 20, 2018): 9. https://doi.org/10.1186/s40779-018-0156-7.

CHAPTER 2: Toxins

Aker, A. M., D. J. Watkins, L. E. Johns, et al. "Phenols and Parabens in Relation to Reproductive and Thyroid Hormones in Pregnant Women." *Environ Res* 151 (2016): 30–37. https://doi.org/10.1016/j.envres.2016.07.002.

Andrianou, X. D., S. Gängler, A. Piciu, et al. "Human Exposures to Bisphenol A, Bisphenol F and Chlorinated Bisphenol A Derivatives and Thyroid Function." *PLOS ONE* 11, no. 10 (2016).

Arakawa, Y. M. Watanabe, N. Inoue, M. Sarumaru, Y. Hidaka, and Y. Iwatani. "Association of Polymorphisms in DNMT1, DNMT3A, DNMT3B, MTHFR and MTRR Genes with Global DNA Methylation Levels and Prognosis of Autoimmune Thyroid Disease." *Clinical and Experimental Immunology* 170 (2012): 194–201. https://doi.org/10.1111/j.1365-2249.2012 .04646.x.

Biedermann, Sandra, Patrik Tschudin, and Koni Grob. "Transfer of Bisphenol A from Thermal Printer Paper to the Skin." *Analytical and Bioanalytical Chemistry* 398 (2010): 571–576. https://doi.org/10.1007/s00216-010-3936-9.

Björnsdotter, Maria, Jacob de Boer, and Ana Ballesteros-Gómez. "Bisphenol A and Replacements in Thermal Paper: A Review." *Chemosphere* 182 (2017). https://doi.org/10.1016/j.chemosphere.2017.05.070.

Blazejewski, C., F. Wallet, A. Rouzé, et al. "Efficiency of Hydrogen Peroxide in Improving Disinfection of ICU Rooms." *Crit Care* 19, no. 1 (February 2, 2015): 30. https://doi.org/10.1186/s13054-015-0752-9.

Blount, B. C., J. L. Pirkle, J. D. Osterloh, L. Valentin-Blasini, and K. L. Caldwell. "Urinary Perchlorate and Thyroid Hormone Levels in Adolescent and Adult Men and Women Living in the United States." *Environ Health Perspect* 114, no. 12 (December 2006): 1865–1871.

Boas, M., U. Feldt-Rasmussen, N. E. Skakkebaek, and K. M. Main. "Environmental Chemicals and Thyroid Function." *Eur J Endocrinol* 154, no. 5 (May 2006): 599–611.

Brent, G. A. "Environmental Exposures and Autoimmune Thyroid Disease." *Thyroid* 20, no. 7 (2010): 755–761. http://doi.org/10.1089/thy.2010.1636.

Calsolaro, V., G. Pasqualetti, F. Niccolai, N. Caraccio, and F. Monzani. "Thyroid Disrupting Chemicals." *Int J Mol Sci* 18, no. 12 (December 1, 2017): 2583. http://doi.org/10.3390/ijms18122583.

Chen, Yichang, Le Shu, Zhiqun Qiu, et al. "Exposure to the BPA-Substitute Bisphenol S Causes Unique Alterations of Germline Function." *PLOS Genetics* 12, no. 7 (2016): e1006223. https://doi.org/10.1371/journal.pgen.1006223.

Choi, A. L., G. Sun, Y. Zhang, and P. Grandjean. "Developmental Fluoride Neurotoxicity: A Systematic Review and Meta-analysis." *Environ Health Perspect* 120, no. 10 (October 2012): 1362–1368.

City of Toronto. "Fluoridation of City Drinking Water." 2018. Accessed August 13, 2019. https://www.toronto.ca/311/knowledgebase/kb/docs/articles /toronto-water/water-treatment-and-supply/operations-efficiency/fluorida tion-of-city-drinking-water-fluoride-levels.html.

Cortesia, Claudia, Catherine Vilcheze, Audrey Bernut, et al. "Acetic Acid, the Active Component of Vinegar, Is an Effective Tuberculocidal Disinfectant." *mBio* 5 (2014). https://doi.org/10.1128/mBio.00013-14.

Edmondson D., M. Nordness, M. Zacharisen, V. Kurup, and J. Fink. "Allergy and 'Toxic Mold Syndrome.'" *Annals of Allergy, Asthma and Immunology*. 94. (2005): 234–249. doi:10.1016/S1081-1206(10)61301-4.

"Emerging Contaminant in Soil, Water and Food." *Chemosphere* 150 (2016): 667–677. http://doi.org/10.1016/j.chemosphere.2016.01.109.

Environmental Working Group. "Safe Sunscreen Guide 2019." https://www .ewg.org/sunscreen/report/executive-summary/.

Grady, Harvey. "Immunomodulation Through Castor Oil Packs." *Journal of Naturopathic Medicine* 7, no. 1 (Year unknown): 84–89.

Harvey, P. W., and D. J. Everett. "Significance of the Detection of Esters of *p*-Hydroxybenzoic Acid (Parabens) in Human Breast Tumours." *J Appl Toxicol* 24 (2004): 1–4.

Houlihan, Jane, Timothy Kropp, Richard Wiles, Sean Gray, and Chris Campbell. "Body Burden: The Pollution in Newborns." July 14, 2005. Washington, DC: Environmental Working Group, May 28, 2007: 1, 13, 16, 27–29, 31, 35. www.ewg.org/research/body-burden-pollution-newborns.

Iheozor-Ejiofor, Z., H. V. Worthington, T. Walsh, et al. "Water Fluoridation for the Prevention of Dental Caries." Cochrane Database of Systematic Reviews 2015, no. 6, art. no. CD010856. https://doi.org/10.1002/14651858 .CD010856.pub2.

"Infection Prevention and Control of Epidemic- and Pandemic-Prone Acute Respiratory Infections in Health Care." Annex G, *Use of Disinfectants: Alcohol and Bleach.* Geneva: World Health Organization, 2014. https://www.ncbi .nlm.nih.gov/books/NBK214356/.

Koeppe, Erika, Kelly Ferguson, Justin Colacino, and John Meeker. "Relationship Between Urinary Triclosan and Paraben Concentrations and Serum Thyroid Measures in NHANES 2007–2008." *Science of the Total Environment* 445–446C (2013): 299–305. https://doi.org/10.1016/j.scitotenv.2012.12.052.

Kumarathilaka, P., C. Oze, S. P. Indraratne, and M. Vithanage. "Perchlorate as an Emerging Contaminant in Soil, Water and Food." *Chemosphere* 150 (2016): 667–677. https://doi.org/10.1016/j.chemosphere.2016.01.109.

Kwa, M., L. J. Welty, and S. Xu. "Adverse Events Reported to the US Food and Drug Administration for Cosmetics and Personal Care Products." *JAMA Intern Med* 177, no. 8 (2017): 1202–1204.

Lagarde, Fabien, Claire Beausoleil, Scott Belcher, et al. "Non-monotonic Dose-Response Relationships and Endocrine Disruptors: A Qualitative Method of Assessment." *Environmental Health* 14 (2015). http://doi.org /10.1186/1476-069X-14-13.

Lanphear, B. P. "Low-Level Toxicity of Chemicals: No Acceptable Levels?" *PLOS Biol* 15, no. 12 (December 19, 2017): e2003066. http://doi.org/10.1371 /journal.pbio.2003066.

Li, Na, Donghong Wang, Yiqi Zhou, Mei Ma, Jian Li, and Zijian Wang. "Dibutyl Phthalate Contributes to the Thyroid Receptor Antagonistic Activity in Drinking Water Processes." *Environmental Science & Technology* 44, no. 17 (2010).

Louis, G. W., D. R. Hallinger, M. Janay Braxton, A. Kamel, and T. E. Stoker. "Effects of Chronic Exposure to Triclosan on Reproductive and Thyroid Endpoints in the Adult Wistar Female Rat." *J Toxicol Environ Health A* 80, no. 4 (2017): 236–249.

Lu, L., T. Zhan, M. Ma, et al. "Thyroid Disruption by Bisphenol S Analogues via Thyroid Hormone Receptor β: in Vitro, in Vivo, and Molecular Dynamics Simulation Study." *Environmental Science & Technology* 52, no. 11 (2018): 6617–6625. https://doi.org/10.1021/acs.est.8b00776.

Malik, R., and H. Hodgson. "The Relationship Between the Thyroid Gland and the Liver." *QJM* 95, no. 9 (September 2002): 559–569. https://doi.org/10 .1093/qjmed/95.9.559.

National Research Council Committee on the Health Risks of Phthalates. "Table 2: Phthalate Exposure Assessment in Humans. Phthalates and Cumulative Risk Assessment: The Tasks Ahead." Washington, DC: National Academies Press, 2008.

Panth, P., G. Guerin, and N. M. DiMarco. "A Review of Iodine Status of Women of Reproductive Age in the USA." *Biol Trace Elem Res* 188, no. 1 (2019): 208–220. http://doi.org/10.1007/s12011-018-1606-5.

Park, Choonghee, Wookhee Choi, Moonyoung Hwang, et al. "Associations Between Urinary Phthalate Metabolites and Bisphenol A Levels, and Serum Thyroid Hormones Among the Korean Adult Population—Korean National Environmental Health Survey (KoNEHS) 2012–2014." *Science of the Total Environment* (2017): 584. https://doi.org/10.1016/j.scitotenv.2017.01.144.

Peckham, S., and N. Awofeso. "Water Fluoridation: A Critical Review of the Physiological Effects of Ingested Fluoride as a Public Health Intervention." *Scientific World Journal* 2014 (2014): 293019. https://doi.org/10.1155/2014/293019.

Roundtable on Environmental Health Sciences, Research, and Medicine; Board on Population Health and Public Health Practice; Institute of Medicine. "Identifying and Reducing Environmental Health Risks of Chemicals in Our Society: Workshop Summary." In *The Challenge: Chemicals in Today's Society*. Washington, DC: National Academies Press, 2014. https://www.ncbi.nlm.nih.gov/books/NBK268889/.

Susheela, A. K., M. Bhatnagar, K. Vig, and N. K. Mondal. "Excess Fluoride Ingestion and Thyroid Hormone Derangements in Children Living in Delhi, India." *Fluoride* 38, no. 2 (2005): 98–108.

United States Environmental Protection Agency. "EPA Releases First Major Update to Chemicals List in 40 Years." 2019. Accessed December 22, 2019. https://www.epa.gov/newsreleases/epa-releases-first-major-update-chemicals-list-40-years.

Wang, J., L. Pan, S. Wu, et al. "Recent Advances on Endocrine Disrupting Effects of UV Filters." *Int J Environ Res Public Health* 13, no. 8 (August 3, 2016): 782. https://doi.org/10.3390/ijerph13080782.

Wang, N., Y. Zhou, C. Fu, et al. "Influence of Bisphenol A on Thyroid Volume and Structure Independent of Iodine in School Children," edited by C.-Q. Gao. *PLOS ONE* 10, no. 10 (2015): e0141248. https://doi.org/10.1371/journal.pone.0141248.

World Health Organization. "Water Sanitization Hygiene: Water Related Diseases." 2019. Accessed August 13, 2019. https://www.who.int/water_sanitation_health/diseases-risks/diseases/fluorosis/en/.

CHAPTER 3: Stress

American Psychological Association. "Gender and Stress." 2010. Accessed July 14, 2019. https://www.apa.org/news/press/releases/stress/2010/gender-stress.

Anderson, E., and G. Shivakumar. "Effects of Exercise and Physical Activity on Anxiety." *Front Psychiatry* 4 (April 23, 2013): 27. https://doi.org/10.3389/fpsyt.2013.00027.

Blue Zones. "What Exercise Is Best for Optimal Health and Longevity?" 2018. Accessed July 20, 2019. https://www.bluezones.com/2018/01/what-exercise -best-happy-healthy-life/.

Breuner, C. W., B. Delehanty, and R. Boonstra. "Evaluating Stress in Natural Populations of Vertebrates: Total CORT Is Not Good Enough." *Funct Ecol* 27 (2013): 24–36. https://doi.org/10.1111/1365-2435.12016.

Brown, R. P., and P. L. Gerberg. "Sudarshan Kriya Yogic Breathing in the Treatment of Stress, Anxiety, and Depression: Part II—Clinical Applications and Guidelines." *J Altern Complement Med* 11 (2005): 711–717. https:// doi.org/10.1089/acm.2005.11.711.

Çiloğlu, Figen, Ismail Peker, Aysel Pehlivan, et al. "Exercise Intensity and Its Effects on Thyroid Hormones." *Neuro Endocrinology Letters* 26 (2006): 830–834.

Cleveland Clinic. "Diaphragmatic Breathing." 2019. Accessed July 20, 2019. https://my.clevelandclinic.org/health/articles/9445-diaphragmatic -breathing.

Georgetown University Medical Center. "Mindfulness Meditation Training Lowers Biomarkers of Stress Response in Anxiety Disorder: Hormonal, Inflammatory Reactions to Stress Were Reduced After Meditation Training, in Rigorous NIH-Sponsored Trial." ScienceDaily, January 24, 2017. www .sciencedaily.com/releases/2017/01/170124111354.htm.

Gottfried, S. *The Hormone Cure*. New York: Scribner, 2013.

Heim, C., U. Ehlert, and D. H. Hellhammer. "The Potential Role of Hypocortisolism in the Pathophysiology of Stress-Related Bodily Disorders." *Psychoneuroendocrinology* 25 (2000): 1–35.

Helmreich, D. L., and D. Tylee. "Thyroid Hormone Regulation by Stress and Behavioral Differences in Adult Male Rats." *Horm Behav* 60, no. 3 (2011): 284–291. https://doi.org/10.1016/j.yhbeh.2011.06.003.

Hill, E. E., E. Zack, C. Battaglini, M. Viru, A. Viru, and A. C. Hackney. "Exercise and Circulating Cortisol Levels: The Intensity Threshold Effect." *J Endocrinol Invest* 31 (2008): 587–591. https://doi.org/10.1007/BF03 345606.

Hunter, MaryCarol R., Brenda W. Gillespie, and Sophie Yu-Pu Chen. "Urban Nature Experiences Reduce Stress in the Context of Daily Life Based on Salivary Biomarkers." *Frontiers in Psychology* 10 (2019). https://doi.org /10.3389/fpsyg.2019.00722.

Lautenbach, Franziska, and Sylvain Laborde. Chapter 19: "The Influence of Hormonal Stress on Performance." In *Performance Psychology*, edited by Markus Raab, Babett Lobinger, Sven Hoffmann, Alexandra Pizzera, and Sylvain Laborde. London: Academic Press, 2016, 315–328.

Luders, E. "Exploring Age-Related Brain Degeneration in Meditation Practitioners." *Annals of the New York Academy of Sciences* 1307 (2013): 82–88.

Luders, E., F. Kurth, E. A. Mayer, et al. "The Unique Brain Anatomy of Meditation Practitioners: Alterations in Cortical Gyrification." *Frontiers in Human Neuroscience* 6 (2012): 1–9.

Ma, X., Z. Q. Yue, Z. Q. Gong, et al. "The Effect of Diaphragmatic Breathing on Attention, Negative Affect and Stress in Healthy Adults." *Front Psychol* 8 (June 6, 2017): 874. https://doi.org/10.3389/fpsyg.2017.00874.

Matud, M. "Gender Differences in Stress and Coping Styles." *Personality and Individual Differences* 37 (2004): 1401–1415. https://doi.org/10.1016/j.paid .2004.01.010.

Mizokami, Tetsuya, Audrey Li, Samer El-Kaissi, and Jack Wall. "Stress and Thyroid Autoimmunity." *Thyroid* 14 (2005): 1047–1055. https://doi.org/10.1089 /thy.2004.14.1047.

Morgan, Nani, Irwin Michael, Mei Chung, and Chenchen Wang. "The Effects of Mind-Body Therapies on the Immune System: Meta-Analysis." *PLOS ONE* 9 (2014): e100903. https://doi.org/10.1371/journal.pone.0100903.

Mullington, J. M. "Endocrine Function During Sleep and Sleep Deprivation." *Encyclopedia of Neuroscience.* 2009. https://doi.org/10.1016B978-008045046 -9.00067-X.

Naik, G. S., G. S. Gaur, and G. K. Pal. "Effect of Modified Slow Breathing Exercise on Perceived Stress and Basal Cardiovascular Parameters." *Int J Yoga* 11, no. 1 (2018): 53–58. https://doi.org/10.4103/ijoy.IJOY_41_16.

Turakitwanakan, Wanpen, Chantana Mekseepralard, and Panaree Busarakum-tragul. "Effects of Mindfulness Meditation on Serum Cortisol of Medical Students." *J Med Assoc Thai* 96, Suppl 1 (2013): S90–95.

Verma, R., Y. P. Balhara, and C. S. Gupta. "Gender Differences in Stress Response: Role of Developmental and Biological Determinants." *Ind Psychiatry J* 20, no. 1 (2011): 4–10. https://doi.org/10.4103/0972-6748.98407.

Walter, K. N., E. J. Corwin, J. Ulbrecht, et al. "Elevated Thyroid Stimulating Hormone Is Associated with Elevated Cortisol in Healthy Young Men and Women." *Thyroid Res* 5, no. 1 (October 30, 2012): 13. https://doi.org /10.1186/1756-6614-5-13.

Wondisford, F. E. "A Direct Role for Thyroid Hormone in Development of the Adrenal Cortex." *Endocrinology* 156, no. 6 (2015): 1939–1940. https://doi .org/10.1210/en.2015-1351.

CHAPTER 4: Electromagnetic Fields (EMFs)

Amin, A. I., N. M. Hegazy, K. S. Ibrahim, H. Mahdy-Abdallah, H. A. Hammouda, and E. E. Shaban. "Thyroid Hormone Indices in Computer Workers with Emphasis on the Role of Zinc Supplementation." *Open Access Maced J Med Sci* 4, no. 2 (2016): 296–301. https://doi.org/10.3889/oamjms .2016.041.

Asl, J. F., B. Larijani, M. Zakerkish, F. Rahim, K. Shirbandi, and R. Akbari. "The Possible Global Hazard of Cell Phone Radiation on Thyroid Cells and Hormones: A Systematic Review of Evidences." *Environ Sci Pollut Res Int* 26, no. 18 (2019): 18017–18031. https:// doi.org/10.1007/s11356-019 -05096-z.

Baby, N. M., G. Koshy, and A. Mathew. "The Effect of Electromagnetic Radiation Due to Mobile Phone Use on Thyroid Function in Medical Students Studying in a Medical College in South India." *Indian J Endocrinol Metab* 21, no. 6 (2017): 797–802. https://doi.org/10.4103/ijem.IJEM_12_17.

Baldwin, M., S. A. Bach, and S. A. Lewis. "Effects of Radio-Frequency Energy on Primate Cerebral Activity." *Neurology* 10 (1960): 178–187. https://doi.org/10.1212/WNL.10.2.178.

Bank of America Newsroom. 2015. Accessed June 30, 2019. https://newsroom.bankofamerica.com/press-releases/consumer-banking/perpetually-plugged-americas-smartphone-obsession-continues-many.

Boscolo, Paolo. "Electromagnetic Fields and Autoimmune Diseases." *Prevention & Research* (2014). https://doi.org/10.11138/PER/2014.3.2.079.

Canadian Initiative for Safe Wireless, Electric and Electromagnetic Policy (WEEP). "What Is Electrohypersensitvity." 2008. Accessed June 28, 2019. http://www.weepinitiative.org/areyou.html.

Cauter, E. V., K. Knutson, R. Leproult, et al. "The Impact of Sleep Deprivation on Hormones and Metabolism." *Medscape Neurology* 7, no. 1 (2005). https://www.medscape.org/viewarticle/502825.

Ely, T. S., D. E. Goldman, and J. Z. Hearon. "Heating Characteristics of Laboratory Animals Exposed to Ten-Centimeter Microwaves." *IEEE Transactions on Biomedical Engineering* 11 (1964): 123–135. https://doi.org/10.1109/TBME.1964.4502322.

Environmental Working Group. "Does Your Cellphone Case Increase Your Radiation Exposure?" 2015. Accessed March 22, 2020. https://www.ewg.org/research/does-your-cell-phone-case-raise-your-radiation-exposure.

German, K. "A Cell Phone Case for Reducing Cell Phone Radiation." 2011. http://www.cnet.com/news/a-cell-phone-case-for-reducing-cell-phone-radiation/.

Government Accountability Office (GAO). "Exposure and Testing Requirements for Mobile Phones Should Be Reassessed." GAO-12-771, 2012. http://www.gao.gov/assets/600/592901.pdf.

Guerriero, F., and G. Ricevuti. "Extremely Low Frequency Electromagnetic Fields Stimulation Modulates Autoimmunity and Immune Responses: A Possible Immuno-modulatory Therapeutic Effect in Neurodegenerative Diseases." *Neural Regen Res* 11, no. 12 (2016): 1888–1895. https://doi.org/10.4103/1673-5374.195277.

Havas, Magda. "Are You Electrically Sensitive." 2009. Accessed June 28, 2019. https://www.magdahavas.com/wp-content/uploads/2009/10/ehs-quiz.pdf.

Hsiao, Y. H., Y. T. Chen, C. M. Tseng, et al. "Sleep Disorders and Increased Risk of Autoimmune Diseases in Individuals Without Sleep Apnea." *Sleep* 38, no. 4 (April 1, 2015): 581–586. https://doi.org/10.5665/sleep.4574.

Johansson, Olle. "Electrohypersensitivity: State-of-the-Art of a Functional Impairment." *Electromagnetic Biology and Medicine* 25 (2006): 245–258. https://doi.org/10.1080/15368370601044150.

Koren, G. "Exposure to Electromagnetic Fields During Pregnancy." *Can Fam Physician* 49 (2003): 151–153.

Koyu, Ahmet, Gokhan Cesur, Fehmi Ozguner, Mehmet Akdogan, Hakan Mollaoglu, and S. Ozen. "Effects of 900 MHz Electromagnetic Field on TSH and Thyroid Hormones in Rats." *Toxicology Letters* 157 (2005): 257–262. https://doi.org/10.1016/j.toxlet.2005.03.006.

Kresser, Chris. "Do You Need to Protect Yourself Against EMF Dangers?" 2019. Accessed June 28, 2019. https://chriskresser.com/do-you-need-to-protect-yourself-against-emf-dangers/.

Kundi, M. "EMFs and Childhood Leukemia." *Environ Health Perspect* 115, no. 8 (2007): A395. https://doi.org/10.1289/ehp.10217.

Li, De-Kun, Hong Chen, Jeannette R. Ferber, Roxana Odouli, and Charles Quesenberry. "Exposure to Magnetic Field Non-ionizing Radiation and the Risk of Miscarriage: A Prospective Cohort Study." *Scientific Reports* 7, no. 1 (2017). https://doi.org/10.1038/s41598-017-16623-8.

Luo, J., N. C. Deziel, H. Huang, et al. "Cell Phone Use and Risk of Thyroid Cancer: A Population-Based Case-Control Study in Connecticut." *Ann Epidemiol* 29 (October 29, 2018): 39–45. https://doi.org/10.1016/j.annepidem.2018.10.004.

Marshall, T. G., and T. J. R. Heil. "Electrosmog and Autoimmune Disease." *Immunol Res* 65, no. 1 (2017): 129–135. https://doi.org/10.1007/s12026-016-8825-7.

Michaelson, Sol M. "Effects of Exposure to Microwaves: Problems and Perspectives." *Environ Health Perspect* 8 (1974): 133–155. https://doi.org/10.1289/ehp.748133.

Mortazavi, S. A., S. Taeb, S. M. Mortazavi, et al. "The Fundamental Reasons Why Laptop Computers Should Not Be Used on Your Lap." *J Biomed Phys Eng* 6, no. 4 (December 1, 2016): 279–284.

National Institutes of Health, National Institute of Neurological Disorders and Stroke. "Brain Basics: Understanding Sleep." 2019. https://www.ninds.nih.gov/Disorders/Patient-Caregiver-Education/Understanding-Sleep.

National Toxicology Program, U.S. Department of Health and Human Sciences. "Cellphone Frequency Radiation." 2019. Accessed June 20, 2019. https://ntp.niehs.nih.gov/results/areas/cellphones/index.html.

Pall, Martin. "Scientific Evidence Contradicts Findings and Assumptions of Canadian Safety Panel 6: Microwaves Act Through Voltage-Gated Calcium Channel Activation to Induce Biological Impacts at Non-thermal Levels, Supporting a Paradigm Shift for Microwave/Lower Frequency Electromagnetic Field Action." *Reviews on Environmental Health* 30, no. 2 (2015). https://doi.org/10.1515/reveh-2015-0001.

Pineault, Nicolas. *The Non-tinfoil Guide to EMFs: How to Fix Our Stupid Use of Technology.* N & G Media, 2017.

Pineault, Nicolas. "Are You Electrosensitive?" 2019. Accessed January 28, 2019. https://nontinfoilemf.com/.

Plante, Amber. "How the Body Uses Electricity." *University of Maryland Gazette*, February 2019. Accessed June 28, 2019. https://www.graduate.umaryland.edu/gsa/gazette/February-2016/How-the-human-body-uses-electricity/.

Pong Research Corporation. Pong May 31, 2012 filing to the Federal Communications Commission, WT Docket 11-186. http://apps.fcc.gov/ecfs/document/view?id=7021921006.

Rod, N. H., A. S. Dissing, A. Clark, T. A. Gerds, and R. Lund. "Overnight Smartphone Use: A New Public Health Challenge? A Novel Study Design Based on High-Resolution Smartphone Data." *PLOS ONE* 13, no. 10 (October 16, 2018): e0204811. https://doi.org/10.1371/journal.pone.0204811.

Sinha, Rakesh. "Chronic Non-thermal Exposure of Modulated 2450 MHz Microwave Radiation Alters Thyroid Hormones and Behavior of Male Rats." *International Journal of Radiation Biology* 84 (2008): 505–513. https://doi.org/10.1080/09553000802085441.

Snutch, T. P., J. Peloquin, E. Mathews, et al. "Molecular Properties of Voltage-Gated Calcium Channels." In *Madame Curie Bioscience Database*. Austin, TX: Landes Bioscience, 2000–2013. https://www.ncbi.nlm.nih.gov/books/NBK6181/.

Spiegel, K., R. Leproult, and E. Van Cauter. "Impact of Sleep Debt on Metabolic and Endocrine Function." *Lancet* 354 (1999): 1435–1439.

Statement by the Advisors to the International EMF Scientist Appeal. August 18, 2017. Accessed June 20, 2019. https://www.emfscientist.org/.

World Health Organization. "Electromagnetic Fields (EMFs)." Accessed June 28, 2019. https://www.who.int/peh-emf/about/WhatisEMF/en/index1.html.

CHAPTER 5: Genes

Abu-Hassan, Diala W., Abdullah N. Alhouri, Nadera A. Altork, et al. "MTHFR Gene Polymorphisms in Hypothyroidism and Hyperthyroidism Among Jordanian Females." *Archives of Endocrinology and Metabolism* 63, no 3 (2019): 280–287. Epub May 2, 2019. https://dx.doi.org/10.20945/2359-3997000000133.

American Association for the Advancement of Science. News release, June 10, 2019. Accessed August 16, 2019. https://www.eurekalert.org/pub_releases/2019-06/mcg-lsn060719.php.

Anand, P., A. B. Kunnumakkara, C. Sundaram, et al. "Cancer Is a Preventable Disease That Requires Major Lifestyle Changes." *Pharm Res* 25, no. 9 (2008): 2097–2116. https://doi.org/10.1007/s11095-008-9661-9.

Arakawa, Y., M. Watanabe, N. Inoue, M. Sarumaru, Y. Hidaka, and Y. Iwatani. "Association of Polymorphisms in DNMT1, DNMT3A, DNMT3B, MTHFR and MTRR Genes with Global DNA Methylation Levels and Prognosis of Autoimmune Thyroid Disease." *Clinical and Experimental Immunology* 170 (2012): 194–201. https://doi.org/10.1111/j.1365-2249.2012.04646.x.

Buhner, S., C. Buning, J. Genschel, et al. "Genetic Basis for Increased Intestinal Permeability in Families with Crohn's Disease: Role of CARD15 3020insC Mutation?" *Gut* 55, no. 3 (2006): 342–347. https://doi.org/10.1136/gut .2005.065557.

Ceccarelli, F., N. Agmon-Levin, and C. Perricone. "Genetic Factors of Auto-immune Diseases." *J Immunol Res* 2017 (2017): 2789242. https://doi.org /10.1155/2017/2789242.

Chopra, I. J., D. H. Solomon, and U. Chopra, "Abnormalities in Thyroid Function in Relatives of Patients with Graves' Disease and Hashimoto's Thyroiditis: Lack of Correlation with Inheritance of HLA B8." *Journal of Clinical Endocrinology and Metabolism* 45, no. 1 (1977): 45–54.

Coppedè, F. "Epigenetics and Autoimmune Thyroid Diseases." *Front Endocrinol* (Lausanne) 8 (June 29, 2017): 149. https://doi.org/10.3389/fendo.2017.00149.

Davies, Terry F., Rauf Latif, and Xiaoming Yin. "New Genetic Insights from Autoimmune Thyroid Disease." *Journal of Thyroid Research* 2012, art. ID 623852 (2012). https://doi.org/10.1155/2012/623852.

DNA Company. "Genome Pulse Report." 2018.

Fasano, A., and T. Shea-Donohue. "Mechanisms of Disease: The Role of Intestinal Barrier Function in the Pathogenesis of Gastrointestinal Autoimmune Diseases." *Nat Clin Pract Gastroenterol Hepatol* 2 (2005): 416–422. https:// doi.org/10.1038/ncpgasthep0259.

Gerenova, J., and S. Stanilova. "IL-12B and IL-10 Gene Polymorphisms in the Development of Hashimoto's Thyroiditis. *Int J Immunogenet* 43 (2016): 397–403. https://doi.org/10.1111/iji.12293.

Goodrich, Julia K., Emily Davenport, Andrew G. Clark, and Ruth Ley. "The Relationship Between the Human Genome and Microbiome Comes into View." *Annual Review of Genetics* 51 (2017). https://doi.org/10.1146 /annurev-genet-110711-155532.

Inoue, N., M. Watanabe, N. Ishido, et al. "The Functional Polymorphisms of VDR, GC and CYP2R1 Are Involved in the Pathogenesis of Autoimmune Thyroid Diseases." *Clin Exp Immunol* 178, no. 2 (2014): 262–269. https:// doi.org/10.1111/cei.12420.

Kevans, David, Williams Turpin, Karen Madsen, et al. "Determinants of Intestinal Permeability in Healthy First-Degree Relatives of Individuals with Crohn's Disease." *Inflammatory Bowel Diseases* 21 (2015). https://doi.org /10.1097/MIB.0000000000000323.

Kippola, P. *Beat Autoimmune.* New York: Citadel Press, 2019.

Korach-Rechtman, H., S. Freilich, S. Gerassy-Vainberg, et al. "Murine Genetic Background Has a Stronger Impact on the Composition of the Gut Microbiota Than Maternal Inoculation or Exposure to Unlike Exogenous Microbiota." *Appl Environ Microb* (2019). https://doi.org/10.1128/AEM .00826-19.

Lynch, Ben. *Dirty Genes.* New York: Harper One, 2018.

Mohammed, Monsoor. Genome pulse report review. Conversation with author, August 14, 2019, Ontario, Canada.

Nagayama, Yuji. "Radiation-Related Thyroid Autoimmunity and Dysfunction." *Journal of Radiation Research* 59 (2017): 1–10. https://doi.org/10.1093/jrr/rrx054.

Paknys, Gintaras, Anatolijus Juozas Kondrotas, and Egidijus Kevelaitis. "Risk Factors and Pathogenesis of Hashimoto's Thyroiditis." *Medicina* (Kaunas, Lithuania) 45 (2009): 574–583.

Piacentini, Sara, Paola Maria Monaci, Renato Polimanti, Dario Manfellotto, and Maria Fuciarelli. "GSTO2*N142D Gene Polymorphism Associated with Hypothyroidism in Italian Patients." *Molecular Biology Reports* 40 (2012). https://doi.org/10.1007/s11033-012-2253-0.

Saranac, L., S. Zivanovic, B. Bjelakovic, H. Stamenkovic, M. Novak, and B. Kamenov. "Why Is the Thyroid So Prone to Autoimmune Disease?" *Horm Res Paediatr* 75 (2011): 157–165. https://doi.org/10.1159/000324442.

Turpin, Williams, Osvaldo Espin-Garcia, Larbi Bedrani, et al. "Analysis of Genetic Association of Intestinal Permeability in Healthy First-Degree Relatives of Patients with Crohn's Disease." *Inflammatory Bowel Diseases* izz116. https://doi.org/10.1093/ibd/izz116.

US National Library of Medicine, Genetics Home Reference. "VDR Gene." 2019. Accessed August 15, 2019. https://ghr.nlm.nih.gov/gene/VDR.

Wartofsky, Leonard. "Combination L-T3 and L-T4 Therapy for Hypothyroidism." *Current Opinion in Endocrinology, Diabetes, and Obesity* 20 (2013). https://doi.org/10.1097/01.med.0000432611.03732.49.

Wernimont, S. M., F. Raiszadeh, P. J. Stover, et al. "Polymorphisms in Serine Hydroxymethyltransferase 1 and Methylenetetrahydrofolate Reductase Interact to Increase Cardiovascular Disease Risk in Humans." *J Nutr* 141, no. 2 (2011): 255–260. https://doi.org/10.3945/jn.110.132506.

Wiersinga, W. M. "Hashimoto's Thyroiditis." In *Thyroid Diseases: Pathogenesis, Diagnosis, and Treatment*, edited by P. Vitti and L. Hegedüs. New York: Springer, 2018.

CHAPTER 6: Infections

Allert, Stefanie, Toni Förster, Carl Svensson, et al. "Candida albicans—Induced Epithelial Damage Mediates Translocation Through Intestinal Barriers." *mBio* 9 (2018): e00915-18. https://doi.org/10.1128/mBio.00915-18.

Buhner, S. *Herbal Antivirals*. North Adams, MA: Storey, 2013.

Caselli, E., M. C. Zatelli, R. Rizzo, et al. "Virologic and Immunologic Evidence Supporting an Association Between HHV-6 and Hashimoto's Thyroiditis." *PLOS Pathog* 8, no. 10 (2012): e1002951. https://doi.org/10.1371/journal.ppat.1002951.

Chedid, V., S. Dhalla, J. O. Clarke, et al. "Herbal Therapy Is Equivalent to Rifaximin for the Treatment of Small Intestinal Bacterial Overgrowth." *Glob Adv Health Med* 3, no. 3 (2014): 16–24. https://doi.org/10.7453/gahmj.2014.019.

Citera, M., P. R. Freeman, and R. I. Horowitz. "Empirical Validation of the Horowitz Multiple Systemic Infectious Disease Syndrome Questionnaire for Suspected Lyme Disease." *Int J Gen Med* 10 (September 4, 2017): 249–273. https://doi.org/10.2147/IJGM.S140224.

Columbia University Irving Medical Center, Lyme and Tick Borne Disease Research Center. "Diagnosis of Lyme Disease." Accessed August 20, 2019. https://www.columbia-lyme.org/diagnosis.

Corapcioglu, Demet, Vedia Tonyukuk, Mehmet Kiyan, et al. "Relationship Between Thyroid Autoimmunity and Yersinia enterocolitica Antibodies." *Thyroid* 12 (2002): 613–617. https://doi.org/10.1089/105072502320288483.

Dagci, Hande, Sebnem Ustun, Memduh S. Taner, Galip Ersoz, Ferit Karacasu, and Seza Budak. "Protozoon Infections and Intestinal Permeability." *Acta tropica* 81 (2002): 1–5. https://doi.org/10.1016/S0001-706X(01)00191-7.

De Bolle, L., L. Naesens, and E. De Clercq. "Update on Human Herpesvirus 6 Biology, Clinical Features, and Therapy." *Clin Microbiol Rev* 18, no. 1 (2005): 217–245. https://doi.org/10.1128/CMR.18.1.217-245.2005.

Dinleyici, Ener, Makbule Eren, Nihal Dogan, Serap Reyhanioglu, Zeynel Yargic, and Yvan Vandenplas. "Clinical Efficacy of Saccharomyces boulardii or Metronidazole in Symptomatic Children with Blastocystis hominis Infection." *Parasitology Research* 108 (2010): 541–545. https://doi.org/10.1007/s00436-010-2095-4.

Dittfeld, A., K. Gwizdek, M. Michalski, and R. Wojnicz. "A Possible Link Between the Epstein-Barr Virus Infection and Autoimmune Thyroid Disorders." *Cent Eur J Immunol* 41, no. 3 (2016): 297–301. https://doi.org/.5114/ceji.2016.63130.

Ercolini, A. M., and S. D. Miller. "The Role of Infections in Autoimmune Disease." *Clin Exp Immunol* 155, no. 1 (2009): 1–15. https://doi.org/10.1111/j.1365-2249.2008.03834.x.

Eschler, D. C., A. Hasham, and Y. Tomer. "Cutting Edge: The Etiology of Autoimmune Thyroid Diseases." *Clin Rev Allergy Immunol* 41, no. 2 (2011): 190–197. https://doi.org/10.1007/s12016-010-8245-8.

Fasano, Alessio. "Leaky Gut and Autoimmune Diseases." *Clinical Reviews in Allergy & Immunology* 42 (2011): 71–78. https://doi.org/10.1007/s12016-011-8291-x.

Gao, X., E. M. Lampraki, S. Al-Khalidi, M. A. Qureshi, R. Desai, and J. B. Wilson. "N-Acetylcysteine (NAC) Ameliorates Epstein-Barr Virus Latent Membrane Protein 1 Induced Chronic Inflammation." *PLOS ONE* 12, no. 12 (December 11, 2017): e0189167. https://doi.org/10.1371/journal.pone.0189167.

Geiler, Janina, Martin Michaelis, Patrizia Naczk, et al. "N-Acetyl-L-cysteine (NAC) Inhibits Virus Replication and Expression of Pro-inflammatory Molecules in A549 Cells Infected with Highly Pathogenic H5N1 Influenza A Virus." *Biochemical Pharmacology* 79 (2009): 413–420. https://doi.org/10.1016/j.bcp.2009.08.025.

Guggenheim, A. G., K. M. Wright, and H. L. Zwickey. "Immune Modulation from Five Major Mushrooms: Application to Integrative Oncology." *Integr Med* (Encinitas) 13, no. 1 (2014): 32–44.

Heyma, P., L. C. Harrison, and R. Robins-Browne. "Thyrotrophin (TSH) Binding Sites on Yersina enterocolitica Recognized by Immunoglobulins from Humans with Graves' Disease." *Clin Exp Immunol* 64, no. 2 (1986): 249–254.

Holz, C., A. Busjahn, H. Mehling, et al. "Significant Reduction in Helicobacter pylori Load in Humans with Non-viable Lactobacillus reuteri DSM17648: A Pilot Study." *Probiotics Antimicrob Proteins* 7, no. 2 (2015): 91–100.

Hou, Yi, Wen Sun, Chengfei Zhang, et al. "Meta-analysis of the Correlation Between Helicobacter pylori Infection and Autoimmune Thyroid Diseases." *Oncotarget* 8 (2015). https://doi.org/10.18632/oncotarget.22929.

Kashimura, H., K. Suzuki, M. Hassan, et al. "Polaprezinc, a Mucosal Protective Agent, in Combination with Lansoprazole, Amoxycillin and Clarithromycin Increases the Cure Rate of Helicobacter pylori Infection." *Aliment Pharmacol Ther* 13, no. 4 (1999): 483–487.

Khangura, Preet. "Superseding SIBO." Seminar and webinar, 2017.

Kippola, P. *Beat Autoimmune.* New York: Citadel Press, 2019.

Kundukad, B., M. Schussman, K. Yang, et al. "Mechanistic Action of Weak Acid Drugs on Biofilms." *Sci Rep* 7, no. 1 (July 6, 2017): 4783. https://doi.org/10.1038/s41598-017-05178-3.

Larouche, V., and M. Tamilia. "Cytomegalovirus-Mononucleosis-Induced Thyroiditis in an Immunocompetent Patient." *Endocrinol Diabetes Metab Case Rep* 2017 (November 24, 2017): 17-0142. https://doi.org/10.1530/EDM-17-0142.

Lauritano, Ernesto Cristiano, Anna Lisa Bilotta, Maurizio Gabrielli, et al. "Association Between Hypothyroidism and Small Intestinal Bacterial Overgrowth." *Journal of Clinical Endocrinology & Metabolism* 92, no. 11 (November 1, 2007): 4180–4184. https://doi.org/10.1210/jc.2007-0606.

Malfertheiner, P., F. Megraud, C. A. O'Morain, et al. "Management of Helicobacter pylori Infection—The Maastricht IV/ Florence Consensus Report." *Gut* 61, no. 5 (April 5, 2012): 646–664.

Matsukura, T., and H. Tanaka. "Applicability of Zinc Complex of L-Carnosine for Medical Use." *Biochemistry* (Moscow) 65, no. 7 (2000): 817–823.

Mayo Clinic Laboratories. "The Past, Present and (Possible) Future of Serologic Testing in Lyme Disease." 2016. Accessed February 5, 2020. https://news.mayocliniclabs.com/2016/05/16/the-past-present-and-possible-future-of-serologic-testing-for-lyme-disease/.

Mehling, H., and A. Busjahn. "Non-viable Lactobacillus reuteri DSMZ 17648 (Pylopass) as a New Approach to Helicobacter pylori Control in Humans." *Nutrients* 5, no. 8 (2013): 3062–3073.

Messina, Giovanni, Teresa Esposito, Jean-Marc Lobaccaro, et al. "Effects of Low-Carbohydrate Diet Therapy in Overweight Subjects with Autoimmune Thyroiditis: Possible Synergism with ChREBP." *Drug Design, Development and Therapy* 10 (2016): 2939–2946. https://doi.org/10.2147/DDDT.S106440.

Namkin, K., M. Zardast, and F. Basirinejad. "Saccharomyces boulardii in Helicobacter pylori Eradication in Children: A Randomized Trial from Iran." *Iran J Pediatr* 26, no. 1 (2016): e3768. https://doi.org/10.5812/ijp.3768.

Naylor, Gregory, and Anthony Axon. "Role of Bacterial Overgrowth in the Stomach as an Additional Risk Factor for Gastritis." *Canadian Journal of Gastroenterology* 17 (2003): 13B–17B. https://doi.org/10.1155/2003/350347.

Patil, A. D. "Link Between Hypothyroidism and Small Intestinal Bacterial Overgrowth." *Indian J Endocrinol Metab* 18, no. 3 (2014): 307–309. https://doi.org/10.4103/2230-8210.131155.

Pender, M. P. "CD8+ T-Cell Deficiency, Epstein-Barr Virus Infection, Vitamin D Deficiency, and Steps to Autoimmunity: A Unifying Hypothesis." *Autoimmune Dis* 2012 (2012): 189096. https://doi.org/10.1155/2012/189096.

Pimentel, M., E. J. Chow, and H. C. Lin. "Eradication of Small Intestinal Bacterial Overgrowth Reduces Symptoms in Irritable Bowel Syndrome." *Am J Gastroenterol* 95, no. 12 (2000): 3503–3506.

Prummel, Mark F., and Wilmar M. Wiersinga. "Yersinia enterocolitica Infections and Autoimmune Thyroid Diseases." *Pediatr Blood Cancer* (2004): 363–372. https://doi.org/10.1016/B978-044451271-0.50029-6.

Rajič, Borko, Jurica Arapović, Kazimir Raguž, Mladen Bošković, Senaida Marina Babić, and Suzana Maslać. "Eradication of Blastocystis hominis Prevents the Development of Symptomatic Hashimoto's Thyroiditis: A Case Report." *Journal of Infection in Developing Countries* 9 (2015): 788–791. https://doi.org/10.3855/jidc.4851.

Shapiro, Eugene, and Gary P. Wormser. "Lyme Disease in 2018: What Is New (and What Is Not)." *JAMA* 320 (2018). https://doi.org/10.1001/jama.2018.10974.

Shmuely, H., I. Shimon, and L. A. Gitter. "Helicobacter pylori Infection in Women with Hashimoto Thyroiditis: A Case-Control Study." *Medicine* (Baltimore) 95, no. 29 (2016): e4074. https://doi.org/10.1097/MD.0000000000004074.

"Takeaways from the 2017 Integrative SIBO Conference: Practice Updates from the Speakers." *Natural Medicine Journal* 9, no. 6 (June 2017).

Virili, Camilla, and Marco Centanni. "Does Microbiota Composition Affect Thyroid Homeostasis?" *Endocrine* 49 (2014). https://doi.org/10.1007/s12020-014-0509-2.

Wasserman, Ellen E., Kenrad Nelson, Noel Rose, et al. "Infection and Thyroid Autoimmunity: A Seroepidemiologic Study of TPOaAb." *Autoimmunity* 42 (2009): 439–446. https://doi.org/10.1080/08916930902787716.

CHAPTER 7: Special Considerations: Fertility, Pregnancy, and Postpartum

Abdel Rahman, A. H., H. Aly Abbassy, and A. A. Abbassy. "Improved in Vitro Fertilization Outcomes After Treatment of Subclinical Hypothyroidism in Infertile Women." *Endocr Pract* 16 (2010): 792–797.

Aghajanova, L., M. Lindeberg, I. B. Carlsson, et al. "Receptors for Thyroid-Stimulating Hormone and Thyroid Hormones in Human Ovarian Tissue." *Reprod Biomed* 18 (2009): 337–347.

Ajayi, A. F., R. E. Akhigbe, and L. O. Ajayi. "Hypothalamic-Pituitary-Ovarian Axis in Thyroid Dysfunction." *West Indian Med J* 62 (2013): 835–838.

Alexander, Erik, Elizabeth N. Pearce, Gregory A. Brent, et al. "2017 Guidelines of the American Thyroid Association for the Diagnosis and Management of Thyroid Disease During Pregnancy and the Postpartum." *Thyroid* 27 (2017). https://doi.org/10.1089/thy.2016.0457.

Al-Katib, Sami, Maisem M. H. Al-Kaabi, Wasen Ghasi Al-Safi, and Aseel Albderi. "Effect of the Relationship Between Vitamin C and Serum Ferritin on Fertility." *Al-Kufa University Journal for Biology* 10 (2018): 33–39.

American Family Physician. "Chasteberry." *Am Fam Physician* 72, no. 5 (September 1, 2005): 821–824. Accessed July 29, 2019. https://www.aafp.org/afp/2005/0901/p821.html.

Baldassarre, M. E., V. Palladino, A. Amoruso, et al. "Rationale of Probiotic Supplementation During Pregnancy and Neonatal Period." *Nutrients* 10, no. 11 (November 6, 2018): 1693. https://doi.org/10.3390/nu10111693.

Bates, Melissa A., Christina Brandenberger, Ingeborg I. Langohr, et al. "Silica-Triggered Autoimmunity in Lupus-Prone Mice Blocked by Docosahexaenoic Acid Consumption." *PLOS ONE* 11, no. 8 (2016): e0160622. https://doi.org/10.1371/journal.pone.0160622.

Benvenga, S., M. T. Vigo, D. Metro, R. Granese, R. Vita, and M. Le Donne. "Type of Fish Consumed and Thyroid Autoimmunity in Pregnancy and Postpartum." *Endocrine* 52 (2016): 120–129. https://doi.org/10.1007/s12020-015-0698-3.

Benzie, I. F. F., and S. Wachtel-Galor, eds. *Herbal Medicine: Biomolecular and Clinical Aspects.* 2nd ed. Boca Raton, FL: CRC Press/Taylor & Francis, 2011.

Carney, Leo, Jeffrey Quinlan, and Janet M. West. "Thyroid Disease in Pregnancy." *Am Fam Physician* 89, no. 4 (2014): 273–278.

Cenksoy, Pinar, Cem Ficicioglu, Ozge Kizilkale, et al. "Can Coenzyme Q10 Supplementation Protect the Ovarian Reserve Against Oxidative Damage?" *Journal of Assisted Reproduction and Genetics* 33 (2016). https://doi.org/10.1007/s10815-016-0751-z.

Chiu, Yu Han, A. E. Karmon, Audrey Gaskins, et al. "Serum Omega-3 Fatty Acids and Treatment Outcomes Among Women Undergoing Assisted Reproduction." *Human Reproduction* (Oxford, England) 33 (2017): 1–10. https://doi.org/10.1093/humrep/dex335.

Cho, M. K. "Thyroid Dysfunction and Subfertility." *Clin Exp Reprod Med* 42, no. 4 (2015): 131–135. https://doi.org/10.5653/cerm.2015.42.4.131.

Di Bari, Flavia, Roberta Granese, Maria Le Donne, Roberto Vita, and Salvatore Benvenga. "Autoimmune Abnormalities of Postpartum Thyroid Diseases." *Frontiers in Endocrinology* 8 (2017): 166. https://doi.org/10.3389/fendo.2017.00166.

Dugoua, Jean-Jacques, Marcio Machado, Xu Zhu, Xin Chen, Gideon Koren, and Thomas Einarson. "Probiotic Safety in Pregnancy: A Systematic Review and Meta-analysis of Randomized Controlled Trials of Lactobacillus, Bifidobacterium, and Saccharomyces spp." *Journal d'obstétrique et gynécologie du Canada (JOGC)* 31 (2009): 542–552. https://doi.org/10.1016/S1701-2163 (16)34218-9.

ERFA. Prescribing Information. 2016. https://pdf.hres.ca/dpd_pm/00034857 .PDF.

Garber, Jeffrey R., Rhoda H. Cobin, Hossein Gharib, et al. "Clinical Practice Guidelines for Hypothyroidism in Adults." Co-sponsored by the American Association of Clinical Endocrinologists (AACE) and the American Thyroid Association, Inc. (ATA). *Thyroid* 22 (2012). https://doi.org/10.1089 /thy.2012.0205.

Gardner, Z., and M. McGuffin. *American Herbal Products Association's Botanical Safety Handbook.* 2nd ed. Boca Raton, FL: CRC Press/Taylor & Francis, 2013.

Greenberg, J. A., and S. J. Bell. "Multivitamin Supplementation During Pregnancy: Emphasis on Folic Acid and l-Methylfolate." *Rev Obstet Gynecol* 4, nos. 3–4 (2011): 126–127.

Greenberg, J. A., S. J. Bell, and W. V. Ausdal. "Omega-3 Fatty Acid Supplementation During Pregnancy." *Rev Obstet Gynecol* 1, no. 4 (2008): 162–169.

Herrick, K. A., C. G. Perrine, Y. Aoki, and K. L. Caldwell. "Iodine Status and Consumption of Key Iodine Sources in the U.S. Population with Special Attention to Reproductive Age Women." *Nutrients* 10, no. 7 (July 6, 2018): 874. https://doi.org/10.3390/nu10070874.

Hsu, Mei-Chi, Chia-Yi Tung, and Hsing-E. Chen. "Omega-3 Polyunsaturated Fatty Acid Supplementation in Prevention and Treatment of Maternal Depression: Putative Mechanism and Recommendation." *Journal of Affective Disorders* (2018): 238. https://doi.org/10.1016/j.jad.2018.05.018.

International Society for the Study of Fatty Acids and Lipids (ISSFAL). "GOED Recommendations for EPA and DHA." Accessed July 26, 2019. https:// www.issfal.org/goed-recommendations-for-epa-dha.

Kim, C. H., J. W. Ahn, S. P. Kang, S. H. Kim, H. D. Chae, and B. M. Kang. "Effect of Levothyroxine Treatment on in Vitro Fertilization and Pregnancy Outcome in Infertile Women with Subclinical Hypothyroidism Undergoing in Vitro Fertilization/Intracytoplasmic Sperm Injection." *Fertil Steril* 95 (2011): 1650–1654.

Le Donne, M., A. Alibrandi, R. Vita, D. Zanghì, O. Triolo, and S. Benvenga. "Does Eating Oily Fish Improve Gestational and Neonatal Outcomes? Findings from a Sicilian Study." *Women Birth* 29 (2016): e50–7. https://doi .org/10.1016/j.wombi.2015.12.005.

Levant, B. "N-3 (Omega-3) Fatty Acids in Postpartum Depression: Implications for Prevention and Treatment." *Depress Res Treat* 2011 (2011): 467349. https://doi.org/10.1155/2011/467349.

Liu, Y., J. J. Alookaran, and J. M. Rhoads. "Probiotics in Autoimmune and Inflammatory Disorders." *Nutrients* 10, no. 10 (October 18, 2018): 1537. https://doi.org/10.3390/nu10101537.

Maraka, S., N. M. Singh Ospina, G. Mastorakos, and D. T. O'Keeffe. "Subclinical Hypothyroidism in Women Planning Conception and During Pregnancy: Who Should Be Treated and How?" *J Endocr Soc* 2, no. 6 (May 3, 2018): 533–546. https://doi.org/10.1210/js.2018-00090

Martin, A., C. Horowitz, A. Balbierz, and E. A. Howell. "Views of Women and Clinicians on Postpartum Preparation and Recovery." *Matern Child Health J* 18, no. 3 (2014): 707–713. https://doi.org/10.1007/s10995-013-1297-7.

Meletis, Chris. "Iodine Health Implications of Deficiency." *Journal of Evidence-Based Complementary & Alternative Medicine* 16 (2011): 190–194. https://doi.org/10.1177/2156587211414424.

Middleton, P., J. C. Gomersall, J. F. Gould, E. Shepherd, S. F. Olsen, and M. Makrides. "Omega-3 Fatty Acid Addition During Pregnancy." Cochrane Database of Systematic Reviews, issue 11 (2018), art. no.: CD003402. https://doi.org/10.1002/14651858.CD003402.pub3.

Miller, Elizabeth. "The Reproductive Ecology of Iron in Women." *American Journal of Physical Anthropology* 159 (2016): S172–S195. https://doi.org/10.1002/ajpa.22907.

Milman, Nils, Thomas Bergholt, Lisbeth Eriksen, et al. "Iron Prophylaxis During Pregnancy—How Much Iron Is Needed? A Randomized Dose-Response Study of 20–80 mg Ferrous Iron Daily in Pregnant Women." *Acta obstetricia et gynecologica Scandinavica* 84 (2005): 238–247. https://doi.org/10.1111/j.0001-6349.2005.00610.x.

Mori, Kouki, Yoshinori Nakagawa, and Hiroshi Ozaki. "Does the Gut Microbiota Trigger Hashimoto's Thyroiditis?" *Discovery Medicine* 14 (2012): 321–326.

Mumford, S. L., J. E. Chavarro, C. Zhang, et al. "Dietary Fat Intake and Reproductive Hormone Concentrations and Ovulation in Regularly Menstruating Women." *Am J Clin Nutr* 103, no. 3 (2016): 868–877. https://doi.org/10.3945/ajcn.115.119321.

National Institutes of Health. "Selenium: Fact Sheet for Health Professionals." 2019. Accessed August 9, 2019. https://ods.od.nih.gov/factsheets/Selenium-HealthProfessional/.

"Negro, R., G. Greco, T. Mangieri, A. Pezzarossa, D. Dazzi, and H. Hassan. "The Influence of Selenium Supplementation on Postpartum Thyroid Status in Pregnant Women with Thyroid Peroxidase Autoantibodies." *J Clin Endocrinol Metab* 92 (2007): 1263–1268. https://doi.org/10.1210/jc.2006-1821.

Nehra, D., H. D. Le, E. M. Fallon, et al. "Prolonging the Female Reproductive Lifespan and Improving Egg Quality with Dietary Omega-3 Fatty Acids." *Aging Cell* 11, no. 6 (2012): 1046–1054. https://doi.org/10.1111/acel.12006.

Quintino-Moro, Alessandra, Denise E. Zantut-Wittmann, Marcos Tambascia, Helymar Machado, and Arlete Fernandes. "High Prevalence of Infertility

Among Women with Graves' Disease and Hashimoto's Thyroiditis." *International Journal of Endocrinology* 2014 (2014): 982705. https://doi.org/10.1155/2014/982705.

Rafieian-Kopaei, M., and M. Movahedi. "Systematic Review of Premenstrual, Postmenstrual and Infertility Disorders of Vitex Agnus Castus." *Electron Physician* 9, no. 1 (January 25, 2017): 3685–3689. https://doi.org/10.19082/3685.

Rao, M., Z. Zeng, S. Zhao, and L. Tang. "Effect of Levothyroxine Supplementation on Pregnancy Outcomes in Women with Subclinical Hypothyroidism and Thyroid Autoimmuneity Undergoing in Vitro Fertilization/Intracytoplasmic Sperm Injection: An Updated Meta-analysis of Randomized Controlled Trials." *Reprod Biol Endocrinol* 16, no. 1 (September 24, 2018): 92. https://doi.org/10.1186/s12958-018-0410-6.

Rao, Meng, Zhengyan Zeng, Fang Zhou, et al. "Effect of Levothyroxine Supplementation on Pregnancy Loss and Preterm Birth in Women with Subclinical Hypothyroidism and Thyroid Autoimmunity: A Systematic Review and Meta-analysis." *Human Reproduction Update* 25, no. 3 (May–June 2019): 344–361. https://doi.org/10.1093/humupd/dmz003.

Raven, J. H., Q. Chen, R. J. Tolhurst, and P. Garner. "Traditional Beliefs and Practices in the Postpartum Period in Fujian Province, China: A Qualitative Study." *BMC Pregnancy Childbirth* 7 (June 21, 2007): 8. https://doi.org/10.1186/1471-2393-7-8.

Saran, S., B. S. Gupta, R. Philip, et al. "Effect of Hypothyroidism on Female Reproductive Hormones." *Indian J Endocrinol Metab* 20, no. 1 (2016): 108–113. https://doi.org/10.4103/2230-8210.172245.

Sathi, P., Shirin Kalyan, C. L. Hitchcock, M. Pudek, and Jerilynn Prior. "Progesterone Therapy Increases Free Thyroxine Levels—Data from a Randomized Placebo-Controlled 12-Week Hot Flush Trial." *Clinical Endocrinology* 79 (2012). https://doi.org/10.1111/cen.12128.

Shonibare, Tolulope, and Alia Munir. "Management of Hypothyroidism in Pregnancy with Armour Thyroid." *Endocrine Abstracts* (2015). https://doi.org/10.1530/endoabs.38.P486.

Tamaki, H., N. Amino, K. Takeoka, et al. "Thyroxine Requirement During Pregnancy for Replacement Therapy of Hypothyroidism." *Obstet Gynecol* 76, no. 2 (August 1990): 230–233.

Trentini, D., and M. Shomon. *Your Healthy Pregnancy with Thyroid Disease*. Boston: Da Capo Press, 2016.

Tuli, H. S., S. S. Sandhu, and A. K. Sharma. "Pharmacological and Therapeutic Potential of Cordyceps with Special Reference to Cordycepin." *3 Biotech* 4, no. 1 (2014): 1–12. https://doi.org/10.1007/s13205-013-0121-9.

van den Boogaard, Emmy, Rosa Vissenberg, Jolande A. Land, et al. "Significance of (Sub)clinical Thyroid Dysfunction and Thyroid Autoimmunity Before Conception and in Early Pregnancy: A Systematic Review." *Human Reproduction Update* 17, no. 5 (September–October 2011): 605–619. https://doi.org/10.1093/humupd/dmr024.

Westphal, L. M., M. L. Polan, and A. S. Trant. "A Nutritional Supplement for Improving Fertility in Women: A Pilot Study." *Journal of Reproductive Medicine* 49 (2004): 289–293.

Xu, Y., V. Nisenblat, C. Lu, et al. "Pretreatment with Coenzyme Q10 Improves Ovarian Response and Embryo Quality in Low-Prognosis Young Women with Decreased Ovarian Reserve: A Randomized Controlled Trial." *Reprod Biol Endocrinol* 16, no. 1 (March 27, 2018): 29. https://doi.org/10.1186/s12958-018-0343-0.

Zhu, Jihe, Blagica Arsovska, and Kristina Kozowska. "Spontaneous Abortion Treatment with Acupuncture and Cordyceps sinensis." *Journal of Case Reports in Practice* 4 (2016): 30–31.

CHAPTER 8: The Thyroid-Healing Diet

Abbott, R. D., A. Sadowski, and A. G. Alt. "Efficacy of the Autoimmune Protocol Diet as Part of a Multi-disciplinary, Supported Lifestyle Intervention for Hashimoto's Thyroiditis." *Cureus* 11, no. 4 (April 27, 2019): e4556. https://doi.org/10.7759/cureus.4556.

Adebamowo, Clement, D. Spiegelman, F. Danby, Lindsay Frazier, W. Willett, and Michelle Holmes. "High School Dietary Dairy Intake and Teenage Acne." *Yearbook of Dermatology and Dermatologic Surgery 2006* (2006): 158–159. https://doi.org/10.1016/S0093-3619(08)70113-8.

Akçay, M. N., and G. Akçay. "The Presence of Anti Glidan Antibodies in Autoimmune Thyroid Disease." *Hepatogastroenterology* 50 Suppl 2 (December 2003).

American Heart Association. "Trans Fats." Accessed May 5, 2019. https://www.heart.org/en/healthy-living/healthy-eating/eat-smart/fats/trans-fat.

Aris, Aziz, and Samuel Leblanc. "Maternal and Fetal Exposure to Pesticides Associated to Genetically Modified Foods in Eastern Townships of Quebec, Canada." *Reproductive Toxicology* (Elmsford, NY) 31 (2011): 528–533. https://doi.org/10.1016/j.reprotox.2011.02.004.

Bajaj, J. K., P. Salwan, and S. Salwan. "Various Possible Toxicants Involved in Thyroid Dysfunction: A Review." *J Clin Diagn Res* 10, no. 1 (2016): FE01–FE3. https://doi.org/10.7860/JCDR/2016/15195.7092.

Baranski, Marcin, Dominika Średnicka-Tober, N. Volakakis, et al. "Higher Antioxidant and Lower Cadmium Concentrations and Lower Incidence of Pesticide Residues in Organically Grown Crops: A Systematic Literature Review and Meta-analyses." *British Journal of Nutrition* 112 (2014): 1–18. https://doi.org/10.1017/S0007114514001366.

Bendsen, N. T., R. Christensen, Else Bartels, and Arne Astrup. "Consumption of Industrial and Ruminant Trans Fatty Acids and Risk of Coronary Heart Disease: A Systematic Review and Meta-analysis of Cohort Studies." *European Journal of Clinical Nutrition* 65 (2011): 773–783. https://doi.org/10.1038/ejcn.2011.34.

Bian, X., L. Chi, B. Gao, P. Tu, H. Ru, and K. Lu. "Gut Microbiome Response to Sucralose and Its Potential Role in Inducing Liver Inflammation in Mice." *Front Physiol* 8 (July 24, 2017): 487. https://doi.org/10.3389/fphys.2017.00487.

Blasbalg, Tanya L., Joseph R. Hibbeln, Christopher E. Ramsden, Sharon F. Majchrzak, and Robert R. Rawlings. "Changes in Consumption of Omega-3 and Omega-6 Fatty Acids in the United States During the 20th Century." *American Journal of Clinical Nutrition* 93, no. 5 (May 2011): 950–962. https://doi.org/10.3945/ajcn.110.006643.

Carman, J. A., H. R. Vlieger, L. J. Steegd, et al. "A Long-Term Toxicology Study on Pigs Fed a Combined Genetically Modified (GM) Soy and GM Maize Diet." *Journal of Organic Systems* 8 (2013): 38–54.

Catassi, C., J. C. Bai, B. Bonaz, et al. "Non-Celiac Gluten Sensitivity: The New Frontier of Gluten Related Disorders." *Nutrients* 5, no. 10 (2013): 3839–3853. https://doi.org/10.3390/nu5103839.

Chang, H. C., and D. R. Doerge. "Dietary Genistein Inactivates Rat Thyroid Peroxidase in Vivo Without an Apparent Hypothyroid Effect." *Toxicol Appl Pharmacol* 168, no. 3 (November 1, 2000): 244–252.

Chavarro, Jorge, Janet Rich-Edwards, B. A. Rosner, and Walter Willett. "A Prospective Study of Dairy Foods Intake and Anovulatory Infertility." *Human Reproduction* (Oxford, England) 22 (2007): 1340–1347. https://doi.org/10.1093/humrep/dem019.

Chen, Qianru, Xiang Gao, Hongwei Zhang, Bafang Li, Guangli Yu, and Bo Li. "Collagen Peptides Administration in Early Enteral Nutrition Intervention Attenuates Burn-Induced Intestinal Barrier Disruption: Effects on Tight Junction Structure." *Journal of Functional Foods* 55 (2019). https://doi.org/10.1016/j.jff.2019.02.028.

Chevrier, J., M. Warner, R. B. Gunier, P. Brambilla, B. Eskenazi, and P. Mocarelli. "Serum Dioxin Concentrations and Thyroid Hormone Levels in the Seveso Women's Health Study." *Am J Epidemiol* 180, no. 5 (2014): 490–498. https://doi.org/10.1093/aje/kwu160.

Collin, P., J. Salmi, O. Hällström, T. Reunala, and A. Pasternack. "Autoimmune Thyroid Disorders and Coeliac Disease." *Eur J Endocrinol* 130 (1994): 137–140. ISSN 0804-4643.

Contempre, B., J. Dumont, B. Ngo, et al. "Effect of Selenium Supplementation in Hypothyroid Subjects of an Iodine and Selenium Deficient Area: The Possible Danger of Indiscriminate Supplementation of Iodine-Deficient Subjects with Selenium." *J Clin Endocrinol Metab* 73, no. 1 (1991): 213–215. https://doi.org/10.1210/jcem-73-1-213.

Cumming, R. G., and R. J. Klineberg. "Case-Control Study of Risk Factors for Hip Fractures in the Elderly." *Am J Epidemiol* 139 (1994): 493–505.

Dadgarnejad, Manouchehr, Shahzad Kouser, and Masoumeh Moslemi. "Genetically Modified Foods: Promises, Challenges and Safety Assessments." *Applied Food Biotechnology* 4, no. 4 (2017): 193–202. https://doi.org/10.22037/afb.v4i4.17244.

Danby, F. W. "Acne Dairy and Cancer." *Dermatoendocrinol* 1, no. 1 (January–February 2009): 12–16.

Davis, Donald R., Melvin D. Epp, and Hugh D. Riordan. "Changes in USDA Food Composition Data for 43 Garden Crops, 1950 to 1999." *Journal of the American College of Nutrition* 23 (2004): 669–682. https://doi.org/10.1080/07315724.2004.10719409.

de Benoist, B., E. Mclean, M. Andersson, and L. Rogers. "Iodine Deficiency in 2007: Global Progress Since 2003." *Food Nutr Bull* 29, no. 3 (2008): 195–202.

De Punder, K., and L. Pruimboom. "The Dietary Intake of Wheat and Other Cereal Grains and Their Role in Inflammation." *Nutrients* 5, no. 3 (2013): 771–787.

De Santis, S., E. Cavalcanti, M. Mastronardi, E. Jirillo, and M. Chieppa. "Nutritional Keys for Intestinal Barrier Modulation." *Front Immunol* 6 (December 7, 2015): 612. https://doi.org/10.3389/fimmu.2015.00612.

Divi, R. L., and D. R. Doerge. "Inhibition of Thyroid Peroxidase by Dietary Flavonoids." *Chem Res Toxicol* 9, no. 1 (January–February 1996): 16–23.

Divi, R. L., H. C. Chang, and D. R. Doerge. "Anti-thyroid Isoflavones from Soybean: Isolation, Characterization, and Mechanisms of Action." *Biochem Pharmacol* 54, no. 10 (November 15, 1997): 1087–1096.

Doerge, D. R., and D. M. Sheehan. "Goitrogenic and Estrogenic Activity of Soy Isoflavones." *Environ Health Perspect* 110, Suppl 3 (June 2002): 349–353.

Ehrman, Jan. "Pesticide Use Linked to Lupus, Rheumatoid Arthritis." *NIH Record*, March 18, 2011. https://nihrecord.nih.gov/sites/recordNIH/files/pdf/2011/NIH-Record-2011-03-18.pdf.

Environmental Working Group. "Clean Fifteen." 2020. https://www.ewg.org/foodnews/clean-fifteen.php.

Environmental Working Group. "Dirty Dozen." 2020. https://www.ewg.org/foodnews/dirty-dozen.php.

Farhangi, M. A., P. Dehghan, S. Tajmiri, and M. M. Abbasi. "The Effects of Nigella sativa on Thyroid Function, Serum Vascular Endothelial Growth Factor (VEGF)-1, Nesfatin-1 and Anthropometric Features in Patients with Hashimoto's Thyroiditis: A Randomized Controlled Trial." *BMC Complement Altern Med* 16, no. 1 (November 16, 2016): 471. https://doi.org/10.1186/s12906-016-1432-2.

Felker, Peter, Ronald Bunch, and Angela Leung. "Concentrations of Thiocyanate and Goitrin in Human Plasma, Their Precursor Concentrations in Brassica Vegetables, and Associated Potential Risk for Hypothyroidism." *Nutrition Reviews* 74 (2016). doi:10.1093/nutrit/nuv110.

Fernandes, Gabriel. "Dietary Lipids and Risk of Autoimmune Disease." *Clinical Immunology and Immunopathology* 72 (1994): 193–197. https://doi.org/10.1006/clin.1994.1129.

Ferrari, S. M., P. Fallahi, A. Antonelli, and S. Benvenga. "Environmental Issues in Thyroid Diseases." *Front Endocrinol* (Lausanne) 8 (March 20, 2017): 50. https://doi.org/10.3389/fendo.2017.00050.

Feskanich, D., H. A. Bischoff-Ferrari, A. L. Frazier, and W. C. Willett. "Milk Consumption During Teenage Years and Risk of Hip Fractures in Older Adults." *JAMA Pediatr* 168, no. 1 (2014): 54–60. https://doi.org/10.1001/jamapediatrics.2013.3821.

Feskanich, D., W. C. Willet, M. J. Stampfer, and G. A. Colditz. "Milk, Dietary Calcium, and Bone Fractures in Women: A 12-Year Prospective Study." *Am J Public Health* 87 (1997): 992–997.

Fortune Business Insights. "Genetically Modified Seeds Market Size, Share and Industry Analysis by Crop (Corn, Soybean, Cotton, Canola and Others), and Regional Forecast 2019–2026." 2018. Accessed November 30, 2019. https://www.fortunebusinessinsights.com/industry-reports/genetically-modified-seeds-market-100389.

Froehlich, Eleonore, and Richard Wahl. "Microbiota and Thyroid Interaction in Health and Disease." *Trends in Endocrinology & Metabolism* 30 (2019). https://doi.org/10.1016/j.tem.2019.05.008.

Fryar, C. D., J. P. Hughes, K. A. Herrick, and N. Ahluwalia. "Fast Food Consumption Among Adults in the United States, 2013–2016." NCHS Data Brief no. 322. Hyattsville, MD: National Center for Health Statistics, 2018.

Gong, Tao, Xiaqiong Wang, Yanqing Yang, et al. "Plant Lectins Activate the NLRP3 Inflammasome to Promote Inflammatory Disorders." *Journal of Immunology* (Baltimore) 198 (2017). https://doi.org/10.4049/jimmunol.1600145.

Hakenen, M., K. Luotola, J. Salmi, P. Laippala, K. Kaukinen, and P. Collin. "Clinical and Subclinical Thyroid Disease in Patients with Celiac Disease." *Dig Dis Sci* 46, no. 12 (December 2001): 2631–2635.

"Harvest of Fears: Farm Raised Fish May Not Be Free of Mercury and Other Pollutants." *Scientific American*, June 15, 2011. https://www.scientificamerican.com/article/farm-raised-fish-not-free-mercury-pcb-dioxin/.

Herforth, Anna, Mary Arimond, Cristina Álvarez-Sánchez, Jennifer Coates, Karin Christianson, and Ellen Muehlhoff. "A Global Review of Food-Based Dietary Guidelines." *Advances in Nutrition* 10, no. 4 (July 2019): 590–605. https://doi.org/10.1093/advances/nmy130.

Hu, Yang, Karen Costenbader, Xiang Gao, et al. "Sugar-Sweetened Soda Consumption and Risk of Developing Rheumatoid Arthritis in Women." *American Journal of Clinical Nutrition* 100 (2014). https://doi.org/10.3945/ajcn.114.086918.

Huang, Z., J. H. Himes, and P. G. McGovern. "Nutrition and Subsequent Hip Fracture Risk Among a National Cohort of White Women." *Am J Epidemiol* 144 (1996): 124–134.

Hyman, Mark. *Food: What the Heck Should I Eat?* New York: Little, Brown, 2018.

Institute for Responsible Technology (IRT). "Health Risks." 2019. Accessed May 5, 2019. https://responsibletechnology.org/gmo-education/health-risks/.

Jeyaraman, M. M., A. M. Abou-Setta, L. Grant, et al. "Dairy Product Consumption and Development of Cancer: An Overview of Reviews." *BMJ Open* 9 (2019): e023625. https://doi.org/10.1136/bmjopen-2018-023625.

Joung, J., Y. Cho, S. Park, et al. "Effect of Iodine Restriction on Thyroid Function in Subclinical Hypothyroid Patients in an Iodine-Replete Area: A Long Period Observation in a Large-Scale Cohort." *Thyroid* 24, no. 9 (2014): 1361–1368. https://doi.org/10.1089/thy.2014.0046.

Kittivachra, Rubporn. "Effects of Cassava on Thyroid Gland in Rats." *Thai J. Pharm Sci* 30 (2006): 57–62.

Kose, Engin, Orkide Guzel, Korcan Demir, and Nur Arslan. "Changes of Thyroid Hormonal Status in Patients Receiving Ketogenic Diet Due to Intractable Epilepsy." *Journal of Pediatric Endocrinology and Metabolism* 30 (2017). https://doi.org/10.1515/jpem-2016-0281.

Kratz, Mario, Ton Baars, and Stephan Guyenet. "The Relationship Between High-Fat Dairy Consumption and Obesity, Cardiovascular, and Metabolic Disease." *European Journal of Nutrition* 52 (2012). https://doi.org/10.1007/s00394-012-0418-1.

Krysiak, Robert, Witold Szkróbka, and Boguslaw Okopien. "The Effect of Gluten-Free Diet on Thyroid Autoimmunity in Drug-Naïve Women with Hashimoto's Thyroiditis: A Pilot Study." *Experimental and Clinical Endocrinology & Diabetes* 127 (2018). https://doi.org/10.1055/a-0653-7108.

Labonté, Marie-Ève, Patrick Couture, Caroline Richard, Sophie Desroches, and Benoît Lamarche. "Impact of Dairy Products on Biomarkers of Inflammation: A Systematic Review of Randomized Controlled Nutritional Intervention Studies in Overweight and Obese Adults." *American Journal of Clinical Nutrition* 97, no. 4 (April 1, 2013): 706–717. https://doi.org/10.3945/ajcn.112.052217.

Lambertz, J., S. Weiskirchen, S. Landert, and R. Weiskirchen. "Fructose: A Dietary Sugar in Crosstalk with Microbiota Contributing to the Development and Progression of Non-Alcoholic Liver Disease." *Front Immunol* 8 (September 19, 2017): 1159. https://doi.org/10.3389/fimmu.2017.01159.

Lerner, A., and T. Matthias. "Changes in Intestinal Tight Junctions in Permeability Associated with Industrial Food Additives Explain the Rising Incidence of Autoimmune Disease." *Autoimmunity Reviews* 14, no. 6 (June 2015): 479–489.

Lerner, A., P. Jeremias, and T. Matthias. "Gut-Thyroid Axis and Celiac Disease." *Endocr Connect* 6, no. 4 (2017): R52–R58. https://doi.org/10.1530/EC-17-0021.

Limbergen, Johan, John Martino, and Leah Cahill. "The Role of Carrageenan and Carboxymethylcellulose in the Development of Intestinal Inflammation." *Frontiers in Pediatrics* 5 (2017). https://doi.org/10.3389/fped.2017.00096.

Lucas, Lisa, Aaron Russell, and Russell Keast. "Molecular Mechanisms of Inflammation. Anti-inflammatory Benefits of Virgin Olive Oil and the

Phenolic Compound Oleocanthal." *Current Pharmaceutical Design* 17 (2011): 754–768. https://doi.org/10.2174/138161211795428911.

Ludwig, D. S., and W. C. Willett. "Three Daily Servings of Reduced-Fat Milk: An Evidence-Based Recommendation?" *JAMA Pediatr* 167, no. 9 (2013): 788–789. https://doi.org/10.1001/jamapediatrics.2013.2408.

McMillan, M., E. A. Spinks, and G. R. Fenwick. "Preliminary Observations on the Effect of Dietary Brussels Sprouts on Thyroid Function." *Human Toxicology* 5, no. 1 (1986): 15–19. https://doi.org/10.1177/096032718600 500104.

Melnik, B. C. "Evidence for Acne Promoting Effects of Milk and Other Insulin Like Dairy Products." *Nestle Nutr Workshop Ser Pediatr Program* 67 (2011): 131–145. Epub February 16, 2011. https://doi.org/10.1159/000325580.

Mensink, R. P., and M. B. Katan. "Effect of Dietary Trans Fatty Acids on High-Density And Low-Density Lipoprotein Cholesterol Levels in Healthy Subjects." *New England Journal of Medicine* 323, no. 7 (August 16, 1990): 439–445.

Nambisan, Padma. "Recombinant DNA Technology and Genetically Modified Organisms." 2017. https://doi.org/10.1016/B978-0-12-809231-6.00004-1.

Natural Resources Defense Council. "The Smart Seafood Buying Guide." 2015. https://www.nrdc.org/stories/smart-seafood-buying-guide.

Nestle, Marion. "Food Lobbies, The Food Pyramid, and U.S. Nutrition Policy." *International Journal of Health Services: Planning, Administration, Evaluation* 23 (1993): 483-496. https://doi.org/10.2190/32F2-2PFB-MEG7 -8HPU.

Ohlsson, B., M. Orho-Melander, and P. M. Nilsson. "Higher Levels of Serum Zonulin May Rather Be Associated with Increased Risk of Obesity and Hyperlipidemia, Than with Gastrointestinal Symptoms or Disease Manifestations." Edited by S. Angelini. *International Journal of Molecular Sciences* 18, no. 3 (2017): 582. https://doi.org/10.3390/ijms18030582.

Olivier, Bruyère, Ahmed H. Serge, and Atlan Catherine, et al. Erratum to "Review of the Nutritional Benefits and Risks Related to Intense Sweeteners." *Archives of Public Health* 73 (2015). https://doi.org/10.1186/s13690-015 -0092-x.

Patterson, E., Rebecca Wall, G. F. Fitzgerald, R. P. Ross, and C. Stanton. "Health Implications of High Dietary Omega-6 Polyunsaturated Fatty Acids." *Journal of Nutrition and Metabolism* 2012 (2012): 539426. https://doi .org/10.1155/2012/539426.

Pew Research Center. "The New Food Fights: U.S. Public Divides over Food Science." 2016. Accessed November 30, 2019. https://www.pewresearch .org/science/2016/12/01/public-opinion-about-genetically-modified-foods -and-trust-in-scientists-connected-with-these-foods/.

Rapin, J. R., and N. Wiernsperger. "Possible Links between Intestinal Permeability and Food Processing: A Potential Therapeutic Niche for Glutamine." *Clinics* 65, no. 6 (2010): 635–643. https://doi.org/10.1590/S1807-5932201 0000600012.

Riehemann, K., B. Behnke, and K. Schulze-Osthoff. "Plant Extracts from Stinging Nettle (Urtica dioica), an Antirheumatic Remedy, Inhibit the Proinflammatory Transcription Factor NF-kappaB." *FEBS Lett* 442, no. 1 (1999): 89–94. https://doi.org/10.1016/s0014-5793(98)01622-6.

Sandström, B., B. Kivistö, and A. Cederblad. "Absorption of Zinc from Soy Protein Meals in Humans." *J Nutr* 117, no. 2 (February 1987): 321–327.

Sategna-Guidetti, Caria, Mauro Bruno, Enrico Mazza, et al. "Autoimmune Thyroid Diseases and Coeliac Disease." *European Journal of Gastroenterology & Hepatology* 10 (1998): 927–931. https://doi.org/10.1097/00042737-1998 11000-00005.

Shlomit, David, Carmit Shani Levi, Lulu Fahoum, et al. "Revisiting the Carrageenan Controversy: Do We Really Understand the Digestive Fate and Safety of Carrageenan in Our Foods?" *Food & Function* 9, no. 3 (2018): 1344–1352. https://doi.org/10.1039/c7fo01721a.

Spaulding, S. W., I. J. Chopra, R. S. Sherwin, and S. S. Lyall. "Effect of Caloric Restriction and Dietary Composition of Serum T3 and Reverse T3 in Man." *J Clin Endocrinol Metab* 42, no. 1 (January 1976): 197–200.

Spencer, M., A. Gupta, L. V. Dam, C. Shannon, S. Menees, and W. D. Chey. "Artificial Sweeteners: A Systematic Review and Primer for Gastroenterologists." *J Neurogastroenterol Motil* 22, no. 2 (2016): 168–180. https://doi .org/10.5056/jnm15206.

Spisák, S., N. Solymosi, P. Ittzés, et al. "Complete Genes May Pass from Food to Human Blood." *PLOS ONE* 8, no. 7 (2013): e69805. https://doi.org /10.1371/journal.pone.0069805.

Stanford Hospital and Clinics Digestive Health Center Nutritional Services. "The Low FODMAP Diet." Accessed August 28, 2019. http://www.marin healthcare.org/upload/Low-FODMAP-Diet.pdf.

Stanford University. "The Specific Carbohydrate Diet." Accessed August 28, 2019. https://med.stanford.edu/content/dam/sm/gastroenterology/documents /IBD/CarbDiet%20PDF%20final.pdf.

Statistica. "Canada: How Often Do You Eat Fast Food (Any Quick Service Restaurant) in a Given Week (on Average)." 2016–2018. Accessed May 5, 2019. https://www.statista.com/statistics/561254/canada-average-fast-food -consumption-per-week/.

Streider, Thea G. A., Mark F. Prummel, Jan G. P. Tijssen, Eric Endert, and Wilmar M. Wiersinga. "Risk Factors for and Prevalence of Thyroid Disorders in a Cross-Sectional Study Among Healthy Female Relatives of Patients with Autoimmune Thyroid Disease." *Clin Endocrinol* (Oxford, England) 59, no. 3 (September 2003): 396–401.

Tobacman, J. K. "Review of Harmful Gastrointestinal Effects of Carrageenan in Animal Experiments." *Environ Health Perspect* 109, no. 10 (2001): 983–994. https://doi.org/10.1289/ehp.01109983.

United States Department of Agriculture (USDA) Economic Research Science. "Sugar and Sweeteners." 2019. https://www.ers.usda.gov/topics/crops/sugar -sweeteners/background.aspx.

Verkaik-Kloosterman, J., P. van 't Veer, and M. C. Ocké. "Reduction of Salt: Will Iodine Intake Remain Adequate in the Netherlands." *Br J Nutr* 104, no. 11 (December 2010): 1712–1718.

Virili, Camilla, and Marco Centanni. "Does Microbiota Composition Affect Thyroid Homeostasis?" *Endocrine* 49 (2014). https://doi.org/10.1007/s12020 -014-0509-2.

Vojdani, A. "Lectins, Agglutinins, and Their Roles in Autoimmune Reactivities." *Altern Ther Health Med* 21 Suppl 1 (2015): 46–51.

World Health Organization. "Healthy Diet." 2018. Accessed December 2, 2019. https://www.who.int/news-room/fact-sheets/detail/healthy-diet.

World Health Organization. "Replace Trans Fat." 2018. Accessed November 28, 2019. https://www.who.int/nutrition/topics/replace-transfat.

Zivkovic, A. M., N. Telis, J. B. German, and B. D. Hammock. "Dietary Omega-3 Fatty Acids Aid in the Modulation of Inflammation and Metabolic Health." *California Agriculture* 65, no. 3 (2011): 106–111. https://doi.org/10.3733/ca .v065n03p106.

CHAPTER 9: Keep Your Microbiome Happy

Asik, Mehmet, Fahri Gunes, Emine Binnetoglu, et al. "Decrease in TSH Levels After Lactose Restriction in Hashimoto's Thyroiditis Patients with Lactose Intolerance." *Endocrine* 46 (2013). https://doi.org/10.1007/s12020-013 -0065-1.

Barbaro, M. R., C. Cremon, V. Stanghellini, and G. Barbara. "Recent Advances in Understanding Non-celiac Gluten Sensitivity." *F1000Res* 7 (October 11, 2018): F1000 Faculty Rev-1631. https://doi.org/10.12688/f1000research .15849.1.

Centanni, Marco, Massimo Marignani, Lucilla Gargano, et al. "Atrophic Body Gastritis in Patients with Autoimmune Thyroid Disease." *Archives of Internal Medicine* 159 (1999): 1726–1730. https://doi.org/10.1001/archinte.159 .15.1726.

Centanni, Marco, Miriam Cellini, Maria Santaguida, et al. "Hashimoto's Thyroiditis and Autoimmune Gastritis." *Frontiers in Endocrinology* 8 (2017). https://doi.org/10.3389/fendo.2017.00092.

Darabi, B., S. Rahmati, M. R. Hafezi Ahmadi, et al. "The Association Between Caesarean Section and Childhood Asthma: An Updated Systematic Review and Meta-analysis." *Allergy Asthma Clin Immunol* 15, no. 62 (2019). https:// doi.org/10.1186/s13223-019-0367-9.

Daulatzai, Mak. "Non-Celiac Gluten Sensitivity Triggers Gut Dysbiosis, Neuroinflammation, Gut-Brain Axis Dysfunction, and Vulnerability for Dementia." *CNS & Neurological Disorders Drug Targets* 14 (2015). https://doi .org/10.2174/1871527314666150202152436.

De Filippo, C., D. Cavalieri, M. Di Paola, et al. "Impact of Diet in Shaping Gut Microbiota Revealed by a Comparative Study in Children from Europe and

Rural Africa." *Proc Natl Acad Sci* (USA) 107 (2010): 14691–14696. https://doi.org/10.1073/pnas.1005963107.

Dudek-Wicher, R. K., A. Junka, and M. Bartoszewicz. "The Influence of Antibiotics and Dietary Components on Gut Microbiota." *Prz Gastroenterol* 13, no. 2 (2018): 85–92. https://doi.org/10.5114/pg.2018.76005.

Dukowicz, A. C., B. E. Lacy, and G. M. Levine. "Small Intestinal Bacterial Overgrowth: A Comprehensive Review." *Gastroenterol Hepatol* (NY) 3, no. 2 (2007): 112–122.

Dunn, A. B., S. Jordan, B. J. Baker, and N. S. Carlson. "The Maternal Infant Microbiome: Considerations for Labor and Birth." *MCN Am J Matern Child Nurs* 42, no. 6 (2017): 318–325. https://doi.org/10.1097/NMC.0000000000000373.

Ebert, Ellen C. "The Thyroid and the Gut." *Journal of Clinical Gastroenterology* 44 (2010): 402–406. https://doi.org/10.1097/MCG.0b013e3181d6bc3e.

Fasano, Alessio. "Leaky Gut and Autoimmune Diseases." *Clinical Reviews in Allergy & Immunology* 42 (2011): 71–78. https://doi.org/10.1007/s12016-011-8291-x.

Fasano, Alessio, and Terez Shea-Donohue. "Mechanisms of Disease: The Role of Intestinal Barrier Function in the Pathogenesis of Gastrointestinal Autoimmune Diseases." *Nat Clin Pract Gastroenterol Hepatol* 2 (2005): 416–422. https://doi.org/10.1038/ncpgasthep0259.

Kellman, R. *The Microbiome Diet*. New York: Da Capo Lifelong Books, 2014.

Khalili, H. "Risk of Inflammatory Bowel Disease with Oral Contraceptives and Menopausal Hormone Therapy: Current Evidence and Future Directions." *Drug Saf* 39, no. 3 (2016): 193–197. https://doi.org/10.1007/s40264-015-0372-y.

Kulnigg-Dabsch, S. "Autoimmungastritis." *Wien Med Wochenschr* 166, nos. 13–14 (2016): 424–430. https://doi.org/10.1007/s10354-016-0515-5.

Lamoureux, E. "Factors Affecting the Gut Microbiome." Dalhousie University, 2017. Accessed August 9, 2019. https://dalspace.library.dal.ca/bitstream/handle/10222/73207/Lamoureux-Emily-MSc_PHAC-Aug-2017.pdf?sequence=5&isAllowed=y.

Lazar, V., L. M. Ditu, G. G. Pircalabioru, et al. "Aspects of Gut Microbiota and Immune System Interactions in Infectious Diseases, Immunopathology, and Cancer." *Front Immunol* 9 (August 15, 2018): 1830. https://doi.org/10.3389/fimmu.2018.01830.

Liang, J., Z. Zhang, W. Yang, et al. "Association Between Cesarean Section and Weight Status in Chinese Children and Adolescents: A National Survey." *Int J Environ Res Public Health* 14, no. 12 (December 20, 2017): 1609. https://doi.org/10.3390/ijerph14121609.

Liu, Y., J. J. Alookaran, and J. M. Rhoads. "Probiotics in Autoimmune and Inflammatory Disorders." *Nutrients* 10, no. 10 (October 18, 2018): 1537. https://doi.org/10.3390/nu10101537.

Lomer, Miranda. Review article: "The Aetiology, Diagnosis, Mechanisms and Clinical Evidence for Food Intolerance." *Alimentary Pharmacology & Therapeutics* 41 (2014). https://doi.org/10.1111/apt.13041.

Maseda, D., J. P. Zackular, B. Trindade, et al. "Nonsteroidal Anti-inflammatory Drugs Alter the Microbiota and Exacerbate *Clostridium difficile* Colitis While Dysregulating the Inflammatory Response." *mBio* 10, no. 1 (January 8, 2019): e02282-18. https://doi.org/10.1128/mBio.02282-18.

Meyer, Rosan, Heather Godwin, Robert Dziubak, et al. "The Impact on Quality of Life on Families of Children on an Elimination Diet for Non-immunoglobulin E Mediated Gastrointestinal Food Allergies." *World Allergy Organization Journal* 10 (2017). https://doi.org/10.1186/s40413-016-0139-7.

Mohajeri, M. H., R. J. M. Brummer, R. A. Rastall, et al. "The Role of the Microbiome for Human Health: From Basic Science to Clinical Applications." *Eur J Nutr* 57 (Suppl 1) (2018): 1–14. https://doi.org/10.1007/s00394-018-1703-4.

Molina-Infante, J., S. Santolaria, D. S. Sanders, and F. Fernández-Bañares. "Systematic Review: Noncoeliac Gluten Sensitivity." *Alimentary Pharmacology & Therapeutics (Review)* 41, no. 9 (2015): 807–820. https://doi.org/10.1111/apt.13155.

Human Microbiome Portfolio Analysis Team, National Institutes of Health. "A Review of 10 Years of Human Microbiome Research Activities at the US National Institutes of Health, Fiscal Years 2007–2016." *Microbiome* 7 (2019): 31. https://doi.org/10.1186/s40168-019-0620-y.

Nylund, Lotta, Katri Kaukinen, and Katri Lindfors. "The Microbiota as a Component of the Celiac Disease and Non-celiac Gluten Sensitivity." *Clinical Nutrition Experimental* 6 (2016). https://doi.org/10.1016/j.yclnex.2016.01.002.

Patil, A. D. "Link Between Hypothyroidism and Small Intestinal Bacterial Overgrowth." *Indian J Endocrinol Metab* 18, no. 3 (2014): 307–309. https://doi.org/10.4103/2230-8210.131155.

Rao, R. K., and G. Samak. "Protection and Restitution of Gut Barrier by Probiotics: Nutritional and Clinical Implications." *Curr Nutr Food Sci* 9, no. 2 (2013): 99–107.

Roy, Abhik, Monika Laszkowska, Johan Sundström, et al. "Prevalence of Celiac Disease in Patients with Autoimmune Thyroid Disease: A Meta-analysis." *Thyroid* 26 (2016). https://doi.org/10.1089/thy.2016.0108.

Ruscio, M. *Healthy Gut, Healthy You.* Las Vegas: Ruscio Institute, 2018.

Sanders, Mary. "Impact of Probiotics on Colonizing Microbiota of the Gut." *Journal of Clinical Gastroenterology* 45 Suppl. (2011): S115–119. https://doi.org/10.1097/MCG.0b013e318227414a.

Santaolalla, R., M. Fukata, and M. T. Abreu. "Innate Immunity in the Small Intestine." *Curr Opin Gastroenterol* 27, no. 2 (2011): 125–131. https://doi.org/10.1097/MOG.0b013e3283438dea.

Schooley, R. T. "The Human Microbiome: Implications for Health and Disease, Including HIV Infection." *Top Antivir Med* 26, no. 3 (2018): 75–78.

Sharma, B. R., A. S. Joshi, P. K. Varthakavi, M. D. Chadha, N. M. Bhagwat, and P. S. Pawal. "Celiac Autoimmunity in Autoimmune Thyroid Disease Is Highly Prevalent with a Questionable Impact." *Indian J Endocrinol Metab* 20, no. 1 (2016): 97–100. https://doi.org/10.4103/2230-8210.172241.

Sigthorsson, G., J. Tibble, J. Hayllar, et al. "Intestinal Permeability and Inflammation in Patients on NSAIDs." *Gut* 43, no. 4 (1998): 506–511.

Singh, Rasnik K., Hsin-Wen Chang, Di Yan, et al. "Influence of Diet on the Gut Microbiome and Implications for Human Health." *Journal of Translational Medicine* 15 (2017): 73. https://doi.org/10.1186/s12967-017-1175-y.

Takiishi, T., C. I. M. Fenero, and N. O. S. Câmara. "Intestinal Barrier and Gut Microbiota: Shaping Our Immune Responses Throughout Life." *Tissue Barriers* 5, no. 4 (2017): e1373208. https://doi.org/10.1080/21688370.2017.1373208.

Telle-Hansen, V. H., K. B. Holven, and S. M. Ulven. "Impact of a Healthy Dietary Pattern on Gut Microbiota and Systemic Inflammation in Humans." *Nutrients* 10, no. 11 (November 16, 2018): 1783. https://doi.org/10.3390/nu10111783.

Virili, Camilla, and Marco Centanni. "Does Microbiota Composition Affect Thyroid Homeostasis?" *Endocrine* 49 (2014). https://doi.org/10.1007/s12020-014-0509-2.

CHAPTER 10: What You Need to Know About Medications

Alberta Medical Association. "Subclinical Hypothyroidism: A Brief Review and Suggested Treatment Approach." 2019. Accessed August 19, 2019. https://www.albertadoctors.org/services/media-publications/newsletters-magazines/ops/subclinical-Hypothyroidism.

Bihari, Bernard. "Low Dose Naltrexone for Normalizing Immune System Functioning." Accessed August 18, 2019. https://todayspractitioner.com/wp-content/uploads/2013/10/Bernard-Bihari-MD-Low-dose-Naltrexone-for-Normalizing-Immune-System-Function-athm_19_2_bihari_56_65.pdf.

Bolk, N., T. J. Visser, J. Nijman, I. J. Jongste, J. G. P. Tijssen, and A. Berghout. "Effects of Evening vs Morning Levothyroxine Intake: A Randomized Double-Blind Crossover Trial." *Arch Intern Med* 170, no. 22 (2010): 1996–2003. https://doi.org/10.1001/archinternmed.2010.436.

Dayan, C., and V. Panicker. "Management of Hypothyroidism with Combination Thyroxine (T4) and Triiodothyronine (T3) Hormone Replacement in Clinical Practice: A Review of Suggested Guidance." *Thyroid Res* 11 (January 17, 2018): 1. https://doi.org/10.1186/s13044-018-0045-x.

Flynn, Robert, Sandra Bonellie, Roland Jung, Thomas Macdonald, Andrew Morris, and Graham Leese. "Serum Thyroid-Stimulating Hormone Concentration and Morbidity from Cardiovascular Disease and Fractures in Patients on Long-Term Thyroxine Therapy." *Journal of Clinical Endocrinology and Metabolism* 95 (2009): 186–193. https://doi.org/10.1210/jc.2009-1625.

Hoang, Thanh, Cara H. Olsen, Vinh Q. Mai, Patrick W. Clyde, and Mohamed K. M. Shakir. "Desiccated Thyroid Extract Compared with Levothyroxine in the Treatment of Hypothyroidism: A Randomized, Double-Blind, Cross-over Study." *Journal of Clinical Endocrinology and Metabolism* 98 (2013). https://doi.org/10.1210/jc.2012-4107.

Jonklaas, Jacqueline, Antonio Carlos Bianco, Andrew Bauer, et al. "Guidelines for the Treatment of Hypothyroidism: Prepared by the American Thyroid Association Task Force on Thyroid Hormone Replacement." *Thyroid* 24 (2014). https://doi.org/10.1089/thy.2014.0028.

LDN Research Trust. "Low Dose Naltrexone." 2017. Accessed August 18, 2019. http://www.ldnresearchtrust.org/.

Lowe, J. C. "Stability, Effectiveness, and Safety of Desiccated Thyroid vs Levothyroxine: A Rebuttal to the British Thyroid Association." *Thyroid Science* 4 (2009): 1–12.

McAninch, E. A., and A. C. Bianco. "The History and Future of Treatment of Hypothyroidism" [published correction in *Ann Intern Med* 164, no. 5 (March 1, 2016): 376]. *Ann Intern Med* 164, no. 1 (2016): 50–56. https://doi.org/10.7326/M15-1799.

McDermott, Michael T., and E. Chester Ridgway. "Subclinical Hypothyroidism Is Mild Thyroid Failure and Should be Treated." *Journal of Clinical Endocrinology & Metabolism* 86, no. 10 (October 1, 2001): 4585–4590. https://doi.org/10.1210/jcem.86.10.7959.

Peterson, Sarah J., Elizabeth A. McAninch, and Antonio C. Bianco. "Is a Normal TSH Synonymous with 'Euthyroidism' in Levothyroxine Monotherapy?" *Journal of Clinical Endocrinology & Metabolism* (2016): jc.2016–2660. https://doi.org/10.1210/jc.2016-2660.

Rush University Medical Center. "Hypothyroidism Symptoms Linger Despite Medication Use, Normal Blood Tests." ScienceDaily, October 12, 2016. www.sciencedaily.com/releases/2016/10/161012132038.htm.

Tariq, A., Y. Wert, P. Cheriyath, and R. Joshi. "Effects of Long-Term Combination LT4 and LT3 Therapy for Improving Hypothyroidism and Overall Quality of Life." *South Med J* 111, no. 6 (2018): 363–369. https://doi.org/10.14423/SMJ.0000000000000823.

WP Thyroid. "Prescribing Information." Accessed August 17, 2019. https://getrealthyroid.com/assets/docs/WP-Thyroid-Prescribing-Information.pdf.

Zijian, Li, Yue You, Noreen Griffin, Juan Feng, and Fengping Shan. "Low-Dose Naltrexone (LDN): A Promising Treatment in Immune-Related Diseases and Cancer Therapy." *International Immunopharmacology* 61 (2018): 178–184. https://doi.org/10.1016/j.intimp.2018.05.020.

CHAPTER 11: Natural Herbs and Supplements

Basciani, N. "Myo-inositol Plus Selenium Supplementation Restores Euthyroid State in Hashimoto's Patients with Subclinical Hypothyroidism." *European Review for Medical and Pharmacological Sciences* 21, no. 2 (2017): 51–59.

Bharthi, V., N. Kavya, M. Shubhashree, and S. Bhat. "Herbal Approach to Management of Thyroid Disease: A Review." *J Ayu Herb Med* 3, no. 1 (2017): 51–55.

Bone, K., and S. Mills. *The Essential Guide to Herbal Safety*. Philadelphia: Elsevier, 2005.

Chaudhary, S., D. Dutta, M. Kumar, et al. "Vitamin D Supplementation Reduces Thyroid Peroxidase Antibody Levels in Patients with Autoimmune Thyroid Disease: An Open-Labeled Randomized Controlled Trial." *Indian J Endocrinol Metab* 20, no. 3 (May–June 2016): 391–398.

Chen, S., Z. Li, R. Krochmal, M. Abrazado, W. Kim, and C. B. Cooper. "Effect of Cs-4 (Cordyceps sinensis) on Exercise Performance in Healthy Older Subjects: A Double-Blind, Placebo-Controlled Trial." *J Altern Complement Med* 16, no. 5 (2010): 585–590. https://doi.org/10.1089/acm.2009.0226.

Cheney, G. "Rapid Healing of Peptic Ulcers in Patients Receiving Fresh Cabbage Juice." *Calif Med* 70, no. 1 (1949): 10–15.

Cheng, Ni, Naiyan Ren, Hui Gao, Xingsheng Lei, Jianbin Zheng, and Wei Cao. "Antioxidant and Hepatoprotective Effects of Schisandra chinensis Pollen Extract on CCl(4)-Induced Acute Liver Damage in Mice." *Food and Chemical Toxicology* 55 (2012). https://doi.org/10.1016/j.fct.2012.11.022.

Collins, J. "Clinical Efficacy of Systemic Enzyme Support." 2009. Accessed August 21, 2019. https://pdfs.semanticscholar.org/c438/5053751b4679135ce 87a65ff5f0b4a7a26c7.pdf.

Farhangi, M. A., P. Dehghan, S. Tajmiri, and M. M. Abbasi. "The Effects of Nigella sativa on Thyroid Function, Serum Vascular Endothelial Growth Factor (VEGF)-1, Nesfatin-1 and Anthropometric Features in Patients with Hashimoto's Thyroiditis: A Randomized Controlled Trial. *BMC Complement Altern Med* 16, no. 1 (November 16, 2016): 471. https://doi.org /10.1186/s12906-016-1432-2.

Gardner, Z., and M. McGuffin. *American Herbal Products Association's Botanical Safety Handbook*. 2nd ed. Boca Raton, FL: CRC Press, 2013.

Gibbert, J., Fabian Kreimendahl, Jennifer Lebert, Reinhard Rychlik, and Inga Trompetter. "Improvement of Stress Resistance and Quality of Life of Adults with Nervous Restlessness After Treatment with a Passion Flower Dry Extract." *Complementary Medicine Research* 24 (2017). https://doi.org /10.1159/000464342.

Groves, M. N. "Herbal Endocrine Support System" AHG Advanced Webinar Intensives. Accessed August 24, 2019. https://www.americanherbalistsguild .com/sites/americanherbalistsguild.com/files/endocrine3thyroid.slides .groves.pdf.

Gupta, Anshita, Suchita Wamankar, Bina Gidwani, Chanchal Deep Kaur. "Herbal Drugs for Thyroid." *International Journal of Pharmacy and Biological Sciences* 6 (2016): 62–70.

Harper, Mary-Ellen, and Erin Seifert. "Thyroid Hormone Effects on Mitochondrial Energetics." *Thyroid* 18 (2008): 145–156. https://doi.org/10.1089/thy .2007.0250.

He, T., R. Zhao, Y. Lu, et al. "Dual-Directional Immunomodulatory Effects of Corbrin Capsule on Autoimmune Thyroid Diseases." *Evid Based Complement Alternat Med* 2016 (2016): 1360386. https://doi.org/10.1155/2016/1360386.

HealthMastersLive.com. Thyroid Masterclass 2015 course content.

Hur, Y. G., C. H. Suh, S. Kim, and J. Won. "Rosmarinic Acid Induces Apoptosis of Activated T Cells from Rheumatoid Arthritis Patients via Mitochondrial Pathway." *J Clin Immunol* 27, no. 1 (2007): 36–45. https://doi.org/10.1007/s10875-006-9057-8.

Jabbar, Abdul, Aasima Yawar, Sabiha Waseem, et al. "Vitamin B12 Deficiency Common in Primary Hypothyroidism." *JPMA: Journal of the Pakistan Medical Association* 58 (2008): 258–261.

Kar, Anand, S. Panda, and Sweta Bharti. "Relative Efficacy of Three Medicinal Plant Extracts in the Alteration of Thyroid Hormone Concentrations in Male Mice." *Journal of Ethnopharmacology* 81 (2002): 281–285. https://doi.org/10.1016/S0378-8741(02)00048-X.

Katagiri, Ryoko, Xiaoyi Yuan, Satomi Kobayashi, and Satoshi Sasaki. "Effect of Excess Iodine Intake on Thyroid Diseases in Different Populations: A Systematic Review and Meta-analyses Including Observational Studies." *PLOS ONE* 12 (2017): e0173722. https://doi.org/10.1371/journal.pone.0173722.

Kumar Sharma, Ashok, Indraneel Basu, and Siddarth Singh. "Efficacy and Safety of Ashwagandha Root Extract in Subclinical Hypothyroid Patients: A Double-Blind, Randomized Placebo-Controlled Trial." *Journal of Alternative and Complementary Medicine* 24 (2017). https://doi.org/10.1089/acm.2017.0183.

Kuo, Jip, Wen-Chyuan Chen, I.-Shiung Cheng, Pu-Hsi Tsai, Ying-Jui Lu, and Ning-Yuean Lee. "The Effect of Eight Weeks of Supplementation with Eleutherococcus senticosus on Endurance Capacity and Metabolism in Human." *Chinese Journal of Physiology* 53 (2010): 105–111.

Lee, S., and D. K. Rhee. "Effects of Ginseng on Stress-Related Depression, Anxiety, and the Hypothalamic-Pituitary-Adrenal Axis." *J Ginseng Res* 41, no. 4 (2017): 589–594. https://doi.org/10.1016/j.jgr.2017.01.010.

Leung, A. M., and L. E. Braverman. "Consequences of Excess Iodine." *Nat Rev Endocrinol* 10, no. 3 (2014): 136–142. https://doi.org/10.1038/nrendo.2013.251.

Li, Y., V. Pham, M. Bui, et al. "*Rhodiola rosea L.*: An Herb with Anti-stress, Anti-aging, and Immunostimulating Properties for Cancer Chemoprevention." *Curr Pharmacol Rep* 3, no. 6 (2017): 384–395. https://doi.org/10.1007/s40495-017-0106-1.

Lin, B., and S. Li. "Chapter 5. Cordyceps as an Herbal Drug." In *Herbal Medicine: Biomolecular and Clinical Aspects*. 2nd ed. Edited by I. F. F. Benzie and S. Wachtel-Galor. Boca Raton, FL: CRC Press/Taylor & Francis, 2011. https://www.ncbi.nlm.nih.gov/books/NBK92758/.

Lull, C., H. J. Wichers, and H. F. Savelkoul. "Antiinflammatory and Immuno-modulating Properties of Fungal Metabolites." *Mediators Inflamm* 2005, no. 2 (2005): 63–80. https://doi.org/10.1155/MI.2005.63.

Mahmoodianfard, Salma, Mohammad Reza Vafa, Fatemeh Golgiri, et al. "Effects of Zinc and Selenium Supplementation on Thyroid Function in Over-weight and Obese Hypothyroid Female Patients: A Randomized Double-Blind Controlled Trial." *Journal of the American College of Nutrition* 34 (2015): 1–9. https://doi.org/10.1080/07315724.2014.926161.

Markou, K., N. Georgopoulos, V. Kyriazopoulou, and A. G. Vagenakis. "Iodine-Induced Hypothyroidism." *Thyroid* 11, no. 5 (2001): 501–510. https://doi.org/10.1089/105072501300176462.

Maxwell, C., and S. L. Volpe. "Effect of Zinc Supplementation on Thyroid Hor-mone Function." *Ann Nutr Metab* 51 (2007): 188–194. https://doi.or/10.1159/000103324.

McGregor, Brock. "Extra-thyroidal Factors Impacting Thyroid Hormone Ho-meostasis: A Review." *Journal of Restorative Medicine* 4, no. 1 (December 1, 2015): 40–49.

Michielan, A., and R. D'Incà. "Intestinal Permeability in Inflammatory Bowel Disease: Pathogenesis, Clinical Evaluation, and Therapy of Leaky Gut." *Mediators Inflamm* 2015 (2015): 628157. https://doi.org/10.1155/2015/628157.

Noori Bashboosh, Nawras. "Correlation Between Hypothyroidism and Iron De-ficiency Anemia in Female Patients." *World Journal of Pharmacy and Phar-maceutical Sciences* 6, no. 7 (2019): 80–89. https://doi.org/10.20959/wjpps 20177-9457.

Osakabe, N., H. Takano, C. Sanbongi, et al. "Anti-inflammatory and Anti-allergic Effect of Rosmarinic Acid (RA); Inhibition of Seasonal Allergic Rhinoconjunctivitis (SAR) and Its Mechanism." *Biofactors* 21, nos. 1–4 (2004): 127–131. https://doi.org/10.1002/biof.552210125.

Panda, S., and A. Kar. "Changes in Thyroid Hormone Concentrations After Ad-ministration of Ashwagandha Root Extract to Adult Male Mice." *J Pharm Pharmacol* 50, no. 9 (1998): 1065–1068.

Panda, S., and A. Kar. "Guggulu (Commiphora mukul) Potentially Ameliorates Hypothyroidism in Female Mice." *Phyther Res* 19, no. 1 (2005): 78–80.

Peterson, C. T., V. Sharma, S. Uchitel, et al. "Prebiotic Potential of Herbal Medicines Used in Digestive Health and Disease." *J Altern Complement Med* 24, no. 7 (2018): 656–665. https://doi.org/10.1089/acm.2017.0422.

Rayman, M. "Multiple Nutritional Factors and Thyroid Disease, with Particular Reference to Autoimmune Thyroid Disease." *Proceedings of the Nutrition Society* 78, no. 1 (2019): 34–44. https://doi.org/10.1017/S002966511800 1192.

Rink, T., H. Schroth, L. Holle, and H. Garth. "Effect of Iodine and Thyroid Hormones in the Induction and Therapy of Hashimoto's Thyroiditis." *Nuk-learmedizin* 38, no. 5 (1999, 2016): 144–149.

Roy Chengappa, K., J. Gannon, and P. Forrest. "Subtle Changes in Thyroid Indices During a Placebo-Controlled Study of an Extract of Withania somnifera in Persons with Bipolar Disorder." *J Ayurveda Integr Med* 5, no. 4 (2014): 241.

Siciliano, G., F. Monzani, M. L. Manca, et al. "Human Mitochondrial Transcription Factor A Reduction and Mitochondrial Dysfunction in Hashimoto's Hypothyroid Myopathy." *Mol Med* 8, no. 6 (2002): 326–333.

Simopoulos, Artemis. "Omega-3 Fatty Acids in Inflammation and Autoimmune Diseases." *Journal of the American College of Nutrition* 21 (2003): 495–505. https://doi.org/10.1080/07315724.2002.10719248.

Skrovanek, S., K. DiGuilio, R. Bailey, et al. "Zinc and Gastrointestinal Disease." *World J Gastrointest Pathophysiol* 5, no. 4 (2014): 496–513. https://doi.org/10.4291/wjgp.v5.i4.496.

Stansbury, Jill, Paul Saunders, David Winston, and Eugene R. Zampieron. "Rosmarinic Acid as a Novel Agent in the Treatment of Autoimmune Disease." *Journal of Restorative Medicine* 2012, no. 1 (2012): 112–116.

Sturniolo, Giacomo, Vincenza Di Leo, Antonio Ferronato, A. D'Odorico, and Renata D'Incà. "Zinc Supplementation Tightens 'Leaky Gut' in Crohn's Disease." *Inflammatory Bowel Diseases* 7 (2001): 94–98. https://doi.org/10.1097/00054725-200105000-00003.

Toulis, Konstantinos, Athanasios Anastasilakis, Thrasivoulos Tzellos, Dimitrios Goulis, and Dimitrios Kouvelas. "Selenium Supplementation in the Treatment of Hashimoto's Thyroiditis: A Systematic Review and a Meta-analysis." *Thyroid* 20 (2010): 1163–1173. https://doi.org/10.1089/thy.2009.0351.

Tripathi, Y. B., O. P. Malhotra, and S. N. Tripathi. "Thyroid Stimulating Action of Z-Guggulsterone Obtained from Commiphora mukul." *Planta Med* 50, no. 1 (1984): 78–80.

Ucan, Bekir, Mustafa Sahin, Muyesser Sayki Arslan, et al. "Vitamin D Treatment in Patients with Hashimoto's Thyroiditis May Decrease the Development of Hypothyroidism." *International Journal for Vitamin and Nutrition Research* 86 (2017): 1–9. https://doi.org/10.1024/0300-9831/a000269.

Ventura, M., M. Melo, and F. Carrilho. "Selenium and Thyroid Disease: From Pathophysiology to Treatment." *Int J Endocrinol* 2017 (2017): 1297658. https://doi.org/10.1155/2017/1297658.

Vernon, Suzanne, Toni Whistler, Barbara Cameron, Ian Hickie, William C. Reeves, and Andrew Lloyd. "Preliminary Evidence of Mitochondrial Dysfunction Associated with Post-infective Fatigue After Acute Infection with Epstein Barr Virus." *BMC Infectious Diseases* 6 (2006): 15. https://doi.org/10.1186/1471-2334-6-15.

Wachtel-Galor, S., J. Yuen, J. A. Buswell, et al. "Ganoderma lucidum (Lingzhi or Reishi): A Medicinal Mushroom." In *Herbal Medicine: Biomolecular and Clinical Aspects*. 2nd ed. Edited by I. F. F. Benzie and S. Wachtel-Galor. Boca Raton, FL: CRC Press/Taylor & Francis, 2011. https://www.ncbi.nlm.nih.gov/books/NBK92757/.

Wang, Bin, Guoyao Wu, Zhigang Zhou, et al. "Glutamine and Intestinal Barrier Function." *Amino Acids* 47 (2014). https://doi.org/10.1007/s00726-014-17 73-4.

Wu, D., Y. Deng, L. Chen, et al. "Evaluation on Quality Consistency of *Ganoderma lucidum* Dietary Supplements Collected in the United States." *Sci Rep* 7 (2017): 7792. https://doi.org/10.1038/s41598-017-06336-3.

Zimmermann, M. B. "Iodine Deficiency." *Endocr Rev* 30, no. 4 (2009): 376–408. https://doi.org/10.1210/er.2009-0011.

CHAPTER 12: Ancient and Emerging Therapies

An, H. J., J. Y. Kim, W. H. Kim, et al. "Therapeutic Effects of Bee Venom and Its Major Component, Melittin, on Atopic Dermatitis in Vivo and in Vitro." *Br J Pharmacol* 175, no. 23 (2018): 4310–4324. https://doi.org/10.1111/bph .14487.

Arsovska, Blagica, Jihe Zhu, and Kristina Kozowska. "Case Report: Acupuncture Treatment for Hypothyroidism." *Imperial Journal of Interdisciplinary Research* 2 (2016): 184–187.

Banerji Homeopathic Research Foundation. "Thyroid and Homeopathy." Accessed August 26, 2019. http://www.pbhrfindia.org/thyroid-and-homeopathy .html.

Bhavanani, Ananda, Zeena Sanjay, and Madanmohan. "Effect of Yoga on Subclinical Hypothyroidism: A Case Report." *Yoga Mimamsa* 43 (2012): 102–107.

Black, D. S., and G. M. Slavich. "Mindfulness Meditation and the Immune System: A Systematic Review of Randomized Controlled Trials." *Ann N Y Acad Sci* 1373, no. 1 (2016): 13–24. https://doi.org/10.1111/nyas.12998.

Booz, G. W. "Cannabidiol as an Emergent Therapeutic Strategy for Lessening the Impact of Inflammation on Oxidative Stress." *Free Radic Biol Med* 51, no. 5 (2011): 1054–1061. https://doi.org/10.1016/j.freeradbiomed.2011.01 .007.

Boukhatem, M. N., A. Kameli, M. A. Ferhat, F. Saidi, and M. Mekarnia. "Rose Geranium Essential Oil as a Source of New and Safe Anti-inflammatory Drugs." *Libyan J Med* 8 (October 7, 2013): 22520. https://doi .org/10.3402/ljm.v8i0.22520.

Boukhatem, M. N., M. A. Ferhat, A. Kameli, F. Saidi, and H. T. Kebir. "Lemon Grass (Cymbopogon citratus) Essential Oil as a Potent Anti-inflammatory and Antifungal Drug." *Libyan J Med* 9 (September 19, 2014): 25431. https:// doi.org/10.3402/ljm.v9.25431.

Budney, A. J., R. Roffman, R. S. Stephens, and D. Walker. "Marijuana Dependence and Its Treatment." *Addict Sci Clin Pract* 4, no. 1 (2007): 4–16. https:// doi.org/10.1151/ascp07414.

Buric, I., M. Farias, J. Jong, C. Mee, and I. A. Brazil. "What Is the Molecular Signature of Mind-Body Interventions? A Systematic Review of Gene

Expression Changes Induced by Meditation and Related Practices." *Frontiers in Immunology* 8 (2017). https://doi.org/10.3389/fimmu.2017.00670.

Chan, J. S. M., R. T. H. Ho, K. Chung, et al. "Qigong Exercise Alleviates Fatigue, Anxiety, and Depressive Symptoms, Improves Sleep Quality, and Shortens Sleep Latency in Persons with Chronic Fatigue Syndrome-like Illness." *Evidence-Based Complementary and Alternative Medicine* 2014, art. ID 106048 (2014). https://doi.org/10.1155/2014/106048.

Chauhan, V. K., R. K. Manchanda, A. Narang, et al. "Efficacy of Homeopathic Intervention in Subclinical Hypothyroidism with or Without Autoimmune Thyroiditis in Children: An Exploratory Randomized Control Study." *Homeopathy* 103, no. 4 (2014): 224–231. https://doi.org/10.1016/j.homp.2014.08.004.

Cheng, Fung Kei. "An Overview of the Contribution of Acupuncture to Thyroid Disorders." *Journal of Integrative Medicine* 16 (2018): 375–383. https://doi.org/10.1016/j.joim.2018.09.002.

Christianson, Alan. "Hydrotherapy." Accessed January 5, 2020. https://drchristianson.com/how-amazing-hydrotherapy-can-strengthen-your-thyroid-and-benefit-your-health/.

Crow, D. "Frankincense and Myrrh: The Botany, Culture and Therapeutic Use of the World's Two Most Important Resins." Accessed August 27, 2019. https://pdfs.semanticscholar.org/3454/440f1160482da4a10bde3cecea0dde67a753.pdf.

Ding, S. S., S. H. Hong, C. Wang, Y. Guo, Z. K. Wang, and Y. Xu. "Acupuncture Modulates the Neuro–Endocrine–Immune Network." *QJM: An International Journal of Medicine* 107, no. 5 (May 2014): 341–345. https://doi.org/10.1093/qjmed/hct196.

"East Meets West in UCLA Medicine." *UCLA Magazine*, 2012. Accessed August 26, 2019. http://magazine.ucla.edu/features/east-meets-west-in-ucla-medicine/.

Elshafie, H. S., and I. Camele. "An Overview of the Biological Effects of Some Mediterranean Essential Oils on Human Health." *Biomed Res Int* 2017 (2017): 9268468. https://doi.org/10.1155/2017/9268468.

Fondin, Michelle. "Speak Your Inner Truth with the Fifth Chakra." Chopra Center, 2019. Accessed August 26, 2019. https://chopra.com/articles/speak-your-inner-truth-with-the-fifth-chakra.

Franzini D., L. A. Cuny L., and S. Pierce-Talsma. "Osteopathic Lymphatic Pump Techniques." *The Journal of the American Osteopathic Association* 118 (7) (2018): e43–e44. doi: https://doi.org/10.7556/jaoa.2018.112.

Government of Canada, Department of Justice. "Cannabis Legalization and Regulation." Accessed May 25, 2019. https://www.justice.gc.ca/eng/cj-jp/cannabis/.

Hasin, D. S., T. D. Saha, B. T. Kerridge, et al. "Prevalence of Marijuana Use Disorders in the United States Between 2001–2002 and 2012–2013." *JAMA Psychiatry* 72, no. 12 (2015): 1235–1242. https://doi.org/10.1001/jamapsychiatry.2015.1858.

Hodge L. M. "Osteopathic Lymphatic Pump Techniques to Enhance Immunity and Treat Pneumonia." *International Journal of Osteopathic Medicine* 15 (1) (2112): 13-21. 21. doi:10.1016/j.ijosm.2011.11.004

Hwang, D. S., S. K. Kim, and H. Bae. "Therapeutic Effects of Bee Venom on Immunological and Neurological Diseases." *Toxins* (Basel) 7, no. 7 (June 29, 2015): 2413–2421. https://doi.org/10.3390/toxins7072413.

Jahnke, R., L. Larkey, C. Rogers, J. Etnier, and F. Lin. "A Comprehensive Review of Health Benefits of Qigong and Tai Chi." *Am J Health Promot* 24, no. 6 (2010): e1–e25. https://doi.org/10.4278/ajhp.081013-LIT-248.

Katz, D., I. Katz, and Y. Shoenfeld. "Cannabis and Autoimmunity—The Neurologic Perspective: A Brief Review." *J Neurol Neuromed* 1, no. 4 (2016): 11–15.

Kaur, Sat Dharam, Mary Danylak-Arhanic, and Carolyn Dean. *The Complete Natural Medicine Guide to Women's Health.* Toronto: Robert Rose, 2005.

Keng, S. L., M. J. Smoski, and C. J. Robins. "Effects of Mindfulness on Psychological Health: A Review of Empirical Studies." *Clin Psychol Rev* 31, no. 6 (2011): 1041–1056. https://doi.org/10.1016/j.cpr.2011.04.006.

Konieczny, E., and L. Wilson. *Healing with CBD: How Cannabidiol Can Transform Your Health Without the High.* Berkeley, CA: Ulysses Press, 2018.

Leafly. "Where Is Cannabis Legal?" https://www.leafly.com/news/cannabis-101 /where-is-cannabis-legal.

Leinow, L., and J. Birnabaum. *CBD: A Patient's Guide to Medical Cannabis— Healing Without the High.* Berkeley, CA: North Atlantic Books, 2017.

Licciardone, J. C., C. M. Kearns, L. M. Hodge, and M. V. Bergamini. "Associations of Cytokine Concentrations with Key Osteopathic Lesions and Clinical Outcomes in Patients with Nonspecific Chronic Low Back Pain: Results from the OSTEOPATHIC Trial." *The Journal of the American Osteopathic Association.* 112 (2012): 596–605.

Malcolm, B. J., and K. Tallian. "Essential Oil of Lavender in Anxiety Disorders: Ready for Prime Time?" *Ment Health Clin* 7, no. 4 (March 26, 2018): 147–155. https://doi.org/10.9740/mhc.2017.07.147.

Malhotra, S., R. A. Heptulla, P. Homel, and R. Motaghedi. "Effect of Marijuana Use on Thyroid Function and Autoimmunity." *Thyroid* 27, no. 2 (2017): 167–173. https://doi.org/10.1089/thy.2016.0197.

Malikov, Damir. "Traditional Chinese Medicine Approach to Hypothyroidism." *International Journal of Complementary & Alternative Medicine* 5 (2017). https://doi.org/10.15406/ijcam.2017.05.00142.

McManus, D. E. "Reiki Is Better Than Placebo and Has Broad Potential as a Complementary Health Therapy." *J Evid Based Complementary Altern Med* 22, no. 4 (2017): 1051–1057. https://doi.org/10.1177/2156587217728644.

McPartland, John, Geoffrey Guy, and Vincenzo Di Marzo. "Care and Feeding of the Endocannabinoid System: A Systematic Review of Potential Clinical Interventions That Upregulate the Endocannabinoid System." *PLOS ONE* 9 (2014): e89566. https://doi.org/10.1371/journal.pone.0089566.

Milton S. Hershey Medical Center, Penn State Hershey. "Hypothyroidism." Accessed January 5, 2020. http://pennstatehershey.adam.com/content.aspx ?productid=107&pid=33&gid=000093.

Mooventhan, A., and L. Nivethitha. "Scientific Evidence-Based Effects of Hydrotherapy on Various Systems of the Body." *N Am J Med Sci* 6, no. 5 (2014): 199–209. https://doi.org/10.4103/1947-2714.132935.

Newman, T. "Everything You Need to Know About Reiki." Medical News Today, 2017. Accessed August 26, 2019. https://www.medicalnewstoday.com /articles/308772.php.

Nichols, James, and Barbara Kaplan. "Immune Responses Regulated by Cannabidiol." *Cannabis and Cannabinoid Research* 5 (2019). https://doi.org/10.1089 /can.2018.0073.

NIDA. "Marijuana." December 24, 2019. Accessed January 4, 2020. https:// www.drugabuse.gov/publications/research-reports/marijuana.

Nilakanthan, Savitri, Kashinath Metri, Nagaratna Raghuram, and Nagendra Hongasandra. "Effect of 6 Months Intense Yoga Practice on Lipid Profile, Thyroxine Medication and Serum TSH Level in Women Suffering from Hypothyroidism: A Pilot Study." *Journal of Complementary and Integrative Medicine* 13 (2016). https://doi.org/10.1515/jcim-2014-0079.

Orr, Catherine, Philip Spechler, Zhipeng Cao, et al. "Grey Matter Volume Differences Associated with Extremely Low Levels of Cannabis Use in Adolescence." *Journal of Neuroscience* 39 (2019): 1817–1827. https://doi.org/10 .1523/JNEUROSCI.3375-17.2018.

Pajai, M., and S. Pajai. "Role of Yoga in Prevention of Hypothyroidism." *JPSI* 3, no. 2 (2014): 111–113.

Pandey, R., K. Mousawy, M. Nagarkatti, and P. Nagarkatti. "Endocannabinoids and Immune Regulation." *Pharmacol Res* 60, no. 2 (2009): 85–92. https:// doi.org/10.1016/j.phrs.2009.03.019.

PDQ Integrative, Alternative, and Complementary Therapies Editorial Board. "Aromatherapy with Essential Oils (PDQ®): Health Professional Version." January 8, 2019. In *PDQ Cancer Information Summaries* [Internet]. https:// www.ncbi.nlm.nih.gov/books/NBK65874/.

Poitevin, B. "Integrating Homeopathy in Health Systems." *Bulletin of the World Health Organization* 77, no. 2 (1999): 160–166.

"Poses for Your Thyroid." *Yoga Journal.* Accessed August 26, 2019. https://www .yogajournal.com/poses/anatomy/thyroid.

Prüss, Harald, Andrea Tedeschi, Aude Thiriot, et al. "Spinal Cord Injury-Induced Immunodeficiency Is Mediated by a Sympathetic-Neuroendocrine Adrenal Reflex." *Nature Neuroscience* 2017. https://doi.org/10.1038/nn.4643.

Rho, Y. H., J. H. Woo, S. J. Choi, Y. H. Lee, J. D. Ji, and G. G. Song. "A New Onset of Systemic Lupus Erythematosus Developed After Bee Venom Therapy." *Korean J Intern Med* 24, no. 3 (2009): 283–285. https://doi.org/10.3904 /kjim.2009.24.3.283.

Riley, Kristen, and Crystal Park. "How Does Yoga Reduce Stress? A Systematic Review of Mechanisms of Change and Guide to Future Inquiry." *Health Psychology Review* 9 (2015): 1–30. https://doi.org/10.1080/17437199.2014.9 81778.

Rogers, P. A., A. M. Schoen, and J. Limehouse. "Acupuncture for Immune Mediated Disorders: Literature Review and Clinical Applications." *Probl Vet Med* 4, no. 1 (1992): 162–193.

Ryan, Marc. *How to Heal Hashimoto's.* Carlsbad, CA: Hay House, 2017.

Sharma, K., K. Udayakumara, P. Thirumaleshwara, and P. Mahabala. "The Effect of Yogic Practices on Thyroid Functions." *Indian Journal of Applied Research* 4 (2014): 7, 526–527.

Su, S., J. Duan, T. Chen, et al. "Frankincense and Myrrh Suppress Inflammation via Regulation of the Metabolic Profiling and the MAPK Signaling Pathway" [published correction in *Sci Rep* 5 (2015): 15597]. *Sci Rep* 5 (September 2, 2015): 13668. https://doi.org/10.1038/srep13668.

Subramanian, Kiruthiga. "Homoeopathic Thyroidinum 3x–An Adjuvant in the Treatment of Hypothyroidism." *International Journal of Complementary & Alternative Medicine* 11 (2019). https://doi.org/10.15406/ijcam.2018.11 .00339.

Sullivan, Amy, Susan Bauer-Wu, and Michael Miovic. "The Tong Ren Healing Method: A Survey Study." *Complementary Health Practice Review* 14 (2009). https://doi.org/10.1177/1533210108329265.

Thyroflex Asia. Accessed August 31, 2019. http://www.thyroflexasia.com/.

White, A., and E. Ernst. "A Brief History of Acupuncture." *Rheumatology* 43, no. 5 (May 2004): 662–663. https://doi.org/10.1093/rheumatology/keg005.

Wilkinson, Jonathan, and Richard Faleiro. "Acupuncture in Pain Management." *Continuing Education in Anaesthesia Critical Care & Pain* 7 (2007). https:// doi.org/10.1093/bjaceaccp/mkm021.

Winters, K. C., and C. Y. Lee. "Likelihood of Developing an Alcohol and Cannabis Use Disorder During Youth: Association with Recent Use and Age." *Drug Alcohol Depend* 92, nos. 1–3 (2008): 239–247. https://doi.org/10.1016 /j.drugalcdep.2007.08.005.

Yin Yang House. "Tam Healing and Tong Ren Therapy for Hashimoto's." Accessed August 25, 2019. https://theory.yinyanghouse.com/treatments /tongren_for_hashimotoss_disease.

CHAPTER 13: Your Thyroid-Healing Plan

Barnes, B. *Hypothyroidism: The Unsuspected Illness.* New York: Harper, 1976.

Gustafson, C. Denis Wilson. "Low Body Temperature as an Indicator for Poor Expression of Thyroid Hormone." *Integr Med* (Encinitas) 14, no. 3 (2015): 24–28.

Wilson's Temperature Syndrome. "Check the Body Temperature." Accessed January 3, 2020. https://www.wilsonssyndrome.com/identify/how-are-body -temperatures-measured/.

Yavuz, Sahzene, Silvia Salgado Nunez del Prado, and Francesco S. Celi. "Thyroid Hormone Action and Energy Expenditure." *Journal of the Endocrine Society* 3, no. 7 (July 2019): 1345–1356. https://doi.org/10.1210/js.2018-00423.

CHAPTER 14: Recipes

Croteau, Etienne, Christian-Alexandre Castellano, Marie Anne Richard, et al. "Ketogenic Medium Chain Triglycerides Increase Brain Energy Metabolism in Alzheimer's Disease." *Journal of Alzheimer's Disease* 64 (2018): 551–561. https://doi.org/10.3233/JAD-180202.

Kregiel, D., E. Pawlikowska, and H. Antolak. "*Urtica* spp.: Ordinary Plants with Extraordinary Properties." *Molecules* 23, no. 7 (July 9, 2018): 1664. https://doi.org/10.3390/molecules23071664.

O'Callaghan, T. F., H. Faulkner, S. McAuliffe, et al. "Quality Characteristics, Chemical Composition, and Sensory Properties of Butter from Cows on Pasture Versus Indoor Feeding Systems." *Journal of Dairy Science* 99, no. 12 (2016): 9441–9460. https://doi.org/10.3168/jds.2016-11271.

Okafor, Gabriel I., and O. Apochi. "Production of Oleoresin from Ginger (Zingiber officinale) Peels and Evaluation of Its Antimicrobial and Antioxidative Properties." *African Journal of Microbiology Research* 7 (2013): 4981–4989. https://doi.org/10.5897/AJMR2013.6125.

Pustjens, A. M., R. Boerrigter-Eenling, A. H. Koot, M. Rozijn, and S. M. van Ruth. "Characterization of Retail Conventional, Organic, and Grass Full-Fat Butters by Their Fat Contents, Free Fatty Acid Contents, and Triglyceride and Fatty Acid Profiling." *Foods* 6, no. 4 (March 31, 2017): 26. https://doi.org/10.3390/foods6040026.

Index

About the Author

Dr. Emily Lipinski is a doctor of naturopathic medicine and is passionate about helping people heal naturally. Emily strongly believes in addressing the root cause of a medical issue and using natural therapies either alone or in conjunction with conventional Western medicine. Her passion for using both science and nature to address medical conditions started from a young age. Her father, a conventional dentist, helped to nurture her love for science and math, while her mother fed her green juices, brought her to naturopathic doctors, and taught her about the importance of organic foods.

After years of feeling unwell despite being on medication for her thyroid, Emily was diagnosed with Hashimoto's thyroid disease, an autoimmune disorder. Using natural therapies and changes in diet and lifestyle, she has dramatically improved her health and has effectively balanced her hormones.

Dr. Lipinski completed her undergraduate degree in biology and her thesis at Dalhousie University in Halifax. Her thesis propelled her to research spinal cord injuries at the University of British Columbia in Vancouver. She then went on to complete her four years of naturopathic medical school at the Canadian College of Naturopathic Medicine in Toronto.

Emily lives in between Ontario, Canada, and the Turks and Caicos Islands with her family. Visit her online at www.emilylipinski.com.